I0415345

THE CONTRIBUTION OF NATURAL LAW THEORY TO MORAL AND LEGAL DEBATE CONCERNING SUICIDE, ASSISTED SUICIDE AND EUTHANASIA

THE CONTRIBUTION OF NATURAL LAW THEORY TO MORAL AND LEGAL DEBATE CONCERNING SUICIDE, ASSISTED SUICIDE AND EUTHANASIA

Craig Paterson

Viewforth Press

Los Angeles, CA

2010

Front cover: Jacques-Louis David, *La Mort de Marat*, 1793.

Originally prepared as a dissertation presented to the Faculty of the Graduate School of Saint Louis University for the degree of Doctor of Philosophy, 2001.

© 2010. This Viewforth edition. All rights reserved.

Published by Viewforth Press, Los Angeles, California. Distributed by www.createspace.com.

ISBN: 1452868395
EAN-13: 9781452868394

For My Parents

Digest

In chapter one, I argue for the important contribution that a natural law based framework can make towards an analysis and assessment of key controversies surrounding the practices of suicide, assisted suicide, and voluntary euthanasia.

In the second chapter, I consider a number of historical contributions to the debate.

The third chapter takes up the modern context of ideas that have increasingly come to the fore in shaping the 'push' for reform. Particular areas focused upon include the value of human life, the value of personal autonomy, and the rejection of double effect reasoning.

In chapter four, I engage in the task of pointing out structural weakness in utilitarianism and deontology. I argue that major systemic weaknesses in both approaches can be overcome by a teleology of basic human goods. John Finnis' work becomes the underpinning of subsequent applied natural law analysis.

In chapter five, I proceed to argue for the defence of the intrinsic good of human life from direct attack. I hold out for the proposition "that it is always a serious moral wrong to intentionally kill a human person, whether self or another, regardless of a further appeal to consequences or motive." In support of this, I defend the validity of double effect reasoning as an indispensable part of applied moral decision making.

In chapter six, I critically assess the arguments of anti-perfectionists that it is not the business of the state to enforce deep or substantive conceptions of the 'good life'. The chapter moves on to argue that the natural law conception of the person in society, centred on the common good, provides a solid framework for assessing both the justification for, as well as the limits on, the role of the state to use its power to legally impose certain moral standards.

In chapter seven, I address the concrete relationship between natural law and legal policy by exploring the issue of assisted suicide in the constitutional context of the United States.

Table of Contents

Chapter One

Introduction

Questions concerning the moral and legal justifications for the practices of suicide, assisted suicide, and voluntary euthanasia are undergoing renewed debate in contemporary Western society. In the United States, the activities of Jack Kevorkian, and pressure groups such as *Exit* and *Compassion in Dying*, ensure that the question will continue to be the object of intense debate. Of course, such pressure groups would be marginalised if there were uniform rejection of the legitimacy of such practices. There is not. There are historical precedents for their viewpoints, and these are fuelled by the realities of pluralism in contemporary life.

Respect for persons, John Rawls claims, must take the 'fact of pluralism' seriously. I agree with this, if it is taken to mean that respectful consideration of persons cannot be demonstrated by imposition of the will, but rather, must seek to provide reasoned and publicly accessible grounds for justifying conclusions reached. No society can justify or tolerate all practices that individuals happen to want to pursue. That much is clear. What really becomes the object of intense debate, however, is the nature of the justifications posed for placing limits on acceptable human conduct, justifications that will themselves be coloured by the view taken of the human person, and what is found fulfilling. As the philosopher Thomas Nagel puts it, there is no "view from nowhere," and we must stand somewhere on key foundational questions concerning our understanding of the human person.[1]

Natural Law Ethics

This book seeks to make a constructive contribution to the current debate concerning the moral and legal status of suicide, assisted suicide, and voluntary euthanasia from the perspective of 'natural law ethics'. This is a perspective that has become marginalised in the eyes of many, due to its

1

perceived dependency on the 'privileged truths' of revealed religion, a source of justification that cannot function as the grounds for morality or law in modern secular society. As this book unfolds, however, it will become clear why I think that such an assessment is unwarranted. Not because I think that religion, whether Christian, or any other, can provide the shared foundational premises for civil life together. Rather, it is because natural law ethics itself (*natural distinguished from super-natural*) presents a body of accessible knowledge for scrutiny, that is derived from nothing other than the operation of reason itself (open, and in principle, accessible to all), that it can indeed justify its claim to give rise to common premises for the co-ordination of respectful life in society with one another.

By my use of the phrase 'natural law ethics', I am referring to a basic theme in ethical theory, that there is a corpus of accessible principles that can be comprehended by the power of human reason to effectively guide the making of personal and societal choices in reasonable, fruitful, and fulfilling ways. It is an 'objectivist' approach that holds on to the basic tenet that there is discernible truth in morality that can be accounted for by the teleological appeal of humanly fulfilling goods. Such goods provide the intelligible starting points for the subsequent operation of human reason, to work out questions of the good and the right in human conduct.

Whilst the phrase 'natural law' may evoke the ready assumption that natural law is necessarily a form of *ethical naturalism* (a form of analysis that seeks to derive ethical 'norms' from 'factual' or 'theoretical' statements about human nature), an assumption supported by ample precedent in much of the tradition of natural law inquiry, it need not be construed as such. In the body of the work, I will argue for an appropriately 'qualified' version of natural law that is 'natural' in the sense that our nature is the ultimate parameter setter for what is considered humanly fulfilling, but that seeks to explain how normativity in relation to our nature is necessarily dependent on the mediating structure of our capacity to *reason practically* about an array of basic human goods. I draw, in particular, on the work of John M. Finnis. His work provides the main normative framework for the approach to natural law ethics adopted in this book. An emphasis on the work of Finnis is especially useful within the parameters of this book because he is recognised as a philosopher who is widely discussed in 'secular' circles, thus cutting across conventional classificatory boundaries. Secondly, his analytical mode of approaching philosophy, with its emphasis on the use of unaided practical reason, is very helpful in promoting the understanding and engagement of a natural law based ethics across different traditions of inquiry. Crucially, he does not lose sight of the important task of positively working towards establishing the 'public reasonableness' of a natural law based ethics beyond the seemingly interminable interstices of metaphysical controversy.

Lastly, in terms of what is meant by the use of the phrase 'natural law' in this work, I also take it to mean a form of 'perfectionism' in political as well as in personal life. Morality, politics, and law are ultimately concerned with the promotion of good persons, making goods choices. Contra the idea of anti-perfectionism, that governments must eschew promoting controversial or contested ideas of goodness, natural law holds on to the idea that promoting intelligible goods (even if contested) is central to the rationale and justification for legitimate government. Natural law is not simply about the promotion of human flourishing in 'our own lives' or in the lives of our 'moral friends'. There are no 'moral strangers'. Its understanding of persons and what fulfils them is socially mediated, through and through. Its understanding of the role of society in fostering and promoting the flourishing of persons mitigates against any radical severance between 'individuals' and their basic interconnectedness to one another in the 'common good'. For natural law ethics, the state, and other instruments of governance, have a positive role to play in promoting social conditions that in fact foster and promote, rather than undermine, the authentic flourishing of the person in society. Natural law, therefore, holds out for the proposition that that the function of government is to help promote the conditions of human flourishing by its co-ordination of amicable life together.

Yet, if natural ethics is perfectionist, an important caveat is in order. It need not be monistic in its understanding of what constitutes an array of worthwhile plans and forms of living compatible with its understanding of what constitutes human flourishing. In short, perfectionism need not be thought of as opposed to an array of worthwhile plurality, and therefore, in conjunction with this array of plurality, it is not an oxymoron to meaningfully talk in terms of 'pluralistic perfectionism' rather than 'monistic perfectionism', when we think of the pursuit of human perfectibility.

Having made a few clarificatory remarks on what is meant by the natural law, the remainder of this introduction will be devoted to the twin tasks of (a) presenting a brief conspectus as to how the chapters of the book will unfold, and (b) engaging in additional definitional analysis concerning the use of terms—suicide, assisted suicide, and voluntary euthanasia.

Arrangement of Chapters

In chapter two, *A History of Ideas Concerning the Morality of Suicide, Assisted Suicide and Voluntary Euthanasia*, I consider a number of historical contributions to the debate concerning the morality of those practices. I have tried to concentrate on the leading protagonists in the history of ideas. The chapter makes no pretence to being complete or exhaustive. Rather, its key purpose is to set the contemporary debate in context. It concludes with a summary of the main historical ideas for and against the morality of suicide and euthanasia.

Chapter three, *Contemporary Justifications for the Practices of Suicide, Assisted Suicide and Voluntary Euthanasia*, takes up the modern context of ideas that have increasingly come to the fore in shaping the 'push' for reform in our traditional ethical and legal prohibition of these acts. Particular areas focused upon concern the value and status of human life, especially the quality of personal life rather than mere biological life; self-determination and the value of personal autonomy; the rejection of concrete moral absolutes; the rejection of double effect reasoning; and the rejection of perfectionist accounts concerning the use of the state's legal apparatus to enforce 'morals law'.

In chapter four, *Natural Law Ethics: Re-establishing Foundations*, I engage in the negative task of pointing out structural weakness in the two leading ethical theories of modern times: Utilitarianism and Kantianism. I argue that major systemic weaknesses in these ethical approaches can be overcome by a teleology of basic goods, rooted in the natural law work of John Finnis. I then turn to the positive task of analysing and explaining this approach to natural law ethics. As the chapter title indicates, Finnis's work becomes the underpinning of subsequent applied natural law analysis concerning the morality of self-directed intentional death.

In chapter five, *Natural Law and the Ethics of Self-Killing*, I proceed to argue for the defence of the intrinsic good of human life from direct attack, whether in self or another. I hold out for a defence of the proposition "that it is always a serious moral wrong to intentionally kill a human person, whether self or another, regardless of a further appeal to consequences or motive." Secondly, I turn to an assessment of the idea of personal autonomy, and seek to place it within a framework of value that does not attempt to exalt the worth of that significant but instrumental (or facilitative) good above its own warranted status. Thirdly, I defend the validity and importance of the criteria of double effect reasoning as an indispensable part of moral decision making concerning the clash resulting from conflicts between obligations. Finally, the chapter briefly concludes with a defence of the need for natural law ethics to promote a consistent ethic of intentional killing across the gamut of life-taking situations, including self-defence and capital punishment.

In chapter six, *Natural Law, State Intervention and the Common Good*, I proceed with a critical assessment of the arguments of anti-perfectionists (H. Tristram Engelhardt; John Rawls) that it is not the business of the state to enforce upon its citizens, deep or substantive conceptions of what constitutes the 'moral life'. A related anti-perfectionist notion, put forward by Ronald

Dworkin, is then addressed, concerning the requirement that the state treat its citizens with equal concern and respect.

The chapter then turns to an assessment of the idea that liberal notions of the state need not be founded on an anti-perfectionism, but rather, can seek to defend liberal goals on the basis of its own thicker notion of human flourishing, constituted by key liberal values—nothing less than a liberal perfectionism upon which to ground limits on the authority of the state to enforce certain kinds of norms on its citizens (Joseph Raz; William A. Galston).

The next part of the chapter then proceeds to argue that the natural law conception of the person in society, centred on the common good, provides a solid framework for assessing both the justification for, as well as the limits on, the role of the state to use its power to legally enforce certain (appropriately qualified) forms of moral standards. The concluding part examines the relevance of slippery slope reasoning to understanding the impact that the legalisation of assisted suicide or euthanasia may have on the common good of society.

In the final chapter, *Natural Law, Judicial Review and the Legalisation of Assisted Suicide in the United States*, I proceed to concretise the relationship between natural law and legal policy by exploring the issue of assisted suicide in the constitutional context of the United States. Turning initially to clarify some questions concerning the relationship between natural law and the positive law of a state, I then move to explore some questions of judicial interpretation relevant to understanding the meaning and scope of the 14th Amendment, especially that amendment's Due Process Clause pertaining to liberty rights. The analysis culminates in a review and analysis of two significant constitutional judgements of the Supreme Court, decided in 1997, that directly centre on the legal status of assisted suicide in the United States— *Washington v. Glucksberg* and *Vacco v. Quill.*

Usage of Other Key Terms

Before turning to the task of historical review and analysis, in chapter one, it is necessary to make some remarks concerning the use of our other key terms in this book—suicide, assisted suicide, and euthanasia, in order to help guide subsequent analysis and discussion. The criteria of specificity, non-arbitrariness, consistency (between various terms), and the avoidance of *strong pejorative* presuppositions, will supply the main standards guiding the usages employed. However, a word of initial caution is necessary. Definitional analysis is inherently problematic when major assumptions are themselves the subject of much debate. Any attempt at defining terms risks exposure to the charge of engaging in the practice of 'sophistry with words'.[2] This is particularly the case when, on the face of it, different actions may have 'identical exterior appearances' but may differ significantly in terms of what can be labelled the 'interior action elements' of 'knowledge', 'intent', and 'motive'.[3]

Wary of such a possible charge, I will state at the outset that questions of definition cannot be viewed independently from an examination of the various components that go into the analysis of an action.[4] Definitional neutrality, in my view, is not possible when faced with differing and competing accounts of action theory, accounts that differ not simply in incidentals but in fundamentals—especially the validity and significance of distinctions drawn between intention and foresight, intention and motive, act and omission, act and consequence, etc.[5] Here I can only state that the reader will need to accept 'on faith,' for the time being, some of those initial problematics. A promissory note is issued to the effect that the burden of substantiating those assumptions will be discharged in chapters four and five of the book.[6]

Suicide. Turning, firstly, to the word 'suicide', the initial use of the word is recorded in the Oxford English Dictionary as occurring in 1651. However, Alfred Alvarez has discovered an earlier use of the word that dates from 1635.[7] The definition that occurs from historical usage is "one who dies by his [or her] own hand; one who commits self-murder." Subsequent usage of the word has reflected, in part, the strong pejorative meaning of earlier phrases used to connote the wrongful killing of oneself, e.g., self-murder and self-slaughter.

There are, however, severe problems with the adoption of any such definition, for it lacks clarity and discrimination with reference to some of the important elements that go into the creation of an act-description. Firstly, too many acts that cannot properly be described as the 'intentional killing of self' would be incorporated under such a description. Yet, in my view, the element of intent, and its scope, is a crucially important element to the process of determining any act-signification. Whether a consequence of an act was intended, or not, is no minor matter, and cuts at the heart of subsequent analysis and interpretation. The question of intention therefore must play an important part in the description of the scope of the act designated by the word suicide. Fundamentally, we are interested in assessing the deeds that a person can be held accountable for. The feasibility of that task crucially depends upon placing intentional behaviour at the forefront of an analysis of human acts.

Secondly, the Oxford definition is unsatisfactory because it seems to arbitrarily exclude the possibility of an omission being the attributable means of intentionally killing oneself—in short, "by his [or her] own hand"—seems too predisposed towards the actual performance of a positive extensional act.[8] It should, therefore, remain an open question for subsequent moral assessment as to whether or not an agent actually intended to kill himself or herself by means of such an omission. It should not be settled by definitional exclusion that a person could not intentionally self-kill by means of, say, refusing life sustaining treatment.

Thirdly, the overly pejorative connotations of the Oxford usage should be avoided so that we can move beyond any ready appeal to rhetoric.[9] It is important, therefore, to avoid the use of strong value loaded terminology of an unduly biased nature—terminology that in an *a priori* fashion settles the question, such as 'self-murder', since the word necessarily connotes wrongfulness. When the word suicide is used in this work, it will not definitionally rule out the possibility that arguments can be made such that the notion of a morally acceptable suicide, is not rendered linguistically absurd.[10]

Following from the above discussion, I would argue that any satisfactory usage of suicide would need to clearly incorporate into a classification both the key elements of intent and omission. The Oxford definition, then is at once too broad and too narrow—too broad since it does not focus upon the necessary action component of intent that would further clarify the definition—too narrow since it seems to inadequately recognise the need to incorporate into the definition of suicide the possibility of bringing about the intended death of self by means of an omission.

Turning to the usage of the French sociologist Émile Durkheim, his influential usage, whatever its merits for sociological investigation, also lacks precision for the purposes of subsequent moral and legal analysis (concerned as they both are with the attribution of responsibility and the apportionment of blame).[11] Durkheim applies the term suicide to "… all cases of death resulting directly or indirectly from a positive or negative act of the victim himself [or herself] which he [or she] knows will produce this result …."[12]

On a positive note, Durkheim's definition at least gives weight to the idea that omissions as well as actions can be suicidal in nature. It avoids such an exclusion. However, the essential problem with Durkheim's definition is that it is still far too vague in its characterisation of basic act-descriptions. For example, all forms of self-sacrifice would automatically be included as part of the very definition of suicide. Thus, say, Jesus would necessarily be said to have committed suicide since he 'knew' of the impending certainty of his own earthly death and yet chose not to avert it in any way. Death acceptance thus becomes suicide in one bold definitional step. However, such an interpretation will not do, since it again fails to give sufficient scope to the importance of intentions in determining the objective of a person's action.

Moving on to consider the definition of suicide offered by Richard Brandt, a philosopher who has written a significant article on rational suicide, his definition has greater specification attached to it since he defines suicide as

"... doing something which results in one's death, either from the intention of ending one's life or the intention to bring about some other state of affairs (such as relief from pain) which one thinks it certain or highly probable can be achieved only by means of death ...."[13]

Notwithstanding that precision, however, his definition will still not suffice either, for it introduces by his secondary use of the word intention the claim that intention should be read as an equivalent to 'foresight with probability'. Such a definition, however, lacks discrimination in terms of an 'anatomy of the will'. It can be said to confuse an *epistemic* distinction with one based on *volition*. At this stage I can only state that for an intentional behaviour to be brought under the act-description of suicide, it should require more than mere knowledge or belief that an action may (even certainly) result in the death of oneself for it to be identified as such. Certainly knowledge is an important prerequisite to the subsequent analysis of action, but it should not rule out the possibility that a consequence of an action can be known, yet not be, as such, intended.

Finally, before moving to a consideration of the term assisted suicide, I will briefly consider an aspect of Tom Beauchamp's definition of suicide. He seeks to build into his definition the idea of non-coercion. Thus, "... an act is a suicide if a person brings about his or her own death in circumstances where others do not coerce him or her to action."[14]

It is understandable that Beauchamp may seek to protect under this aegis, certain acts that are not always conventionally classified as suicides, e.g., certain forms of altruistic self-sacrifice. Yet, tempting as it is to write into the very definition of an action—freedom from coercion—this seems unduly narrow and restrictive. Coercion is most usually taken into account as an important circumstance pertaining to the degree of responsibility born by the agent for intentionally acting the way he or she did. Certainly it is possible to envisage circumstances in which responsibility can be diminished significantly (even to the point of exoneration). Anyone familiar with the history of Anglo-American criminal law will be familiar with the classic case of *Regina v.*

Dudley. In this case a cabin boy was killed by his fellow shipwrecked crew members in order to use his body for food.[15] Whilst the judge was prepared to exercise leniency in sentencing, he was not prepared to 're-describe' the conduct of the men on the basis of coercive circumstance. In short, many actions are performed under pressure, and we do not seek to redefine them simply on the basis of coercion. Thus, an act of rape (penetrative sexual intercourse with a woman contrary to her will), is still considered an act of rape, even if a gun was held to the head of the agent, and he had every reason to believe he would be shot dead unless he behaved as he was bidden.

In consequence, it seems to stretch the plausible description of an action too far to build a 'coercion exception clause' into the very definition. The question of an agent's degree of culpability for an act performed, is most usually regarded as a second order question, to be assessed once it has been determined what the nature of the intended act or omission undertaken was.

On the basis of the above analysis, I will adopt the following usage to signify what is connoted by the word suicide (and other linguistic synonyms). Here, suicide is to be taken to mean: *an act or omission whose proximate effect results in the person's own bodily death, voluntarily undertaken, with the intended objective (whether as an end-in-itself or as a means-to-some-further- end) that one's bodily life be so terminated.*

Assisted Suicide. The term 'assisted suicide' attempts to classify the role played by a third party in the suicide of another person. The phrase can receive additional specification, as is the phrase—'physician assisted suicide'— whereby a designated class of person performing the assistance is referred to as a qualifier. The term has come to prominence due to an apprehended difference in act-description between the analysis of an act of assisted suicide and one of voluntary euthanasia. In an act of assisted suicide the final 'act of killing' in a 'chain of acts' is said to be left to the suicide, and is not actually performed by the third party—the assister. A typical case of assisted suicide would entail a physician furnishing a patient with a lethal dose of narcotics in order to end his or her own life. The final act of ministration would be performed by the patient and not the physician.

In addition to what has already be said on suicide above, I will confine myself here to some initial clarifying reflections on the status of intent. To furnish another person with the necessary means to take their own life, following a suicide request, can usually be described as intending that the other person in fact be killed by the provision of such means (since the provision of such means is a *conditio sine qua non* central to the attainment of that objective). Now, it is often said that the assister need not intend death as an end-in-itself but only as a means to some further end, e.g., the ending of suffering in the context of the physician-patient relationship. However, it is surely odd to say that an intended end can simply lead to the re-description of a whole class of acts under, say, the phrase 'mercy killing.' The question is best stated as one of whether or not it is justifiable to intentionally provide lethal means to another person so that the other person may act to terminate their life *as a means* to some further intended end (the end being the collusive motive of eliminating pain and/or suffering).

Basic questions of intent pertaining to the end of an action, *for the sake of which* a means is being employed, should be distinguished from questions pertaining to the intentional election of means. Consider the question of the relationship between means and ends with reference to the following example: A woman seeks a position as an administrator at a hospital. A friend is the personnel manager. The applicant claims a crucial qualification that she does not have. The proverbial blind eye is turned. She is a single mother with several dependent children to support. She, and her friend, are motivated by an altruistic concern to provide for her family. Yet, notwithstanding that motive of altruism, it would render violence to our basic understanding of relationships between means and ends to claim anything other than that a deliberate deceit was employed as an intended shared means to some further intended end (leaving aside all questions of whether or not such deceit can, in certain circumstances, be morally justified). Questions pertaining to the moral assessment of means cannot be avoided by linguistic turns that seek to redescribe such actions on the basis of the intended end, for means themselves are a distinguishable and highly significant bearer of moral significance in their own right.

It is also argued that it need not always be the case that an assister in a suicide need intend the death of the other person *even as a means*. It seems possible to say that a person provided the means 'reluctantly', and 'hopes' that the other person, intent on committing suicide, does not go through with the final act. Yet, what is being intentionally willed here, even though wishes or desires might be expressed to the contrary, is precisely an act intimately and strategically bound to the performance of the final act by the suicide. The act is still an intimate part of a common enterprise of the provision of lethal means in order to terminate the life of the patient.

Hopes and desires cannot avoid questions of responsibility for what the likely effects of the provision of such means are going to be on a given patient population. Consider the following case that illustrates the point at stake. A man sells heroin to a drug addict. He may hope that the drug addict may not overdose on the drug. However his act of selling the drug was undertaken in the context of knowledge as to the subsequent effects that selling those drugs is likely to have on many drug users. It can be no defence to state that he merely sought to pursue his trade for money and was not responsible for the subsequent use made of the drugs he supplied. He intentionally sold drugs to those he had good reason to believe would run a high risk of overdosing. By analogy, a physician can hardly be said to be able to absolve himself or herself from culpability on the grounds of not intending the death of the patient but of merely having sought to furnish the required means, perhaps out of respect for patient choice.

On the basis of our analysis above, I will use the term assisted suicide to connote: *an act or omission by a third party, voluntarily and knowingly undertaken, whose intent (at the very least) is to furnish a potential suicide with the lethal means necessary to commit suicide.*

13

<u>Voluntary Euthanasia.</u>Turning lastly to the usage of 'voluntary euthanasia', in its classic Greek usage, the Oxford Dictionary points out that the term euthanasia simply meant "a gentle and easy death." It is only within the latter decades of the 19th century that we find the term being used in the modern sense of "the action of inducing a gentle and easy death."[16]

Such a usage, again, however, has several problems attached to it. Firstly, it makes no direct reference to the analysis of a series of acts that falls under the broad category of 'intentional homicide'. This is an important detail, and must be included as part of a serviceable usage. Under the above usage, too many actions of a different kind are simply lumped together under the banner of a non-specific description as to motive. Such a description also fails to adequately account for the importance of including in a definition the possibility of an omission's being the means of killing.

When both of these elements are introduced, it becomes apparent that euthanasia is a species of the class—homicide. A third party, the 'euthanizer,' undertakes the final act of killing the other person. What is said to differentiate euthanasia from the description of assisted suicide is precisely the performer of this final act.

What the Oxford definition does point to, is the sense in which motive plays a peculiar role in the characterisation of this form of homicide. The motive of the third party is said to be the good one of seeking to relieve pain and/or suffering and points out the emphasis placed on motive. Death is not sought as an end-in-itself, but rather as a means of putting the person out of his or her woes.

The definition of euthanasia offered by Tom Beauchamp and Arnold Davidson seems to accurately describe the act-classification of euthanasia, overcoming the deficiencies of intent and omission present in the Oxford definition. They define an act as one of euthanasia if and only if:

> A's death is intended by at least one other human being, B, where B is either the cause of death or a causally relevant feature ... (whether by action or omission) ... [and] there is sufficient evidence for B to believe that A is acutely

> suffering ... [and] B's primary reason for intending A's
> death is the cessation of A's (actual or predicted) ...
> suffering ...[17]

This definition certainly is heading in the right direction for our purposes, since it expresses much of the needed non-arbitrariness, clarity, and discrimination needed in order not to confuse the act-classification of euthanasia with other situations in which death is certainly foreseen, but is not, as such, intended. It also directly brings into play the relevance of omissions as well as acts. Although they do not use the language of 'active' and 'passive' euthanasia common in the literature, these can be broadly interpreted as being the equivalent of act and omission. For our purposes, however, the description is still not specific enough, for it will focus upon a particular form of euthanasia called 'voluntary euthanasia'. This term is somewhat queer at face value since the qualifier—voluntary—refers not to voluntariness on the part of the euthanizer but to the request of the candidate being euthanized. Secondly, the term 'voluntary' is being loosely used, for more than the merely voluntary is being supposed, i.e. consent. Nevertheless, what the qualifier is drawing attention to is the co-operative nature of the final act of killing with the expressed will of the suicide, so we can let that pass providing it is borne in mind that what is being signified is the element of consent and not just voluntariness.

Given the consensual nature of the act characterised here, such an act can be said to entail both an act of intentional self-killing on the part of the suicide and an act of intentional killing on the part of the euthanizer. An act of voluntary euthanasia, can be differentiated from an act of 'non-voluntary' or 'involuntary' euthanasia. An act of non-voluntary euthanasia would entail the intentional killing of a person not capable of granting consent, and an act of involuntary euthanasia would entail the intentional killing of a person who expressly withheld consent.

Since we are, for the most part, interested in the task of the moral and legal evaluation of proposals for the legitimacy, at least under certain circumstances, of the practices of assisted suicide and voluntary euthanasia, I will simply concentrate on adopting a usage for voluntary euthanasia (it would not be hard to adapt this usage, *mutatis mutandis,* to other forms of euthanasia). Voluntary euthanasia can be defined using the vocabulary consistent with our previous definitions as: *an act or omission voluntarily and knowingly performed by a third party, whose intended proximate effect is the suicide's bodily death, undertaken with the motive of relieving acute pain and/or suffering, and expressly consented to by the suicide.*

In concluding this discussion, I will again reiterate the point that such analysis is not intended to settle the question of the moral and legal licitness of any of the acts by means of definitional fiat. Equally, it is not possible to discuss a subject matter without making some attempt to explain what it is that we will be assessing and in doing so, laying down at least some parameters of meaning. Again, I will ask the reader to bear in mind the earlier promissory note made regarding the need to justify the strength of some of the assumptions made in the body of the work. Where my usages are clearly seen to be major points of contestation in the second and third chapters, the reader can, so to speak, bracket them in the conditional pending further justification.

Notes to Chapter One

[1] Thomas Nagel, *The View from Nowhere* (Oxford: Oxford University Press, 1986).

[2] See John Donnelly, "Suicide and Rationality," in *Language, Metaphysics, and Death,* ed. John Donnelly (New York: Fordham University Press, 1978), 87-105.

[3] Whilst my vocabulary is different here from the *fonts moralitatis* of the Thomistic tradition, its structural similarities will become apparent, especially in chapter five of the work.

[4] Throughout this book I will use the terms action(s) and act(s) interchangeably. Nothing is meant to be signified by the use of one word rather than the other.

[5] See Joseph Kupfer, "Suicide: Its Nature and Moral Evaluation," *The Journal of Value Inquiry* 24 (1990): 67-81. Whilst Kupfer defines suicide in a way that leave open the possibility of justifiably intending to killing oneself, he acknowledges the point that how one characterises an action will inevitably affect its moral evaluation. Normative implications will necessarily be influenced by the way in which an action is characterised. An implication of Kupfer's analysis is that definitions of suicide, etc. cannot function in a 'neutral' way.

[6] On the 'open-texture' of the language associated with this topic in the different languages of the Western tradition (Hebrew, Greek, Latin, etc.) see David Daube, "The Linguistics of Suicide," *Philosophy and Public Affairs* 1 (1972): 387-437. See also the detailed study on the use of various terms and euphemisms for 'self-willed death' in the classical languages by Anton J.L. van Hooff, *From Autothanasia to Suicide: Self-killing in Classical Antiquity* (New York: Routledge, 1990), esp. 135-56.

[7] "Herein are they in extreme, that allow a man to be his own assassin, and so highly extol the end and suicide of Cato" (Sir Thomas Browne, *Religio Medici*. 1635, sect. XLIV). Work cited in Alfred Alvarez, *The Savage God: A Study of Suicide* (New York: Random House, 1972), 50. On the equivalent Latin neologism 'suicidium' see van Hooff, *Autothanasia*, 136-37. According to van Hooff, the neologism is attributed to L. Caramuel in his *Theolgia Moralis Fundamentalis* (Rome, 1656). Caramuel uses the word under the title *De Homicidio* in the context of a discussion concerning the scope of the biblical fifth commandment.

[8] By omission I mean the non-performance of an action that was within the scope of a person's power of agency to perform.

[9] For an interesting examination of the place of rhetoric in historical and contemporary discussions concerning the use of the word 'suicide' and its various euphemisms, see Suzanne Stern-Gillet, "The Rhetoric of Suicide," *Philosophy and Rhetoric* 20 (1987): 160-70.

[10] A significant usage of suicide that does not definitionally rule out the possibility of all suicides being immoral is seen in the Roman Catholic tradition whereby a distinction is made between cases of *direct* and *indirect* suicide. Only direct suicides are condemned as an illicit taking of human life. See Robert Barry, "The Development of the Roman Catholic Teachings on Suicide," *Notre Dame Journal of Law, Ethics and Public Policy* 9 (1995): 449-501.

[11] Émile Durkheim, *Suicide,* trans. J.A. Spaulding and G. Simpson (Glencoe: Free Press, 1951).

[12] Durkheim, *Suicide*, 44.

[13] Richard Brandt, "The Morality and Legality of Suicide," in *A Handbook for the Study of Suicide,* ed. Seymour Perlin (New York: Oxford University Press, 1975), 117.

[14] Tom L. Beauchamp, "Suicide," in *Matters of Life and Death: New Introductory Essays in Moral Philosophy*, ed. Tom Regan (New York: McGraw-Hill, 1994), 77.

[15] Case of *Regina v. Dudley and Stephens*, discussed by Alan Donagan in his *Theory of Morality* (Chicago: Chicago University Press, 1977), 175-77.

[16] W. E. H. Lecky, *A History of European Morals from Augustus to Charlemagne* (London: Longmans, 1869), vol. I, 233.

[17] Tom Beauchamp and Arnold Davidson , "The Definition of Euthanasia," *Journal of Medicine and Philosophy* 4 (1979): 294-312, 304.

Chapter Two

A History of Ideas Concerning the Morality of Suicide, Assisted Suicide and Voluntary Euthanasia

Introduction

Questions concerning the legitimacy of the practices of suicide, assisted suicide, and voluntary euthanasia are some of the most controversial currently debated in Western society.[1] However, the issues raised by those debates are not new, and have a long history informed by many centuries of thought.[2] The challenge of engaging in an exhaustive review and analysis of that history would, however, take us way beyond the limited scope of this work.

The aim of this chapter, rather, is the more modest one of identifying some of the main historical protagonists, and delineating some of the key arguments that have been used concerning the acceptance or rejection of those practices. Due to practical limitations concerning the scope of the chapter, our analysis will be confined to the 'stage' of the Western tradition. Consequently, questions of insight and differences in perspective from other traditions, e.g., Eastern and Oriental, will not be engaged.[3]

Further, concerning questions of scope, it should be pointed out that this chapter will not give any substantive consideration to an evaluation of the claims of Christian faith concerning the existence or non-existence of prohibitions contained in Hebrew or Christian Scripture against the practices of suicide and euthanasia. The evaluation of such special or privileged sources of knowledge concerning morality are beyond the scope of our inquiry, based as it is on philosophy, not theology. This question of scope is not to discount the importance of such lines of inquiry concerning the relationship between faith and reason.[4] Rather, it is merely to state that the scope necessarily has to be limited to questions of what can and cannot be justified by natural reason in the light of our attempt to pose publicly accessible reasons that can, in principle, inform 'secular' morality and law in this area.[5]

The history of suicide and euthanasia practices may, at first glance, seem to have only a distant influence upon the contemporary debate. Yet, the historical development of thinking on the subject is vital if we are to adequately contextualise the contemporary arguments made against traditional negative prohibitions; prohibitions that have hitherto formed the status quo in the West.[6] Being able to claim historical support lends credence to claims, especially when those figures or sources appealed to have had a significant impact on contemporary patterns of thought.[7] It is to the task of reviewing and analysing those historically rooted ideas, that I now turn.

Ideas from Greek and Roman Thought

Socrates/Plato

In the thought of Socrates and Plato, the idea of an objective order of moral truth, based upon an examination of human nature, as apprehended by the use of human reason, is discussed and defended.[8] The human person is not merely an instinctual creature, but is also a creature of reason. The human person possesses a higher power or intellect that is capable of apprehending knowledge of an array of concerns, including a knowledge of what constitutes good human conduct.[9]

For Socrates and Plato, ignorance of objective truth concerning the good life is ultimately a constitutive source of misery and unhappiness.[10] The exercise of wisdom in the conduct of life is the central focus of Socratic ethics. The good life was not merely the useful or the pleasant. Rather, at is most perfect, it was to be equated with the noble good of the interior life of the human soul.[11]

Turning to a brief assessment of the characterisation of Socrates' view on the human soul, it is important to consider a text that relates the last days of his life—the *Phaedo* [61d]-[62d]. Here Socrates presents something of a Pythagorean opposition to the idea of suicide.[12] Life is not the possession of the person, to be taken or disposed of at will. As dependent beings, we have

20

been placed in the body by the gods and are therefore not free to abandon this station.[13] Socrates certainly recognises the many impediments to wisdom that the human body can place in the path of a seeker of truth—pain, suffering, desires, etc. However, the body cannot ultimately be despised, since it is a necessary instrument.[14] Any dualism between body and soul that exists in Socrates' thought does not therefore entail the *necessary conclusion* that the care of the body can be readily rejected once certain impediments to the flourishing of the person come into play.[15]

For Socrates and Plato, there is a fundamental teleological good in overcoming deficiencies in this life in preparation for life after death. For, if this were not so, why could not death be more quickly sought by intentional design? It is precisely this sort of challenge that Augustine would subsequently make to those over-eager for the choice of martyrdom.[16] Here, I think, Socrates is relating something of an embryonic discrimination between wishing or anticipating an outcome and deliberately and intentionally acting to bringing that outcome about. [17]

Critics of Socrates' opposition to suicide in the *Phaedo* turn to Plato's *Republic* as offering some support for the licitness of suicide or voluntary euthanasia under certain circumstances. Does not Plato argue that rational suicide is possible where there is an incurable and wasting disease or disability that the person is suffering from?[18]

It does not follow, however, as Cooper perceptively argues, that Plato's argument in Republic III 405a-410 leads to that conclusion.[19] The discussion is set within the boundary of what is just, a term that has a deep, objective teleological reality for Plato. Plato understood that there was a natural law, or a natural justice, which was the foundation of all law. The laws of a state should be just in that they should reflect and participate in the Ideal Laws, and justice should reflect and participate in those ideals. It is not ideal justice to strive officiously with every possible means to keep alive.[20] The soul has an ultimate purpose beyond bodily life. To maintain the body at all costs may actually harm, not further, the perfection of the soul. There is, for Plato, a *via media* to be discerned (albeit somewhat anachronistically) between the use of every means to sustain bodily life and what can be termed 'reasonable means' based on an assessment of the person's benefits and burdens. The tenor of what Plato is advocating here is more a case of what we would now call cases of allowing to die rather than cases of intentional self-killing.[21]

Our concise analysis of Plato's thought derives an added layer of complexity due to his discussion of suicide in the Laws [873c-d].[22] Some commentators have argued that Plato, when he is removed from the context of a deep metaphysic, influenced by mysticism, states his support for certain acts of suicide and euthanasia.[23]

I find such a conclusion unconvincing, however, since the apparent exceptions listed in support of this claim—compulsion, misfortune, disgrace—need not be interpreted as dispensations from the general ground shared by Socrates and Plato for opposition to those practices.[24] Rather, they can be plausibly interpreted as enacting ameliorative legal measures designed to show some compassion towards those who have acted in taking their own lives. They should not, for example, be denied a burial by family members. This hardly seems to imply a condonation of the practice but rather an easing of the otherwise harsh effects of Athenian law.[25]

Aristotle

Moving on to consider the thought of Aristotle, we see that he raises the question of the licitness of suicide in the Nicomachean Ethics [1138a].[26] For Aristotle, every human act, performed voluntarily and intentionally, has a built in purposefulness—a teleology. His ethics is, therefore, an inherently teleological one, the purpose being a good life centred on the pursuit of human happiness (flourishing).[27] Intellectual and moral virtues are required in order to promote the integral pursuit of full human development.[28] It is the task of prudence to discern in the particular context of action, the practical undertaking, of 'doing', what is an appropriate fit between the action and the goods that form the proximate ends of the action.[29]

For Aristotle, one of the moral virtues to be considered in relation to suicide is justice—the moral virtue of rendering to each person his or her due. As with Plato, Aristotle also considered the act of suicide to be an act of injustice, but he reached that judgement on different grounds. Suicide *per se* is not considered an act of injustice against the person who takes his or her own life (i.e., against the interests of perfecting the human soul, as it was for Socrates and Plato), but rather, is considered an act of injustice against the very state or society that is deprived of the shared participatory life of that person.[30] For Aristotle, justice requires an interpersonal dimension. Thus, whilst persons, strictly speaking, cannot render unto themselves an injustice, such an injustice can be visited upon forms of human society.[31]

Aristotle's analysis concerning justice does not end here, for he thinks that laws should help to render people virtuous and suppress vice. If suicides generally were determined to be acts contrary to virtue in other ways, the law could seek to function to justly suppress that vice. Aristotle makes such a judgement under the heading of a vice against moderation (or temperance) in the *Nicomachean Ethics* at [1116a]. Suicide is considered wrong because it is not a moderate act, but rather, is judged an excessive act. It can be summarised by the judgement that he considered suicide to result from a lack of courage, a weakness in the face of affliction, or from the contrary excess, rashness, i.e., an excess of courage.[32] The person of practical wisdom (the *phronimos*) is the very person, who, by the cultivation and application of the intellectual virtue of right reason, is able to discern the mean between excesses. Thus, for Aristotle, no right thinking, well balanced person, would commit the immoderation of suicide.[33]

This passage seems to illustrate a general opposition to suicide (*per se*) since a person is said to lack the requisite fortitude needed to put up with the trials and tribulations of life's lot. James Rist and Droge and Tabor, however, assert that Aristotle's remarks should not be taken as a condemnation of suicide as such.[34] They suggest that Aristotle appears to recognise exceptions, since the list of exclusionary categories covered does not appear to be exhaustive.[35]

Yet, contrary to their interpretation on this point, it seems entirely plausible to argue that an act of 'rashness' could also cover, say, the ignominy of loss in battle, dishonour, etc., and that, in consequence, Aristotle does not endorse "the normal Greek view," that certain categories of suicide were morally acceptable to the *phronimos*, the standard setter of right reason.[36]

Stoicism

The Stoic philosophy of life and death was in large measure responsible for the intellectual justification of suicide in later Greek and subsequent Roman society.[37] In Roman society, many of the famous 'cults' of suicide could trace their inspiration to Stoic doctrines via the examples of the deaths of some of its leading exponents.[38] The founder of the school, Zeno of Citium, was said to have committed suicide by holding his breath because he had suffered a fall and had fractured one of the digits of his foot.[39]

The Stoic philosophy was centred on the idea of determining the reason or order of things—the *logos*—a kind of eternal metaphysical rationality governing the structures of the universe. The primary object of life was to discern this rationality, and to conduct both one's life and one's death in conformity to this. Thus the goal of all human beings was to live in accordance with this reasoned understanding of nature, as given by the *logos*. Decisions made should not be governed by reactions to the world surrounding the individual, but by a cultivated indifference to the things of the world as they can impinge upon the individual will centred on the *logos*.[40]

The only goods present in human life were acts of virtue in conformity with the *logos*, and the only evil, vice. All other acts were indifferent. Of indifferent acts, there was a further categorisation into 'indifferent but preferred' and 'indifferent but not preferred'.[41] Life was normally to be preferred and death not normally to be preferred. For a transition from one preference category to another, however, the presence of a virtuous reason was required. For the Stoics, only suicide in accordance with reason was morally acceptable, since it alone instantiated the necessary virtue to justify the act.[42] What then were those conditions?

Firstly, there was the notion of suicides in fulfilment of obligations to others. Since life in itself was *only a preference*, a virtuous reason could be provided by appealing to suicide for the sake of country, friends, family, causes, etc.[43]

Secondly, suicides associated with shame or dishonour. A good example of this kind of suicide would be the death of Cato. After Cato's troops, in the service of Pompey, were defeated by Caesar, he decided to take his own life by stabbing himself, thus absolving himself from the ignominy of defeat in battle.[44]

Thirdly, cases in the more contemporary sense of 'rational' suicide—self-killing in order to offset the effects of pain, mutilation, or incurable illness. Suicide was rational for anyone faced with an imbalance in the kind of things likely to threaten the ability of the individual will to remain properly indifferent to them. Death, so to speak, was an act of reasserting control, thus acting virtuously in defeating the threat to indifference.[45]

Whilst there was a general acceptance amongst the Stoics that suicide could indeed be a morally justifiable practice, there is a notable exception to this in the thought of Cicero.[46] Cicero affirmed that there is indeed a natural law, accessible to human inquiry, by the function of right reason to apprehend the ends of human goodness. Whilst he agreed that there is a primacy to the internal good of self-mastery over the impact of external contingencies, and with it a fostering of the virtues necessary to achieve this, he affirmed the importance of recognising the integration of the person in mind and body.[47] In a manner somewhat reminiscent of the thought of Socrates and Plato, Cicero believed that bodily life could not be treated as a dispensable instrumentality, a mere preference, in the pursuit of the more 'noble good' (i.e., the perfectibility of the human soul). A person could not, in consequence, take his or her own life, even in more extreme cases, unless there was a clear sign from the gods that the act was in conformity with the natural law dictated by right reason (human reason in conformity with the will of the eternal).[48]

Epicureanism

Certain accounts of Epicureanism, such as the account posed by Robert Barry, suggest that the Epicureans granted approval to suicides under any circumstances.[49] Yet this is a somewhat overstated claim (coloured, no doubt, by later contemporary images as to what adherence to a doctrine of 'hedonism' necessarily entailed). For example, the founder of the school, Epicurus, died in quite a different manner from the death of Zeno of Citium. Epicurus died of natural causes that resulted in immense pain during his last days.[50] On the face of it, this seems odd, since the Stoic school taught that virtue was the good to be pursued and the Epicureans hedonistic pleasure. Yet, the key to understanding Epicurus's stance is that he was in fact rather more wary of embracing suicide than Zeno. He taught, for example, that an important part of the goal of meeting our desires was to overcome fear of death (death representing annihilation or extinction) and to resist the physical impulses of pain in order to achieve the 'higher pleasure' of overcoming this fear of death.[51]

Such nuances of thought can easily be glossed over under the belief that Epicureanism was necessarily a narrowly hedonistic doctrine. Rather than being heavily permissive towards the practice of self-killing, their attitude can be better described as more one of toleration for those who were not able to demonstrate the necessary degree of control.[52] It was far from being regarded as an ideal or model to follow.[53] In Epicureanism, therefore, there was no widespread enthusiasm for the practice of suicide, an enthusiasm present amongst many of the Stoic writers. The boldest statement permitting certain suicides was made by Hegesias who taught the desirability of suicide as a means of ending painful existence that could no longer be endured.[54] Yet, even this endorsement was significantly more restrained than the general impression current amongst popular conceptions as to what Epicureanism actually entailed.[55]

Ideas from Augustinian and Thomistic Thought

Problem of Martyrdom

One of the perplexities to confront early Christian communities was the question of human conduct in the face of persecution. Margaret Battin, for example, makes the claim that prior to the teaching of Augustine, there was practically an epidemic of "voluntary martyrdom" that threatened the very survival of early Christian communities.[56] In my view, however, such a statement serves to confuse more than it illuminates, for it fails to adequately consider the complexity of the issue of what was deemed to constitute suicide.[57]

In analysing further questions of martyrdom, such cases almost have to be judged on a case-by-case basis. Here, I will simply point out one possible model that could be used, in certain cases, to justify martyrdom, and thus differentiate it from cases of intentional self-killing. When faced with the challenge of renouncing faith or facing death (or other punishment), the martyr accepts the latter. Death may be foreseen as a certainty. The 'call of eternal salvation' can even be 'wished for' and be a source of consolation. However, it does not necessarily follow from a foreknowledge of the consequences, that death is, as such, intended. Whilst the choice made is voluntary, to accept death rather than deny faith, death itself need not be said to form a part of the scope of the martyr's intention.[58] In analysing cases of 'voluntary martyrdom' (whatever the cause; defence of religion, defence of political goals, etc.),[59] the term merely stresses a willingness to accept death for the sake of a 'just' cause, and does not sufficiently discriminate between cases where martyrdom has been brought about by means of self-intended death from those where it has not.[60]

Augustine of Hippo

Although Augustine was heavily influenced in his thought by neo-Platonic influences (e.g., by Plotinus and Boethius), he resisted any strong tendency to devalue the corporeal body in anticipation of eternal life.[61] He stressed the gift of life as a free gift of God to be reverenced and respected. [62] The incarnation was a profound truth for Augustine as it was for Christians generally. Jesus accepted death and in doing so brought about the redemption of the world.[63]

Augustine's understanding of the significance of the life of Jesus was in contrast to those zealously eager for martyrdom (e.g., the Circumcellions and the Donatists) a zealotry that, to his mind, neglected the gift of earthly life and the duties of responsible stewardship.[64] Such responsible stewardship for Augustine was evident in the case of Christian virgins who did not seek revenge for their defilement by killing themselves, as had often been the Roman practice (Lucretcia being the prototype of this form of martyrdom).[65] Their refusal to kill themselves demonstrated the virtues of heroism and courage in the face of adversity. Thus, for Augustine, such is the value of bodily life, that even such a grave affront to human dignity could not justify an act of suicide.[66] Whilst he expressed compassion for their predicament, such is the value of bodily life and the call of responsible stewardship, that even those circumstances could not empower a private individual with a right of authority to determine the manner and timing of his or her own death.[67]

In Augustine's interpretation, authentic martyrdom required a *limitation of means* in witnessing faith. Death, even certain death, can be accepted or even welcomed in anticipation of the good being pursued. However, it cannot be attained by a resort to intentional self-killing (in contravention of his understanding of the scope of the Fifth Commandment).[68] In contrast, authentic martyrdom was considered to be an act which was aimed at the good of witness and not at self-destruction. In Augustine's thought here we can see the implied use of the principle of double effect as it became known in subsequent tradition, and which was itself considered to be a refinement of the Pauline maxim that evil may not be done that good may come of it.[69]

Thomas Aquinas

In Aquinas's thought, we can observe a synthesising of Aristotelian philosophy and Christian revelation.[70] With Aristotelian metaphysics, Aquinas was able to more systematically explain the relationship of the soul and body in one 'body-person'.[71] The soul constituted the form of the body. The human being, therefore, was neither essentially soul or body but rather a unique synthesis of two principles of form and matter in one unitary substance.[72] Aquinas, therefore, rejected any dualistic tendency to devalue the corporeal body instrumentally in the name of the immortality of the soul (although dualism, as we have seen with our discussion of Plato, need not be *logically compelled* to reach such a conclusion).[73]

Aquinas insisted that the elemental norms of the *Decalogue* can (in principle at least) be apprehended by the use of right reason, accessible to all.[74] As such, reason need not appeal to such special or privileged sources of knowledge to inform common morality. Through the use of right reason, the human person can recognise the goodness of certain basic inclinations of human existence. The first self-evident precept apprehended by reason, operating practically, is that "good is to be done and pursued and evil is to be avoided."[75] Such a precept is apprehended by the insight of practical reason. In pursuing and doing the good, Aquinas means precisely the pursuit of those goods, apprehended by our capacity for practical reason, as being genuine goods of the human person. Aquinas enumerated (at least) five such primary goods perfective of the human person, including the inclination to preserve human life in its existence.[76] Taken together, these *bona humana* are directed to the intermediate end of human flourishing (apprehended by reason), and are ultimately considered by Aquinas to be ordered towards the final end of heavenly beatitude (apprehended by faith).[77]

Concerning the preservation of human life, Aquinas, as with Augustine, made certain exceptions for divine command intervening in the life of the person (e.g., Abraham's sacrifice of his son Isaac), for the conduct of just war, and for the use of delegated authority for the punishment of criminals.[78]

Aquinas, however clearly denies the licitness of any private use of intentional killing, whether self inflicted or inflicted by another.[79]

Such denial of the private use of intentional killing can be seen in his discussion of self defence, and can be said to represent the *locus classicus* of the principle of double effect.[80] A person can use force, even lethal force, if necessary (undertaken as a last resort), to protect human life from the action of an aggressor.[81] A crucial qualifying point here, however, is that the use of lethal force need not have the intended object of inflicting death as the means of bringing about the good of protecting human life from unjust attack. Aquinas stressed the scope of the person's intention relating to the order of goodness. The object intended needs to be self protection and not the actual death of the aggressor.[82]

Turning now to his analysis of suicide in *II-II, q. 64. a 5*, Aquinas posits four reasons for a condemnation of suicide. In Aquinas's first non-philosophical argument, he rejected suicide on the basis of a claim to have dominion. Such a power belongs to God (and in certain limited circumstances to God's delegates in civil government), not to the individual.[83]

Secondly, he considered suicide to be an act of injustice against the community. Drawing upon Aristotle, he developed the notion that the individual does not exist as an isolate, whose individual actions consequently cannot be severed from their impact on the wider community, instantiated in the framework of a shared participatory common good.[84] Such is the value of innocent human life that a community may never justly sanction its taking. One of the primary rationales for the justification of state authority and the force vested in it is precisely to protect innocent human life from all threats of private killing that disturb the order of a common framework of mutual obligation.[85]

Thirdly, Aquinas's main natural law argument against suicide *in and of itself*, concerns the basic apprehension of the good of human life itself, one of the *bona humana*, corresponding to the natural inclination to preserve life. Being human, for Aquinas, entails an apprehension of the nature of this good as understood by our capacity for practical human reason.[86] To intentionally act against such a good is therefore to disrupt the order of moral goodness communicated to us by our capacity for practical reason, that grasps the nature of certain goods, and with it, the duties imposed upon choice that we have in relation to the proper apprehension of those values.[87]

Fourthly, to act contrary to this good was to act against charity—love owed to all—including the self. Suicide was regarded as an infliction of harm against this charity owed to self. One cannot truly love the self (in terms of the full signification of what is said to truly perfect or actualise the self) and yet intentionally seek the very destruction of self (an act of ontological deprivation that intentionally wounds the self by self-inflicted destruction).[88]

Finally, in an earlier article of the *Summa,* II-II q. 58, a. 1, Aquinas reiterates Aristotle's objection to suicide as an act against the virtue of fortitude. All people have a responsibility to develop the required virtue to do what is right even under the most pressing of circumstances. This requires the cultivation of resolve in the face of pressure to the contrary. In an act of suicide, there is not the required resolve present to suffer the effects of adversity and thus hold on to that which is constantly good—the innocent life that continues to inhere in the body of the person.[89]

Francisco de Vitoria

To inquire in to the subsequent development of scholastic and neo-scholastic thought would take us too far afield, limited as we are by the constraints of length.[90] It must suffice, for our purposes, to note the work of Francisco de Vitoria as indicative of the trend of further refinement in the arguments already essentially adduced by Aquinas—firstly, the development of casuistry in the differentiation of seemingly similar cases (informed by an analysis of the principle of double effect), and secondly, the extent to which a person was subjected to measures to preserve his or her own life.[91]

In his *De Homicidio* and his Commentary on the *Summa Theologiae* II-II q. 64, we find Vitoria ruling out all forms of direct self-killing as contrary to the inclination to preserve human life.[92] However, certain forms of self-killing which may apparently be considered intentional acts of self-killing cannot be regarded as such. It is here that Vitoria introduces a certain 'fleshing out' of Aquinas's thought on the legitimacy of, and scope for, the operation of the principle of double effect.

It is sufficient here for the purposes of illustration to consider only one case—the martyr, Apollonia. She is said to have leapt into the fire prepared by her tormentors to kill her. Did she not intentionally will the hastening of her own death? Vitoria, argues, however, that such a judgement would be mistaken. Firstly, she did not intentionally co-operate in her own death. She was assuredly going to be executed shortly anyway and there was no possible means of escape. Rather, in acting the way she did, she intended only to deprive her tormentors of the further pleasure of holding unjust power over her life. Her precise scope of intention then could be described as ending the spectacle, and in doing so, preserve her dignity in the face of it, whilst bearing witness to her faith in God.[93]

Turning to the second question, of duties to preserve life, Vitoria makes the important point that "in order to preserve life, it is not necessary to use all means—but only those which of themselves are both fitting and suitable."[94] Vitoria is essentially making the claim that a person is not obliged to use all possible means to preserve life (a point, as already noted, that can in fact be traced, embryonically, to Plato), and that the use of means must be judged in relation to a consideration of a person's contingent circumstances. Whilst there is always considered to be a direct negative obligation never to intentionally take innocent human life, there was an obligation to be realistic in the claims made concerning the duties of action to positively preserve life. It is important to be clear here that this claim *did not entail* that there could not be an intention to self-kill by omission. Rather, there is recognition here that some omissions are consistent with the purpose of avoiding certain burdens and that death need not, therefore, be intended.[95]

Ideas from Renaissance and Early Modern Thought

Ideational Change

During the Renaissance it is possible to detect the first signs of an intellectual and cultural weakening on the prohibition against suicide found in Latin Christianity. The impact of learning derived from the Stoic and Epicurean visions of humanity led to a renewed questioning of the grounds for its moral condemnation under all circumstances.[96] Typical of this renewed interest in Greek and Roman learning was a questioning and searching for answers to the meaning of life independently of the answers provided by the attempts to synthesis faith and reason in the Mediaeval schools of thought.[97] It was during the Renaissance that we can observe the first strains of what can be described as a 'turn to the subject', and with it the idea that humanity is more beholden to its own created image of self than of any external design (whether that design be imposed by nature or by divinity).[98]

In his *Oration on the Dignity of Man*, for example, Pico della Mirandola, expressed the idea that the human person is more the shaper and fashioner of its own being than any extrinsic source.[99] For Mirandola, suicide could be a sign of the dignity of the human person as effective sculptor of his or her own life, for whilst life depended on the will of others to bring it to be, death was dependent largely on the self.[100]

Michel de Montaigne

It is with the *Essays* of Montaigne that the question of approval of suicide is taken up as a subject for detailed examination.[101] Whilst not original, he expressed a blending of Stoic and Epicurean views to support the licitness of suicide under certain circumstances.[102] Through the guise of an essay on events practised on the Isle of Cea (an Ancient Greek society that kept a public store of poison for suicide), he took to task, by weight of example, the prohibition on all forms of suicide. From the tenor of his examples it is clear that he finds unconvincing the notion that the manner and timing of death are

33

left in the hands of God, for "death is a remedy against all evils: it is a most assured haven, never to be feared, and often to be sought. ... The most voluntary death is the finest. Life depends on the pleasure of others; death upon our own."[103]

What is significant in Montaigne's account of suicide is his desire to separate it from the context of theological speculation and place it's assessment firmly within an 'experiential' mould.[104] When viewed through the light of so many renowned ancient authors who justified the practice, he came to the conclusion that questions of pain, suffering, and fear of a worse death, could justify suicide and kindly assistance in suicide.[105]

Here we can see some affinity with the idea of the plasticity of the human condition remarked upon earlier by Pico della Mirandola. The clear implications of this thought are not hard to draw, and have an 'unmistakable ring' that resounds today.[106] The question of suicide should be viewed more as a question of personal decision making, to be left to the judgement and conscience of the individual, and should not, therefore, be the subject for any sort of absolutist imposed norm prohibiting the practice (at least in circumstances where the act of killing is informed by a merciful motivation in conditions of pain and suffering).

John Donne

The primary weakening of opposition to the immorality of suicide, in the early modern period, took place amongst some Anglican clerics.[107] Amongst their number can be included Robert Burton's *Anatomy of Melancoly* and John Donne's *Biathanatos*. (Only Donne's text will be considered.)[108]

Donne's work was notable for its attempt to demonstrate that suicide was not incompatible with the law of nature or the law of reason.[109] As such, it takes the form of an implicit attempt to refute the arguments made by Aquinas in the *Summa Theologiae*, on the immorality of suicide.[110] His treatise, in several key respects, foreshadowed the subsequent attack on Aquinas's arguments made by David Hume a century and a half later.[111]

In Part one of *Biathanatos*, Donne argued, contrary to Aquinas, that everything does not always seek naturally to preserve itself, regardless of circumstance. If life can be said to be natural, so too can death itself. There can be said to be a natural desire for dying that is part and parcel of the human condition. On natural grounds, therefore, it cannot be demonstrated that the claims of a tendency to 'self-preservation' must always, so to speak, 'trump' this other tendency inherent in nature. He drew upon many classical instances of self-induced death to demonstrate that the desire for 'death as release' is also part of 'nature's fabric'.[112]

In Part Two of *Biathanatos*, Donne turned to argue that suicide cannot in all circumstances be regarded as against the law of reason as found in civil and canon law. There was no necessary wrong in suicide such that it must necessarily be regarded as a crime against the state or the community. Certain forms of suicide do not endanger the state or the community. There was therefore no necessary relationship between suicide and the claim that it necessarily entailed an act of injustice. Whilst Donne was against certain forms of suicide, e.g., suicides motivated by vengeance, atonement for past sins, avoidance of future sin, etc., he was highly doubtful of the efficacy of the law to deter them.[113]

Thomas Hobbes

Notwithstanding those arguments of Donne, inspired by sympathetic motivations towards the relief of intense human suffering, the onset of the new materialist oriented scientific outlook (inspired by the method of Francis Bacon), initially brought in its wake a rejection of ideas of suicide.[114] This rejection can be seen most forcefully in the work of Thomas Hobbes and his understanding of what constituted the "law of human nature."[115]

Unlike previous natural law based theories (i.e., Plato, Aristotle, and Aquinas), based as they are on a teleological understanding of the good ends of the human person, as apprehended by human reason, Hobbes saw human nature as essentially a complex of material sense perceptions and passions, chief amongst them being drives of egotistical desire.[116] This led Hobbes to deny that the human person was capable of grasping the traditional fonts of natural law theory based on teleology and reason, "[f]or there is no such *finis ultimus*, utmost aim, or *summum bonum*, greatest good, as is spoken of in the books of the old moral philosophers. ... Felicity is a continual progress of desire, from one object to another ...."[117]

Given Hobbes's materialist view of human nature reduced to a consideration of desires and aversions, it is simply a recurring drive of human nature, so conceived, for human beings to seek the means of their own self-preservation.[118] The central aim of his political philosophy was to create sets of conditions whereby peace and security would promote the self-interested conditions necessary to sustain the self in existence, viz., the promotion of peace and security in the Leviathan state.[119] Reason was understood only to operate in an instrumental fashion in order to further the pursuit of the self-interested drives of human nature.[120]

Since Hobbes considered it axiomatic that the human bundle of desires and aversions necessarily seeks to perpetuate itself in existence, it would be contrary to this law of our nature to positively act against this impulse. Thus, as we have this strong perpetual desire, so it would be acting against this law of our nature to thwart it. [121] For Hobbes, only the state of madness itself (*non compos mentis* by virtue of inner torment), could bring a person to reach the conclusion that the 'unnaturalness' of acting against the impulse towards self-preservation, could possibly be opted for.[122]

Ideas from Enlightenment Thought

General Overview

With the rise of enlightenment thought in the 18th century, there were several notable proponents of suicide who thought that there was nothing essentially contrary to reason in the idea of suicide.[123] In this regard they represented an increasing 'secular' challenge to the waning traditional opinion that suicide and assistance in death were necessarily immoral acts. Several authors whose names can be mentioned here include Robeck, Montesquieu, Voltaire, Rousseau, Beccaria, Helvetius, Vauvenargues, D'Holbach, Condorcet, and Charron.[124] Here it can be summarily stated that all those authors saw suicide as a legitimate practice for a variety of life's predicaments, e.g., unremitting pain, uncontrollable suffering, and deep-seated melancholia. Space prevents any detailed elaboration on the many nuances of thought expressed by those thinkers. Suffice it to make the following remarks. Charles Montesquieu, stressed the point that it was absurd to think that a good and loving God could wish to see a person suffer and pretend to turn it in to a blessing for the afflicted.[125] Voltaire (François Marie Arouet) recognised that suicidal thoughts were often symptoms of physical illness and a loss of control over self. In such circumstances, the act was beyond punishment or moral condemnation.[126] Jean Jacques Rousseau returned to the ancient theme that by an act of suicide we do not destroy the person, only the body, and thus we should not view the mater with such significance.[127]

For the remainder of this section I shall restrict myself to the views of two prominent philosophers, who, in differing ways, stand at the apex of enlightenment thought—David Hume and Immanuel Kant.

David Hume

Hume's scepticism concerning the claims made on behalf of human reason to acquire knowledge, especially moral knowledge, led him to reject the possibility of deriving or 'reading off' normative claims from descriptive propositions of human nature—whether based upon Aristotelian natural teleology or Hobbes's materialist framework of egoistic self-interest.[128]

In the first book of his *Treatise of Human Nature*, Hume forcefully presented the distinction between 'fact' and 'value', and the logical non-derivability of the latter from the former, in the following terms:

> In every system of morality, which I have hitherto met with,
> I have always remark'd, that the author proceeds for some
> time in the ordinary way of reasoning, and ... makes

observations concerning human affairs; when of a sudden I am surpriz'd to find, that instead of the usual copulations of propositions, is, and is not, I meet with no proposition that is not connected with an ought, or an ought not … [as] this ought, or ought not, expresses some new relation or affirmation, 'tis necessary that it shou'd be observ'd and explain'd; and at the same time that a reason should be given, for what seems altogether inconceivable, how this new relation can be a deduction from others, which are entirely different from it.[129]

In his posthumously published essay, *On Suicide*, Hume argued that suicide could in principle be justified, since none of the prevailing arguments against its universal prohibition were sound.[130] In the text, Hume applies both his sceptical epistemology and his moral theory of natural sentiment (essentially emotivist approval and disapproval) to his evaluation of the subject. Reason cannot discover what is good or bad in life. Rather, the 'good' is that which we are inclined to think useful based on our sentiments, and badness that which does not hold for the satisfaction of sentiments.[131]

In the first philosophical argument tackled by Hume, that suicide be contrary to nature (the argument from self-preservation), Hume makes the point that human kind interferes constantly with all manner of natural laws, so why should the question of life or death be viewed any differently from all other manner of interference? If there be such a tendency in nature towards the preservation of life, this cannot dictate whether or not it is right or wrong to end a life any more that it is right or wrong to interfere with any other natural occurrences in the scheme of things.[132] Hume therefore claims that an act of committing suicide is as much an interference against nature as treating, say, a naturally occurring disease of the body. In the words of Hume, "if I turn aside a stone which is falling upon my head, I disturb the course of nature", so why should that change of a natural course be any different from ending one's life?[133] Hume, therefore, concluded that if it is acceptable to interfere with a law of nature, then suicide cannot be held to be wrong on account of disturbing such laws.[134]

Hume's second philosophical argument (contrary to the claim that suicide was an act of injustice against society) was designed to demonstrate that suicide did not entail any necessary act of injustice against neighbour.[135] Society, in Hume's view existed to ensure mutual benefit, and the bonds that tied a person to society cease when there was no longer a mutuality of benefit to be derived. An individual faced with great suffering was in just such a situation, and any claim on the individual by society was extinguished, for there was no longer any bond that must be preserved.[136]

In Hume's defence of suicide, there can be discerned clear lines of argumentation utilised in the contemporary debate concerning acts of assisted suicide and euthanasia. In short, suicide need not be considered an 'irrational' or 'unnatural act' contrary to reason, but rather can be viewed as an act perfectly compatible with a broadly utilitarian outlook rooted in natural sentiment towards contentment. As the toils and tribulations on an individual's life increase, so the claims made on behalf of society for that life's preservation, diminish to the point of extinction.[137]

Immanuel Kant

In Kant's *Groundwork of the Metaphysic of Morals*, we see an attempt to provide an alternative foundation to morality based on the idea of pure reason divorced, from any attempt to root morality in the passions (Hume), in selfish drives (Hobbes), or in a teleological theory of the good (Aristotle, Aquinas).[138] For Kant, a will that is governed by passion or feeling is not an autonomous will but a heteronomous will.[139] Desires or other extrinsic attractions, as such, cannot be rational, since they only arise due to the contingent and changeable aspects of the human condition. If we are to find a will in correspondence with his ideal of rationality, it is a will in conformity with the call of duty.[140] For Kant, the source of morality is located in a will that acts only out of the pure guiding light of rationality, which is nothing less than a will that conforms to the imperatives of human reason.[141]

Having stressed the importance Kant attached to the notion of a will acting in conformity with duty, Kant details for us the nature of the test that is required if the will is to act in conformity with the call of duty—the Categorical Imperative.[142] The Categorical Imperative commands action, not as a means to any end, but by delimiting action that is right by reference to its form. The will therefore does not determine morality by any external appeal beyond its own necessitating structure.[143]

The key feature that underpins Kant's Categorical Imperative is form driven universality. This is the form imposed upon the concrete particulars of the empirical world brought to bear by the agent.[144] In order to test the legitimacy of a proposed maxim, it is necessary to subject it to the objective order manifested in the Categorical Imperative.[145]

What then is this supreme principle of morality? Kant states it as follows: (1) "act only on that maxim through which you can at the same time will that it should become a universal law."[146] Immediately following on from this formulation, however, a second variant follows: (2) "act as if the maxim of your action were to become through your will a universal law of nature." In fact, Kant thought that there were three variations of the Categorical Imperative.[147] The third variation can be stated as follows: (3) "so act as to treat humanity, whether in your own person or in that of any other, always at the same time as an end, and never merely as a means."[148]

In his analysis of morality, Kant applied his moral law to the case of suicide and concluded that it cannot be adopted as a universal law. With reference to the first and second formulations of the Categorical Imperative he stated that:

> A man reduced to despair by a series of misfortunes feels wearied of life, but is still so far in possession of his reason that he can ask himself whether it would not be contrary to his duty to himself to take his own life ... His maxim is: From self-love I adopt it as a principle to shorten my life when its longer duration is likely to bring more evil than satisfaction. It is asked then simply whether this principle founded on self- love can become a universal law of nature.

Now we see at once that a system of nature of which it should be a law to destroy life by means of the very feeling whose special nature it is to impel to the improvement of life would contradict itself, and therefore could not exist as a system of nature; hence that maxim cannot possibly exist as a universal law of nature.[149]

Further, when considering the application of the Categorical Imperative in its third form, he argued that:

He who contemplates suicide should ask himself whether his action can be consistent with the idea of humanity as an end in itself. If he destroys himself in order to escape from painful circumstances, he uses a person merely as a means to maintain a tolerable condition up to the end of life. But a man is not a thing, that is to say, something which can be used merely as means, but must in all his actions be always considered as an end in himself.[150]

For Kant, therefore, it is evident that he opposed the legitimacy of suicide on the grounds that such an act could not be reconciled with the moral order apprehended by the imperatives inherent in reason. Suicide offends the moral order precisely because it denies in the person the proper regard for duties to self and to others.[151] In committing suicide, the person denies his or her own objective worth, that resonates throughout his or her being, and secondly, denigrates that worth to others, who are part and parcel of the wider picture of humanity, and who bear witness to the act of self-destruction. In short, to deny the image of humanity in self is to become a kind of bearer of false image that offends against the worth of persons generally.[152]

Ideas from Classical Utilitarian Thought

Jeremy Bentham

In turning to this school of thought, we encounter a movement in moral and political philosophy, foreshadowed by Hume, that sought to place the locus of value on the idea of utility.[153] Actions or rules are to be assessed in terms of their ability to maximise utility and minimise disutility.[154] The key founder of classical utilitarianism was Jeremy Bentham who adopted a narrowly hedonistic approach to his 'felicific calculus'. People seek pleasure and avoid pain:

> Nature has placed mankind under the governance of two sovereign masters, pain and pleasure. It is for them alone to point out what we ought to do as well as what we shall do. On the one hand the standard of right and wrong, on the other the chain of cause and effect are linked to their throne. They govern us in all we do, every effort we can make to throw off their subjection will serve but to demonstrate and confirm it. In a word man may pretend to abjure their empire; but in reality he will remain subject to it all the while. The principle of utility recognises this subjection, and assumes it for the foundation of that system the object of which is to rear the fabric of felicity by the hand of reason and law.[155]

Happiness for Bentham was more narrowly construed than any account of hedonism posed by classical Epicureanism.[156] Bentham's views on the question of suicide were essentially those stated by David Hume, that if life became too much of a burden of suffering, it could be morally justifiable to seek to end it, the life having outlived its benefit or usefulness. Society's claim on the life of the individual loses its hold. [157]

Bentham's work can be seen as a practical translation of the idea of utility into the governance of law. Contrary to the 'superstitions' of the age, Bentham thought that law should be based on the purely rational foundation of utility. Laws should be enacted that promote the greatest happiness for the greatest number.[158] Upon such a principle, the laws of a state ought to be framed and should be the basis for their validity. On the basis of this line of reasoning, therefore, Bentham opposed, in principle, the imposition of criminal sanctions that prohibited the practice of suicide.[159] Such a law would not be conducive to promoting the greatest happiness for the greatest number of people, for, as Hume had recognised, once life loses its beneficiary powers, due to pain and suffering, it ceases to be an overall good and instead can become a positive harm to the affected person.[160]

Bentham was a strong opponent of the idea of natural law and natural rights, regarding such notions as "nonsense on stilts." [161] For Bentham, a hedonism based on an assessment of the outcomes of an action was the sole basis for judging the rightness and wrongness of an action.[162] Bentham, for example, opposed the notion of the centrality of good or bad intentions to the moral assessment of an action. Much of his key criticism of natural law and natural rights theory was directed at its manifestation in the English legal system under the influence of William Blackstone's *Commentaries on the Laws of England*. Bentham's notion of action assessment radically turned on its head the emphasis of existing legal categories centred on the notion of the agent's *mens rea*.[163] For Bentham, we need not ask whether an agent's intention in performing an action was good or bad—such subjectivity and prejudice should be eschewed. Rather, the scientific approach of the utilitarian would be an objective assessment of the net benefits and/or harms to proceed from an action in terms of its consequences.[164] As Bentham stated, only the happiness (consequences) of the result of an action is "the right and proper, and the only right and proper and universally desirable end of human action."[165]

The morality of assessing the consequences of an action led Bentham to be highly critical of what he took to be major systemic inconsistencies in traditional natural law theory concerning the evaluation of actions concerning killing. For example, what was it exactly about *non-innocent* human life that justified killing another person? Why did that life cease to have sanctified protection? Was there any coherent systematic theory of justification for innocent life's immunity? Bentham thought that traditional natural theory was riddled by inconsistency due to the exceptions it tried to create around the notion of innocent human life, inconsistencies further compounded by its object-intention centred account of action theory that radically downplayed the significance of consequences in moral assessment.[166]

John Stuart Mill

The influence of utilitarianism in the contemporary era is linked to the extensions made to the philosophy by John Stuart Mill.[167] Whilst Mill rejected Bentham's narrow hedonistic account of value, opting for a eudemonistic account that admitted of qualitative distinctions between pleasures and not simply quantitative distinctions, he nevertheless embraced the essential pillar of Bentham's moral and political philosophy, namely, that the evaluation of actions ought to be tied to the promotion of the greatest happiness for the greatest number.[168]

Mill, however, contrary to Bentham, was aware of the ambiguities of pursuing such a principle when confronted with the realities of a myriad of permutations of choice concerning the weighing and balancing of the consequences of human actions.[169] Mill's solution was to focus on *individual liberty and freedom from constraint* as the best mechanism for promoting the maximisation of human happiness.[170] Allowing for freedom of choice and self-development would provide the best conditions for promoting this general utilitarian goal. Liberty enhances "the permanent interests of man as a progressive being" and in so doing promotes the general end of human happiness to the many.[171]

Mill's defence of liberty of action is famously expressed in the so-called *harm principle*, "the only purpose for which power can be rightfully exercised over any member of a civilised community, against his will, is to prevent harm to others. *His own good, either physical or moral* is not sufficient warrant (my emphasis)."[172]

For Mill, only significant *other regarding* harms could justify the imposition of the coercion of the law on adults retaining a capacity for rational/deliberative thought.[173] To coerce an adult with deliberative capacity into accepting a particular course of self-regarding action does not generally promote human happiness, since it forces people into moulds of restriction that basically affect only them, not other people. The spread of human happiness, for Mill, was increased by the recognition of such a principle.[174]

Whilst this was a general principle in Mill's moral and political philosophy, he nevertheless thought that some primarily self-regarding harms could be restricted for the sake of preserving liberty itself where they went manifestly against the promotion of greater good of "the permanent interests of man as a progressive being."[175] Thus Mill, for example, justified laws prohibiting slavery on the grounds that it was sometimes necessary to restrict choice for the sake of preserving the robust idea of liberty for the greater good, even of those who would care to voluntarily relinquish it.[176] Restriction for the very sake of liberty itself could provide sufficient warrant to restrict some self-regarding harms, in narrow circumstances.[177]

Mill nevertheless was heavily circumspect about the use of state coercion in general to restrict the activities of its citizens. The basic idea of Mill is that the state should preserve a large penumbra of neutrality about enforcing theories of coercion based on narrow perfectionist accounts of the good life. Mill's utilitarianism admitted of far greater diversity and balance between an array of goods than Bentham's hedonism would permit. The limits on liberty, for Mill, are therefore drawn at wide margins. Yet margins are indeed drawn, for to claim that government should be neutral about imposing a narrow thick overarching sense of the good, is not to claim that government should be neutral about everything. The case for neutrality draws on a distinction between the *right and the good*: the state should be neutral with respect to a wide range of competing conceptions of the good, though not with respect to the right. In Mill's thought, it is therefore possible to discern the idea that neutrality supposes that individuals are free to pursue their conception of the good without governmental interference, within broad limits, and that these outer limits are set by the need to prevent other regarding harm that infringes on the rights of others (or, some narrowly circumscribed categories of self-regarding harm).

Whilst Mill never directly argued the point that a regulated scheme of assisted suicide or voluntary euthanasia could be permitted by the state, others in the contemporary era have advocated this idea on the basis of his thought. It is, of course, not difficult to draw that conclusion, for once it is admitted that there is a general liberty to live or die as one wishes (providing one does not significantly and directly harm another individual, and provided that the choice is rationally and voluntarily undertaken), it is but a short step to justify the provision of assistance by third parties to facilitate the execution of such a choice. If a rationally thinking person chooses to die quickly, especially for motives of intense pain or suffering, then that should be viewed as a legitimate exercise of liberty and should not fall within the purview of state authority to ban the practice. [178]

With this Millian turn on the problematic of liberty and the strong limitations imposed by it on the right of the state to interfere paternalistically with its exercise, we have now encountered, in outline form, many of the strong ideational impetuses arising in the West that have helped to shape more contemporary arguments for and against the practices of assisted suicide and voluntary euthanasia. Before turning to the task of examining contemporary arguments for the practices of assisted suicide and voluntary euthanasia in our next chapter, I shall, by way of conclusion, finish this chapter with a brief *synthesising summary* of the main arguments made.

Summary of the Main Ideas

Ideas Against Self-Killing

The human soul. **W**ith the thought of Socrates and Plato we can observe the influential idea that self-killing is considered to be contrary to the notion of the perfectibility of the human soul. Plato's influence was expanded and extended with the rise of Neo-Platonism and its reception into subsequent Christian thought. With the thought of Augustine, in particular, the notion of the perfectibility of the human soul is synthesised into the Judaeo-Christian idea of God's dominion over human life. Such a theme recurs in the thought of the West, and informs a significant part of the thought of Aquinas and the subsequent tradition of scholasticism.

46

Value of human life. In the thought of Aristotle, we can observe the judgement of the wise man, the man of practical reason, regarding the valuational status of human life. Human life is a natural good to be respected and promoted. Such a good can be objectively apprehended by human reason, independently of Plato's metaphysically ambitious claims concerning the immortality of the soul. The human being is naturally ordered to the preservation of life and the avoidance of threats to life. To protect that good, the cultivation of human virtue is required. Courage is needed in the face of suffering and adversity to resist the temptation to act against this good, one of the primary constituents of integrated human flourishing or well-being.

In the thought of Aquinas, the inclination of life-preservation, apprehended by reason as a human good, is considered to be intrinsically valuable, a good valued for its own sake, a *bonum honestum*, not a *bonum utile*. Given such a status, to act against such a good was thought to run contrary to the foundational precept of the natural law, that good is to be done and evil avoided. The intentional taking of innocent human life was thus considered to be an evil.

The good of preserving human life expressed in Aquinas, and in the subsequent tradition of scholasticism, was given an overtly materialist turn in the metaphysics of Thomas Hobbes. For Hobbes, the human person is basically a being driven by egoistic instincts that control and influence basic patterns of human behaviour. Since the human person is one governed by egoism, egoism being natural, Hobbes concluded that an attack on the self would be bad since the end of action is the perpetuation of selfish interests. Interests could not be perpetuated without the existence of the subject, therefore, intentional self-killing was wrong.

Killing and letting die. In the thought of Plato, we observed the first signs of awareness of a distinction between the provision of active means to intentionally bring about death and the notion of the withdrawal or non-provision of treatment due to its burdensomeness. Turning to the thought of Augustine and the question of martyrdom, and also the thought of Aquinas concerning the conditions of self-defence, the importance of the direction of intention concerning its impact on human goods was increasingly regarded as crucial. Vitoria, at the height of the scholastic natural law tradition, draws out in greater detail the implications of negative and positive duties concerning the preservation of human life, placing the question of intention into central focus for an action's moral evaluation. In this tradition the conditions associated with the framework of double effect reasoning were developed.

Justice and societal demands. Aristotle and Aquinas both considered suicide to be a act of injustice against the state and society. If individuals are distinct substances, they are also social beings whose duties surpass individual interests. An act of self-killing deprives society of the existence of one of its members. The radical contribution that a person makes to society is not to be judged upon that person's usefulness or utility to society. Individuals belong in part to the community and cannot divorce their individual actions from the interests of the state in fostering and promoting respect for the foundational good of protecting human life. The private lethal use of force, even when directed against self, has many potentially disruptive ramifications for wider society. These ramifications are especially acute when the act of self-killing is supported by the actions of third parties, who assist in, or actually administer, the death dealing means.

Idea of universal humanity. Kant considered suicide and assistance in suicide a self contradiction based on his formulations of the Categorical Imperative—the universal moral law of reason. It is not consistent to will that it become a universal law that an individual may chose to kill himself or herself by intentional design. For Kant, it was illogical for a person to seek to abolish his or her life on the basis of the challenges that life itself presents to us. If self-love be the motivation informing such an act, why does this motive of self-love attack the very nature of self that gives rise to the notion in the first place, the condition of all possibility?

Kant thought that self-killing cannot be a respectful means in pursuing a goal to be free from suffering, because any individual is an exemplar of humanity. By attacking humanity in the subjectivity of his or her own person, one is attacking the idea of humanity generally.[179] The individual cannot readily be treated as a discrete self-standing monad, who can be viewed independently from his or her fundamental connectedness with the rest of humanity.

Ideas Permitting Self-Killing

<u>Soul not hindered</u>. For the Stoics, with the notable exception of Cicero, the human soul is perfected by its ability to remain indifferent to the trials and tribulations of life. If the circumstances of life radically impinge on the person's ability to remain indifferent to them and master them, then earthly life may be ended in the service of this indifference. For the Stoic, bodily life was not to be regarded as an indispensable good, but rather as a preference only in the service of the projects of the person in line with the person's understanding of the ends of the *logos*. The soul could be perfected by protecting the indifference of the person to the impinging events of the world.

Influenced by Stoic ideas, Montaigne found no essential incompatibility between the idea of self-inflicted death and preserving a person from the trials and tribulations of life. Why would such an action ultimately harm the soul? For Montaigne, such an act could be a way of preserving the soul from further unwarranted contumely, and give it a release from what would otherwise be an overly burdensome life.

Such a theme is also strongly echoed in the work of John Donne. Donne did not think that the soul of a person would necessarily be harmed by a self-inflicted act of suicide in conditions where the person was subjected to intolerable impositions of suffering. Surely, the ending of earthly life in such circumstances would be a blessing for the soul as it was released from its attachment to bodily life; a bodily life that could no longer serve the best interests of the soul. If God has dominion over life, then why is it wrong to end that life in conditions where it is possible to suppose that ending life need not be viewed as an act contrary to the will of God?

Life's intolerable burden. For the Epicureans, life was a valued good as long as it was possible to cultivate the higher pleasures of life. Once life ceased to be able to provide that balance for the individual, life itself could be severed. The preference of life itself can be commensurated with other goods such as freedom from pain and suffering to judge whether or not life was worth continuing with.

This Epicurean theme, of life ceasing to be an overall good, and instead becoming an unbearable burden, is manifested in most subsequent arguments in favour of intentional self-inflicted death. Montaigne, Donne, Hume, Bentham, and Mill, all thought that suicide, in some circumstances, could be justified by some form of a commensuration of goods whereby the good of life itself could be outweighed by the burdens of its continuation.

The notion that the ending of human life by intentional design is contrary to human nature, is strongly challenged by the work of David Hume. For Hume, as well as Immanuel Kant, who followed Hume on this, there is a logical fallacy in proceeding from a descriptive claim relating to human nature to the subsequent creation of normative obligations from such description. For Hume, the *naturalism* of the natural law tradition (including Hobbes's 'state of nature' approach) rested on the mistaken presupposition that one could proceed from factual and descriptive observations of human nature to the derivation of normative obligations. For Hume, therefore, to suppose that there was a natural inclination to preserve life, could in and of itself tell us nothing about the extent of our duties to preserve life, especially when those duties conflicted with other contrary inclinations.

Consequences of an action. With the thought of David Hume, Jeremy Bentham, and J.S. Mill, there is a rejection of the notion that the morality of an action can be determined by the notion of the intended object of an action. If other forms of killing can be justified upon the basis of the value of the consequences appealed to, then why not suicide or euthanasia? If authors in the natural law tradition have justified killing on the basis of self-defence and capital punishment, is it not really a case of justifying an action on the basis of an appeal to its resultant consequences?

Hume, Bentham, and Mill eschewed all notions that an action can be regarded as intrinsically right or wrong depending on the object of the action. Consequently, there was no need for anything resembling the principle of double effect. For Bentham, in particular, the morality of the action is to be determined by the foreseeable and predictable consequences that the action performed will bring in its wake. Where certain types of action would bring about a greater balance of utility rather than disutility as a result of their performance, they were justifiable and should not be the focus of condemnation or disapproval, especially by state intervention by criminal sanction.

State Non-Interference. With the thought of J.S. Mill, there is a strong articulation of the notion of limits on government to pursue a perfectionist account of what constitutes the good life for human beings to pursue. Government interference with the exercise of liberty should be restricted to actions and activities that significantly impinge on the rights of others. Given the importance of liberty to the promotion of human happiness, there needs to be preserved a wide penumbra of freedom for the individual to pursue his or her own judgement as to what human happiness should concretely mean. Suicide is simply seen as one of the last options available to the individual to assert self control in the face of adverse events that affront the person. Paradoxically, whilst Kant first gave rise to the notion of the autonomous will, it is in fact J. S. Mill whose thought has given this notion most fully over to individual self-determination, and with it, a large claim for freedom of action, especially self-regarding action, in the face of external impositions.

Notes to Chapter Two

[1] Margaret P. Battin, *Ethical Issues in Suicide* (Englewood Cliffs: Prentice-Hall, 1995), 1-3.

[2] Jack C. Willke, Assis*ted Suicide and Euthanasia: Past and Present* (Cincinnati: Hayes, 1998), 2-6; Georgia Noon, "On Suicide," *Journal of the History of Ideas* 39 (1978): 371-73.

[3] For an interesting comparative account engaging some of those other traditions (Buddhist, Hindu, Shinto, etc.) see generally, Jennifer M. Scherer and Rita J. Simon, *Euthanasia and the Right to Die: A Comparative View* (Lanham: Rowman & Littlefield, 1999). See also, *To Die or Not to Die: Cross-Disciplinary, Cultural and Legal Perspectives on the Right to Choose Death*, eds. Arthur S. Berger and Joyce Berger (New York: Praeger, 1990); Kenneth L. Vaux, *Death Ethics: Religious and Cultural Values in Prolonging and Ending Life* (Philadelphia: Trinity Press International, 1992).

[4] Tensions with my own position concerning the relationship between faith and reason exist on two fronts: firstly, certain authors such as Ronald Dworkin blur the line between the kinds of truth that can be know by reason and kinds of truth that can be known only by an appeal to faith based considerations; secondly, there is the problem of thinkers and politicians who support the state sanctioning of religion, at least in the 'broad sense' of the Judaeo-Christian heritage. For a stimulating account of the general relationship between faith and reason, somewhat sympathetic to my own perspective, see Philip Devine, *Natural Law Ethics* (Westport: Greenwood Press, 2000), 1-13.

[5] Devine, *Natural Law*, 1-13. For sources on the question of whether or not the Hebrew and Christian Scriptures supported a strong prohibition on suicide and euthanasia, see Norman L. Farberow, "Cultural History of Suicide," in *Suicide in Different Cultures*, ed. N. L. Farberow (Baltimore: University Park Press, 1975), 3-4; George Rosen, "History," in *A Handbook for the Study of Suicide*, ed. Seymour Perlin (New York: Oxford University Press, 1975), 4-5 [previously published as "History in the Study of Suicide," *Psychological Medicine* 1 (1971): 267-85]; Jacques Choron, *Suicide* (New York: Charles Scribner, 1972), 13-14; Georges Minois, *History of Suicide: Voluntary Death in Western Culture* (Baltimore: Johns Hopkins University Press, 1999); Arthur Droge and James Tabor, *A Noble Death: Suicide and Martyrdom Among Christians and Jews in Antiquity* (San Francisco: Harper San Francisco, 1992); Robert Barry, *Breaking the Thread of Life* (New Brunswick: Transaction, 1994); Edward J. Larson and Darrel W. Amundsen, *A Different Death: Euthanasia and Christian Tradition* (Downers Grove: InterVarsity Press, 1998).

[6] Minois, *History*, 5-9.

[7] Minois, *History*, 5-9; G. Gruman, "An Historical Introduction to Ideas About Voluntary Euthanasia," *Omega* 4 (1973): 87-91.

[8] See Terence Irwin, *Plato's Ethics* (New York: Oxford University Press, 1995), 25-49.

[9] Irwin, *Plato*, 25-49. See also Alfonso Gómez-Lobo, *The Foundations of Socratic Ethics* (Indianapolis: Hackett, 1994), ch.2.

[10] Pamela Huby, "Greek Ethics," in *New Studies in Ethics*, ed. W.D. Hudson (New York: St. Martin's Press, 1971), 17-42.

[11] Such a position contrasted strongly with the position of many Sophists who extolled human impulses at the expense of reasons discernment of the perfectibility of the human soul. See Irwin, *Plato*, 23-37; Huby, "Greek Ethics," 28-41.

[12] Plato, *Complete Works: Phaedo*, trans. John M. Cooper (Indianapolis: Hackett, 1997).

[13] John M. Cooper, "Greek Philosophers on Euthanasia and Suicide," in *Suicide and Euthanasia: Historical and Contemporary Themes*, ed. Baruch Brody (Dordrecht: Kluwer Academic, 1989), 16.

[14] Michael M. Uhlmann, "Western Thought," in *Last Rights?: Assisted Suicide and Euthanasia Debated*, ed. Michael H. Uhlmann (Washington, D.C.: Ethics and Public Policy Center; Eerdmans, 1998), 14-18.

[15] David Novak, *Suicide and Morality: The Theories of Plato, Aquinas and Kant* (New York: Scholars Press, 1975), 11-13. The problem for later thought, especially modern thought after Descartes, was a tendency to devalue more directly the body into a mere machine like instrumentality at the behest of the "conscious substantiality" of the human person.

[16] See the discussion on martyrdom and Augustine of Hippo *infra*.

[17] That death should be intentionally hastened is nowhere argued by Socrates, nor by Plato. On the contrary, a careful reading of the *Phaedo* concerning the relationship of body and soul, strongly suggests that the pains and tribulations of life are necessary to bear in the process of acquiring wisdom, for it is *highly unlikely* that the soul can be improved by an act that intentionally seeks to destroy the body in the name of the soul's benefit. See Novak, *Sucide and Morality*, 17; Cooper, "Greek Thought," 16.

[18] Paul Carrick, *Medical Ethics in Antiquity: Philosophical Perspectives on Abortion and Euthanasia* (Boston: D. Reidel, 1985), 138-40.

[19] Plato, *The Republic*, trans. G. M. A. Grube (Indianapolis: Hackett, 1992); Cooper, "Greek Thought," 12-14.

[20] Christopher Rowe, *Greek Ethics* (London: Hutchison, 1976), 55-60.

[21] Cooper, "Greek Thought," 12-14; Novak, *Suicide*, 27-31; Uhlmann, "Western Thought," 16-18. Plato's account in book III of the *Republic* is, therefore, compatible with the view that not everything must be done in the context of family and society to preserve life at all costs. This does not mean that, for Plato, it is just to intentionally kill a dying person. His words are compatible with the idea that death can be said to occur by reason of the underlying pathology due to cessation of treatment no longer deemed in the best interests of the patient.

[22] A later treatise dealing with the practicalities of governance. See Plato, *The Laws*, trans. G. M. A. Grube (Indianapolis: Hackett, 1984).

[23] Droge and Tabor, *Noble Death*, 20-22; Battin, *Ethical Issues*, 58-59. See also Alfred Alvarez, *Savage God* (London: Weidenfeld and Nicolson, 1971), 59-60; R. Garland, "Death Without Dishonour. Suicide in the Ancient World," *History Today* 33 (Jan. 1983): 33-37; D. Gourevitch, "Suicide Among the Sick in Classical Antiquity," *Bulletin of the History of Medicine* 43 (1969): 501-18.

[24] Carrick supports this general interpretation. See his *Medical Ethics*, 140.

[25] Plato is very much concerned with questions of social order and the practicalities of governance—of what may be called the teleology of the political common good. By granting a dispensation to these categories, he was recognising that powerful psychological forces are at work that often compel people to act. His chief object of prohibition by the framing of law this way can plausibly be seen to be one of rational suicide prevention and not the punishment of those overcome with passion or mental disorder, whom he insightfully thought could not be deterred by the power of the law to punish. Plato's work brings out the importance of motive and the psychological dimension to suicide. He does not think the law should punish in those cases, for it cannot deter. He is concerned with rational and deliberate acts of self-killing since they are considered more amenable to control by the social order. In the *Laws*, therefore, he presents a tempering of the limits on what the *operation of the law* can reasonably seek to protect and promote for the good of society, without conceding that suicide need be considered a morally acceptable species of act on the part of the individual citizen. See further Novak, *Suicide and Morality*, 20-25.

[26] Aristotle. *Nicomachean Ethics. The Basic Works of Aristotle*, ed. Richard McKeon, trans. W. D. Ross (New York: Random House, 1941).

[27] J.L. Ackrill, *Aristotle* (Oxford: Clarendon Press, 1981), 135-55.

[28] W. F. R. Hardie, *Aristotle's Ethical Theory*. 2nd ed. (Oxford: Clarendon Press, 1980), 73-89.

[29] Ackrill, *Aristotle*, 135-41.

[30] See Cooper "Greek Philosophers," 22-34.

[31] On the nature of justice in Aristotle see further Fred. D. Miller, *Nature, Justice, and Rights in Aristotle's Politics* (Oxford : Clarendon Press, 1995); Curtis Johnston, *Aristotle's Theory of the State* (New York: St. Martin's Press, 1990).

[32] Carrick, *Medical Ethics*, 143.

[33] Uhlmann, "Western Thought," 18-21; A.W. Mair, "Suicide (Greek and Roman)," in *Encyclopaedia of Religion and Ethics*, vol. 12, ed J. Hastings (Edinburgh: T & T. Clark, 1992), 26-30. See further Kenneth W. Kemp, "Euthanasia," *American Catholic Philosophical Quarterly* 72 (1998): 315-27.

[34] James Rist, *Stoic Philospohy* (Cambridge: Cambridge University Press, 1969), 236; Droge & Tabor, *Noble Death*, 23.

[35] Rist, *Stoic Philospohy,* 236; Droge & Tabor, *Noble Death*, 23.

[36] Cooper "Greek Philosophers," 22-34.

[37] Michael J. Seidler, "Kant and the Stoics on Suicide," *Journal of the History of Ideas* 44 (1983): 429-32. He points out that Kant was influenced by the Stoic doctrines but rejected them on the ground that his moral law made suicide a contradiction of humanity and could not be justified.

[38] Rist, *Stoic Philosophy*, 233-35; Henry Romilly Fedden, *Suicide: A Social and Historical Study* (London: P. Davies, 1938), 85.

[39] Rist, *Stoic Philosophy*, 242-43.

[40] Miriam Griffin, "Roman Suicide," in *Medicine and Moral Reasoning*, eds. K. W. M. Fulford, Grant R. Gillett and Janet Martin Soskice (Cambridge:

Cambridge University Press, 1994), 109-10. See also F. H. Sandbach, *The Stoics,* 2nd ed. (Indianapolis: Hackett, 1989), 48-52.

[41] Sandbach, *Stoics,* 48-52.

[42] Miriam Griffin, "Philospohy, Cato, and Roman Suicide," *Greece and Rome* 33 (1986): 64-66.

[43] Griffin "Philosophy," 72-75. See also Russell Noyes, "Seneca on Death," *Journal of Religion and Health* 12 (1973): 223-40.

[44] Griffin, "Roman Suicide," 119-20; Sandbach, *Stoics,* 48-52.

[45] Griffin, "Roman Suicide," 115; Sandbach, *Stoics,* 48-52.

[46] Fedden, *Suicide,* 83-84.

[47] Cicero, *De Senectute,* xx, stating Pythagoras's view that people should not "depart from their guard or station in life without the order of their commander, that is, of God").

[48] Unless there was a sign of divine permissibility, therefore, life should be pursued and not intentionally ended.

[49] Robert Barry, "The Development of the Roman Catholic Teachings on Suicide," *Notre Dame Journal of Law, Ethics and Public Policy* 9 (1995): 449-501, 486.

[50] Choron, *Suicide,* 112-14.

[51] Choron, *Suicide,* 112-14.

[52] Cooper, "Greek Philosophers," 29.

[53] Griffin, "Roman Suicide," 113.

[54] Griffin, "Roman Suicide," 114.

[55] E.g. Barry, "Roman Catholic Teaching," 486-87.

[56] Battin, *Ethical Issues,* 1-5. For similar lines of argumentation see Droge and Tabor, *Noble Death,* 129-31, 138-40; Robert Martin, "Suicide and Self-Sacrifice," in *Suicide: The Philosophical Issues,* eds. Margaret P. Battin and David J. Mayo (New York: St. Martin's Press, 1980), 48-68.

[57] It also fails to take cognisance of the attempts of several of the Church Fathers who preceded Augustine to seek to constrain certain forms of martyrdom. Justin Martyr, for example, discouraged the impulse to hasten departure by one's own action and abandon earthly existence simply in order to embrace eternal life. Such an action instead of being said to fulfil the will of God was said to instantiate an opposition to the will of God as it neglected the value of earthly life and the duties of stewardship. A similar point is echoed by Clement of Rome, Lactantius, John Chrysostom, Ambrose, and Jerome. The Christian ought not to take his or her own life, and whilst the Christian should be ready to accept martyrdom and not deny faith, such acceptance should not translate into a disregard for earthly life and a proper attention to duties of self-preservation. The one exception that appears in Orthodox thought concerning suicide, approved of by Ambrose and Jerome, was the case of the Virgin who took her own life rather than suffer a violation of virginity (such was the regard held for the preservation of this good). It took a thinker of the stature of Augustine to eventually iron some of those inconsistencies. See Amundsen, "Suicide and Early Christian Values," 96-122.

[58] See Augustine Regan, "The Worth of Human Life," *Studia Moralia* 6 (1968): 220-29. See also Regan, "The Accidental Effect in Moral Discourse," *Studia Moralia* 16 (1978): 99-127.

[59] Consider, for example, the case of Bobby Sands, a well known IRA hunger striker who starved himself to death rather than accept the authority of the British Government to imprison and detain him. See James W. McGray, "Bobby Sands, Suicide, and Self-Sacrifice," *Journal of Value Inquiry* 17 (1983): 65-76. See also Christopher Kaczor, "Faith and Reason and Physician-Assisted Suicide, " *Christian Bioethics* 4 (1998): 183-201.

[60] Of course I realise that this begs the question of the credibility of such an account of action theory, an account that needs to be argued for and not simply assumed. As was said in the introduction, this is the task of later analysis. For now it is sufficient for our purposes to demonstrate an alternative account of such deaths in order to avoid the *ready conclusion* that acts of suicide here are being *disingenuously shrouded* under the guise of martyrdom or self-sacrifice. See Regan, "Worth," 220-29; Kaczor, "Faith and Reason," 184-87.

[61] Christopher Kirwan, *Augustine* (New York: Routledge, 1989), 61-63.

[62] Darrel. W. Amundsen, *Medicine, Society, and Faith in the Ancient and Medieval Worlds* Baltimore: Johns Hopkins Press, 1996), 103-20.

[63] Larson and Amundsen, *Different Death,* 116-23. See also Augustine Regan, "Human Body in Moral Theology: Some Basic Orientations," *Studia Moralia* 17 (1979): 151-88.

[64] William E. Stempsey, "Laying Down One's Life for Oneself," *Christian Bioethics* 4 (1998): 204-8.

[65] Kirwan, *Augustine,* 204-8.

[66] Augustine of Hippo, *City of God,* trans. H. Bettenson (London: Penguin, 1972), I, 19; I, 20.

[67] Indeed, such was the value of life, for Augustine, that it could never be abandoned in the face of atonement for sin. Such was the gravity of suicide for Augustine that the suicide was said to deprive himself or herself of the gift of salvation, for in an effort to atone for previous sins, they compounded their earlier action by a final act of severance from God's grace. See Augustine, *City of God,* I, 22-7.

[68] Larson and Amundsen, *Different Death,* 121-23; Stempsey, "Laying Down One's Life," 213-14. See also Barry, *Breaking the Thread of Life.*

[69] Romans 3:8. On the historical development of the principle of double effect see J. T. Mangan, "An Historical Analysis of the Principle of Double Effect," *Theological Studies* 10 (1949): 41-61. See also Anthony Kenny, "The History of Intention in Ethics," in *Anatomy of the Soul* (Oxford; Basil Blackwell, 1973).

[70] Vernon J. Bourke, *Ethics* (New York: MacMillan, 1966), 8-13, 41-3. For further elaboration of the relationship between faith and reason from an analytical perspective see John Haldane, "What Future Has Catholic Philosophy?" *American Catholic Philosophical Quarterly* 71 (1997): S79-90. Whilst I focus only on Aquinas, scholastics of all philosophical stripes were generally opposed to suicide. For example, Bonaventura saw the act of suicide as one of unrestrained self-love. In acting thus, the suicider places his own apprehension of love over true self-effacing love that alone is consonant with placing oneself in the mercy of God's hands. Duns Scotus placed particular emphasis on the question of the usurpation of power claimed by someone that commits an act of homicide on himself or herself. Only the direct intervention of God can dispense a person from this commanded obedience. See Minois, *History,* 32-36.

[71] Armand Maurer, "Descartes and Aquinas on the Unity of a Human Being," *American Catholic Philosophical Quarterly* 67 (1993): 497-511.

[72] Regan, "Human Body," 161-6; Maurer, "Descartes and Aquinas," 505-9.

[73] There may of course be a psychological tendency that flows from dualism to underestimate the worth of the body. See Mary Rousseau, "Elements of a Thomistic Philosophy of Death," *The Thomist* 43 (1979): 582-601. See also Frederick Copleston, *Aquinas* (London: Penguin Books, 1955); Patrick Lee, "Human Beings are Animals," in *Natural Law and Moral Inquiry*, ed. Robert P. George (Washington, DC: Georgetown University Press, 1998), 135-51.

[74] The derivation of the commandments from the first precept of the natural law is therefore possible for Aquinas although passions and errors in reasoning can corrupt or distort the process of recognising the precepts of the natural law that flow from its first principle.

[75] Thomas Aquinas, *Summa Theologica*, trans. English Dominican Fathers (New York: Benziger, 1948), I, II q. 94, a. 2.

[76] *Summa Theologica* I, II q. 94, a. 2.

[77] See Servais Pinckaers, *Sources of Christian Ethics*, trans. Mary Noble. 3rd ed. (Washington, DC: Catholic University of America, 1995), 405-8; Benedict Ashley, *Living the Truth in Love* (New York: Alba House, 1996), 108; Craig Paterson, "Renewing the Moral Life: Some Recent Work in Virtue Theory," *New Blackfriars* 81 (May 2000): 238-44.

[78] See for example the following commentaries on Aquinas's thought concerning some of those issues: George I. Mavrodes, "Innocence and Suicide," *Faith and Philosophy* 16 (1999): 315-35; Matthew J. Kelly, and George Schedler, "St. Thomas and the Judicial Killing of the Innocent," *Journal of Thought* 14 (1979): 17-22; Garrett Barden, "Defending Self-Defence," *Irish Philosophical Journal* 1 (1984): 25-35; Steven A. Long, "St. Thomas Aquinas and the Death Penalty," *Thomist* 63 (1999): 511-52. On the question of the intervention of God changing the moral species or nature of an act, building upon the theological and philosophical reflections of St. Augustine and St. Thomas Aquinas, see Patrick Lee, "Permanence of the Ten Commandments," *Theological Studies* 42 (1981): 422-43.

[79] Joseph Boyle, "*Praeter Intentionem* in Aquinas," *Thomist* 42 (1978): 649-65.

[80] Boyle, "*Praeter Intentionem*," 649-65.

[81] Joseph Boyle, "Towards Understanding the Principle of Double Effect," *Ethics* 90 (1980): 527-38.

[82] See John Finnis, "Object and Intention in Moral Judgements According to St. Thomas Aquinas," in Finalité intentionnalité: doctrine Thomiste et perspectives modernes (Paris: Éditions Peeters, 1992), 127-48.

[83] Stempsey, "Laying Down Ones' Life," 215; Barry, *Breaking the Thread,* 127, 137-44. As with Augustine, he accepts the intervention of God as a grounds for killing. However, unlike Augustine he considered that the nature of a divine intervention changed the 'moral species' of the action. It ceased to be an act of homicide and instead became an act of obedience to the will of God.

[84] See Augustine Regan, "Moral Argument on Self-Killing," *Studia Moralia* 18 (1980): 301-7.

[85] John Finnis, *Aquinas* (Oxford: Oxford University Press, 1998), 275-94.

[86] Joseph Boyle, "Sanctity of life and Suicide: Tensions and Developments within Common Morality," in *Suicide and Euthanasia: Historical and Contemporary Themes*, ed. Baruch Brody, 221-50.

[87] *Summa Theologica* II-II, q. 64. a 5.

[88] Rousseau, "Elements," 584-88; Regan, "Moral Argument," 301-7. For Aquinas, therefore, all forms of private homicide whether by one's own hand or at the hand of another have a basic deprivation attached to them They represent a disorder against the order of goodness.

[89] Bourke, *Ethics*, 354.

[90] On the development of neo-scholastic thought generally see Joseph Donceel, "A Survey of Some Neo-Scholastic Theories," *New Scholasticism* 39 (1965): 295-315.

[91] Gary M. Atkinson, "History of Catholic Teaching on Prolonging Life," in *Moral Responsibility in Prolonging Life Decisions,* eds. Donald G. McCarthy and Albert Moraczewski (St. Louis: Pope John Center, 1981), 95-115.

[92] Francisco de Vitoria, *Reflection on Homicide & Commentary on Summa Theologiae II-II Q. 64*, intro. & trans. John P. Doyle (Milwaukee: Marquette University Press, 1997).

[93] Vitoria, *Reflection on Homicide*, 30-1, 174-5.

[94] Vitoria, *Reflection on Homicide*, 55.

[95] However, even if some omissions are not intended to cause death they may still entail some culpability. Whilst a patient or physician may not precisely intend death they can be culpable through a failure to address the proportionality of means to the end of life preservation. See Atkinson, "History," 95-115.

[96] Jacques Choron, "Death as a Motive of Philosophic Thought," in *Essays in Self-Destruction*, ed. Edwin S. Shneidman (New York: Science House, 1967), 62-63.

[97] See Brian P. Copenhaver and Charles B. Schmitt, *Renaissance Philosophy* (Oxford: Oxford University Press, 1992), 24-37.

[98] Gary B. Ferngren, "The Ethics of Suicide in the Renaissance and Reformation," in *Suicide and Euthanasia: Historical and Contemporary Perspectives*, ed. Baruch A. Brody, 155-81.

[99] Giovanni Pico della Mirandola, *Oration on the Dignity of Man*, trans. A. Robert Caponigri (Washington, DC: Regnery/Gateway, 1956).

[100] Jacques Choron, *Death and Western Thought* (London: Macmillan, 1963), 96-101; Copenhaver and Schmitt, *Renaissance*, 162-77. The impact of Stoic and Epicurean ideas on Renaissance humanism were captured in the literature of the period. Thus, for example, William Shakespeare wrote no less than eight tragedies containing some fourteen suicides. See M. D. Faber "Shakespeare's Suicides: Some Historic, Dramatic and Psychological Reflections," in *Essays in Self-Destruction*, ed. Edwin S. Shneidman, 30-58.

[101] Michel de Montaigne, *The Essays*, trans. Charles Cotton (Chicago: Britannica, 1952). For commentary on Montaigne in historical context see Jakob Amstutz, "Philosophers on Death," *Essence* 2 (1978): 129-38.

[102] On rekindled Roman influences and their influence on later Renaissance humanism see Mark Sacharoff, "Suicide and Brutus," *Journal of the History of Ideas* 33 (1972): 115-22.

[103] Montaigne, *Essays*, 25.

[104] Amstutz, "Philosophers on Death," 32-6; Choron, *Death*, 98-102.

[105] Ferngren, "Ethics of Suicide," 159-62.

[106] Minois, *History*, 89-92.

[107] Although there was little toleration of suicide amongst the Anglican clergy generally during this period. Indeed, several treatises were written employing the arguments against suicide already made by Augustine and Aquinas (e.g., Thomas Cranmer, John King, George Abbot, and John Sym). See Ferngren, "Ethics of Suicide," 168-73; Minois, "History," 127-35.

[108] Robert Burton, *Anatomy of Melancholy*, 3 vols. (Oxford: Clarendon Press, 1989-94); John Donne, *Biathanatos*, ed. Michael Rudick and Margaret P. Battin (New York: Garland, 1982).

[109] Or the law of God. In Part Three of *Biathanatos*, Donne argued that there is no necessary contravention between suicide and the will of God. He argued that suicide is nowhere prohibited in the canon of the Bible. Moreover, humanity is a co-operator in discerning the will of God in the circumstances of a person's own life. Given the natural tendency also to die, there seemed to be no necessary contravention in an individual hastening his or her own death

[110] Samuel E. Sprott, *The English Debate on Suicide from Donne to Hume* (La Salle: Open Court, 1961), 2-5, 66. See further David Daube, "The Linguistics of Suicide," *Philosophy and Public Affairs* 1 (1972): 387-437.

[111] See latter section for discussion on Hume.

[112] Donne, *Biathanatos*, 45-83.

[113] Donne, *Biathanatos*, 84-144.

[114] Michael MacDonald and Terence R. Murphy, *Sleepless Souls: Suicide in Early Modern England* (Oxford: Clarendon Press, 1990), 165-69.

[115] Minois *History of Suicide*, 159-60.

[116] Thomas Hobbes, *On the Citizen*, trans. Richard Tuck and Michael Silverthorne (Cambridge: Cambridge University Press, 1998), viii-xxxii. See further the commentary on Hobbes's moral philosophy by Richard Tuck "Hobbes's Moral Philosophy," in *The Cambridge Companion to Hobbes*, ed. Tom Sorell (Cambridge: Cambridge University Press, 1996), 184-93.

[117] Thomas Hobbes, *Leviathan*, (Cambridge: Cambridge University Press, 1996), 70.

[118] See Gary B. Herbert, "Fear of Death and the Foundations of Natural Right in the Philosophy of Thomas Hobbes," *Hobbes Studies* 7 (1994): 56-68.

[119] See Charles D. Tarlton, "To Avoid the Present Stroke of Death: Despotical Dominion, Force, and Legitimacy in Hobbes's "Leviathan"," *Philosophy* 74 (1999): 221-45.

[120] Bernard Gert, "Hobbes's Psychology," in *Cambridge Companion to Hobbes*, 169-71.

[121] Herbert, "Fear of Death", 56-68.

[122] Thomas Hobbes *A Dialogue Between a Philosopher and a Student of the Common Laws of England* (Chicago: University of Chicago Press, 1971), 88-89.

[123] See generally Lester G. Crocker, "The Discussion of Suicide in the Eighteenth Century," *Journal of the History of Ideas* 13 (1952): 47-72.

[124] Minois, *History*, 210-66; Choron, *Suicide*, 124-27.

[125] Crocker, "Discussion," 61; Minois, *History*, 228-30.

[126] Crocker, "Discussion," 61-62; Choron, *Suicide*, 124-25.

[127] Crocker, "Discussion," 67-69; Choron, *Suicide*, 126; Minois, *History*, 221-23.

[128] See David Fate Norton, "Hume, Human Nature, and the Foundations of Morality," in *The Cambridge Companion to Hume* (Cambridge: Cambridge University Press, 1993), 148-59.

[129] David Hume, *A Treatise of Human Nature*, ed. L.A. Selby-Bigge and P.H. Nidditch (Oxford: Clarendon Press, 1978), 469-70.

[130] Published posthumously in 1784. David Hume, "Of Suicide," in *Applied Ethics*, ed. Peter Singer (Oxford: Oxford University Press, 1986), 19-27. As with the approach of John Donne, discussed above, the structure of Hume's text can loosely be seen as a reply to the arguments made by Aquinas against the moral licitness of suicide.

[131] See R. G. Frey, "Hume on Suicide," *Journal of Medicine and Philosophy* 24 (1999): 336-51; Tom Beauchamp, "An Analysis of Hume's Essay 'On

Suicide'," *Review of Metaphysics* 30 (1976): 73-95. See also John Immerwahr, "God and Morality in Hume's Suppressed Essays," *International Studies in Philosophy* 11 (1979): 91-102.

[132] Hume, "Suicide," 22.

[133] Hume, "Suicide," 22.

[134] Hume, "Suicide," 23.

[135] This is not Hume's second textual argument, for he makes also a theistic argument that is chronologically second. In this he points to the utter insignificance of human life from the perspective of the rest of creation, "the life of a man is of no greater importance than that of an oyster." Further, he states that since God uses all manner of natural phenomenon to bring about death then why not an act of suicide? See Hume, "Suicide," 23.

[136] Hume, "Suicide," 25-27.

[137] See Kenneth R. Merrill, "Hume on Suicide," *History of Philosophy Quarterly* 16 (1999): 395-412. See also R G. Frey, "Hume," 74-77.

[138] Immanuel Kant, *Groundwork of the Metaphysic of Morals*, trans. H. J. Paton (New York: Harper & Row, 1964), 56-60. On Kant's moral theory generally see B. E. A. Liddell, *Kant on the Foundation of Morality* (Bloomington: Indiana University Press, 1970).

[139] Kant, *Groundwork of the Metaphysic of Morals*, 109-10.

[140] Kant, *Groundwork of the Metaphysic of Morals*, 64-68.

[141] Kant, *Groundwork of the Metaphysic of Morals*, 121-23.

[142] Kant, *Groundwork of the Metaphysic of Morals*, 82-84.

[143] Liddell, "Kant," 112-24, 119-22.

[144] J.B. Schneewind, "Autonomy, Obligation, and Virtue: An Overview of Kant's Moral Philosophy," in *The Cambridge Companion to Kant*, ed. Paul Guyer (Cambridge: Cambridge University Press, 1992), 317-18; T. C. Williams, "The Traditional Interpretation of the Categorical Imperative," in T.C. Williams, *The Concept of the Categorical Imperative: A Study of the Place of the Categorical Imperative in Kant's Ethical Theory* (Oxford: Clarendon Press, 1968), 37-41.

145 Kant, *Groundwork of the Metaphysic of Morals*, 88; Williams, "Traditional Interpretation," 37-38.

146 Kant, *Groundwork of the Metaphysic of Morals*, 88.

147 Kant, *Groundwork of the Metaphysic of Morals*, 103-4.

148 Kant, *Groundwork of the Metaphysic of Morals*, 96.

149 Kant, *Groundwork of the Metaphysic of Morals*, 83-84.

150 Kant, *Groundwork of the Metaphysic of Morals*, 83-84.

151 Novak, *Suicide and Morality*, 132-38.

152 Michael J. Seidler, "Kant and the Stoics," 429-32. In making such an argument, we can see strong affinities here between Kant's thought and the philosophy of Benedict de Spinoza. For Spinoza, everything that exists is a manifestation of the one ultimate reality that existed, a manifestation of one universal substance. The desire to be cannot be extinguished arbitrarily at the will of the person since it offends against the very humanity that resides in all persons as a manifestation of universal substance. On Spinoza see Regan, "Moral Argument," 311; cf. Choron, *Death*, 121-28.

153 On Hume and utility see A.J. Ayer, *Hume* (Oxford: Oxford University Press, 1980), 82-83.

154 See Geoffrey Scarre, *Utilitarianism* (London: Routledge, 1993), 10-14.

155 Jeremy Bentham, *An Introduction to the Principles of Morals and Legislation*, in *Utilitariarism*, ed. Mary Warnock (London: Fontana, 1979), 33.

156 Scarre, *Utilitarianism*, 72-91.

157 See Mary P. Mack, *Jeremy Bentham* (New York: Columbia University Press, 1963), 112-13, 213. The comparison with Hume is made by the utilitarian James Rachels in his *End of Life* (New York: Oxford University Press, 1986), 19.

158 Bentham, *Principles of Morals and Legislation*, 34-35.

159 Mack, *Jeremy Bentham*, 112-13.

160 See discussion of Hume *supra.*

161 See Ross Harrison, *Bentham* (London: Routledge, 1983), 77-78.

162 Bentham, *Principles of Morals and Legislation*, 35-7.

163 Gerald J. Postema, *Bentham and the Common Law Tradition* (Oxford: Clarendon Press, 1986), 308-13.

164 See A.J.P. Kenny "Intention and Purpose in Law," in *Essays in Legal Philosophy*, ed. R.S. Summers (Berkeley: University of California, 1968), 146-63.

165 Bentham, *Principles of Morals and Legislation*, 33.

166 See Harrison, *Bentham*, 77-105.

167 John Stuart Mill, *Utilitarianism. On Liberty*, ed. Mary Warnock (London: Fontana, 1962).

168 Wendy Donner, *The Liberal Self* (Ithaca: Cornell University Press, 1991), 37-41.

169 Scarre, *Utilitarianism*, 90-95.

170 See discussion of this in David Lyons, "Liberty and Harm to Others," *Mill's On Liberty: Critical Essays,* ed. Gerald Dworkin (Lanham: Rowman & Littlefield, 1997), 115-36.

171 Mill, *On Liberty*, 136.

172 Mill, *On Liberty*, 135.

173 C.L. Ten, "Mill on Self-Regarding Actions," *Philosophy* 43 (1968): 29-37.

174 See Max Charlesworth, *Bioethics in a Liberal Society* (Cambridge: Cambridge University Press, 1993), 15-20.

175 Mill, *On Liberty*, 136.

176 Jonathan Riley, *Mill on Liberty* (London: Routledge, 1998), 132-35.

177 Riley, *Mill*, 132-35.

[178] See for example Dan Brock, "Physician-Assisted Suicide is Sometimes Morally Justified," *Physician-Assisted Suicide*, ed. Robert Weir (Bloomington: Indiana University Press, 1997), 86-103; James Rachels, "Euthanasia," in *Matters of Life and Death*, ed. Tom L. Beauchamp and Tom Regan, 3rd ed. (New York: McGraw-Hill, 1993), 30-68; Margaret P. Battin, *The Least Worse Death* (New York: Oxford University Press, 1994), 3-29, 101-29.

[179] G.K. Chesterton expressed well Kant's reasoning here when he stated, albeit somewhat dramatically, that "he who kills himself kills all men."

Chapter Three

Contemporary Justifications for the Practices of Suicide, Assisted Suicide and Voluntary Euthanasia

Introduction

In the preceding chapter, significant historical perspectives on the moral legitimacy of suicide and assistance in suicide have been discussed. History is never far away from the context of the contemporary debate. It is against the background of the history of ideas that modern forms of argumentation are derived and advanced. The basis for the analysis of this chapter will be just such a consideration of those contemporary lines of argumentation for the moral legitimacy of those practices that spring from, and further extend, the key conceptual ideas of the previous chapter. The order of engagement here will broadly correspond to the enumeration of ideas encountered in summary form at the end of the previous chapter.

Firstly, I will consider the idea that the worth of human life is commensurable with other values, or disvalues, such that the value of life itself can diminish or wane to the point that intending death itself becomes a valid choice worthy option.

Secondly, I will consider arguments arising from ideas relating to self-determination and spheres of subjectivity that are said to preclude intervention in the exercise of choice by means of coercion, due to the significance and priority of this value in the face of other competing values.

Thirdly, I will consider accounts of action theory that reject the principle of double effect, a principle designed to resolve potential conflict between negative moral prohibitions. If that principle were unsustainable, then the maintenance of exceptionless moral norms in the natural law tradition concerning killing would result in a *reductio ad absurdum*, for it would entail the imposition of impossibly rigorist demands on the agent.

Fourthly, I will address the argument that the sanctity of life perspective, most closely associated with natural law theory, lacks consistency, for it is considered contradictory for that perspective to uphold rights to self defence and capital punishment and yet deny certain forms of consensual killing on the basis of altruistic motive.

Lastly, I will consider the claim that once we have removed the yoke of 'divine imperatives' on contemporary secular society, only narrow forms of 'public secular reasoning' can prevail in shaping public life together. I will address 'anti-perfectionist' accounts of the state that call for neutrality, viz. competing theories of the good life reflected in the fragmentary nature of contemporary pluralism.

Before turning directly to this task of exploring contemporary ideas under these broad classificatory rubrics, a caveat concerning scope is called for. I will refrain from subsequently discussing the idea of the immortality of the human soul. Its inclusion in the previous chapter was designed to assist in delineating context, and in demonstrating the interstices of the historical development of ideas relating to our subject matter generally. As is now clear, from the analysis of the preceding chapter, attempts to infer the immorality of suicide from the immortality of the soul, *do in fact* 'trade on' or 'smuggle in' special or privileged assumptions in order to put normative flesh on otherwise bare speculative bones.

I defend this subsequent exclusion on the same ground upon which I have excluded theological lines of argumentation from underpinning our inquiry. Only appeals to natural reason (in principle) can be relevant to the moral assessment of suicide, when the question is framed within the context of justifications for imposing limits on action in conditions of pluralism. To the extent that the question is tied to insights derived from special or privileged claims of knowledge, it cannot function as a publicly accessible ground for assertions of immorality (or morality for that matter).

Plato's account of the soul, for example, is rendered normatively inconclusive when it is severed from the religious influence of Pythagorean mysticism.[1] When severed from such a religious context, why does the fact that the soul may be immortal render it immoral to hasten its departure from the body? Since the bodily habitation of the soul is considered a transitory state, why is it wrong to release the soul from the body in conditions where considerable burdens are imposed? Answers to such questions, in order to have content, depend on implied religious assumptions. Remove such content, and the 'metaphysical fact', in my view, is incapable of doing the work required of it one way or the other in the debate.

Lest my position be misunderstood in making such an exclusion, let me make it clear that I am far from denying *the possibility* of rational argument demonstrating either the existence of the human soul or its subsequent immortality.[2] Rather, I simply see such claims as being indeterminate and inconclusive with regard to addressing the central task of this work—the critical evaluation of natural and publicly accessible reasons advanced for and against the legitimacy of suicide and assistance in suicide—reasons that must be independently supported and justified apart from any express or implied reference to, or dependence on, faith based considerations concerning the contentful significance of the soul's immortality.

A Life Not Worth Living

Invalid Quasi-Religious Appeals

A rhetorically influential line of attack on the notion of the inviolable dignity of human life (going significantly further than my own weak exclusionary steps) is to decry the whole gambit of traditional sanctity of human life concerns as being essentially religious in nature and thus not capable of structuring forms of appeal that can function as a set of accessible public reasons in contemporary secular society. The influence of the work of David Hume is the most significant historical progenitor of this line of critique. Other important historical influences include the critique of natural law forms of reasoning advanced by Jeremy Bentham and J.S. Mill.[3] Dan Brock and Helga

Kuhse carry Hume's torch, and are typical of the rejection of appeals to sanctity of life to instil objective inviolable worth in human life regardless of the quality of life of the patient.[4] Life, as with any other presumptive value, is not a value that can be held up for reification independently of the quality of life to be assessed.[5] The judgement as to whether or not a life is actually worth living, in the face of intractable pain and suffering, is one that can and should be made by the individual patient in determining whether his or her life is essentially one worth continuing with or not.

Since we permit an assessment of benefit and burden for each patient in terms of the discontinuation of treatment, we should permit the same calculation of benefit and burden in the decision of whether or not to intentionally terminate that life, if necessary, with the active assistance and co-operation of a third party.[6]

Life's Instrumental Goodness

The main opposition to the sanctity of human life perspective, closely associated with natural law theory, relates to the question of the status of the good of human life itself. Stripped from its quasi-religious context and relying on a broad array of factors to determine its value vis-à-vis the appeal of other values, how can it make sense to talk of human life as an intrinsic good that can never be intentionally acted against?

The predominate theme in current moral philosophy, as G.E.M. Anscombe has noted, is one that heavily relies on consequentialist and mixed consequentialist systems of reasoning.[7] Such an approach is not new, of course, and can in fact trace its historical roots to both the Stoic and Epicurean emphasis on indifference or hedonism, respectively, as the sole ultimate sources of human value by which other subordinate values are assessed. In such systems, human life cannot be the bearer of any intrinsic value attached to it. Life is a positive value so long as it can hold its own against other competing considerations such as the disvalue of human suffering. It is even a weighty presumptive value since it underpins all of life's significant projects.

However, when life itself manifests ever increasing evils, life itself ceases to be a positive value that must prevail against other competing values.[8] The classic modern form of such commensuration or proportionality between competing values and disvalues can be seen in Utilitarianism.

J.J.C. Smart, a contemporary Utilitarian, has stated that the right-making properties of an action can only be judged by an assessment of the consequences.[9] Right actions are those that have the best consequences, and wrong actions are not maximising in their consequences.[10] The worth of outcomes is determined solely by consequences, and not by other moral standards. The Benthamite 'ring' to this account of the moral evaluation of an action is unmistakable.[11] This account of moral evaluation of course presupposes that diverse consequences are indeed commensurable. This in turn presupposes that there must be a common means of weighing various values that allows the person to objectively determine what is the best value outcome in a given situation.[12]

Consequentialist based systems, therefore, clearly reject the principle that life itself can have any intrinsic (*per se*) value attached to it. Such an approach is similarly evident in Joseph Fletcher's ethics of Situationalism.[13] The context of a person's life is supremely important. The only general non-specific absolute is love. In individual situations there need be no contradiction between the balancing of values and the service of love. Suicide and assisted suicide can, in the unique situation of the individual, constitute a loving act.[14] Such an act may well be manifested in the decision of a person to give witness to their rational 'personhood function' over the indignity of losing their consciousness or other ignominies.[15]

Mixed deontological/consequentialist systems also admit of commensuration between all forms of value, although not in such overtly obvious ways. In those systems life can have high value. However, that value is not considered to be fully basic and incommensurable, in that it can be intentionally acted against in certain compelling circumstances.

Take, for example, the work of Tom Beauchamp and James Childress, influential authors of a leading bioethics textbook.[16] They argue that certain principles, like the non-killing of the innocent, are valid for the most part. However, exceptions arise in which the value of human life itself is 'trumped' by the disvalues in a given situation. The value of life can be outweighed by the force of other disvalues.[17] The basic approach adopted in that text draws heavily on the influential work of the early 20th century Oxford philosopher W.D. Ross.[18]

W.D. Ross addressed the problem of value commensuration within the deontological tradition by incorporating the call of duty within the framework of intuitionalism and *prima facie* obligation.[19] The appeal of certain duties gives rise to conflicts of obligation. In any concrete situation, rules based on duties conflict. When faced with such a conflict, the agent has to decide which duty has priority. Whilst on the face of it, to act against a duty is always *prima facie* wrong, one duty will be able to override another duty.[20] The weighing of duties cannot take place in a vacuum divorced from consequences, but must consider consequences in justifying the overriding of one *prima facie* duty with an appeal to the other.[21]

Ross's basic method for resolving conflicts between duties has been extremely influential, although it is presented under various disguises.[22] It has become a near orthodoxy in deontological circles, that 'tragedy' or 'disaster' or 'escape clause' overrides are an essential part of the fabric of any practical morality.[23]   Ross's influence can be further demonstrated with reference to the work of bioethicists Bernard Gert, Charles Culver, and Danner Clouser.[24] Common morality can apprehend the reasonableness of the general rule that prohibits 'unjustified killing.' Yet, the challenges of pain and suffering and other pressures place the terminally ill patient in such a predicament that the normal rule can be said to accede to 'tragic situations'.[25] Whilst there are practical difficulties in satisfactorily regulating the relationship between respecting patients in this predicament and unjust pressures on other patients who are all too easily marginalised, competent patients can, in principle, sensibly make a choice to intentionally end life by forgoing treatment or by positively seeking to end life by suicide and assisted suicide. Thus, the rule against no 'unjustified killing' is still preserved since such circumstances render such an act of killing justified.[26]

Further Assessing Life's Worth

The notion of 'quality of life' was traditionally used to measure environmental conditions that either improved or impaired the quality of a person's life. Reformers used this traditional concept to increase the standard of living by improving working conditions, health care, education, and other living conditions, etc.[27] In the wake of contemporary movements, however, the dynamic of quality of life concerns has now been significantly altered. Now, rather than measuring conditions that improve life, the notion of quality of life has increasingly come to signify the measurement of the worth of a person's life itself.[28]

Jonathan Glover, James Rachels, and Peter Singer, all utilitarians, for example, make a distinction between 'being alive' and 'having a life'.[29] Again, the influence of historical antecedents here is not hard to trace. The ideas of Stoicism, Epicureanism, Michael de Montaigne, David Hume, Jeremy Bentham, and J.S. Mill, have all cumulatively contributed to the seeming plausibility of this distinction. The first, being alive, is merely the last vestiges, the near cadaver, of biological function, and the second, having a life, is an expression of the worthwhile biographical characteristics of the person. Having a life equals personal life. Having a life consists in all the plans, aspirations, preferences, memories, dreams, etc., of personality. These are what we value, not mere biological life as such. It is this complex of psychological and emotional features that makes a life worth living not simply being alive or barely alive.[30]

Negative quality thresholds are effectively established for having a life rather than being merely alive. Objectivity, in such a framework, points to an array of personal values that need to be factored in as to whether or not a life beyond the negative minimum has sufficient value. For competent patients, at

75

least, the actual weighing of those values, their relational strengths, is resolved, for they ought to be determined by the individual patient in the context of a *de facto* self-assessment exercise.[31]

Ronald Dworkin's mixed-rights-based system also represents a form of balancing the value of life with an interpretation of what constitutes the value of a life, via the notion of investment.[32] Human life, objectively, can be said to have value in so far as the person, whose life it is, is in a position to derive value from it. Human life takes on value from the life projects of the person. Dworkin claims that nearly all people seek to honour a sense in which life is 'sacred'. However, a reasonable interpretation of this value is that life's 'inherent' value depends on the creative investment of the person.[33] It is this sense of life that is 'sacre', not the biological life of the person, which has failed to sustain personal creativity.

There is no intrinsic value to be had in bodily life, only in conscious control of that life, through which the individual can shape it and give it significance and meaning. Thus, when the condition of the body no longer acts in the service of this creative life of authorship, it can be reasonable to reject the ensuing condition and seek to end it via suicide or assisted suicide. Such an act can be a last testament to that life of authorship, representing a final seal to the values of personal choice and control determined by the agent.[34]

For Dworkin, not unlike Rachels and Glover, the objective notion of life's worth, at least for competent patients (within the very broad brush strokes of the idea of investment), is also readily passed into the hands of a *de facto* self-assessment exercise. For the incompetent, life's value is judged by something akin to a 'minimum creativity standard', and the fate of a patent suffering from, say, advanced senility, is determined by a judgement, made by a third party, that that person's life indeed falls below the minimal threshold needed for any form of personal creativity.

An appeal to a thoroughgoing value commensuration in the evaluation of life's worth can be further demonstrated in the work of Helga Kuhse and John Harris.

Helga Kuhse shares the direct rejection of the sanctity of life approach, which holds that innocent life must be valued such that it cannot be directly attacked by an act of intentional killing. She points out what she regards as the hypocrisy of 'allowing' patients to die by the withdrawal of treatment, yet refusing to assist patients by positively reaching the same chosen outcome.[35]

In determining whether a life is worth living or not, attention should be focused upon an array of 'interests' of the person, and these, for the competent patient at least, are going to vary considerably, since they will be informed by the patient's underlying dispositions, and, for the incompetent, by a minimal quality threshold. It follows that for competent patients, a broad ranging assessment of quality of life concerns is the trump card as to whether or not life continues to be worthwhile. Different patients may well decide differently. That is the prerogative of the patient, for the only unpalatable alternative is to force a patient to stay alive.[36]

For Harris, life can be judged valuable or not when the person assessing his or her own life determines it to be so.[37] If a person values his or her own life, then that life is valuable, precisely to the extent that he or she values it. Without any real capacity to value, there can be no value. As Harris states, "... the value of our lives is the value we give to our lives."[38]

It follows that the primary injustice done to a person is to deprive the person of a life he of she may think valuable. Objectivity in the value of human life, for Harris (in line with the other thinkers discussed above), essentially becomes one of negative classification (ruling certain people out of consideration for value), allied positively to a broad range of 'critical interests'; interests worthy of pursuing—friendships, family, life goals, etc.— which are subjected to de facto self-assessment for the further determination of meaningful value.[39]

Suicide, assisted suicide, and voluntary euthanasia, can therefore be justified, on the grounds that once the competent nature of the person making the decision has been established, the thoroughgoing commensuration between different values, in the form of interests or preferences, is essentially left up to the individual to determine for himself or herself.[40] Harris, as with Kuhse and Dworkin, approves of such a strong core of wide-ranging value commensuration in the determination of life's value, since only such a large area of ball-park choice is actually considered compatible with the notion of respect for persons.[41]

At the risk of some simplification, the common thread running through such accounts can be expressed as follows. Life's worth is subject to a *de minimus* threshold that must be crossed. Any objectivity to life resides in 'personal', 'biographical', or 'creative' life, not mere biological life. Personal life represents the minimal threshold for any objective worth. The further determination of life's worth is established by a series of weighing exercises, a balancing of an array of values, under very broad criteria, such as 'creative investment' or 'critical interests', and the task of determining the further application of those broad criteria is left to the devices of the individual.

Arguments Based on Self-Determination

Basic Argument

The basic line of argumentation concerning the idea of self-determination concerning the manner and timing of a person's death will be briefly stated. I will then flesh out some prominent accounts for the grounding of a right to self-determination, encompassing the manner and timing of death, by drawing on several key thinkers who have supported such a right.

The basic line of argument here places great store in a widespread right to non-interference in the making of self-directing choices concerning the self and what constitutes well-being.[42] Consequently, it is said that decisions individuals make affecting the course of their own lives should be respected as long as they do not significantly threaten, injure, or harm others. The influence of J.S. Mill's historical work *On Liberty* looms powerfully here.[43] The right to self-determination seems to apply particularly to medical decision making, as questions pertaining to the timing and circumstances of a person's death are said to be intimate to the person and his or her conception of self and well-being. Allowing an individual to control his or her death is therefore said to further advance the cause of self-determination.[44] As Dan Brock states, "... the great variability among people on this question [of the licitness of consensual killing] makes it especially important that individuals control the manner, circumstances, and timing of their dying and death."[45]

"Philosophers' Brief"

This document, written by six prominent philosophers—Ronald Dworkin, Thomas Nagel, Robert Nozick, John Rawls, Thomas, Scanlon, and Judith Jarvis Thomson—is one of the most significant co-operative documents to have appeared on the subject in recent years, and places the concept of self-determination at the heart of its appeal to recognise a right to physician assisted suicide.[46]

The *Brief* argues from an analogy concerning a woman's right to determine the continuation or termination of a pregnancy, claiming that since such a right to termination is generally recognised, consistency must seek out the underlying principle—a right to self-determination—and apply it to decision making at the end of life as well as to decision making at the beginning of life.[47] In support of such a claim, the philosophers approve of and make a central appeal to the following passage from the US Supreme Court abortion case of *Planned Parenthood v. Casey*:

> ... matters, involving the most intimate and personal choices a person may make in a lifetime, choices central to personal dignity and autonomy, are central to ... liberty ... *At the heart of liberty is the right to define one's own concept of existence, of meaning, of the universe, and of the mystery of human life* (my emphasis)[48]

Following from such a moral claim, it is argued that the state must respect an individual's right to determine fundamental concepts concerning the meaning of life and death from a person's own, essentially subjective, perspective. On such a foundation, it is claimed, the very notion of respect for persons depends. To coerce fundamental choices of that nature is to deny a person an equality of self-worth.[49] Here the language of J.S. Mill is at its strongest. In forcing such choices we impose violence upon another person and rob the person of a profound sense of self-worth. By prohibiting the option for assisted suicide, for example, the state denies the legitimacy of a person's own conception of profound religious or metaphysical values, and thus ceases to treat that person equally.

Equal Concern and Respect

Ronald Dworkin, one of the authors of the above *Brief*, has advanced most forcefully the claim that the right to make momentous personal decisions is a claim that is derived from the notion of the equality of persons. In failing to respect another person's conception of what constitutes the good life, we devalue that person as an equal. As Dworkin states in *Taking Right Seriously*, "Government must not only treat people with concern and respect, but with *equal concern and respect* ... It must not constrain liberty on the ground that one citizen's conception of the good life is nobler or superior to another's (emphasis added)."[50]

By depriving a person of an opportunity to determine such significant questions concerning life and death for himself or herself, we literally disrespect a person's worth. This principle is so fundamental to a person's sense of self and well-being that its compromise is an affront to the basic dignity that ought to prevail between persons.[51] For Dworkin, self-determination in such matters must be allowed to prevail, for to do otherwise is to inform people that the most profound beliefs about themselves are ultimately either base or degrading.

Since the societal enforcement of a particular conception of the meaning of death, including its manner and timing, requires another to accept a central proposition that is rejected, it forces that person to abandon his or her sense of self-worth. Following J.S. Mill closely here, Dworkin concludes that only choices that deny another's equal right to self-constituting choice, or choices

80

that harm another person, can plausibly become candidates for a restriction on the exercise of liberty.[52]

In his book *Life's Dominion*, Dworkin directly employs his conception of equal worth to the assisted suicide debate, and reaches a conclusion very similar to the argument encountered in the *Philosophers' Brief* above. A right to equal concern and respect requires acknowledgement of the importance of deep constitutive choice concerning the meaning of life.[53] Acceptance of such requires the right, in some circumstances at least, to act intentionally to terminate life. Life is in many respects a narrative, a novel in which the person is the primary author or lead character.[54] No one wants do die out of character and lose control over the writing of the last chapter. Thus, "making someone die in a way that others approve, but he believes a horrifying contradiction of his life, is a devastating, odious form of tyranny."[55]

Suicide and assisted suicide constitute a claim to control, in the face of medical technology and a paternalistic medical establishment that is committed to the relentless extension of life.[56] It represents a conscious effort to empower the individual over these external forces that fail to respect the choices of the individual over "the final act of life's drama."[57] A person's sense of authorship over life is compromised and not assisted by a medical establishment that insists upon imposing its values upon the person. Personal decision making is, therefore, compromised in such a situation and the person is not treated as a person of equal worth and respect.[58]

A 'right to die' is therefore derived from a conception of the worth of the person in which persons, so conceived, are entitled to.[59] Thus, self-directing persons are entitled to make certain decisions for themselves, without undue interference from others. Here, persons are defined not simply by their capacities or their active powers to exercise choice, but by their rights—the responsibility of others to allow them to choose regarding matters significantly affecting their lives, assuming their choices are appropriately respectful of the similar rights of others.[60]

Idea of Personal Autonomy

One of the most pressing accounts of argumentation concerning a right to suicide and assistance in suicide flows from conceptions of personal autonomy. Personal autonomy in relation to an individual's conception of life is considered vital if a person is to be respected.[61] Such a right can extend to the manner and timing of death, since such an exercise of self-determination is deeply expressive of the values of the person. [62]

Joel Feinberg has advanced one of the most comprehensive accounts of the personal autonomous self.[63] He lists the qualities that inhere in a personal autonomous life: qualities such as authenticity, integrity, and distinct self-identity. These qualities provide a kind of overview of the self in whom these qualities inhere. The autonomous individual, described by Feinberg, strives to maintain self-direction in a world where external factors impinge on the deliberation of the agent. This self is not radically disconnected from social influence or free of relationships with others.[64]

In discussing the extent to which autonomous persons are self-created, Feinberg acknowledges social influences that help to form character and parental influences that help implant the potential for authenticity. Feinberg states that the "moral independence" that characterises autonomy should not be read to require non-commitment to the demands of others.[65] In important ways, though, these provisos form the 'exceptions' rather than the rule. Of the characteristics that distinguish the autonomous individual, most highlight forms of self-directedness and distinguish them from the condition of being subject to the controlling influence of others, e.g., the autonomous person forges his or her own tastes, opinions, and values.[66]

For Feinberg, an autonomous person can reach a decision consonant with self, to be free from the burdens of life itself, providing that the exercise of that choice is genuinely an expression of self and not the result of other factors that radically impinge and distort or incapacitate that person's considered judgement. Further, Feinberg thinks that a request for assistance in suicide can be justified as long as a suitable framework is in place to ensure that choices made are genuinely reflective of the settled and abiding disposition of person, and are not the result of undue external influences.[67]

In *Harm to Self*, Feinberg rejects the notion that others can know better what is in another person's own interest other than the person him or herself. The paternalist treats the other as not being an independent agent capable of self-guidance. Feinberg draws on a strong analogy with state sovereignty to support this line of reasoning.[68] Just as a state's territorial boundaries can be invaded by border infringement without permission, so too can a person be the subject of such unwelcomed 'invasion'. As it is part of the very constitution of the nation state to protect the state from border infringements that undermine sovereignty, so it is part of the constitution of a person to have the necessary protection to repel unwanted infringements on his or her sovereignty. "Sovereignty is an all or nothing concept: one is entitled to absolute control of whatever is within one's domain however trivial it may be."[69]

Along with Joel Feinberg, D.A.J. Richards has been one of the most outspoken opponents of paternalistic intervention in the light of what he understands to be the pluriform good of a diversity of different personal choices. It is in the context of a consideration of the value of personal autonomy that a right to engage in a variety of diverse and incompatible practices arises. He reasons in a similar fashion to Feinberg, that if personal autonomy is at the heart of a person's identity, that core notion justifies a high importance attached to a duty to respect non-interference.[70]

Richards believes that his account of personal autonomy is in fact derived from the legacy of Immanuel Kant, not J.S. Mill, as first appearances might suggest.[71] Whilst Richards maintains that the parameters of insight have moved on since the time of Kant, Richards claims that Kant is, so to speak, the 'spiritual ancestor' of the modern theory of personal autonomy and its theory of rights. Freudian and other psychological work has deepened our understanding of the subjective will. Kant, was in consequence, too narrow in his strictures concerning the purely rational basis governing the direction of choice. In contrast, choice and its influences have a decidedly more diverse flavour as dispositions and preferences are brought into the core of personal autonomy. Via a decidedly more marked turn to the subject (influenced by historical currents from Romanticism and 19th century Germanic Philosophy), the will is no longer to be governed by the pure guiding light of reason itself, as had Kant maintained in his various formulations of the Categorical Imperative. Richards maintains that we can recognise that autonomy is now properly situated in the very ends set by the person himself or herself, and not by ends imposed by the stamp of abstract reason.[72]

Richards instantiates this in the language of rights, by stating that the core of personal identity, and the respect for that core alone, constitute the stuff of moral rights. In consequence, the only restrictions that can be placed on an action are those that clearly manifest a lack of autonomous decision making capacity, and entail direct harm, or directly and significantly interfere with the rights of another to make self-determining choices for him or herself.[73]

By such a robust defence of a right to non-interference, Richards is able to make an appeal to the licitness of a variety of sexual practices, drug taking, and assisted suicide. Since the drug taker sees value in an artificially induced state of euphoria, and his or her actions need not cause direct harm to third parties, so the practice can be seen to be morally right, since it emanates from that person's own self-constituting choice (even if that choice entails the resultant consequence that the person subsequently becomes drug dependent).[74] By such a line of argumentation, Richards thus defends an overtly anti-paternalistic circumscription on the power of the state or any third party to interfere with the centrality of autonomous choice.[75]

Rationality of Intentional Suicide

At its core, it is argued that the concept of personal autonomy involves the freedom of the individual to making profound constitutive decisions regarding life, including death itself. In order to make decisions, an individual must choose between options, and this requires a certain amount of self-awareness in terms of current location and where it is thought desirable to be in the near future. In order to be autonomous in one's decisions, one must possess the capacity to make autonomous decisions, a certain independence, and be presented with an adequate range of options.[76]

The derived argument, in the light of personal autonomy, concerning the rationality of suicide/assisted suicide, contends that questions of 'rationality' are essentially 'instrumental' in the service of the patient's set goals. If the patient expresses a persistent plan for self-initiated death, and is able to consistently articulate that plan, suicide and assisted suicide can form a rational means to pursue that articulated goal.[77]

Whilst caution is required in cases of, say, depression, or the undue influence of others, creating internal and external pressures that can radically affect the autonomous nature of a proposed course of action, these barriers can, in many cases, be overcome. If 'instrumental' rationality can be determined with reference to the agent's persistent plan that proceeds from autonomous self-deliberation, then suicide and assisted suicide can be justified, notwithstanding practical difficulties concerning the determination of a person's settled frame of mind in a given instance.[78]

Margaret Battin and James Margolis, amongst many others, are typical representatives of this kind of approach concerning the conditions for determining the rationality of an act of suicide. Battin claims that an act of suicide or assisted suicide would be rational if the suicide can articulate a consistent worldview, and can articulate the rational information for and against a choice to commit suicide or seek assistance to that end. Providing the person can articulate these factors, and the nature of the effects an act of suicide would have, the person has a rationally informed basis to justify suicide and to seek support from others, such as physicians or nurse practitioners.[79]

James Margolis argues that suicide can be a rational means if it can be the only realistic way of enabling a person to attain settled and articulated goals. Such a form of rationality does not presuppose that the patient be in 'perfect sound mind', but rather that he or she is competent enough to have a settled articulation of disposition and is able to demonstrate how suicide is the most rationally efficient means to attain the articulated goals.[80]

Such a line of justification for rational suicide finds endorsement in the popular text in biomedical ethics written by Beauchamp and Childress, and they spell out its implications for assisted suicide. For Beauchamp and Childress, the key is the autonomy based notion of the valid consent of the competent patient. If a competent patient can, for example, refuse treatment, then a competent patient can commission another to render assistance in order to perform the task of procuring death. Assuming, therefore, that consent can be exercised on autonomy grounds, both forms of act and omission can be seen as symmetric. In consequence, Beauchamp and Childress argue that both death by omission and death by active intervention can (in principle at least) be rationally justified.[81]

Rejection of Double Effect Reasoning

Background

A number of ethicists, especially in the natural law tradition, make use of the principle of double effect as a set of criteria for making decisions in conflict situations between one or more negative prohibitions. They make use of this form of reasoning in order to enable an agent to make a judgement, which has the practical effect of a destruction against a good or norm that is said not to admit of direct attack.

The use of double effect reasoning is particularly prevalent in analysis concerning the value of human life when it comes into conflict with other goods. If double effect reasoning is undermined, it places the continued maintenance of concrete moral absolutes in a decidedly unpromising light. Indirectly then, the denial of double effect reasoning is a *de facto* denial of the sustainability of exceptionless concrete moral norms.[82]

The starting point for a discussion of double effect reasoning as we saw in the historical chapter is usually traced to Aquinas in his analysis of self-defence (S.T. II-II, q. 64, a. 7). Whilst it is not licit to intend to kill an aggressor, it is licit to use lethal force to repel an attack, if the intention is not to cause the death of the aggressor, but simply to use proportionate force in order to stop the attack.[83] The principle of double effect, in its modern guise, itself the result of subsequent development at the hands of Neo-Scholastic scholars (e.g., Thomas de Vitoria), can be stated in terms of the following necessary and sufficient criteria:

1) The object of the action must be morally good or indifferent in itself;
2) the bad effect(s), though foreseen (permitted), cannot be intended;
3) the bad effect(s) cannot be the causally antecedent means of achieving the good effect(s)—the good effect(s) must either precede or at least be collateral with the bad effect(s);
4) there must be a sufficiently grave proportionate reason to justify the causation of the foreseen bad effect(s).[84]

Double Effect Criteria Explained

As the first criterion of double effect makes clear, double effect cannot be appealed to in order to justify an action that intentionally contravenes an express prohibition of the kind—'it is always illicit to intend to perform action X regardless of circumstances Y for the sake of Z'. Thus, the intentional killing of an innocent person is said to function as such an express prohibition, since the objective of the action is always considered illicit regardless of the circumstances in which the action is performed and regardless of the motive for which it is performed.[85]

The second criterion is designed to express a perceived morally relevant distinction between the direction of a person's intention and the significance of that intention for the goodness of the action (evil cannot intentionally be done that good may come). The bad effects cannot be intended but can only be permitted. If a bad effect is intended (even along with the good effects) then this cancels out any claim to integrity of intention in acting only for the sake of the good (good is to be done and evil avoided).

The third criterion is designed to express the concern that in order to channel the direction of the will in choosing to perform a given action, a proper intention cannot seek to bring about the good effect by the precise causal means of the bad effect. The bad effect cannot be the causal antecedent of the good. To do so would be to say that one can intentionally cause evil for the sake of a good to be pursued. Good intentions cannot simply fly in the face of the causal order manifest in the physical world.

The fourth criterion expresses the key requirement that the causation of a bad effect is not a neutral or irrelevant consideration, once the direction of the intention of an action has been established. Responsibility does not end there. The causation of harm must be undertaken for sufficiently serious reasons to justify the collateral (side) effects that may result.

No Moral Absolutes

As has already been mentioned, modern systems of ethical thought, almost without exception (particularly in the area of bioethics), reject the notion that there can be concrete exceptionless moral norms that always prohibit certain concrete courses of action. The first major line of attack on the principle of double effect is thus the consequentialist or mixed deontological/ consequentialist turn of denying that there can ever be specific concrete exceptionless moral norms in the first place that are always binding (*semper sed non ad semper* not *semper et ad semper*).[86]

Double effect reasoning is considered to be the unique Byzantine creation of a system of morality hedged in by rigid moral norms of its own devising. Abolish the prohibitions and the need for the principle is removed.[87] It is argued that there, can, *ceteris paribus,* be a strong presumption against the permissibility of intentional killing. However, it is a norm that can be overridden in certain circumstances. Such circumstances can extend to the condition of an autonomous patient, with intractable pain and suffering, who consents to the taking of his or her own life.[88]

Erroneous Act Characterisation

Another major prong of attack on the principle of double effect is to challenge its basic method of classifying human actions, thus drawing upon the historical influence of Jeremy Bentham and his alternative account of act characterisation. Jonathan Bennett, for example, argues that the distinction between the thing done and the resultant consequences is merely a verbal one and not therefore substantive.[89] Since there is so much fluctuation and capacity for an *accordion like* re-description of an act, in short, the radical potential for elision between the 'object' of an action and its 'consequences', that way of characterising an action is considered to be deeply misguided. It is better to consider the 'state of affairs' produced, and to ascribe responsibility to an agent on the basis of an assessment of the knowingly foreseeable consequences that result.[90]

Consider the following facts and the different resultant description generated by a Benthamite-Bennettian assessment. Physician X gives a lethal dose of barbiturates to patient Y. He knows that the dose will kill the patient quickly in the causal order. He further foresees the consequence of ending the patient's suffering via the administration of the dose. The patient is aware of the reason for the administration of the drugs and has consented to it. Bennett would classify the action in terms of the foreseeable beneficial consequences and resultant harm. The good of alleviating suffering with the consent of the patient outweighs the resultant bad effects such as the loss of life, or the grief of family, etc. The act can thus properly be classified as one of, say, 'mercy induced death'.

By challenging the description of actions and characterising them in terms of what was reasonably foreseeable as a resultant state of affairs, Bennett purports to be able to 'level' the different traditional requirements of an act description into a weighing of resultant consequences.[91]

Intention and Foresight

As the above description of double effect pointed out, a crucial aspect of the tenability of double effect reasoning is the distinction drawn between intention and foresight—between what the agent intends to happen as a result of his or her action and what is unintended, that is, what is said to stand outside the scope of the agent's intention—that is, what is considered to be *praeter intentionem*. However, this distinction is also rejected as being incapable of substantively grounding the limitation on moral liability sought for resulting bad effects.[92]

Glanville Williams[93], John Mackie[94], Alan Donagan[95], and Roderick Chisholm[96] reject the moral relevance of the distinction between what the agent is said to directly intend and what is said to be collateral or only 'obliquely' intended. They think that the distinction reeks of artificiality.[97] It seems absurd to say that one can use a means to an end which will almost (even) certainly result in death, but not intend those consequences.[98] Such a distinction is said to lead to a 'moral blindness' whereby means are wrenched from their relationship to the knowledge we have about their effects.

This difficulty is resolved in their minds by effectively stating that one intends also the consequences that predictably flow from an action, voluntarily and knowingly undertaken.[99] It is only in the area of uncertainty, where consequences are unforeseen or hazy, that it becomes possible to say that an effect was not intended, due to lack of knowledge.[100]

Tom Beauchamp and James Childress similarly reject the intention/foresight distinction on the basis of the artificiality of the distinction between intended and merely accepted consequences. The agent intends all that can reasonably be expected to flow from the act itself.[101] A similar position is taken by Roderick Chisholm and by Michael Bratman. If an agent acts with the intention of bringing about state-of-affairs A, and if it is reasonable to assume that A implies B...Z, then in order to act logically, the agent must intend both A and B...Z.[102]

A medical case will help to illustrate their argument for rejecting the distinction between intention/foresight. Physician X is faced with a dying patient whose cancer is very advanced. The physician administers ever increasing doses of morphine. She knows that in giving such large doses of morphine, death will likely follow due to respiratory depression (A implies B). The physician is said to intend all the consequences that flow from this; both the relief of pain and the hastening of death.[103] It is therefore argued that the intention/foresight distinction is nothing other than a confusion in such circumstances where the foreseeable effects are reasonably known (again, A implies B...Z). Therefore, the distinction between intention/foresight is not capable of doing the work that its supporters think it capable of doing.

James Rachels advances a further argument about the role of intention that centres on the distinction between the rightness and the goodness of an action. Rightness/wrongness pertains to the extrinsic act objectively understood. Goodness/badness pertains to the interior character of the agent.[104] It would be an impossible situation were moral analysis to primarily concern itself with the interior subjective states of the agent acting where the external manifestations of two acts are identical. Therefore, even if the intention/foresight distinction had some moral relevance (a point *not* conceded by Rachels) it cannot go towards the objective rightness of the act. Intentions can only relate to the interior culpability of the judgement of conscience. As a distinction, relating to external observable acts, it is an irrelevant one. In the example given above, the agent can have different intentions while the external act remains identical. For this reason, according to Rachels, intention/foresight is a distinction that can have no practical moral import in our judgement of the rightness of an action.[105]

Causality

A further critique of double effect reasoning is made with reference to the third criterion concerning causality. Intentions apart, the withdrawal of, say, life support treatment, is indeed the immediate and proximate cause of death of the patient, since it was foreseeable, even certain, to result in the patient's death. It matters not whether the cause precedes, is concomitant with, or follows any good effect of the action since they still flow from the unitary nature of the action being performed. Adapting an example from Dan Brock, we can illustrate this argument for moral equivalence by means of a paired set of cases.[106]

Firstly, a non-competent sclerosis patient is dependent on a respirator due to a critical illness, but may have several years still to live. A critical care nurse, acting on medical instruction, removes the treatment since it is considered medically futile. The patient dies. Secondly, a son judging that his mother (also non-competent and sclerotic) would live for several years and is anxious to inherit her fortune, terminates her treatment by unplugging the respirator. The patient dies. Both actions are seen to be equivalent in terms of their relationship to bringing about a particular state-of-affairs—the death of the patient. There is said to be an equivalence since both actions are immediate in causally contributing to the death of the patient. *But for* the withdrawal of artificial respiration, the patient would have gone on living. Both adopt causal means to bring about death.[107]

What of the argument that the critical care nurse is simply allowing nature to take its course? This can similarly be argued in the son's case. He merely wishes to accelerate the inevitable outcome. Both agents causally contribute to death in the same way.

Such moral equivalence is also said to be demonstrated in the classic case of morphine administration. Physician X administers to a patient an increasingly high dose of morphine in order to tackle symptoms of pain, knowing that such doses of pain medication will, in all probability, hasten death due to respiratory depression. Physician Y administers increasing doses of morphine in order to bring about death as a 'merciful' release for the patient. Intentions apart, both agents are identically situated in terms of the positive act. Both physicians, by providing high doses of pain medication, causally contribute to hastening the death of the patient.[108]

By the use of such paired sets of cases, therefore, it is concluded that it is erroneous to talk of a morally relevant distinction between 'killing' and 'letting die', since in both paired sets, the agents who withdrew treatment are identically placed since they are similarly responsible for causing the death of the patient.

Veiled Consequentialism

A common criticism of the fourth criterion of double effect is that it is really consequentialist in outlook. Is the fourth criterion not simply one of commensurating different good and bad effects in order to reach a judgement that, on balance, more good that evil will occur? Peter Singer makes this objection to double effect reasoning. The preceding criteria are a distraction from the consequentialism that is only thinly concealed in the last criterion. The real work being done in double effect reasoning is the last criterion and the others are merely veiled distractions from this.[109] An action can be considered right or wrong depending on the nature of the state of affairs it would produce. By weighing the various values and goods being sought, the agent focuses on the proportion acknowledged between the good and bad effects, with a view to the greater good or lesser evil actually possible in a particular situation. When all is said and done, morality effectively reduces itself to this.

Acts and Omissions

A distinction related to discussions of double effect reasoning concerns act and omission as they are used in the 'killing' and 'letting die' debate. It is often argued in that debate that the distinction as such is morally significant, sufficient to ground a qualitative difference between the two. Yet, Michael Tooley,[110] Judith Lichtenberg,[111] and James Rachels,[112] amongst others,[113] argue for their essential equivalence. A popular misconception prevalent in contemporary bioethics discourse, it is argued, is due to the belief that culpable killing requires a positive act rather than an omission. Once it is admitted that intentional killing can also be performed by omission, a symmetry can be said to prevail between the two, and since it is widely regarded as legitimate to intentionally kill by omission, in some contexts, so it should also be licit to intentionally kill by positive act.

Again, as with causality, the classic approach rejecting the sustainability of the distinction is to posit two parallel cases that are deemed to be equivalent and thus refute any practical distinction between the two cases in terms of act or omission.

Turning first to Tooley's parallel cases.[114] Two sons seek to inherit a substantial amount of money from their wealthy father. They both decide, independently of each other, to bring about his death by poisoning their father's favourite tipple—whisky. As one son is adding poison to the whisky, the other observes and does nothing further. He allows his father to drink the whisky without intervention. Tooley concludes that both actions are, as far as common understanding goes, morally equivalent. Thus, any moral significance between act and omission is erroneous.[115]

As with the example of Tooley above, Lichtenberg contends that there is no distinction to be drawn between the two kinds of case. Both act and omission are similarly regarded as moral equivalents.[116] Lichtenberg posits the following parallel cases. A boat fully equipped with resources lands on a desert island where a person has been stranded for a few days. There are no other resources and the person is sure to die if not helped. In the first case, the crew refuses to render any assistance in the form of provisions or a passage to safety. In the other case, there is no omission but a positive act. The crew decides to shoot and kill the person. Lichtenberg concludes that both cases are morally equivalent to one another. The person in the first case is as surely killed by the decision of the crew as is the person in the second case.[117]

How does this translate into the distinctions between treatment and non-treatment in clinical cases? Take, for example, the withdrawal or non-provision of hydration and nutrition. Critical care nurse X, acting on a physician's instruction, withdraws hydration and nutrition. Y, another critical care nurse, is not authorised to start treatment since it is judged medically futile. Since both the actor and the omitter are permitting a particular course of action to happen (certain in its consequences to result in death), there is said to be equivalence between the two courses of action.[118] Thus, the conclusion is reached that moral equivalence runs throughout questions of act and omission and nothing of significance can turn upon it. To talk of acts and omissions as if they were capable of grounding a distinction between killing and letting die, is therefore considered a confusion that distracts from a proper consideration of the real moral determinants of the situation. Those determinants are the quality of life of the patient in his or her own assessment of the balance of burdens and benefits. Death itself may legitimately be aimed at by act or omission according to the particular circumstances of an individual patient.

Inconsistency in Killing

It is argued by Margaret Battin, Marvin Kohl, Richard Norman, and others, that the Western tradition concerning the sanctity of life is flawed in terms of its internal consistency.[119] The sanctity of life tradition, forbids the direct killing of the innocent, yet it is nowhere satisfactorily stated how the 'quality' of innocence can fu*nction so as to remove the value of the life being taken, and thus create the sole exception to a general prohibition on intentional killing. What is it about the quality of innocence that renders a life devalued such that it can be intentionally destroyed? Does non-innocent life cease to be sacred?[120]

Self defence, for example, has historically been justified by the moral status of the aggressor, yet there is no satisfactory account of how an intrinsic good such as human life itself can be directly acted against, even in the person of a perpetrator committing a life threatening act.[121] Indeed the radical dignity of the human person, is often stated as something that can never be alienated. Do those who are non-innocent therefore lack this radical dignity? How is this ontological transformation achieved? There therefore seems to be inconsistency between the claim that a person's life is 'sacred' on the one hand, and the claim that it can be justifiable to intentionally seek to end that life on the other.[122]

Another key inconsistency pointed out in the justification of intentional killing is the use of capital punishment. The sanctity of life tradition has historically supported the right of the state to use lethal force in the execution of criminals.[123] How can 'non-innocence' on the part of a criminal who has offended against society remove the essential humanity that remains, and with it, the sanctity of that person's life? Moreover, how can such means possibly claim the 'last resort' caveat that is usually inserted as a justification for self defence? States usually have a variety of other means at their disposal to protect society from future acts, and perhaps in the process rehabilitate the criminal.[124] Is this not the more loving act compatible with the appeal made to the sanctity of human life?

The conclusion is therefore reached that the sanctity of life tradition, closely associated with natural law theory, has indeed justified a variety of acts that are considered to be acts of intentional killing, and the tradition is consequently inconsistent, either it its characterisation of the value of life, or its creation of exceptions.[125] It can of course be argued that self defence is not justifiable, and there is a long tradition of pacifism in the West that would make just such a claim. However, rather than abandon a right to self defence, Norman argues that we should forthrightly accept that it is indeed justifiable to intentionally kill another in self-defence, for good reason, and apply that justification of killing to other situations where it would be deemed appropriate.[126]

Such a justifiable situation would obtain for Norman where a person was faced with a life of intractable pain and suffering, and sought to end it. A motive of ending life for the sake of stopping considerable suffering would be a justifiable form of intentional killing. If an aggressor can be said to waive his or her life to immunity from protection from the lethal use of force against his or her person, then why can a person not voluntarily waive his or her right to continue with life in the face of intractable pain and suffering? If a right can be waived in one set of conditions then why not in other appropriate conditions?[127]

Secularism and State Neutrality

Another argument to be considered is the question of the continuing imposition of 'divine imperatives' or 'thick doctrine' on the condition of liberated secular society.[128] It is claimed that the last vestiges of an attempt to hold on to a 'quasi-religious' form of those divine imperatives can be seen in the contemporary sanctity of life position carried on under the banner of natural law. Such a position, it is argued, seeks to smuggle in religious considerations under the 'cloaking device' of a neutral appeal to thick forms of natural reason. The public sphere at least must remain impartial to such thick sources of knowledge and focus on the idea of minimal rationality, that alone is suitable for underpinning publicly accessible reasoning.[129]

Such a form of minimalist reasoning precludes appeals to thick conceptions of the good life. By an acceptance of such a limitation, all major political implications of natural law theory essentially fall by the wayside. Public policy, particularly that which emanates from the construct of different versions of social contract theory, starts from the perspective of the person's own dominion over himself or herself. Restrictions on that dominion only become justifiable to the extent that they provide mutually beneficial opportunities to pursue an array of divergent life plans, or secondly, to prevent the infliction of significant direct harm on others.[130]

The seeds of this thought can be traced back to an amalgam of ancient Stoic and Epicurean perspectives, spurned on by a strong turn to the subject inspired by early modern thought, further fuelled with an alliance to Millsian political philosophy that became inherently distrustful of the claims of authority to impose its will upon the people subjected to it.

In taking up the question of the use of reason in the public sphere via social contract theory, I will illustrate this notion by drawing on the work of John Rawls and H. Tristam Engelhardt.

Rawls and Public Reason

In his first significant work, *A Theory of Justice*, Rawls's major aim was to derive neutral or impartial premises upon which contemporary society could be founded.[131] Rawls's approach was to adopt a form of contractarian pact that sought to resolve conflicts between values of liberty and equality. Rawls argued for an original position in which individuals were placed under a 'veil of ignorance', so that they were ignorant as to their specific interests.[132] The individual in this original state was free, basically rational, and essentially self-interested. What would these individuals chose as principles for guiding justice? Rawls argued that two principles would emerge. Firstly, each person would have the most extensive liberty compatible with similar liberty for others (liberty principle).[133] Secondly, social and economic inequalities would be ordered so that they would be to the advantage of everyone, and be attached to positions open to all (difference principle).[134] These principles were ranked lexically so that liberty could only be restricted for the sake of liberty, and that liberty concerns be fulfilled first, before addressing social and economic inequalities.[135]

By such a social construct, based on notions of procedural fairness, Rawls was to argue that extensiveness of liberty would be a principle that all could agree upon, as basically rational self-interested individuals, in order to pursue a diversity of rich and yet incompatible life plans. Such a range of permissiveness was essential in order to encompass a sense of neutrality or impartiality on the part of the state to the kinds of life style that each might engage upon (apart from the need to recognise certain limitations on what can be pursued in the name of liberty in order to protect its worth).

In his later work, *Political Liberalism*, Rawls sought to overcome what he, in response to critics, considered to be the rather unwarranted 'thicker' forms of assumption that laid behind that initial project.[136] In *Political Liberalism*, Rawls sought to hold on to the essential tenet of neutrality, yet place it on a footing that required no 'doctrinal grounding'.[137] Rawls now argues for the conduct of public debate from within the perspective of a political conception of justice that centres around basic conceptions of 'legitimacy' and 'reciprocity'.[138] For Rawls, terms of co-operation amongst citizens are fair if reasons are offered for engagement that are publicly accessible and are not dependent on a further appeal to substantive and comprehensive doctrines. The basic conceptions of legitimacy and reciprocity are fair because they recognise that *respect for citizens* is legitimately exercised only by offering people from diverse view points accessible reasons to guide action that can be reciprocally shared.[139] Public reason cannot depend on substantive or thick reasons, but on what can be endorsed by an appeal to common limited human reason that is not dependant on substantive doctrine.[140]

Rawls's central project is to demonstrate that public reason is necessarily restricted, and that appeals to substantive doctrine are illegitimate because they fail to respect the "fact of reasonable pluralism."[141] The need for accessibility excludes claims from private sources of knowledge, as well as claims that are decidedly robust in nature. Thus, believers cannot appeal to substantive doctrine to justify the imposition of their values if they are to treat people fairly, since they must be treated in a manner that is compatible with the limited and heavily circumscribed reach of public reason.[142]

By engaging in the common task of building up and responding with public reason, Rawls thinks we can develop circles of overlapping consensus that can form a minimally cohesive social glue, sufficient to loosely hold society together. Since policy is erected upon the foundation of public reason, people are respected in their capacity to forge patterns of consensus concerning, abortion, euthanasia, and many other areas of disagreement.[143]

Engelhardt and Moral Disagreement

Rawls is not alone in his scepticism concerning a shared sense of 'thick' rationality by which to engage in moral and political inquiry. H. Tristam Engelhardt is similarly convinced that there is no light to be cast on the question of a common thick source of rationality.[144] His claim is even more minimalist than Rawls's, for he further discounts even Rawls's optimistic attempt to ground the public square in 'public reason'. He points to the problems faced by any of the existing moral theories and traditions to come up with rationally compelling grounds for the adoption of their system in contemporary pluralistic society. If ever there were a golden age of shared standards, e.g., of Christian hegemony, it has long gone.[145] Such approaches can, of course, provide a context for those who accept their assumptions (i.e. a religious faith community that recognises the authority and binding nature of the Ten Commandments). Since they are not shared by others, however, they can have no public status, and thus no public warrant to ground the use of the coercive apparatus of the state.[146]

In the face of such intractable moral disagreement, Engelhardt proposes a retreat to a contentless procedural platform, a version of social contract theory, on which people can minimally agree. He adopts a kind of 'state of nature' approach in which the "principle of permission" becomes operative.[147] It cannot have any substantive or thick conception in any perfectionist guise. Instead it is replaced by minimal standards of co-operation.

Since there is no universal substantive conception of the good upon which to model the state, it must be replaced by an artificial procedural construct. This artificial construct is necessarily a limited one in which 'moral strangers' can agree upon minimal obligations.[148] On Engelhardt's account, therefore, this public sphere would jealously guard against the imposition of substantive values, such as a hegemonic sense of the meaning of life itself, and *a fortiori,* the control of a person's self-regarding death. Preservation of this public space would depend on protecting people from impositions they have not directly consented to, for otherwise it would undermine the operative condition of agreement that holds the whole enterprise together.[149]

By such a construct, Engelhardt seeks to provide a justification for the minimal state that can be seen as one of the key hallmarks of libertarianism. It is permissive in allowing consenting people to perform a wide array of actions (providing they are not directly harmful to others who have not consented), but it is restrictive in that it doesn't allow the imposition of thick theories of value upon others who have not consented to them.

In the thought of both Rawls and Engelhardt, divergent thinkers in many respects, we can see clear attempts to construct a 'neutral' vision of the state and the exercise of state power over the lives of citizens. Both thinkers are committed to a thoroughgoing anti-perfectionism in the foundations of their political thought. Both thinkers construct their visions of society on the grounds of a diverse plurality of value, and with it, a lack of agreement concerning the imposition of any thick or substantive vision of the good. Both thinkers limit the ground for interference in another person's conception of the good life to what they think can be agreed to in order to best preserve the exercise of the widest possible array of choice.

The conclusion drawn by such lines of argumentation for any substantive natural law position, should be obvious. With direct respect to its implications for many of the traditional lines of argumentation encountered in the historical chapter concerning the purpose of human life, its worth and inviolability, such are simply considered to be the private non-public claims of individual pockets of 'believers', binding on them alone.[150]

Notes to Chapter Three

[1] Margaret Battin, "Ethical Issues in Physician-Assisted-Suicide," in *Last Rights: Assisted Suicide and Euthanasia Debated,* ed. Michael M. Uhlmann (Washington, DC: Ethics and Public Policy Center, 1998), 121-23.

[2] See Don T. Asselin, "A Weakness in the "Standard Argument" for Natural Immortality," in *Freedom, Virtue, and the Common Good*, eds. Curtis L. Hancock and Anthony O. Simon (Notre Dame: American Maritain Association, 1995), 17-27.

[3] See chapter two *supra*.

[4] See for example Dan W. Brock, *Life and Death: Philosophical Essays in Biomedical Ethics* (New York: Cambridge University Press, 1993); Helga Kuhse, *The Sanctity of Life Doctrine in Medicine: A Critique* (Oxford: Clarendon Press, 1987).

[5] Dan W. Brock, "A Critique of Three Objections to Physician-Assisted Suicide," *Ethics* 109 (1999): 519-54.

[6] Brock, *Life and Death,*, 268-324. See also his "Euthanasia," in *Arguing Euthanasia*, ed. Jonathan D. Moreno (New York: Simon & Schuster, 1995), 196-210.

[7] G. E. M. Anscombe, "Modern Moral Philosophy," [reprinted] in *Virtue Ethics*, eds. Roger Crisp and Michael Slote (Oxford: Oxford University Press, 1997), 26-44.

[8] Dan W. Brock, "The Value of Prolonging Human Life," *Philosophical Studies* 50 (1986): 401-28.

[9] See J.J.C. Smart, "An Outline of a System of Utilitarian Ethics," in J.J.C. Smart and Bernard Williams, *Utilitarianism: For and Against* (Cambridge: Cambridge University Press, 1973), 1-25.

[10] Smart, "Outline of a System," 1-25. See also D. W. Hodgson, *Consequences of Utilitarianism* (Oxford: Oxford University Press, 1967), ch. 2.

[11] See Jonathan Bennett, "Whatever the Consequences," in *Ethics*, eds. J. J. Thompson and Gerald Dworkin (New York: Harper and Row, 1968), 211-36; *The Act Itself* (Oxford: Oxford University Press, 1995).

[12] See John Finnis, *Fundamentals of Ethics* (Washington, DC: Georgetown University Press, 1983), ch. 4. This point will be explored in the fourth chapter of the book.

[13] Joseph Fletcher, *Situation Ethics: The New Morality* (Philadelphia: Westminster Press, 1966).

[14] Fletcher, *Situation Ethics*, 73-79.

[15] Joseph Fletcher, *Morals and Medicine* (Boston: Beacon Press, 1966), 192-3, 207-10.

[16] Tom Beauchamp and James Childress, *Principles of Biomedical Ethics*. 4th ed. (New York: Oxford University Press, 1994).

[17] Beauchamp and Childress, *Principles*, 219-38.

[18] Beauchamp and Childress, *Principles*, 33, 36, 103-7.

[19] W. D. Ross, *Foundations of Ethics* (Oxford: Oxford University Press, 1939), 40-42, 316-25.

[20] Ross, *Foundations of Ethics*, 316-25.

[21] Ross, *Foundations of Ethics*, 316-25.

[22] See by way of example the following: Charles Fried, *Right and Wrong* (Cambridge: Harvard Press, 1978), 7-29. Fried argues that deontological approaches to ethical deliberation are concerned with boundary setting on the basis of defining the meaning and parameters of norms. In each case we need to establish the boundaries of a given type of action. In ordinary circumstances, the norm prohibiting murder, excludes the killing of another person, the norm against lying prohibits telling an untruth, and so on. Within the boundaries of ordinary situations, therefore, our rules of morality are preserved within a process of defining limits to what constitutes respectfulness of persons. For Fried, however, these limits can only be breached by tragedy.

[23] See discussion in chapter four.

[24] Bernard Gert, Charles Culver, and K. Danner Clouser, *Bioethics: A Return to Fundamentals* (New York: Oxford University Press, 1997), 15-50.

[25] Gert, Culver, and Clouser, *Bioethics*, 279-306.

[26] Gert, Culver, and Clouser, *Bioethics*, 279-306.

[27] William Aiken "The Quality of Life," in *Quality of Life: The New Medical Dilemma*, ed. James J. Walter and Thomas A. Shannon (New York: Paulist Press, 1990), 17-25.

[28] See Edward W. Keyserlingk, "The Quality of Life and Death," in *Quality of Life*, 35-53.

[29] Jonathan Glover, *Causing Death and Saving Lives* (London: Penguin, 1977), 51-53, 158-62, 192-94; James Rachels, *The End of Life* (New York: Oxford University Press, 1986), 60-77; Peter Singer, *Practical Ethics*. 2nd ed. (New York: Cambridge University Press, 1993), ch. 7., esp. 184-86.

[30] Rachels, *End of Life*, 88-105.

[31] Glover, *Causing Death*, 158-62, 173-75.

[32] Ronald Dworkin, *Life's Dominion* (London: Harper Collins, 1993), 68-101.

[33] Dworkin, *Life's Dominion*, 199-213.

34 Dworkin, *Life's Dominion*, 199-213.

35 Helga Kuhse, *Sanctity-of-Life,* 198-220.

36 Kuhse, *Sanctity-of-Life*, 198-220.

37 John Harris, *Value of Life* (London: Routledge & Kegan Paul, 1985), 87-110.

38 John Harris, "Euthanasia and the Value of Life," in *Euthanasia Examined*, ed. John Keown (New York: Cambridge University Press, 1995), 11.

39 Harris, *Value of Life*, 198-220.

40 Harris, *Value of Life*, 64-86.

41 Helga Kuhse, "Why Killing Is Not Always Worse—and is Sometimes Better—Than Letting Die," *Cambridge Quarterly of Healthcare Ethics* 7 (1998): 371-74.

42 David A. J. Richards, *Sex Drugs, Death and the Law* (New Jersey: Rowman & Littlefield, 1982), 248-49.

43 See Jonathan Riley, *Mill on Liberty* (London: Routledge, 1998), 91-103.

44 Rachels, *End of Life*, 88-105; Ronald Dworkin, "Autonomy and the Demented Self," *Millbank Quarterly* 64 (1986): 4-15.

45 Brock, *Life and Death*, 206. See also Thomas Szasz, *Fatal Freedom: The Ethics and Politics of Suicide* (Westport: Praeger, 1999), 110-15; John Lachs, "When Abstract Moralising Runs Amok," *Journal of Clinical Ethics* 5 (1994): 10-13.

46 Ronald Dworkin et al., "Assisted Suicide: The Philosophers' Brief," *New York Review of Books* (27 March 1997): 41-47.

47 *Philosophers' Brief*, 43-44.

48 *Philosophers' Brief*, 43, quoting *Planned Parenthood v. Casey* 505 U.S.833 (1992), 851.

49 *Philosophers' Brief*, 44.

[50] Ronald Dworkin, *Taking Rights Seriously* (Cambridge: Harvard University Press, 1977), 272-73.

[51] Ronald Dworkin, *A Matter of Principle* (Cambridge: Harvard University Press, 1985), 205-6.

[52] Ronald Dworkin, *Freedom's Law: The Moral Reading of the American Constitution* (Cambridge: Harvard University Press, 1996), 130-46.

[53] Dworkin, *Dominion*, 179-217.

[54] Dworkin, *Dominion*, 190-92.

[55] Dworkin, *Dominion*, 217.

[56] Dworkin, *Dominion*, 180-83; *Philosophers' Brief*, 42.

[57] *Philosophers' Brief*, 44.

[58] Dworkin, *Dominion*, 190-95.

[59] David A. J. Richards, "Autonomy and Rights," *Ethics* 92 (1981): 3-20; Richards, *Sex Drugs, Death*, 59-62.

[60] Richards, "Autonomy," 6-8. See also R. Lindley, *Autonomy* (Highlands: Humanities Press, 1986), 63-70.

[61] Thomas E. Hill, *Autonomy and Self-Respect* (Cambridge: Cambridge University Press, 1991), 1-3, 19-24, 43-51, 85-103.

[62] Richards, *Sex, Drugs, and Death*, 59-62.

[63] Joel Feinberg, *Harm to Self*, 27-51; Feinberg, "Autonomy," in *The Inner Citadel: Essays on Individual Autonomy*, ed. John Christman (New York: Oxford University Press, 1989), 27-49.

[64] Feinberg, *Harm to Self*, 33-44. See also his *Freedom and Fulfillment: Philosophical Essays* (Princeton: Princeton University Press, 1992), 260-82.

[65] Feinberg, *Autonomy*, 46-49.

[66] Feinberg, *Autonomy*, 28-34. See also his "Suicide and the Inalienable Right to Life," in *Suicide: The Philosophical Issues,* ed. Margaret Battin and David Mayo (New York: St. Martin's Press, 1980), 223-28.

[67] Feinberg, *Harm to Self*, 344-74.

[68] Feinberg, *Harm to Self*, 52-57.

[69] Feinberg, *Harm to Self*, 55.

[70] Richards, *Autonomy*, 3-20.

[71] Richards, *Autonomy*, 10-11.

[72] David A. J. Richards, "Moral Rationality," *Synthese* 72 (1987): 91-101; Richards, *Sex, Drugs, and Death*, 177.

[73] Richards, "Autonomy," 11-17.

[74] Richards, *Sex, Drugs, and Death*, 174-77.

[75] D. A. J. Richards, *Toleration and the Constitution* (New York: Oxford University Press, 1986), 71-85, 237-42.

[76] For further discussion on the value of personal autonomy see Gerald Dworkin, *The Theory and Practice of Autonomy* (New York: Cambridge University Press, 1988), 21-33.

[77] Richard B. Brandt, "The Rationality of Suicide," in *Suicide: The Philosophical Issues* ed. Margaret Battin and David Mayo (New York: St. Martin's Press, 1980), 117-32.

[78] E.W. Kluge, *The Ethics of Deliberate Death* (New York: Kennikat Press, 1981), 30-51.

[79] Battin, *Ethical Issues,* 132-53.

[80] James Margolis, *Negativities: The Limits of Life* (Columbus: Charles Merrill, 1975), 24-28.

[81] Beauchamp and Childress, *Principles,* 219-25. See also Tom L. Beauchamp, "The Justification of Physician-Assisted Deaths," *Indiana Law Review* 29 (1996): 1173-1200. I recognise that the authors have additional problems with the legalisation of assisted suicide concerning genuine consent and the protection of vulnerable groups, and that these may justify its continued prohibition.

[82] See for example, Kuhse, *Sanctity*, 90-123; Rachels, *End of Life*, 16-17, 27-28, 92-93; Robert Martin, "Suicide and Self-Sacrifice," in *Suicide: The Philosophical Issues*, eds. Margaret P. Battin and David J. Mayo, 48-68; Gerald Dworkin and R.G. Frey "Distinctions in Death," in Dworkin, Frey, and Bok, *Euthanasia and Physician-Assisted-Suicide* (New York: Cambridge University Press, 1998), 17-42.

[83] On the pedigree of the principle see Alfred Wilder, "The Meaning and Place of the Principle of Double Effect in St. Thomas Aquinas," in *Sanctus Thomas De Aquino Doctor Hodiernae Humanitatis,* ed. Leo Elders (Rome: Pontificia Accademia di S. Thommaso, 1995), 571-80.

[84] My criteria are somewhat adapted from the discussion of the principle in various sources. It is incorrect to classify it a 'doctrine' since it is really a set of operative conditions that are capable of being grasped by practical reasoning.

[85] Later in the book I argue against the use of innocent as a qualifier in the norm. See discussion in chapter five.

[86] See discussion in chapter five.

[87] For example R.G. Frey, "Some Aspects of the Doctrine of Double Effect," *Canadian Journal of Philosophy* 5 (1975): 259-83.

[88] Howard Brody, "Assisted Death—A Compassionate Response to Medical Failure," *New England Journal of Medicine* 327 (1992): 1384-88; "Causing, Intending and Assisting Death," *Journal of Clinical Ethics* 4 (1993): 112-17.

[89] Bennett, "Whatever the Consequences," 211-36.

[90] Bennett, "Whatever the Consequences," 211-36.

[91] Bennett, "Whatever the Consequences," 211-36. See also Jonathan Bennett, "Morality and Consequences," in *Tanner Lectures on Human Values, v. 2* (Salt Lake City: University of Utah, 1981), 47-116.

[92] John Finnis in his "On the Practical Meaning of Secularism," *Notre Dame Law Review* 73 (1998): 491-516, at 511, points out how the utilitarianism of Jeremy Bentham, tended to collapse intention and foresight together by focusing on the consequences produced by an action.

[93] Glanville Williams, *The Sanctity of Life and the Criminal Law* (New York: A. Knopf, 1968), 286-90.

[94] J. L. Mackie, *Ethics: Inventing Right and Wrong* (London: Penguin, 1977), 160-68.

[95] Alan Donagan, *The Theory of Morality* (Chicago: University of Chicago Press, 1977), 163-64.

[96] Roderick Chisholm, "The Structure of Intention," *Journal of Philosophy* 67 (1970): 636-52.

[97] Mackie, *Ethics*, 166.

[98] Williams, *Sanctity of Life*, 286-88.

[99] Donagan, *Theory*, 157-64.

[100] Bennett, "Whatever the Consequences," 221-24.

[101] Beauchamp and Childress, *Principles,* 206-11.

[102] Chisholm, "Structure of Intention," 636-40. See also Michael Bratman, *Intention, Plans and Practical Reason* (Cambridge: Harvard University Press, 1987), 146-48.

[103] See for example Timothy E. Quill, "The Ambiguity of Clinical Intentions," *New England Journal of Medicine* 329:14 (1993): 1039-40.

[104] James Rachels, "More Impertinent Distinctions and a Defense of Active Euthanasia," in *Biomedical Ethics*, eds. Thomas A. Mappes and Jane S. Zembaty (New York: McGraw-Hill, 1981), 55-56.

[105] Rachels, "Impertinent Distinctions," 55-56.

[106] D. W. Brock, "Voluntary Active Euthanasia," *Hastings Center Report* 22 (1992): 10-22.

[107] See Timothy E. Quill, B. Lo, and D. W. Brock, "Palliative Options of Last Resort: A Comparison of Voluntarily Stopping Eating and Drinking, Terminal Sedation, Physician-Assisted Suicide, and Voluntary Active Euthanasia," *Journal of the American Medical Association* 278:23 (1997): 2099-104.

[108] See David Orentlicher, "The Supreme Court and Terminal Sedation: Rejecting Assisted Suicide, Embracing Euthanasia," *Hastings Constitutional*

Law Quarterly 24 (1997): 947-68; J. Andrew Billings and Susan D. Block, "Slow Euthanasia," *Journal of Palliative Care* 32 (1996): 21-22.

[109] Singer, *Practical Ethics*, 209-12.

[110] Michael Tooley, "An Irrelevant Consideration: Killing Versus Letting Die," in *Killing and Letting Die*, eds. Bonnie Steinbock and Alastair Norcross. 2nd ed. (New York: Fordham University Press, 1994), 103-11.

[111] Judith Lichtenberg, "The Moral Equivalence of Action and Omission," *Canadian Journal of Philosophy* 8 (1982): 19-36.

[112] James Rachels, "Active and Passive Euthanasia," *New England Journal of Medicine* 292 (1975): 78-80.

[113] See for example Jonathan Glover, "It Makes no Difference Whether or Not I Do It," *Proceedings of the Aristotelian Society* 49 (1975): 171-90; Michael Phillips, "Are Killing and Letting Die Adequately Specified Moral Categories?" *Philosophical Studies* 47 (1985): 151-58.

[114] Tooley, "Irrelevant Consideration," 103-5.

[115] Rachels posits the following pair in similar terms: Smith and Jones both stand to inherit large sums of money should their six year old cousin shuffle of this mortal coil. Smith drowns the child whilst taking a bath and then makes it look like accidental death. In the second, Jones who also happens to have a six year old cousin observes the cousin in the bathroom. He intends to drown the child. However, as he enters the bathroom he sees the child slip, and rendered unconscious, drowns. See his "Active and Passive Euthanasia," 78-80.

[116] Lichtenberg, "Moral Equivalence," 19-36.

[117] Lichtenberg, "Moral Equivalence," 23-27.

[118] Howard Brody, "Causing, Intending and Assisting Death," 112-25.

[119] Battin, *Ethical Issues*, 114-30, 212-15; Marvin Kohl, *The Morality of Killing* (New York: Humanities Press, 1974), 3-38; Richard Norman, *Ethics, Killing and War* (Cambridge: Cambridge University Press, 1995), 36-116; Williams, *Sanctity of Life*, 311-28; R. A. Duff, "Intentionally Killing the Innocent," *Analysis* 34 (1973): 16-19.

[120] Kohl, *Morality*, 28-31.

[121] See David Wasserman, "Justifying Self-Defense," *Philosophy and Public Affairs* 16 (1987): 356-78.

[122] Duff, "Innocent," 16-19.

[123] J. C. Murphy, "Cruel and Unusual Punishments," in *Law, Morality and Rights* (Dordrecht and Boston: D. Reidel, 1979), 373-404.

[124] Murphy "Cruel," 401-3.

[125] See for example Hugo Bedau, "The Right to Life," *Monist* 52 (1968): 550-72.

[126] Norman, *Killing*, 40-44, 50-54.

[127] See for example Brock, "Euthanasia," in *Arguing Euthanasia*, 196-210; Rachels, *End of Human Life,* 61-77.

[128] See Chantal Mouffe, "Political Liberalism, Neutrality and the Political," *Ratio Juris* 7 (1994): 314-24; Peter De Marneffe, "Liberalism, Liberty, and Neutrality," *Philosophy and Public Affairs* 19 (1990): 253-74.

[129] Mouffe, "Political Liberalism," 314-24.

[130] Feinberg, *Harm to Self*, 3-26.

[131] John Rawls, *Theory of Justice* (Cambridge: Harvard University Press, 1971), 11-17.

[132] Rawls, *Theory of Justice*, 17-22.

[133] Rawls, *Theory of Justice*, 60-65.

[134] Rawls, *Theory of Justice*, 60-65.

[135] Rawls, *Theory of Justice*, 61-62.

[136] John Rawls, "Justice as Fairness: Political not Metaphysical," *Philosophy and Public Affairs* 14 (1985): 223-51.

[137] John Rawls, *Political Liberalism* (New York: Columbia University Press, 1996), 191-94.

[138] Rawls, *Political Liberalism*, xliv-xlvi .

[139] Rawls, *Political Liberalism*, 15-22.

[140] Rawls, *Political Liberalism*, 213-54.

[141] Rawls, *Political Liberalism*, 24.

[142] Rawls, *Political Liberalism*, 89-127.

[143] Rawls, *Political Liberalism*, 133-72.

[144] H. Tristram Engelhardt, *The Foundations of Bioethics*, 2nd ed. (New York: Oxford University Press, 1996), 11-17.

[145] Engelhardt, *Foundations*, 40-64.

[146] Engelhardt, *Foundations*, 74-77.

[147] Engelhardt, *Foundations*, 103-21.

[148] Engelhardt, *Foundations*, 74-80, 121-23.

[149] Engelhardt, *Foundations*, 68-74.

[150] See Max Charlesworth, *Bioethics in a Liberal Society* (Cambridge: Cambridge University Press, 1993), 15-20; Roger Paden, "Democracy and Liberal Neutrality," *Contemporary Philosophy* 14 (1992): 17-20.

Chapter Four

Natural Law Ethics: Re-establishing Foundations

Introduction

In the previous chapter, having delineated the main contemporary lines of argumentation used to support a moral, political, and jurisprudential right to suicide and assistance in suicide, at least in certain circumstances, I now turn to the task of justifying a contemporary natural law based approach, by which to critically analyse and assess the justifications made for the licitness of those actions. The main concern of the present chapter will be to lay out and defend the key parameters of such a methodological framework for the assessment of important foundational ethical questions. The task of the three following chapters of the book will be the application of this natural law based ethics, firstly, to understanding the status of the good of human life, secondly, to the grounds it provides for the moral and legal protection of this good from intentional acts of direct killing, and thirdly, its concrete relevance to contemporary constitutional debate in the US polity.

Before turning to the task of analysing this approach to natural law theory, it is important to point out that a common underlying theme running through lines of argumentation used to support a right to suicide and assistance in suicide. This is the rejection of what can be termed 'concrete exceptionless moral norms', of the general form "it is always morally wrong to do action X, regardless of a further appeal to consequences Y, or motive Z." No author discussed in the preceding chapter would defend the capacity of natural human reason to support the following moral proposition that "it is always a serious moral wrong to intentionally kill and take [innocent] human life, whether of self or another, regardless of a further appeal to consequences or motive."[1] Such a rejection, I will argue, is mistakenly founded. I will initially proceed to locate the rejection of concrete moral absolutes in central methodological weaknesses inherent in both consequentialist and deontological modes of

113

thought, the two moral traditions most frequently invoked in contemporary ethical analysis.

These two sets of theory, as any standard ethics textbook will explain, are considered to be the principal leading moral systems.[2] In this chapter, therefore, it is clearly necessary to establish the 'credentials' of natural law theory as a live and practicable alternative for ethical analysis (notwithstanding its comparative lack of exposition in standard ethics texts).[3] I will attempt this task, negatively and then constructively. Negatively, I will demonstrate what I think are major structural weaknesses inherent in the kinds of ethical analysis proposed by consequentialist and deontological systems of thought (although not without plausibility, as they both contain significant kernels of truth). It will be argued that their failure to substantiate concrete moral absolutes is due to an inadequate understanding of the sources of human goodness, and a failure to identify how the imposition of duty arises from those sources. This failure to properly ground ethical theory in an adequate characterisation of human goods, and with it, a failure to recognise the appropriateness of practically reasonable deliberative choice concerning these goods, is, in my view, responsible for the inadequate grounding of concrete exceptionless moral norms in the arena of contemporary ethical discourse.

Positively, I will undertake the task of interpreting, defending, and building on the natural law theory proposed by John Finnis (with the help of other collaborators). I will argue that his account of basic human goods and the criteria of practical reason that underpin choice, overcome these deficiencies and credibly justify the derivation of concrete exceptionless moral norms. This credibility significantly distinguishes his method from those of Kantian deontology or from forms of absolutism derived from different versions of divine command theory.[4]

Rejection of Concrete Moral Absolutes

G.E.M. Anscombe's famous 1958 article on the state of modern moral philosophy contained a challenge as fresh today as when it was originally made.[5] One of the currents of thought that she was rebelling against in the article was termed consequentialism. [6] Anscombe used this label to identify any moral system that denied the existence of concrete moral absolutes, since consequences are ultimately said to override rules or principles in hard cases. It is, therefore, by this measure that a system purporting to be non-consequentialist should be evaluated—the acceptance or non-acceptance of a few but strategic negative concrete moral absolutes.[7]

The nub of the seeming appeal of consequentialism is that there are at least certain hard cases that can override certain *prima facie* exceptionless concrete prohibitions, e.g., that it is always wrong to intend to kill an innocent human being.[8] Due to the closeness of the association between hard cases and unacceptable outcomes in terms of the state-of-affairs produced, such qualifications are often termed 'exceptions clauses', 'disaster overrides', 'escape clauses', etc.

Anscombe lays down a powerful challenge to (but not a refutation of) current styles of ethical theory that seek to deny specific moral absolutes. What differentiates the varieties of contemporary deontology and utilitarianism loses it significance when compared to this feature that unites them—an ultimate appeal to overriding consequences.[9] This is of course not to deny that differences between these systems can be very important.[10] However, when placed against the backdrop of specific moral absolutes, the denial of their existence places this common element in a much higher relief, and with it the grounds upon which such denials are based.

Critique of Utilitarianism

Commensuration

J. J. C. Smart has stated that utilitarianism's definition of the good is one that stresses the ability to compare diverse outcomes and impartially assess the rightness of an action on the basis of a weighing of consequences.[11] The worth of outcomes is determined solely by consequences and not by other moral standards. This of course presupposes that diverse consequences are indeed comparable. The nature of values needs to be comparable in an objective way. This in turn presupposes that there must be a common means of weighing various values that allows the agent to determine what is the greater good or best outcome in a given situation.[12] In the light of this structure, the hegemony that consequences assert over any other form of assessment of an action, becomes clear. Utility is usually cited as the call of the good with which this system identifies. Yet, this covers up deep divisions amongst utilitarians as to what is the unit of measurement that provides the means for identifying the greatest utility.

Jeremy Bentham associated the utility principle with pleasure as a form of sensation. J. S. Mill took a more expansive view of utility in terms of the maximisation of happiness where happiness admitted of qualitative and not merely quantitative analysis.[13] Others seek to define utility in terms of the satisfaction of desires or the satisfaction of preferences.[14]

Hedonistic Accounts

J.J.C. Smart argues that there is indeed a univocal sense in which hedonism is the common denominator that allows an assessment of diverse states. Pleasure is the one aspect of human experience that has intrinsic value. Smart, therefore, concludes that a world in which a sadist is the only person who is alive and enjoys the suffering of tormented souls in hell, is a preferable world to a world in which this person is suffering, say, the sorrows of the pains of the dammed.[15] Utilitarianism, for Smart, is such a method of pleasure maximisation. Pleasure and pain are experiences we all have as sentient beings.

Now, it would be plainly contrary to human experience to deny that as sentient human beings, we do indeed seek pleasurable experiences in our lives. Yet conceding this point does not really advance Smart's (and Bentham's) case very far. For it presupposes that the diversity and range of pleasurable human experiences is actually a manifestation of the same phenomenon. Whilst we may classify many activities as in some way pleasurable, it does not follow that the range and diversity of pleasures is capable of being ranked univocally on a single scale of comparison. How does one rank and compare, for example, the pleasure derived from a profound aesthetic experience and the pleasure of perceived ecstatic union in spiritual harmony with the creator of the universe? Secondly, it supposes that we cannot seek to participate in the pursuit of certain values simply because they are rewarding to us in any complex way that doesn't simply equate to the directedness of pleasure or the avoidance of pain.[16]

Rather, as Mill recognised, we participate in certain values for their own sake, precisely because they are in some sense different ends-in-themselves and therefore appear to us as worthwhile for their own sake.[17] Mill claimed that utilitarianism can accept that values can differ in quality as well as quantity, and that in the judgement of those who have experience of different pleasures, some are better than others. For example, it is better to be a human being dissatisfied than a pig satisfied; better to be Socrates dissatisfied than a fool satisfied.[18] If quantitative pleasure alone were to represent such a common denominator of reducibility, it seems to deny other human values their inherent meaningfulness. Is authentic knowledge or friendship really only sought because these values can be said to result in pleasurable experiences for the individual?

Robert Nozick has voiced a powerful (and I think successful) counter-argument to such an identification of pleasure with fulfilment. His description of a series of experiments with a pleasure machine is designed to show just how inauthentic and non-constitutive such a goal really is. A life tied to such a pleasure inducing machine would be a degradation of deeper and profound senses of worth that we deeply identify with.[19] When faced with such a prospect, of a life tethered to such a pleasure inducing machine, we are quickly confronted with the inadequacies of this form of reductionism.

Eudemonistic Accounts

Happiness, rather than hedonism, seems to provide a more embracing sense of the good of human persons, as Mill recognised. However, if happiness is used in a wider sense of what at least seems fulfilling to persons and their well-being (as it is used in Aristotle and Aquinas), it seems quite implausible to claim that it is being used in anything like a univocal sense that can supply a common unit of measurement for consequentialist purposes of calculation.[20] Happiness refers not only to different means by which we can achieve some common shared end, but also to a real diversity in the proximate ends of what seems to make human actions worthwhile. Happiness seems to offer no univocal sense of commonality, such that it could provide the means for reducing complex states to a common measuring rod.[21]

Preferences or Wants

Attempts to supply a common frame of reference to utilitarian calculations have latterly focused on preference or want satisfaction.[22] R. M. Hare provides one of the most sophisticated versions of this.[23] Hare's establishment of preference utilitarianism depends on his claim that moral judgements based on wants can be calculated impartially.[24] If an agent faces a moral situation in which two of his or her intuitions conflict, a universal judgement, not a subjective judgement, must be made.[25] In resolving a clash of intuitions, the agent must make an objectively preferential choice. A solution needs to be posed that would be commendable to all those involved.[26]

The core of Hare's approach is his use of imaginary representations of the preferences of all persons involved with the action. Hare proposes a thought process where the preferences of all those agents affected by any proposed judgement are to be evaluated and weighed according to intensity of preferences. Crucially, for Hare, he does not think that such a weighing involves impossible comparisons.[27] On the contrary, he claims that all inter-personal clashes of preference are, in principle, resolvable in the same sort of way an individual settles on his or her own hierarchies of preference. Since individuals are able to determine in a given situation what they would most prefer, even though they have conflicting orientations, it is possible to gather together the preferences of others affected and weigh them in terms of their intensity.[28]

Tenability of Ideal Observation

How does this account of preferences answer our difficulties with establishing a common means of reconciling the diverse appeals of many values?

Individuals do commensurate different values. No one could plausibly seek to deny this. They do indeed rank and order different preferences in the conduct of their own lives. Such a subjective commitment, however, is not the form of impartial weighing that Hare's argument needs if it is to justify his method.[29]

Hare seeks to bridge the gap between personal commitments and the impartial standpoint by making an illicit move from the view of the agent (first person) to that of an archangel (third person). Yet we are not archangels and do not view the world with such disinterestedness. Crucially, it is difficult to see why certain forms of preference should be treated by an agent as worthy of attention at all if they are repellent to the agent assessing the action.[30] It is certainly true that for certain purposes, for example economics, it is possible to establish the strength and range of preference for a particular outcome. For certain limited practical questions such as the pricing of consumer goods, there is indeed a justification for responding to such preferences in a market situation. Yet how can this be said to provide an adequate foundation for moral value? Some people have intense preferences for sadistic pleasure, torture, etc. Are these preferences to be weighed equally in the calculation of the most optimific outcome?

Hare's impartial standpoint, in the face of assumed equality between preferences, merely seems to beg the point. Crucially, for agents who commensurate values in their own choices, weights are already assigned and there is no such assumed equality between preferences. The preference utilitarian may reply that 'bizarre' preferences may be discounted as being 'contrary to knowledge' or to 'rational standards'.[31] This, however, also merely begs the question. On what objective non-moral criteria does the rejection of the preferences of sadists depend? The preferences of the sadist seem perfectly rational in terms of a Humean means-end relationship (where reason is viewed as a question of efficiency in the pursuit of desired goals). To accept additional moral principles at this crucial stage of establishing the possibility of the objective preference criterion is destructive of the whole project since it radically undermines the essential claim to impartiality.[32]

Individuals commend their judgements to others, but not for the reasons that it will maximise preferences in the fashion stated by Hare. Rather, individuals commend a certain form of action rather than another because it is a worthwhile account of what seems good and worthwhile in a given situation. Despite all the attempts of utilitarians to find the single font of morality based on a common denominator, their attempts have proved unconvincing. Either the source of the value is not univocal, as is the case with happiness; is univocal but too base as in the case of hedonism; or we accept preferences as a source of value but are forced to engage in commensurations based on preferences that no individual could begin to accept or weigh in the impartial terms that utilitarianism requires.

Integrity of Character

There is no space here to develop the different forms of utilitarianism that have been proposed viz. the distinction between its act and rule based forms. However, I find convincing the line of argumentation that seeks to demonstrate how rule based forms of utilitarianism ultimately collapse into act based forms of utilitarianism.[33] To obey a rule is said to have general utility since it refers to a class or type of action whose product is generally optimific. Consequences flow out like ripples into the distant future. If a rule is not optimific in a given instance, the longer term consequences are said to balance it out. However, as Bernard Williams argues, for the rule utilitarian, the exact opposite can as also readily be assumed. If the rule is broken, why can it not be said that the negative consequences will balance themselves out in the longer term? It seems illogical, therefore, to idolise the act of rule keeping where in the given case it is not optimific. To the extent that factors other than consequences are appealed to in order to justify rule keeping, for example, common intuitions, 'the logic' of consequentialism is displaced.[34]

In what follows, I shall therefore restrict myself to problems associated with act-based forms of utilitarianism. These problems relate directly to what Williams calls problems of integrity, and take the form of a *reductio ad absurdum*.[35] Act-utilitarianism exhorts us to choose the option that is seen to have the best outcome given the choices available to the agent. A rule that states that one is always permitted but not always required to perform the action that has the most desirable outcomes can be termed an agent centred prerogative, since it gives the agent a power that can be exercised under certain conditions, so as to not always require the agent to optimise.[36] A stronger version of agent centredness, which I seek to defend, is called agent centred restrictiveness.[37] It goes beyond the prerogative approach. It requires in certain cases that not only is one not required to perform actions perceived as optimific, but that it can indeed be wrong to act optimifically.[38]

When Williams appeals to integrity, he is referring to the inability of consequentialism to accommodate a broad sense of integrity of character—the sense of wholeness or unity in one's life.[39] Crucial to this sense of integrity is the unity that prevents a life being essentially one of disparate episodes. Secondly, there is the important existential sense of the distinctiveness or uniqueness of that life—a sense of non-replaceability.[40]

In order to have a sense of unity, a person must have some ground projects. These projects evolve in a person's life, and unless they are allowed to evolve with the life of the person, there is no essential continuity in that life. Projects may be diverse and multifarious, but we are often deeply committed to them.[41] For example, Joe, a student, may be deeply committed to a future career as an academic. It is a deeply held commitment on his part. It necessarily leads to a certain partiality. To be human is necessarily to identify with life's projects as a constitutive part of what we are. This pursuit on Joe's part has continuity with the past in the form of many years of study and reflection. It promises to have continuity with the future if he diligently pursues his studies. Distinctiveness is equally a part of his life. His sense of distinctiveness would be radically undermined if he thought that his life was dispensable to his friends or readily substituted by someone else. Both unity and distinctiveness, therefore, seem vital to integrity in the form that Williams defines it.

Imagine, however, that a 'rebel' archangel was always looking over Joe's shoulder and exhorting him always to maximise outcomes in each of his actions. Life's meaning is always to be judged with reference to the archangel's demands. Joe's family, friends, work commitments, etc., stand in constant scrutiny to the demands of the archangel. Such scrutiny would indeed radically undermine his integrity as a person. His life would always be at the beck and call of this extrinsic source always telling him to optimise consequences. The unity in his life would be nothing more than a specious form of unity that would amount to satisfying the calls of the archangel.[42] A person who adopts act-utilitarianism as a guide to action would seem to be in precisely this untenable predicament.

Samuel Scheffler, responds to this by proposing that one is not always required to choose the option that is optimific, but may always do so. He states that agent-centred prerogatives operate in such a fashion. They give the agent a veto over always having to so participate in optimising consequences.[43]

On the face of it, Scheffler makes a plausible case. A prerogative is recognised which grants relief and seems to restore some control to the agent. However, there is, I think, a key reason for doubting that such a prerogative is sufficiently strong to adequately preserve a person's sense of integrity. Scheffler leaves the following problem essentially unanswered. Supposing someone were to offer Joe continuing support in pursuing his studies. They promised him this support since it seemed optimific at the time it was offered.

Supposing a brighter, better, scholar were to come along than Joe. Can the promise simply be broken? By Scheffler's estimation, that agent is always entitled to act optimifically. Yet, Scheffler does not adequately tackle the problem of commitments already made. These commitments (antecedent promises), made by one party to another, are also important to our sense of integrity—a life that is not rendered eventistic or episodic by the deeds of others. One needs a stronger rule to the effect that once basic commitments have been formed, as in the case of the above promise, it is generally wrong to act against them. Scheffler's formulation of an agent prerogative fails to adequately account for this potential to undermine integrity.

Due to the inability of consequentialism to furnish anything like a plausible ground for articulating a common denominator to its forms of calculation, and its inability to take character formation seriously as an indispensable requirement of morality, its basic method of approach is seriously flawed as an ethical method. Can a deontological approach overcome these deficiencies in a credible way that either does not manifest other serious weaknesses, or when pushed, does not collapse into a tendency to make a *de facto* appeal to consequentialism when faced with the problem of resolving hard cases?

Evaluation of Deontology

Concept of Duty

Utilitarianism makes a powerful appeal to our intuitions due to the fact that a credible system of morality does concern itself with the consequences of our actions. Any system of morality would be unsustainable were it not to seriously address the question of consequences in human conduct. Deontology, however, relates the primary moral building blocks to the concept of duty, and consequences are said to play a generally subordinate role to the call of duty.[44]

For Kant, a disposition of the will tied to the production of states-of-affairs is heteronomous not autonomous.[45] Unlike Aristotle and Aquinas, whose ethical systems were primarily aimed at the goods of human flourishing, Kant rejected such an extrinsic end for the human will. The autonomous will must be located inside itself. The will is, therefore, a self-legislator based on the notion of the intrinsic call of the will itself. This is expressed in only a slightly misleading fashion by saying it is the call of duty for duty's sake [46]

Kant's Universal Law

Kant derives from the autonomy of the will his Categorical Imperative—"act only on that maxim whereby you can at the same time will that it should become a universal law."[47] Actions are only to be commended if they are done under the call of the Categorical Imperative and not out of heteronomous considerations, e.g., emotions or feelings.[48] There is no substantive theory of the good in the Kantian system, for an action performed out of a response to goods would represent a heteronomous and not an autonomous will.

Kant evidently thought that his delineation of the Categorical Imperative could be a rational basis upon which to account for the kinds of absolute prohibitions located in the Judeo-Christian tradition.[49] However, as G. E. M. Anscombe points out, such assertions are useless without specific and detailed characterisation of what counts as the relevant description of an action.[50] The following example will help spell out the inadequacy of such 'contentless' formalism. Could it not be willed that in ordinary circumstances it is wrong to kill another innocent human being, but in extraordinary circumstances (e.g., a hostage situation where many lives are at stake), it could be morally justified? Such an abstract formulation of principle seeks to banish an agent's teleological purpose from a consideration of the moral assessment of the worth of an action. It removes from central focus the pursuit of intelligible human goods as sought ends. Kant's principle, due to lack of specificity, is incapable of doing the kind of work that Kant requires of it in directing the will of the agent.[51] In his desire to overcome the Humean solution of simply deriving moral considerations from the observable generalities of empirical human behaviour, he unfortunately removed from moral evaluation the intrinsic appeal of certain human goods; human goods that are capable of evoking a kind of direct intelligible attractiveness in the practical reasoning of the agent.[52]

Whilst Kant sought to derive rigorous standards from this principle, as we saw in chapter two with reference to the question of suicide, that principle can in fact be used to support decidedly 'laxist' conclusions. There is, therefore, a wide incongruence between Kant's attempt to justify traditional moral absolutes and the justification for such absolutes via the principle of universal form contained in the first formula of the Categorical Imperative. Whilst Kant sought to oppose the tendency to reduce morality to matters of consequentialist analysis, his own solution to the problem failed to provide intelligible insights into reason's own directly apprehended motivating role (as intelligibly attractive) in concretely shaping and guiding human actions; actions shaped and informed by practical reason in response to the intrinsic appeal of an array of basic teleological goods.

Respect for Humanity

In an attempt to tackle such deficiencies in the Kantian system, Alan Donagan turns to Kant's other formulation of the Categorical Imperative—respect others as ends in themselves and do not treat them merely as a means.[53] Donagan argues that such a formulation is able to provide more substantive content to generate specific first order precepts. He equates the second formulation of the Categorical Imperative with the Christian neighbour-love principle. The fundamental principle of conduct is, therefore, respect for humanity. From this principle of respect for humanity, Donagan attempts to derive more specific maxims that apply the basic foundational principle.[54]

For Donagan, such a deontological starting premise, inherent in common morality, leads to the wrongness of acting so as to treat people merely as means to one's own end. Thus, voluntarily killing another innocent human being is always objectively wrong and always impermissible.[55] Whilst this seems somewhat plausible, does it in fact show that it is wrong to kill another person for the sake of, say, saving additional lives à la consequentialism? It seems unlikely that it does.

The whole question for Donagan is that it is impermissible for anybody at will to use force upon another.[56] It seems, however, that a consequentialist could reasonably argue that in killing another person who is innocent, the killer is not merely using another person as a mere means to his or her own end and thus disrespecting them. To kill another in special circumstances, such as a shipwreck, is not simply to kill at will, but posits another special reason—the survival of several lives. Donagan needs to argue that such killing is not a legitimate exception, and needs to explain just why it falls foul of respect. However, he never directly faces this question. The problem stems from exclusive stress on the notion of respect itself. It is too indeterminate and general a notion to generate the kind of substantive claim he wishes to make regarding what exceptions are licit and what exceptions are not.[57]

Such a principle is too thin to generate the kind of substantive conclusion that Donagan wishes to generate. Donagan shares in the Kantian suspicion of a theory of the good. He falls back onto duty as respect. Yet this notion is still too contentless to convincingly generate the specific kinds of conclusion that he needs. The direct incommensurable appeal of the good of human life itself is not addressed. Such an appeal would provide the kind of substantive content needed if the worthy, but inadequate, general notion of respect for humanity is to be adequately fleshed out. Both Kant and Donagan appeal to a notion of human reason as a basis for the generation of foundational maxims, yet their foundation is not tied to the diversity of goods that can provide intelligible reasons to act. As such it is really an extrinsic approach that stresses bare rationality of form and ignores a dynamic range of intrinsic possibilities for action. Rationality stands apart from the interior purposes of our well-being. Respect for persons is simply not sufficiently rooted in the diversity of humanly good purposes that an agent can act towards—friendship, beauty, play, religion, etc. These goods are not merely heteronomous inclinations and contingencies that 'corrupt' the purity of rational form. Rather, they are the very sources of worthwhile choice that allow us to expand and flourish in all aspects of our lives.[58]

Evaluation of "Mixed Systems"

Prima Facie Obligation

W. D. Ross addressed the problem of moral absolutes within the deontological tradition by incorporating the call of duty within the framework of intuitionalism and *prima facie obligation*.[59] Ross concluded that such primary duties were indefinable characteristics. Like the colour red, duties seem to have such properties that are not further definable.[60] The appeal of certain duties, however, gives rise to conflicts of obligation. In any concrete situation, rules based on duties conflict. When faced with such a conflict, the agent has to decide which duty has priority. Whilst on the face of it, to act against a duty is always *prima facie* wrong, one duty will be able to override another duty. The weighing of duties cannot take place in a vacuum, divorced from consequences, but must consider consequences in justifying the overriding of one *prima facie* duty with an appeal to the other.[61] By the use of the device of *prima facie* wrong, Ross tries to preserve the notion in common morality that duties normally have a claim on our action, whilst at the same time recognising that duties conflict and choices need to be made. In such situations, Ross states that we can only do what seems to us to be the right course of action.[62] *Prima facie* duties cannot be overruled lightly, but given the complexities of human experience, it is sometimes essential to do so.

At first sight, Ross seems to offer a practical solution to the formalism of Kant, the call of duty tempered by the complexities of moral judgement.[63] However, it is far from clear how such a system is practically distinguishable from consequentialist theories, although, to be sure, it has a different starting point within the deontological tradition, since it directly permits a trade between different values. As Peter Geach has remarked, whilst seemingly rigorist in its form of duty orientation, it can produce laxist conclusions that deny any absolutist principles unless those principles are so general as to amount to little other than exhortations.[64]

Ranking and Assigning Weights

Crucially, in my view, mixed systems have been unable to rank and assign due weights in anything like a satisfactory assessment of what an objective proportionality between conflicting obligations would require. When faced with a choice to do something, and weights between obligations are assigned by what intuitively seems right, it amounts to saying do what you think appropriate as long is there is some sort of rationalisation that can be offered for so doing.[65] This problem can be further demonstrated in the work of Charles Fried, and Beauchamp and Childress.[66] In examining these approaches, I seek to show the systemic nature of this central weakness.

Fried, and Beauchamp and Childress, argue that deontological approaches to ethical deliberation are concerned with boundary setting on the basis of defining the meaning and parameters of norms. In each case we need to establish the boundaries of a given type of action. In ordinary circumstances, the norm prohibiting murder excludes the killing of another person, the norm against lying prohibits telling an untruth, and so on.[67] Within the boundaries of ordinary situations, therefore, our rules of morality are preserved within a process of defining limits to what constitutes respectfulness toward persons. Within limits, these prohibitions apply and are 'categorical' within the limits of ordinary circumstances.[68] In this sense they bear strong similarity to Ross's notion of *prima facie* obligation. For Fried, however, these limits can only be breached by tragedy. The threshold for Beauchamp and Childress seems set at a somewhat lower level concerning the impact of consequences. For both, there are hard cases that render adherence to the norms in such (threshold) circumstances, a kind of 'moral fanaticism'. The absoluteness of right and wrong is said to yield to the demands of extraordinary situations. Absolutes can only be absolutes in the sense that they point to certain acts we should not perform in ordinary situations.[69] For Fried, and Beauchamp and Childress, morality is essentially about an analysis of actions within boundaries of normal functioning. Thus, for example, killing an innocent person in order to save the lives of several persons would be morally wrong.

What is curious, however, in the two mixed system accounts discussed, is the complete lack of any non-conventional standard for establishing just when the break-down in the 'ordinary functioning' of a prima facie norm occurs. Both are clear that it is fanatical to insist that it is wrong to intentionally kill another person for the sake of, say, the survival of a nation. Yet what of the ratio say of 100:1 or 1000:1? How many lives are enough to abandon the binding nature of the principle? No answers to such questions are forthcoming, and we are effectively left to fend for ourselves upon an open sea of different competing conventional hunches.

Both Fried, and Beauchamp and Childress are unable to answer this question of what objectively constitutes sufficient proportion, and in doing so effectively abandon principle upon the alter of conventionalism, because a precise answer will leave them directly exposed to the kinds of problem seen in the adoption of full blown consequentialist systems, such as utilitarianism, discussed above. To the extent that they abandon Kant's notion of perfect duties, they merely graft onto their systems consequentialist rationalisations under the guise of appeals to 'intuition' or 'convention'.

Natural Law Ethics

General Remarks

In the preceding sections, we have pointed out a number of deficiencies in consequentialist and deontological approaches to ethical reasoning. The critiques have been negative in nature. Nevertheless, important kernels of truth are contained in both. Consequentialist theories are teleological in that they try to ground moral decisions in some form of conception of what constitutes human goodness. Kantian deontology attempts to ground moral decisions in the rational nature of the human person, whose dignity is stressed. What is needed to reconcile these two important insights is a theory that holds both that ethics is grounded in human goods and that a person's inherent dignity is protected by exceptionless moral norms that prevent a person being instrumentalised and being treated as a mere means. This part of the chapter will proceed to analyse and defend John M. Finnis's alternative foundationalist approach to the construction of ethical theory. The project is firmly rooted in the natural law tradition. However, it is far from synonymous with a traditional neo-scholastic interpretation of natural law theory whereby natural law is essentially viewed as a theory that directly and reductively seeks to 'read off' normative conclusions from the blueprint tendencies of our given human nature.[70]

Neo-Scholasticism

Neo-scholastic natural law thinkers such as Heinrich Rommen, Jacques Maritain, Henry Veatch, and Ralph McInerny claim the authority of Aquinas to support their claims for natural law theory. The naturalistic 'function of the human being' approach, often attributed to Aquinas, is given additional weight by the invocation of Aristotle's metaphysics or philosophical anthropology.[71] Consider the following quote of Heinrich A. Rommen: Good is to be done: such is the supreme commandment of the natural moral law. The highest and basic norm of the natural law in the narrow sense, then, may be stated thus: Justice is to be done. Yet this principle is altogether general. It needs still to be determined to what extent the object striven for by means of a concrete action is a true good. ...Good is that which corresponds to the essential nature. The being of a thing reveals its purpose in the order of creation, and in its perfect fulfillment it is likewise the end or goal of its growth and development. The essential nature is thus the measure. What corresponds to it is good; what is contrary to it is bad. The measure of goodness, consequently, is the essential idea of a thing and the proportionateness thereto of actions and of other things. That is, "Good is to be done" means the same as "Realize your essential nature." Morever, since this essential nature issued from God's creative will and wisdom in both its existence and its quiddity, the principle continues: "You thereby realize the will of God, which is truly manifested to you in the knowledge of your essential nature." [p. 43] [72]

As the above quote illustrates, Neo-scholastic authors have a common core of argumentation running through their approach to natural law theory. It is this. They identify and derive objectively binding moral norms from the interpretation of factual-descriptive propositions concerning human nature— natural inclinations, tendencies, appetites, etc. According to their interpretation of the central tradition of natural law, 'practical wisdom' or 'practical reasoning', that is, reasoning about what 'ought to be done' by the agent, necessarily hinges on what is variously termed either 'theoretical' or 'speculative' reasoning, that is, reasoning about what 'is' human nature. [73]

Its implication for ethical analysis is pretty direct. We derive our ethical understanding from our prior analysis of the study of what human beings essentially are in terms of their ontological make up. Only after we come to understand what it is to have the nature that we have, can we then compare and judge human acts by the standards set by our human nature. Actions that we perform in conformity with our nature are morally good, and therefore worthy of performance, and actions that are contrary to nature are therefore morally bad and ought not to be performed. [74]

Neo-scholastics take it as a near given that the authority of Aquinas directly supports their interpretation of human nature as the regulative standard setter for the derivation of moral norms. Acts that are in conformity with nature are morally good, and acts that are not in conformity are defective and therefore morally bad. [75] They argue that Aquinas's crucial first principle of practical reason, "*bonum est faciendum et prosequendum et malum vitandum*," is a moral command incumbent on the agent to pursue the functions of our nature. The agent works out what is good by the standard of nature and this is what is normative for the agent to perform. The standard for judging human conduct here is therefore clearly considered to be naturalistic through and through.[76]

Rejecting Naturalism

Regarding the neo-scholastic position just briefly elucidated, there is good reason to point to a central methodological difficulty running throughout its account of meta-ethical foundations. Post-Humean philosophy has rejected naturalistic appeals as being erroneously dependent on a fallacy of illicitly trying to infer moral norms from factual (including speculative) premises about what is.[77] In the first chapter of this book, we saw Hume's statement of the problem. Hume's central point was that if you want to give a valid argument for a normative conclusion, you need to add a normative or evaluative premise to the argument. From strictly non-moral premises (about what is), you cannot derive a normative conclusion (about what 'ought' or 'should' be, and conversely, about what 'ought not' or 'should not' be).[78]

The key problem has been further defined by G.E. Moore who argued against the 'naturalistic fallacy' with his 'open question argument'.[79] Take any naturalistic definition of an ethical term ('good' is 'x, y, z', where 'x, y, z' means 'pleasurable' or 'fitting', or 'successfully fulfilling its function', or any other natural property). It is always seems an intelligible question to further ask: "is x, y, z good?" (or the converse). If 'good' really meant 'x, y, z' as a *natural property*, as naturalism claims, then this should not be an open or meaningful question to subsequently pose. Rather, it should be a closed question.[80] Suppose 'x, y, z' stands for 'fulfil our natural functioning' (aspects of our human nature)—so the naturalistic definition offered is that 'bad' means 'contrary to nature'. It seems a perfectly reasonable question to ask "x (e.g., interrupting a natural function such as terminating our life) is contrary to our nature (inclination to preserve life), but is it bad"? If good, therefore, really meant 'conformity with nature' this sort of question should be tautological, but it is not.

The standard response from the neo-scholastic position is tantamount to a dismissal of the nature of the fallacy as a sign of the extent to which modern scepticism, flowing from Hume, has distorted the landscape of modern and contemporary ethical theory.[81] In short, it is said that proponents of the naturalistic fallacy fail to recognise the 'fallacious nature' of the naturalistic fallacy. Since facts must indeed be related to norms, and thus the two do not belong to separate parallel universes, the nature of the fallacy must ultimately be ill-founded.[82]

Was Aquinas a Naturalist?

John Finnis and others have accepted the central validity of the naturalistic fallacy.[83] It is illicit to derive or deduce a normative proposition from a factual premise pertaining to theoretical or speculative reasoning about the natural constitution of human beings as such. Normative conclusions can only be derived from prior normative premises. For Finnis, naturalistic appeals confuse two senses of 'good'. The first sense is 'what-is' sought after. The second sense is 'what-ought-to-be' sought after. The two are logically distinct.[84] When one sees and recognises the basic nature of this division, one truly starts to recognise just why attempts to establish the moral enterprise need to begin with what can be termed necessary, objective, and non-contingent 'goods for us', as recognised by human reason—the goods that human beings spontaneously seek to instantiate as intelligible starting points for the pursuit of human flourishing.[85]

Finnis is refreshingly forthright in agreeing with critics of neo-scholastic natural law theory, in so far as it attempts to reduce the *sui generis* structure of practical normative beginnings to the realm of the speculative. [86] Finnis takes seriously the insights of contemporary analytical philosophy, and does not seek to discount the implications of this corpus for contemporary ethical analysis.[87] The key question that can be posed, however, is whether the ethical theory of Aquinas is similarly naturalist, and thus prone to the same problematic concerning the deduction of norms from factual statements? On the basis of the re-interpretation of Aquinas's ethical theory by Finnis and others, there is reason to think that Aquinas did not (and that contemporary natural law ethics need not) simply adopt a thoroughgoing naturalism, for example, the naturalism of Aristotle, whereby the operation of practical reason is limited in scope, concerned only with working out a prudential choice of means in order to realise the given trajectories of the human *ergon*.[88]

Finnis argues that Aquinas actually conceived of the ethical quest as being thoroughly practical in all dimensions of its genesis and operation. The key error in conventional interpretations of Aquinas, for Finnis, concerns the very meaning of the first self-evident principle of practical reason, "good is to be done and pursued and evil is to be avoided."[89] Unlike most conventional interpretations of Aquinas, Finnis does not interpret this as a moral command. Rather, it is a not-yet-moral directive for human action. In a manner analogous to the first principle of speculative reasoning (the principle of non-contradiction), the first principle of practical reasoning is presupposed in all acts of practical thinking (whether morally good or not). In consequence, the principle cannot be interpreted as a moral command, for not all practical thinking is moral in nature.[90]

For Finnis, therefore, the first principle in Aquinas refers not to what is morally good, but to all good forms of what is considered to be intelligibly worthwhile for the human agent to pursue. All kinds of good worth pursuing are presupposed by this practical principle, not simply moral goods. The principle informs and sums up the pursuit of intelligible goods in general.[91]

As a directive (though not-yet-moral) principle, a gerundive is-to-be, it is nevertheless a normative principle, for not all normative principles are moral. For Finnis, this point is crucial in the interpretation of Aquinas. If it were a moral principle commanding us to do moral good and avoid moral evil, it would lose its credibility as a self-evident principle presupposed in all acts of practical reasoning. We would simply be able to raise the question, why pursue the morally good?, for such a principle would not be self evident and would not be presupposed in all acts of practical reasoning. The self evidence of the principle is dependent on its involvement in all acts of the operation of practical reason *simpliciter.*[92]

Since the principle is normative but-not-yet-moral, it simply directs us to pursue genuinely constitutive human goods in the practical decision making that we undertake in all aspects of our lives. On Finnis's interpretation of Aquinas, in-so-far as Aquinas is viewed as a philosopher (operating under the light of natural reason, and not as a theologian presupposing heavenly beatitude), the good to be pursued in general (happiness or flourishing), is a conjunction or synthesis of several goods that are directly (*per se nota*) apprehended and found to be intrinsically fulfilling to us—goods like human life, knowledge, friendship, etc.[93]

How then do we move from the several goods that constitute identifications of the general form of the first principle of practical reason, for example, 'x' (human life) is a good to be pursued and preserved, to the moral realm? For Finnis, Aquinas bases his understanding of what constitutes the morally good on the degree of full reasonableness instantiated in the choices made by agents. Practical reason becomes a principle of morality by the apprehension that certain choices that we make (whilst still engaging the good of practical reason itself) are less practically reasonable than they could otherwise be. Morally good choices are choices that openly and integratively seek to participate in and embrace the *bona humana.* Conversely, bad choices are choices that unduly limit or restrictively foreclose the agent's integral pursuit of those goods.[94]

On the basis of Finnis's interpretation of Aquinas, therefore, Aquinas is seen to understand that the genesis of moral decision making concerns the degree of reasonableness of choices made, by which we more perfectly or less perfectly shape our lives in an expansive and open way to the appeal of those *bona humana.* Too be sure, bad choices still appeal to an array of intrinsic human goods, but engage those goods in ways that are less reasonable than they ought-to-be.[95]

If the above sketch of Finnis's interpretation of Aquinas's ethical theory is credible, as several other Aquinian scholars (minor quibbles aside) affirm it to be, then it can be plausibly asserted that Aquinas (contra the naturalistic approach of neo-scholastic natural law theory) does not proceed to derive (or otherwise deduce) normative conclusions from the foundations of speculative reasoning.[96] He accords to practical reason what may be termed its own 'unique normative structure', based on the underived, self-evident, intelligibly attractive appeal of basic human goods. Whilst original, Finnis's interpretation is not esoteric. Only recently, a detailed study of Aquinas's use of practical reason, entitled *Natural Law and Practical Reason,* by Martin Rhonheimer, substantiates Finnis's central claim that practical reason is practical through and through and that moral norms are not derived or deduced from any direct appeal to the blueprint of human nature.[97]

Alas, it is beyond the scope of this work to become entangled in the interstices of Aquinian scholarship on this point (a substantial monograph in itself). Suffice it to say, that even if Finnis's account of Aquinas was held in doubt, this would clearly not be fatal to the foundational aspects of his own approach to natural law ethics. Finnis would be entitled to claim, to the extent that his interpretation of Aquinas was found wanting, that Aquinas's approach would need to be departed from or augmented by his own meta-ethical account.

Finnis's Account of Natural Law Ethics

Development of Basic Human Goods

In *Natural Law and Natural Rights*, Finnis re-evaluates various theories of the good. He points out a number of key confusions that inadequate theories of the good have given rise to. Firstly, the search for a common denominator; secondly, attempts to establish a thin theory of the good on the basis of largely instrumental and therefore non-intrinsic values.[98] Finnis rejects the former on the basis that there is no common denominator to be established in an impartial and objective way, that is not inherently question begging. For Finnis, free choice is dependent on the incommensurability of intrinsic goods. Such goods offer the acting person diverse horizons of possible choices that cannot be exhausted. Free choice is free choice, precisely because the basic human goods are attractive in diverse non-reducible ways.[99]

Without the reality of incommensurability, it would in theory be possible to make the sorts of weighing between goods that consequentialist methodology appeals to. Yet what would this do to free choice? If there is always a correct solution in terms of what constitutes the maximisation of good, this would always be the right course of action to follow (viz. our earlier characterisation of a rebel archangel). [100] Yet, free choice is choice between options that appeal to us in diverse and non-reducible ways. Commensurability properly understood, would remove free choice from the agent, since it would in theory reduce all choice to a common denominator of the maximum good (or the least bad).[101] Free choice would become delusional, essentially the result of errors in calculation.

Secondly, he rejects thin theories of the good such as John Rawls's *Theory of Justice*, on the basis that they are fundamentally confused about the primary divisions that exist between goods valued for their own sake (*bonum honestum*) and goods that whilst important (and are significant ancillary means for human fulfilment), are not ultimate sources of value (*bonum utile*).[102]

By searching for the ultimate reasons that lie behind values, we reach a point in the chain of implication whereby we can identify irreducibly foundational goods. Thus, knowledge, for example, is such an irreducibly basic good, since it is capable of being valued for its own sake and not merely as an instrumental source of value. This is, of course not to deny that basic goods can also be used in an instrumental fashion, e.g., reading a car manual in order to repair a fault in the engine of your car. It is simply to make the point that such a good is capable of being understood as being intrinsically sought after for its own sake and not simply as a means to some further end.[103] By searching for the values that we are capable of grasping for their own sake, we can arrive, so to speak, at the primary classification of what is constitutive of 'human flourishing', or as Finnis terms it in later works 'integral human fulfilment'.[104]

In *Natural Law and Natural Rights*, Finnis enumerates seven such basic human goods.[105] However, the explanation of these goods has undergone clarification since that account was given. My enumeration here is based on *Practical Principles, Moral Truth, and Ultimate Ends.*[106]

Finnis, *et al.*, identify seven basic human goods divided into two basic categories. The first category are called 'substantive' goods, and the second category are called 'reflexive' goods.[107] There are three substantive goods. Firstly, there is the good of life itself. As animate beings we are able to grasp this essential good about our own existence. Secondly, as rational beings, we are able to grasp the good of knowledge, of truth (theoretical and practical), and the good of aesthetic experience, to wonder at the beauty of the world that surrounds us. Thirdly, as both animate and rational beings, we necessarily create and shape the world that surrounds us through our actions in work and play.[108]

As substantive goods, these above goods do not necessarily involve the agent in the prior exercise of choice for their initial actualisation, and can therefore be said to precede the exercise of reflexive choice. However, whilst these basic human goods precede choice, they are radically expanded and improved upon by our subsequent intelligent realisation of choices that invoke and affect those goods.[109] The final four goods are the 'reflexive goods'. These goods directly relate to the deliberating and choosing aspects of human agency. [110] Since these goods are dependent on deliberate acts of choice for their actualisation, they are made manifest through it. Firstly, harmonious relations with others. This includes friendship and justice. Secondly, authenticity between conscience and its outward expression. Thirdly, inner peace between emotions and feelings. Fourthly, the reflexive good of contemplation and apprehension of ultimate meaning. This is nothing other than a wonderment of the wider dimensions of meaning to life that lie within human attempts to frame value into a deeper reality that goes beyond self.[111]

Knowledge of the Basic Human Goods

How does the agent come to have knowledge about the basic human goods? For Finnis (as with his interpretation of Aquinas), this knowledge is grasped in and through practical pursuit. It is not to be confused with the apprehension of speculative reasoning, such as theoretical inquiry into the nature of existence (ontology, the speculative science of understanding being). Building upon key insights from Aquinas (ST I-II, q. 94 a. 2), he separates the epistemic requirements of practical knowledge, centred on the question of what constitutes a practical reason for action, from the principles of theoretical reason.[112]

Practical reasoning is not concerned with the explanation of phenomena as with theoretical reasoning. Rather, its purpose is to guide human action. Finnis is making the point that practical reason truly has its own unique 'starting points', which are nothing other than the response of practical reasoning itself to the basic goods of human fulfilment.[113] Whilst there is only one indivisible intellect of the person, the object of living well 'generates', or 'gives rise to', practical truths that are meant to guide action and not theoretically explain it.

For Finnis, the basic human goods are grasped by a self-evident apprehension on the part of the acting person (*propositio per se nota*). This grasp of self-evidency is necessary if we are not to fall either (i) into an infinite regress, or (ii) into an untenable reductionism that seeks to derive the normative directivity of 'ought' statements from the indicative 'is' statements of speculative reason. The starting point must, therefore, entail self-evidence. For Finnis, the basic human goods are just such self-evident starting points. If they were not underived they would not serve as primary starting points, that is, ultimate reasons for human action itself.[114] This is not to leave such goods without further support, however. Dialectical arguments can 'shore up' the appeal to such goods. Yet, of their nature, dialectical arguments (whilst

139

indispensable in the explanation of reality, and therefore to the fleshing out of specific moral obligations) are theoretical, and thus cannot substitute for self-evidence as a basic starting point for ethical foundations.[115]

First Principles of Practical Reason and Morality

In *Natural Law and Natural Rights* and *Fundamentals of Ethics*, Finnis moved directly from an enumeration of the basic human goods to identifying several principles of practical reasoning. However, at this stage in the development of his thought, he did not explicitly spell out either a first principle of practical reason or a first principle of morality. These came later. Nevertheless, this should not be taken as in any way a rejection of his earlier presentation of practical reasoning, particularly the detailed enumeration of the criteria of practical reasonableness.[116] Rather, it represents an explicit statement of linkages clearly assumed but not adequately expressed in earlier works.

He argues that since the basic human goods make appeals to both good and bad choices, their status is not- yet- moral. They represent attractive possibilities, and there are many ways of shaping and unfolding these goods in the choices we make. Human action always makes appeal to the basic human goods in diverse ways. However, we can not yet formulate moral principles until the implications of the first principle of practical reason are understood. Finnis, drawing here on the influence of Aquinas, formulates the first principle of practical reason as "good is to be done and the bad is to be avoided."[117] At this stage of inquiry, this principle is an 'is-to-be' and not yet normative, for 'good' here refers generally to all that can intelligibly be understood by the acting person as in some sense a worthwhile thing to pursue. Similarly, its opposite refers to a deprivation of the good, that is, actions which are not open to the basic forms of human good. The first principle of practical reason then simply points out that in acting for purposes and goals in life, it is possible to choose in ways that are muddled, lack coherence, arbitrarily restrict opportunities for further development, and so on. Such choices are bad (in a not-yet-moral sense) since they are restrictive of the attractive horizon of possibilities. Thus, all agents, whether good or bad, appeal to practical reasoning in the choices they make concerning the basic human goods.[118]

How do we move from the first principle of practical reason and enter the moral sphere? This is the transition from the first principle of practical reason (what can be done) to the first principle of morality (what ought to be done).[119] This takes us to the crux of the matter. The directivity of practical reason itself points to a self-evident primary principle of morality.

There are two fundamental options relating to choice. Either we act in ways that are open to the possibilities of integral human fulfilment, instantiated in and through the basic human goods, or we chose in ways that constrict those possibilities. Bad choices fetter or restrict the fulsome interpretation of the basic human goods. Here the transition from the directivity of practical reason to the normativity of morality takes place. It is immoral to act in ways that stunt or neglect the application of practical reason in guiding the choices we make.[120] In a manner analogous to Aquinas, immorality consists in a deprivation in the measure of reason used to guide practical conduct. Moral choices are expansive and open to the basic human goods, and immoral choices are stunted in their appeal to or use of the basic human goods. [121]

What then is the first principle of morality? The principle is stated as follows: "in voluntarily acting for human goods and avoiding what is opposed to them, one ought to choose and otherwise will those and only those possibilities whose willing is compatible with a will toward integral human fulfilment."[122]

There can be little doubt that such a principle is general. However, it is capable of further specification, and these specifications stand as parts stand in relation to participation in the whole. Specifications of this principle are nothing other than determinations derived from practical reason itself when reflecting on the possibilities of choice relating to the uses of the basic human goods as constitutive aspects of integral human fulfilment.

It might seem at first instance that Finnis is practically appealing to a conception of human fulfilment as a 'state' that is somehow an immediately achievable end of life. Yet this is not the case. It is a guiding teleological horizon that is mediated through the proximity of the basic human goods.[123] By pointing to a horizon of possibility, the principle encourages us to be open to the basic human goods in an expansive and integrative way that is never exhausted but always worth striving relentlessly towards.[124]

Specifications of the First Moral Principle

What, then, are some of the specifications entailed by the first principle? These specifications are the outcome of further determinations reached by the operation of the intermediate principles of practical reason that act as a bridge between the first principle of morality and the derivation of specific norms that direct concrete behaviour. Finnis enumerates nine such intermediate principles of practical reason in *Natural Law and Natural Rights*, and a tenth principle in *Fundamentals of Ethics*.[125]

First, practical reasonableness is itself a basic good. It structures our pursuit and engagement in all the other basic human goods. To act in ways that promote the all round flourishing of the agent, the full application of this good is required in decision making about what is to be done. Second, one needs a coherent plan of life. A life that simply drifts from one episode to another is uncreative and does not further stretch or develop our potentialities in a variety of different ways.[126] Third, whilst an agent may place less (or more) of an emphasis on some of the basic goods, there should be no arbitrary (unduly restrictive) preferences for or against goods, such that there is a distorted (over/under) focus on certain goods at the unreasonable expense of remaining open to a continuance of participation in the others. Fourth, in order to act in a practically reasonable fashion, it is wrong to act in ways that are arbitrarily dismissive of the concerns and interests of other people. There should be no arbitrary preferences amongst persons. This is classically expressed in the Golden Rule (don't do unto others what you would not like done unto you).[127]

Fifth, the agent needs to display appropriate commitment to, as well as appropriate detachment from, life-plans. The collapse of life-plans is not the collapse of the person. Both extremes of singular fanaticism and diffuse indecision need to be avoided. Sixth, there is a firm recognition of the important but limited role that an appeal to consequences can have within the context of choice. Consequences have limited relevance within the structure of action, since consequences must be assessed under the architectonic aegis of all the criteria of practical reasonableness in guiding human choice.[128] Seventh, since the basic human goods are equally irreducible, and there is no hierarchical ordination amongst them, there can never be an adequate justification (sufficient reason) for intentionally or directly attacking, harming, or otherwise intentionally destroying, the instantiation of a basic human good.[129] Eighth, the requirements of the common good. This requirement is necessary in order that the acts of individuals be open to the needs of coordinating individual interests with one another in mutually enhancing ways. Ninth, the importance of the agent adhering to the judgements of an informed conscience. This entails adhering to judgements that the agent profoundly believes to be correct in the face of passion or social pressures to the contrary. Tenth, the reasonableness of integrity and authenticity in the agent's engagement with the basic human goods. It is unreasonable to make an option for simulations of apparent illusionary goods rather than for real genuine goods in a substitutive way that replaces authentic encounter with the artificially contrived.

Derivation of Exceptionless Moral Norms

Due to the incommensurability thesis that Finnis supports, and the operation of the intermediate principles of conduct that result from the deliberation of practical reason, Finnis is able to reach specific and detailed prohibitions concerning certain forms of action. Finnis characterises moral absolutes as 'exceptionless moral norms' that prohibit the execution of certain kinds of action, kinds of action that are capable of being specified in descriptive (non-morally evaluative) ways.[130] Given this characterisation of exceptionless moral norms, it is clear that their justification must proceed in two stages. Firstly, it is necessary to provide a characterisation of the kind of action that is in question. Secondly, it is necessary to demonstrate how any action that answers to that characterisation is necessarily a morally wrong action.[131]

Since Finnis identifies morally right action with action that is fully practically reasonable, it follows that if a correct description of a kind of action is provided, such that the action necessarily is not fully practically reasonable, then the action is morally prohibited. Anyone, therefore, who defends the existence of an exceptionless moral norm against the intentional killing [of the innocent] will first have to defend a particular account of what the act of killing consists in and will then have to show that any action of this sort is not fully practically reasonable.

Regarding the first criteria, Finnis does indeed provide, for our subject matter, a non-moral characterisation prevalent in common morality of the kind of action that is the subject of an exceptionless prohibition. It can be expressed as an intentional act of killing [the innocent], regardless of a further appeal to consequences or motive.[132] This description is not merely a tautological absolute of the form that it is wrong to intentionally perform all actions of 'unjust killing'. Finnis does not smuggle into his definition the use of morally loaded terminology in the very definition of the act of intentional killing. Further analysis of the structure of human action and its characterisation pertaining to killing will be the object of further discussion and analysis in the following chapter. Suffice it for present purposes to be able to see here that the act is not characterised in a tautological way. The question, concerning the second criteria, is, why would the assertion of committing an act of intentional killing [of the innocent] be practically unreasonable in all circumstances and thus absolutely morally prohibited?

To understand why Finnis holds that intentional killing (as an end or as a means) is never fully practically reasonable, it is necessary to draw on the foundational features of his account of practical reasoning. On Finnis's account, there are a variety of basic goods—human life, knowledge, friendship, practical reasonableness, etc., which serve as the starting points for practical reasoning. These goods are the fundamental reasons for action. Each of these is self-evidently a form of intrinsic good. Now, the good of practical reasonableness is both a basic good and also the regulatory means by which the pursuit of the basic goods (including practical reasonableness itself) is participated in. Acting in a way that is practically reasonable consists in adhering to a number of self-evident criteria of practical reasoning which have previously been emphasised. Thus, to act morally is simply to act in accordance with all of these requirements of practical reasonableness.[133]

Since to act morally is to act in accordance with all of the requirements of practical reasonableness, the defence of the moral absolute against killing must rely on one or another of these principles of practical reason. Amongst the basic principles of practical reasonableness is what Finnis (and others) have called the "Pauline principle"—that one must not do evil in order to achieve good.[134] In other words, for Finnis, basic human goods must be respected in every action performed. An agent must never perform an action whose intention is to damage an instantiation of a basic human good. This principle is considered self-evident, for agents are able to recognise that the basic goods, and all distinct instantiations of basic goods among which choices are possible, are indeed incommensurable. If instantiations of basic goods were commensurable, an agent might think it reasonable to intentionally destroy one instantiation of a basic good in order to secure another instantiation that contains 'greater goodness'. However, since distinct instantiations of basic goods are incommensurable, this sort of justification for acting against an instantiation of a basic good must be ill founded.[135]

We are now in a position to formulate Finnis's account of the exceptionless moral norm against intentional killing.[136] Killing is an act whose intention is to extinguish human life. To intend to extinguish human life is to intend to cause damage to an incommensurable basic human good—the good of human life (whether instantiated in self or another). As we have pointed out, for Finnis, acting against any basic good is unreasonable according to the Pauline principle, an important criteria of practical reasoning. Therefore, an agent who intentionally kills, acts in a way that is not fully practically reasonable, and thus acts immorally. Intentional killing, it can be concluded, is therefore exceptionlessly morally forbidden because of the kind of action that killing is. The agent ought not to intentionally act against the basic good of human life under any circumstances.[137] Thus consequences and motive cannot be appealed to in order to override basic concrete negative prohibitions of this nature. To do so is to make a choice characterised by a deprivation of practical reason. As a manifestation of such deprivation such actions display a necessary mark of wrongfulness. They propose to make reasonable that which is objectively unreasonable. To make such a choice would be to say that it is right to act in a manner that is closed to an essential aspect of practical reason itself (e.g., not to directly attack a basic human good), and can therefore be judged immoral on that count.[138]

By an appeal to the basic human goods under the architectonic guidance of practical reason, Finnis, in my view, provides a solid framework supporting the reasonableness of many of the traditional specific moral absolutes comprehended by common morality, especially for our purposes, the prohibition on the intentional killing [of the innocent].

Evaluation of Finnis

Implications of His Approach

What Finnis is able to achieve in his method is considerable, if it can indeed be sustained. I think it can, and will consider some critiques shortly. However, before turning to this task, it is worth spelling out just what the implications of Finnis's method actually are concerning the two proceeding theories. Unlike utilitarianism and other forms of consequentialism, his theory flatly denies the possibility of commensuration between 'competing' forms of basic human goods. He places the integrity of good character formation as central to questions of human conduct. He is, therefore able to overcome the limitations of method earlier directed at consequentialism. Secondly, his theory is able to overcome key deficiencies in deontological ethics. The primary building blocks are located in a full theory of human goods that can substantiate, when combined with the operation of practical reason, highly specific moral norms in robust form. There is, as it were, sufficient flesh on the bones of principle to convincingly argue that the intentional killing of another is always morally wrong. It is not wrong à la Donagan simply because it treats people as a mere means and is therefore disrespectful, though, in a sense, his intermediate principles are indicative of many of the factors that a properly grounded notion of respect would require. Rather, it is wrong because it is a direct rejection of the incommensurable good of human life itself, an essential aspect of flourishing that we can recognise in ourselves and others.

Given the scope of the attack that Finnis makes on alternative methodologies, and his insistence upon a 'full-content' theory of human goods, it is not surprising that his theory has come in for sustained criticism. I will consider criticisms made under four heads. Firstly, the status of the basic goods. Secondly, the adequacy of justifications concerning self-evidence. Thirdly, the incommensurability of the basic goods. Fourthly, the attempt to sever the operation of practical reason itself from a foundationalism that insists that the truths of practical reason must ultimately be derived from the truths of speculative reason.

Status of the Basic Goods

Jean Porter has criticised Finnis's presentation of the basic human goods as some form of mysterious entity.[139] In her first argument, she asserts that it is fundamentally unclear as to what is the ontological or logical status of the basic goods. She accuses Finnis of speaking of the basic human goods almost as Platonic forms that have an independent existence of their own.[140] Consequently, she concludes that Finnis is guilty of a 'hypostatisation' of the basic human goods. Porter finds the language of attacks upon the basic goods as inimical of the tendency of Finnis to place these goods in an extrinsic relationship to the agent. This leads Porter to suggest that they represent more the projection of personal conviction than of solid argument. Secondly, Porter argues against the credibility of the assertion that all rational human actions must be explained in terms of the basic human goods.[141] For Porter, such an argument seems blatantly counter-intuitive in the face of conventional understandings of human motivation.

These would be serious criticisms of Finnis if they could indeed be substantiated. However, I do think they can be met. Finnis is initially evaluating forms of human fulfilment from the agent centred first person perspective. What is it that agents would (implicitly at least) have to admit to as being necessary goods for them to act towards? The basic goods are not abstract theoretical concepts, but practical (rationally attractive) possibilities, apprehended by the acting purposeful agent.[142] They are reasoned practically from human experience. It is the task of practical reason to grasp and make sense of this primary data under its own mode of apprehension. Reason (including practical reason) is pre-eminently an ordering and directing activity. It classifies and organises the primary starting points of attractive possibility and groups them into meaningful clusters.[143] For example, there is sufficient congruence between the animation of life, its transmission, and its preservation, to meaningfully classify together such intelligibly attractive aspects of human possibility. They are not 'entities', but rather constitute the apprehensions of practical reason itself operating on the 'insights' or 'preambula' arising from human nature in the form of capacities or needs (for we most assuredly have a nature, and are not therefore plants or cats). This apprehending and ordering aspect of practical reason is the structure we have for grasping just what needs and tendencies are genuinely (not merely apparently) good or not, and as such are truly worthy of being pursued as basic constituents of human flourishing.[144]

Perhaps a latent concern lying behind some of Porter's thoughts here is the following problem, raised by James M. Dubois, that if Finnis proceeds from an agent centred first person perspective, all that Finnis may be able to claim for the basic human goods would be propositions of the kind that 'X ... Z are intrinsic goods for me'.[145] They are goods for me to pursue because I perceive them to be good. If the agent ceases to value the goods as 'intrinsic goods for me', does that not imply that the goods cease to be goods worthy of pursuit for the agent? For example, if human life ceases to be perceived as continuing to be a 'good for me', does it not cease to be a good for the agent, and can it not therefore be intentionally acted against, say, in an act of suicide? This problem can, I think, be overcome by what Finnis terms the 'transparency' of assertions, in short, what an agent must necessarily assert by acting in a practically reasonable manner.[146] Thus, in claiming that "X is an intrinsic good for me," that claim is also transparent for "it is the case that X is an intrinsic good," and this is in turn transparent for the claim that "X is an intrinsic good for human agents generally." By virtue of the operation of the agent's practical reason, and by subsequent reflection upon its normative insights, the agent is able to apprehend that the basic human goods are not simply 'goods for me', to be participated in or not as the case may be, but are necessary goods applicable to all human agents *qua* human.[147] Once we (fully reasonably) recognise that certain goods are generally applicable to the flourishing of all persons (given further reflection on the commonality of the nature that we have), and that the agent is most assuredly a human person, the agent *cannot subsequently discount* the status of those goods in terms of their applicability to all persons (including himself or herself).

Once the significance of certain goods to human persons is apprehended, the objectively understood status of the goods *cannot subsequently* be abandoned by the agent in subsequent acts of choice (*except on pain of practical unreasonableness*, e.g., a breach of the requirement not to intentionally act against or undermine a basic human good; to continue to be open to participation in the basic human goods; to avoid undue bias in discounting the significance of all the basic human goods, and so on). This is a clear implication flowing from practical reason's own necessitating structure.

To be sure, the suicide, for example, may no longer see the good left in human life as a good 'for them'. Such choices are certainly possible to make (and are not therefore to be discounted as 'incomprehensible'). However, once it is realised that the suicider is no longer being transparently open to the continuing appeal of the good of human life (a good for all humans to pursue and promote), practical reason is, so to speak, short circuited, and the agent can be said to be unreasonably circumventing the importance of maintaining a continuing openness to the constant appeal of this good.

Turning now to Porter's second argument, that all rational human actions need not be explained in terms of the basic human goods, this can be addressed by means of dialectical argumentation, as an indirect support mechanism (for the basic human goods as underived cannot therefore be directly deduced from *theoria*). Porter does not examine supportive arguments concerning 'chains of reasoning' back to ultimate reasons that help grant foundational intelligibility to human actions. She simply does not address this issue. An example will help to clarify matters further. A student is busy working at a number of jobs in order to earn additional money. When asked why do you want this additional money, he may simply say that money is in itself a good thing. This would not be a satisfactory answer if we pressed him further and asked why having money was a good thing to have. Such an answer lacks adequate explanation. The answer would be intelligible, however, if he said that he needed the money in order to help pay for his studies, or if he was saving in order to go on holiday, and so on. By such steps we can arrive at ultimate reasons for action that are full explanations behind the nature of human activities. Of course, we do not always concretely think in those terms. Habits and training circumvent the necessity for such processes. Yet, the possibility for such chains of reasoning provides dialectical support for the basic human goods as ultimate justifications underpinning the ends that guide human action.[148]

Self-Evidence

Criticisms relating to Finnis's appeal to self-evidence, state that he is really trying to cover up his attempt to project his own concerns onto a supposedly objective structure of practical reasoning. As such, he appeals to groundless intuitions in order to cover up the lack of persuasiveness concerning the status of his basic human goods and his principles of practical reason and morality. This line of criticism is advanced by Lloyd Weinreb and Russell Hittinger, amongst others.[149] Weinreb, for example, argues that Finnis's foundationalism rests on the mistaken belief that if a person reflects carefully on the human predicament, they will arrive at self-evidence without further proof.[150] Hittinger argues that such appeals to self-evidence are mere appeals to untethered intuitions, without any foundation in reality. They amount to little other than naked assertion with a rhetorical mask.[151]

Some such suspicion is indeed to be welcomed, and is understandable up to a point. It is not the case however that the basic human goods are directly asserted by the naked force of Finnis's personality. We have a nature and speculative reasoning can tell us much about the nature we have. Speculative reasoning can provide complementary lines of argument to support practical reason's direct understanding of the basic human goods, including the good of practical reason itself. Practical reason does not spring forth miraculously, as if Finnis were Moses walking down the mountain with tablets of stone, making a declaration that we have a new moral system based on self-evidence. Finnis uses speculative reason to dialectally support the claims made relating to self-evidence.[152] Thus, as human beings with a nature of our own, we are able to rationally describe the inclinations of nature. This data, so to speak, provides indirect support for the conclusions that the operation of practical reason itself generates under its own mode of apprehension. Clear lines of complementarity can be said to exist (between nature and praxis) because we have a constitution that gives rise to different modes of apprehension, in sync with one another, proceeding from a reality that is ultimately unitary.[153]

The conception of self-evidence is not, as it were, an empirical statement of the actual acceptance of those practical truths by those who have capacity to know, whether philosophers or field labourers. Rather, it is an assertion of the capacity, in principle, to know. Several reasons can account for this fissure between capacity to know and acceptance, e.g., prior cultural or intellectual commitments already made that colour our vision.[154] What Finnis is claiming, is that their *per se nota* character means that they are not derived from more foundational propositions and can, in principle, be grasped as such.[155] If incredulity still follows from this, then we must agree to disagree. Finnis, in my view, would be entitled to conclude that those thinkers have not sufficiently understood or reflected upon either the epistemic foundations for practical knowledge itself as the source of normativity, or upon his use of dialectical reasoning as indirect support for the claim that certain truths do indeed need to rest on self-evidence as an indispensable starting point.

Commensurability

Garth Hallett, and McKim and Simpson, contest Finnis's incommensurability thesis (a basic statement that X and Y are incommensurate if it is not true that one is objectively 'more valuable' than the other).[156] They argue that preferences can indeed be arranged and objective rational choices made concerning those preferences. They further argue that Finnis is mistaken in his argument contra consequentialism concerning free choice. The establishment of a greater good does not make it irrational to choose the lesser good. Thus, for example, Hallett suggests the case of a philosopher, happily married for a number of years who is strongly attracted to other women. He recognises that the greater good resides in keeping fidelity with his wife and supporting her. However, he chooses the lesser good, the promise of pleasure, so enticing, in the arms of the other woman.[157] McKim and Simpson appeal to a similar rationale to argue that Finnis is posing a false dilemma.[158]

A second line of criticism concerns what may be termed Finnis's value egalitarianism. This argument is made by, amongst others, Jean Porter, Russell

Pannier, and George Wright.[159] Take for example the argument made by Pannier. Suppose that a person is drinking a cup of coffee and sees his friend drowning. If Finnis's strong commensurability thesis is true, then it is meaningless to say that the person ought to save his friend from drowning rather than enjoy the drinking of his cup of coffee.[160] Wright offers a similar example of playing a game of golf whilst a young child is seen drowning in a near by pond.[161]

Again, I think that both these lines of criticism can be effectively met. Finnis does not deny (as a matter of fact) that people can and do make (sub-rational) choices of the kind Hallett supposes that they do. The key question that Hallett has to address, is why one is rationally entitled to prefer one course of action rather than another course of action in a way that provides an objective basis for the comparison of values?

In his rejoinder to McKim and Simpson, Finnis is able to effectively demonstrate that the commensurability assumed by consequentialism is not the rational form of commensurability required, but rather rests upon (sub-rational) emotional commitment or feelings.[162] This merely begs the question as to what objective standard is that is designed to justify such commensuration. The philosopher in Hallett's example is not rationally choosing the lesser good, but is responding emotionally. His passions (sub-rational temptations) have the better of him. This is tantamount to an abandonment of what constitutes rational choice, in their own terms. Finnis is therefore able to conclude that if their argument is about rational choice, then the incommensurability of basic human goods holds true. If it is about the fact that individuals can and do make choices on the basis of emotions, and therefore choose sub-rationally, there is no case to answer. It simply smuggles in assumptions that cannot be assumed if preferences are to be ordered rationally as consequentalist theories claim they can.[163]

What of the second line of criticisms under this head? Take, for example, the 'principle of fairness' to others (a criteria of practical reasonableness). Acting out of fairness to a friend is a prime example of fairness directing the attention of the acting person away from one good and to the priority of another good, in a given context. When faced with a choice between saving a friend and drinking coffee, fairness clearly points to saving the friend. Coffee is not an instantiation of a basic good, but merely an instrumental means to an instantiation of a basic human good. This example, therefore, does not presuppose incommensurability between basic goods. Wright's example does. In such a circumstance, there need be no reason to act against the basic good of play in order to save the life of a girl drowning in a nearby pond. There need be no intention to act against the basic human goods of play or of life. This is an example of the intention/foresight distinction (whose basis we will seek to justify in the next chapter, and which Finnis endorses).[164] In addition, there is positive reason to save the life of the girl on the basis of fairness.[165] He can resume his golf game at a latter date. The life of the girl, short of a miracle, cannot be resurrected. Should the individual chose to play golf and not save the girl, he would be guilty of an immoral act of omission, where he could have reasonably saved the girl's life without major risk to his own. This example serves to illustrate how the Finnisian method is capable of dealing in a practical and sensible way with clashes between the basic human goods. To understand the method adequately requires due attention to all the criteria of practical reasonableness involved in moral decision making, and not just to edited highlights.

Kantianism in Disguise?

Russell Hittinger, Henry Veatch, and Ralph McInerny, amongst others, criticise Finnis's supposed wall of divide between theoretical knowledge of the world and the operation of practical reason.[166] It is claimed that this is a form of Kantianism, since practical reason seems to be self-contained in its own discrete world, divorced from necessary realities about ourselves and the world around us. The categories of practical reason impose themselves on the person and create the necessary grounds of obligation. Does this not give rise to an impossible foundation in the same way that Kant thought that things-in-themselves were unknowable, and located morality in introspective reason divorced from the reality of nature?

In responding to this line of objection, the following clarificatory points can be made to point out the unhelpful nature of such a comparison. Firstly, Finnis, unlike Kant, is overtly teleological in his account of the fonts of attractive purposefulness that arise out of human experience, purposes that constitute basic human goods and provide an intelligible directedness to human action. Finnis does not deny that the data of human experience are crucial to moral decision making.[167] Human experience provides the basis upon which the practical intellect grasps what is genuinely good and worthwhile to pursue (or not). These goods arise out of the complex of human experience itself (including experience of what constitutes our source of normative directedness).[168]

This represents a structural dynamic that moves from the data of experience, to insights of intelligible attractiveness, to non-inferential acts of understanding. The latter, so to speak, is the 'click of normative recognition,' that establishes and affirms what needs and tendencies arising from our nature are genuinely to be pursued as the basic constituents of human flourishing. This represents a dynamic teleological purposefulness to the genesis of normative conduct in a manner quite unlike the formalistic 'boiler press stamping' associated with the notion of Kant's Categorical Imperative (especially the first form).

Secondly, practical reason *is a part of human nature*. As Finnis states, "were man's nature different, so would be his duties."[169] To be human is to participate in the requirements of practical reason. Given the nature that we have, there is no means of entailing normative propositions from theoretical speculation. That task of our human nature is part and parcel of the operation of the practical intellect. It cannot be set apart from human nature, and cannot be radically juxtaposed with it, for it is an indispensable and integral part of the human nature that we have. As beings of the type that we are, our mode of apprehension of normative value is dependent on this mode of practical knowing.

Thirdly, as Robert George points out, Finnis does not deny the dialectical relevance of metaphysical or anthropological inquiry as a systematic into the origin of the needs and potentialities of human nature. No doubt, many of the goods that we recognise as genuinely worthy of practical pursuit have a corresponding ontological basis. An ontological mode of inquiry can fruitfully establish lines of complementary comparison between the apprehension of ontological goods (via speculative reason) and the apprehension of basic human goods (via practical reason).[170]

When we move from an ontological to an epistemological mode of inquiry, however, it is important to recognise that there is no inconsistency in claiming that our normative recognition of basic human goods proceeds from its own direct non-reductive beginning of self-evidence, and that such a separate epistemological distinction is not incompatible with an ontological mode of inquiry (inquiry that theoretically helps to explain why those goods can be said to be perfective of the nature of our being, given the kinds of being that we are with the nature that we have).[171]

Notes to Chapter Four

[1] The use of the bracket around the qualifier innocent is significant. The use of the bracket is designed to mark and reserve for subsequent clarification the problematic of including this word as a qualifier. In chapter five I will argue that the specific concrete exceptionless norm is the wrongfulness of intentional killing *simpliciter* and not just the intentional killing of the innocent.

[2] See for example Montague Brown, *The Quest for Moral Foundations* (Washington, DC: Georgetown University Press, 1996), chs. 4 & 5.

[3] Philip E. Devine, *Natural Law Ethics* (Westport: Greenwood Press, 2000), 1-7.

[4] I will not further consider questions of divine command theory in this book. For an analysis and discussion of divine command theory see Paul Rooney,

Divine Command Morality (Aldershot: Avebury, 1996); Paul Helm, *Divine Commands and Morality* (Oxford: Oxford University Press, 1981).

[5] G. E. M. Anscombe, "Modern Moral Philosophy," in *Virtue Ethics,* eds. Roger Crisp and Michael Slote (Oxford: Oxford University Press, 1997), 26-44. Anscombe further addresses the question of moral absolutes in "War and Murder." In her *Ethics, Religion and Politics*, vol. III (Oxford: Blackwell, 1981), 51-64.

[6] Anscombe, "Modern Moral Philosophy," 37.

[7] The term "concrete" is a necessary insertion. It is possible to admit of exceptionless moral norms at a high degree of generality, e.g., be just, be good, be chaste, etc. and yet still deny the bindingness of specific concrete norms.

[8] This definition of consequentialism can incorporate under this label primarily deontological moral systems such as that posed by Charles Fried in *Right and Wrong* (Cambridge: Harvard University Press, 1978). Fried argues that when faced with such catastrophies the usual rules of right and wrong cease to apply. Thus, for Fried, we cannot in such circumstances assert the view *fiat justitia, ruat coelum.* This of course presupposes that the Stoics ever thought that by following moral absolutes, the heavens could ever in fact fall. See for example, Alan Donagan, "Comment on Wheeler's 'Donagan on Fiat, Justitia, Ruat Caelum'," *Ethics* 96 (1986): 876-77. See also John Finnis, *Moral Absolutes: Tradition, Revision, and Truth* (Washington, DC: Catholic University of America Press, 1991), 105-6.

[9] Anscombe, "Modern Moral Philosophy," 35.

[10] An example of this difference would be when the rules of right and wrong could be departed from in the course of non-disaster avoidance situations, and the respective strengths of their agent centred restrictions where 'extreme' consequences are not seen to apply as overrides. See the discussion on agent centred restrictions *infra.*

[11] J. J. C. Smart, "Extreme and Restricted Utilitarianism," in The*ories of Ethics* ed. Philippa Foot (Oxford: Oxford University Press, 1967), 171-83. See Alistair MacIntyre, *After Virtue* (London: Duckworth, 1981), 62-66, 70-71, for a concise exposition of this key feature of major consequentialist systems.

[12] MacIntyre, *After Virtue*, 62-66, 70-71. *See also* John Rawls, *A Theory of Justice* (Cambridge: Harvard University Press, 1972), 22-27, for a concise overview of classical utilitarianism.

[13] See Mary Warnock, *Introduction to Utilitarianism* (London: Fontana, 1962), 7-31.

[14] D. W. Hodgson, *Consequences of Utilitarianism* (Oxford: Oxford University Press, 1967), ch. 2.

[15] J. J. C. Smart, "An Outline of a System of Utilitarian Ethics," in J. J. C. Smart and Bernard Williams, *Utilitarianism For & Against* (Cambridge: Cambridge University Press, 1973), 25.

[16] For Henry Sidgwick, a Victorian utilitarian, the greatest general happiness is the greatest sum of happiness of individuals, or, according to Sidgwick, the greatest possible surplus of pleasure over pain. If we are to calculate such surplus consciously, we need to perform *objective interpersonal comparisons of pleasures*. See his *Methods of Ethics* (Chicago: University of Chicago Press, 1962), 411-13.

[17] J. S. Mill, *Utilitarianism*, ed. Mary Warnock (London: Fontana, 1962), 257-61.

[18] Mill, *Utilitarianism*, 260.

[19] Robert Nozick, *Anarchy, State and Utopia* (New York: Basic Books, 1974), 42-43.

[20] Bernard Williams, "A Critique of Utilitarianism," in Smart and Williams, *Utilitarianism For & Against*, 112-14.

[21] See Michael Slote, *From Morality to Virtue* (Oxford: Oxford University Press, 1992), 227-38 for an excellent discussion of the diversity of things that makes a good life admirable. See also MacIntyre, *After Virtue*, 64-65.

[22] For varieties of preference formulation see Dan W. Brock, "Recent Work in Utilitarianism," *American Philosophical Quarterly* 10 (1973): 241-76, at 245-46.

[23] R. M. Hare, *Moral Thinking: Its Levels, Method and Point* (Oxford: Clarendon Press, 1981).

[24] Hare, *Moral Thinking*, 4.

[25] Hare, *Moral Thinking*, 108.

[26] Hare, *Moral Thinking*, 95.

[27] Hare, *Moral Thinking*, 110.

[28] Hare, *Moral Thinking*, 110.

[29] Thomas Nagel, *The View From Nowhere* (Oxford: Oxford University Press, 1986), 150-56.

[30] Nagel, *View From Nowhere*, 150-56. See also Bernard Williams, *Ethics and the Limits of Philosophy* (London: Fontana, 1985), 83-84, 87-88, 89-91.

[31] Hare, *Moral Thinking*, 101.

[32] See for example John Findlay, *Values and Intentions* (Atlantic Highlands: Humanities Press, 1978), 234-37. He argues that this way of arguing simply ignores one of the most fundamental aspects of our self-understanding, we are incapable of interpreting the universe thus. See further Thomas Nagel, *Moral Questions* (Cambridge: Cambridge University Press, 1979), 202; Williams, *Critique of Utilitarianism*, 118.

[33] See Smart & Williams, *Utilitarianism For & Against*; David Lyons, *Forms and Limits of Utilitarianism* (Oxford: Clarendon Press, 1965); Slote, *From Virtue to Morality* who in various ways support such a thesis of collapse. Cf. Richard B. Brandt, "Toward a Credible Form of Utilitarianism," in *Contemporary Utilitarianism*, ed. Michael Bayles (Garden City: Doubleday, 1968); Brandt, *Morality, Utilitarianism and Rights* (Cambridge: Cambridge University Press, 1992); J. H. Sobel, "Rule-Utilitarianism," *Australasian Journal of Philosophy* 48 (1968): 33-39. See also J. L. Mackie who argues that whilst there is in principle a separation that can be maintained, it loses out on plausibility grounds: J. L. Mackie, *Ethics: Inventing Right From Wrong* (London: Penguin, 1977).

[34] Williams, *Ethics*, 75-77, 105-6.

[35] Williams, *Critique of Utilitarianism*, 116-17.

[36] Samuel Scheffler, *The Rejection of Consequentialism* (Oxford: Clarendon Press, 1982), 14-17, 22-23.

[37] Scheffler, *Rejection of Consequentialism*, 24-26, 35-36.

[38] Scheffler, *Rejection of Consequentialism*, 38-39.

[39] Williams, *Critique of Utilitarianism*, 108-18.

[40] Williams, *Critique of Utilitarianism*, 108-18.

[41] Williams, *Critique of Utilitarianism*, 108-18.

[42] On this eventistic or episodic theory of action see Anselm W. Müller, "Radical Subjectivity: Morality Versus Utilitarianism," *Ratio* 19 (1977): 115-32. See also the excellent statement of the 'eventist' position in John Finnis, *Fundamentals of Ethics* (Washington, DC: Georgetown University Press, 1983), 116-20.

[43] Scheffler, *Rejection of Consequentialism,* 5, 14-17, 19-21, 83-84.

[44] See for example Barbara Herman, "On the Value of Acting from the Motive of Duty," *Philosophical Review* 90 (1981): 358-82. On general terminological distinctions between ethical theories see W. K. Frankena, *Ethics.* 2nd ed. (Englewood Cliffs: Prentice-Hall, 1973).

[45] Immanuel Kant, *Groundwork of the Metaphysic of Morals*, trans. H. J. Paton (New York: Harper & Row, 1964), 56-60. See also the primacy of duty in the commentary by Marcia Baron, "On the Alleged Repugnance of Acting from Duty," *The Journal of Philosophy* 81 (1984): 179-219.

[46] *Groundwork for the Metaphysics of Morals,* 121-23.

[47] *Groundwork for the Metaphysics of Morals,* 88.

[48] Contra the Scottish School, e.g., Adam Smith and Francis Hutchison. See further The *"Science of Man" in The Scottish Enlightenment: Hume, Reid, and Their Contemporaries,* ed. Peter Jones (Edinburgh: Edinburgh University Press, 1989).

[49] Immanuel Kant, "On a Supposed Right to Lie from Altruistic Motives," in *Critique of Practical Reason,* ed. Lewis White Beck (Chicago: University of Chicago Press, 1949).

[50] Anscombe, "Modern Moral Philosophy," 27. See also her *Intention* (Oxford: Blackwell, 1957), 11-12. See also Eric D'Arcy, *Human Acts: An Essay in Their Moral Evaluation* (Oxford: Clarendon Press, 1963), ch. 1.

[51] Cf. Stephen Darwall, *Impartial Reason* (Ithaca: Cornell University Press, 1983). See also his "Kantian Practical Reason Defended," Ethics 96 (1985): 89-99.

52 See David Sobel, "Full Information Accounts of Human Well-Being," *Ethics* 104 (1994): 784-810.

53 Alan Donagan, *The Theory of Morality* (Chicago: University of Chicago Press, 1977).

54 Donagan, *Theory of Morality*, 57-66

55 Donagan, *Theory of Morality*, 57-66.

56 Donagan, *Theory of Morality*, 76-78, 87-88.

57 See Shelly Kagan, *Normative Ethics* (Boulder: Westview Press, 1998), 240-304. This line of criticism has been simplified from his much more detailed analysis of the notion of respect.

58 At bottom, Kantian ethics seeks the impossible—to derive moral absolutes upon an inadequate foundationalism not based on a teleological understanding of the direct intrinsic appeal of basic goods constitutive of the integral well-being of the human person. See Germain Grisez, Joseph Boyle, and John Finnis, "Practical Principles, Moral Truth, and Ultimate Ends," *American Journal of Jurisprudence* 32 (1987): 99-151, 101.

59 Richard Norman, *The Moral Philosophers* (New York: Oxford University, 1998), 98-100; Jonathan Dancy, "An Ethic of Prima Facie Duties," in *A Companion to Ethics* (Oxford: Blackwell, 1991).

60 W. D. Ross, *Foundations of Ethics* (Oxford: Oxford University Press, 1939), 42. I shall not pursue the justification Ross offers for his appeal to intuitionalism any further within this work.

61 W.D. Ross, *Right and the Good* (Oxford: Clarendon Press, 1930), 16-34.

62 Ross, *Foundations of Ethics*, 320-21.

63 See H.J. McCloskey, "The Concept of a Prima Facie Duty," *Australasian Journal of Philosophy* 41 (1963): 336-45.

64 Peter T. Geach, "Good and Evil," *Analysis* 17 (1956): 33-42.

65 See John Atwell, "Ross and Prima Facie Duties," *Ethics* 88 (1978): 240-49; Donagan, *Theory of Morality*, 23-24.

[66] Fried, *Right and Wrong*, 7-29. Tom Beauchamp and James Childress, *Principles of Biomedical Ethics*. 4th ed. (New York: Oxford University Press, 1994). Similar criticism would also apply to the 'mixed rights' consequentialism of Ronald Dworkin discussed in chapter three.

[67] Fried, *Right and Wrong*, 7-29; Beauchamp and Childress, *Principles*, 32-36, 99-106.

[68] Fried, *Right and Wrong,* 14-18.

[69] Fried, *Right and Wrong,* 14-18.

[70] See generally Anthony Battaglia, *Toward a Reformulation of Natural Law* (New York: Seabury Press, 1981); Robert George, *In Defence of Natural Law* (Oxford: Clarendon Press, 1999).

[71] Heinrich Rommen, *The Natural Law* (St. Louis: Herder, 1947); Jacques Maritain, "Defense of Natural Ethics," *Proceedings of the American Catholic Philosophical Association* 29 (1955): 206-18; *The Degrees of Knowledge* (New York: Fordham, 1938); Henry Veatch, *For and Ontology of Morals* (Ivanston: Northwestern University Press, 1971); *Swimming Against the Current in Contemporary Philosophy* (Washington, DC: Catholic University of America Press, 1990); Ralph McInerny, *Ethica Thomistica,* Rev. ed. (Washington, DC: Catholic University of America Press, 1997); *Aquinas on Human Action* (Washington, DC: Catholic University of America Press, 1992)

[72] Heinrich A. Romme, *The Natural Law, a Study in Legal and Social History and Philosophy,* trans. Thomas R. Hanley, Liberty Fund, Indianapolis, 1998, 34.

[73] McInerny, *Ethica Thomistica,* 12-34; Henry Veatch, *Swimming Against the Current,* 293-311. See also D.J. O'Connor "Aquinas and Natural Law," in *New Studies in Ethics*, ed. W.D. Hudson (New York: St. Martin's Press, 1974), 137-59; R. A. Armstrong, *Primary and Secondary Precepts in Thomistic Natural Law Thinking* (The Hague: Martinus Nijhoff, 1966), 41-51.

[74] Anthony J. Lisska, *Aquinas's Theory of Natural Law* (Oxford: Clarendon Press, 1996), 188-200.

[75] Alan Donagan, "The Scholastic Theory of Moral Law in the Modern World," in *Aquinas*, ed. Anthony J. P. Kenny (Notre Dame: University of Notre Dame Press, 1976), 325-39.

[76] ST I-II q. 94, a. 2; For a strong affirmation of this interpretation of the question, see Thomas J. Higgins *Man As Man: The Science and Art of Ethics* (Milwaukee: Marquette University Press, 1958), 88-100, 120-26.

[77] E. M. Adams, *Ethical Naturalism and the Modern World-View* (Westport: Greenwood, 1973), 41-70.

[78] Hume himself did not consistently follow his own principle regarding the derivation of an 'ought' from an 'is'. See Jonathan Harrison, *Hume's Moral Epistemology* (New York: Oxford University Press, 1976), 110-25.

[79] G. E. Moore, *Principia Ethica* (Cambridge: Cambridge University Press, 1903, repr. 1984), 64-81.

[80] Cf. Douglas B. Rasmussen, "The Open Question Argument and the Issue of Conceivability," *Proceedings of the American Catholic Philosophical Association* 56 (1982): 162-72.

[81] McInerny, *Ethica Thomistica*, 48-54.

[82] Lisska, *Aquinas*, 195-200.

[83] John Finnis, *Natural Law and Natural Rights*. Corr. ed. (Oxford: Clarendon Press, 1982), 33-42.

[84] John Finnis, "Natural Inclinations and Natural Rights: Deriving 'Ought' from 'Is' According to Aquinas," in *Lex et Libertas*, eds. L.J. Elders and K. Hedwig (Vatican City: Pontificia Accademia di S. Tommaso, 1987), 45-47; "Natural Law and the "Is -"Ought" Question: An Invitation to Professor Veatch," *Catholic Lawyer* 26 (1981): 266-77.

[85] In Aquinas's natural law theory, something is good, right, or just "by nature" to the extent that it is in accordance with the measure of reason. See Aquinas, *Summa Theologiae* I-II, q. 71, a. 2, "The good of the human being is being in accord with reason, and human evil is being outside the order of reasonableness." As Finnis points out (*Natural Law and Natural Rights*, 36), regarding the role of practical reason in Aquinas "... for Aquinas, the way to discover what is morally right (virtue) and wrong (vice) is to ask, not what is in accordance with human nature, *but what is reasonable* (my emphasis)."

[86] Robert George, "Recent Criticism of Natural Law Theory," *University of Chicago Law Review* 55 (1988): 1410-14; Patrick Lee, Is Thomas's Natural Law Theory Naturalist?" *American Catholic Philosophical Quarterly* 71 (1998): 567-87.

[87] Charles Covell, *The Defence of Natural Law* (New York: St Martin's Press, 1992), 198-206.

[88] At least according to the most common interpretation of Aristotle's ethics, e.g., Henry Veatch, *Rational Man: A Modern Interpretation of Aristotelian Ethics* (Bloomington: Indiana University Press, 1962). For a non-naturalistic interpretation of Aristotle see John McDowell, "The Role of Eudaimonia in Aristotle's Ethics," in *Essays on Aristotle's Ethics*, ed. Amélie O. Rorty (Berkeley: University of California Press, 1980), 359-76.

[89] Thomas Aquinas, *Summa Theologica*, trans. English Dominican Fathers (New York: Benziger, 1948), I, II q. 94, a. 2. Finnis's interpretation is significantly influenced by the earlier work of Germain Grisez. See Grisez, "The First Principle of Practical Reason," in *Aquinas: A Collection of Critical Essays*, ed. Anthony J.P. Kenny, 340-82.

[90] John Finnis, *Aquinas* (Oxford: Oxford University Press, 1998), 86-94.

[91] Finnis, *Aquinas*, 86-94.

[92] Finnis, *Aquinas*, 103-10.

[93] Finnis, *Aquinas*, 103-10.

[94] Finnis, *Aquinas*, 123-29.

[95] Finnis, *Aquinas*, 79-83, 118-23.

[96] See, for example, Lee, "Thomas's Natural Law Theory," 567-87; George, *Defence of Natural Law*, 17-30.

[97] Martin Rhonheimer, *Natural Law and Practical Reason* (New York: Fordham University Press, 2000).

[98] Finnis, *Natural Law and Natural Rights*, 81-85, 92-95, 112-19; Finnis, *Fundamentals of Ethics*, 48-50, 81-82, 124.

[99] Finnis, *Natural Law and Natural Rights*, 92-95; Finnis, *Fundamentals of Ethics*, 136-44. See also George, Defence of Natural Law, 92-101; Andrew Reeve, "Incommensurability and Basic Values," *Journal of Value Inquiry* 31 (1997): 545-52.

[100] Finnis, *Natural Law and Natural Rights*, 111-18; Finnis, *Fundamentals of Ethics*, 50-53, 90-94.

[101] Reeve, "Incommensurability," 545-48.

[102] Finnis, *Fundamentals of Ethics*, 48-55.

[103] Finnis, *Natural Law and Natural Rights*, ch. III.

[104] Finnis, *Natural Law and Natural Rights*, 23; Fundamentals of Ethics, 8, 38, 52. Finnis first uses the phrase integral human fulfillment in his 1984 essay "Practical Reasoning, Human Goods and the End of Man," *Proceedings of the American Catholic Philosophical Association* 58 (1984): 23-36.

[105] Finnis, *Natural Law and Natural Rights*, ch. 4.

[106] Grisez, Finnis and Boyle, "Practical Principles," 99-151.

[107] Grisez, Finnis and Boyle, "Practical Principles," 106-8. They are called 'reflexive' because they require the exercise of making choices in our activities in order to begin to effectively actualise these goods. Ther are not 'reflective' goods in the sense that they must be actualised only though the conscious deliberation of the agent.

[108] Grisez, Finnis and Boyle, "Practical Principles," 106-8.

[109] See also the discussion of the basic human goods in Finnis, Boyle and Grisez, *Nuclear, Deterrence, Morality and Realism* (Oxford: Clarendon Press, 1987), 277-81.

[110] Benedict Ashley raises a point concerning the 'reflexive' goods. Since choice is a very part of the definition of such goods, they can only have the status of means and not ends in themselves. Choice pertains to means and not ends. Ends cannot be chosen. However, as I see it, the claim is not that *we have a choice to take or leave these goods as necessary perfections*, but rather, acts of choice are necessary to the *actualisation of those fixed perfections* in a way that the 'substantive' goods do not as such depend on the exercise of choice for some of their actualisation (although they too are further perfected in the exercise of choices we make). All of the reflexive goods therefore have the requisite quality for being considered 'final ends' since they represent non-negotiable aspects of human flourishing informing and helping to shape the nature of the choices that we ought to make. See his "What is the End of the Person? The Vision of God and Integral Human Fulfillment," in *Moral Truth and Moral Tradition*, ed. Luke Gormally (Dublin: Four Courts, 1994), 85-86.

[111] "Practical Principles, Moral Truth, and Ultimate Ends," 106-8; Finnis, *Nuclear, Deterrence, Morality and Realism*, 277-81. The good of religion is often misunderstood. This good is not religion in itself but the good that people are after when they perform some form of religious act. It is not necessary to prove the truth of any religion first prior to the intelligibility of this good.

[112] Finnis, *Natural Law and Natural Rights*, 100-3; Finnis, *Fundamentals of Ethics*, 10-19; Finnis, "Practical Reasoning, Human Goods," 23-36.

[113] Grisez, Finnis and Boyle, "Practical Principles," 103-5.

[114] Finnis, *Natural Law and Natural Rights*, 126-27; Grisez, Finnis and Boyle, "Practical Principles," 119-20.

[115] Finnis, *Natural Law and Natural Rights*, 32-33, 64-69, 77-78; Grisez, Finnis and Boyle, "Practical Principles," 103-5, 113.

[116] Finnis, *Natural Law and Natural Rights*, ch. v.

[117] Grisez, Finnis and Boyle, "Practical Principles," 119.

[118] Grisez, Finnis and Boyle, "Practical Principles," 119-20.

[119] Finnis, *Nuclear Deterrence, Morality and Realism*, 281-84; Finnis, *Fundamentals of Ethics*, 71-73; Grisez, Finnis and Boyle, "Practical Principles," 121-25.

[120] Finnis, *Aquinas*, 72-78.

[121] Finnis, *Nuclear Deterrence, Morality and Realism*, 281-84; Finnis, *Fundamentals of Ethics*, 71-73; Grisez, Finnis and Boyle, "Practical Principles," 121-25.

[122] Grisez, Finnis and Boyle, "Practical Principles," 128; Finnis, *Nuclear Deterrence, Morality and Realism*, 283.

[123] Benedict Ashley raises a thought provoking point pertaining to just what may be said to provide the unity in any natural (contra supernatural) end for humanity if there are several basic goods that can be said to function as their own 'sovereign ends' without a overarching substantive unifying principle. Without it, Ashley contends, there is not a teleology but several teleologies— hence the coining of the term 'polyteleologism'. A full response would take us

too far into a realm of inquiry not warranted for the purposes of this work. The following analogy (suffering the inevitable imperfection associated with this device) must therefore suffice as indicative of a possible answer to the problem. We can recognise a *single teleology* for the human person, human flourishing (integral human fulfilment), as a sought after end state, and yet retain the idea of an array of goods as intelligible *per se* ends *that may yet* (in a non-reductionistic fashion) further promote the pursuance of a *more complete good.* That more complete end, may be regarded as a 'harmonious symphony' comprised of several parts for different instruments. Integral human fulfilment is like a human symphony with practical reasoning providing the orchestration of the basic goods as individual instruments. The harmony, of a blending of the different sounds generated by the different instruments, is *more complete, more perfect,* than the contributions of the different instruments. Nevertheless the whole symphony is dependent on the performance of each of the orchestrated parts and cannot be adequately realised without them. The whole of the symphony does not cancel out the contribution of each instrument, and when each instrument is focused upon in terms of its own contribution, it can intelligibly be viewed, not merely a means to something else, but something worthwhile for its own sake. The symphony does not simply represent a formal unity that could exist, say, between different lines of notation on a score sheet written for different parts without reference to one another. Rather, a symphony stands for an integrative harmony between basic human goods, a perfectibility, of many possible sounds coming together via intelligent orchestration. Practical reason itself provides the orchestration within the limits of what it is possible and worthwhile for the human person to intelligibly strive towards in guiding human conduct. See his , "End of the Human Person," 70.

[124] Grisez, Finnis and Boyle, "Practical Principles," 128-29; Finnis, *Nuclear Deterrence, Morality and Realism*, 283-84.

[125] Finnis, *Natural Law and Natural Rights*, ch. v.

[126] Finnis, *Natural Law and Natural Rights*, 103-5.

[127] Finnis, *Natural Law and Natural Rights*, 106-9.

[128] Finnis, *Natural Law and Natural Rights*, 111-17.

[129] Finnis, *Natural Law and Natural Rights*, 118-25.

[130] John Finnis, *Moral Absolutes: Tradition, Revision, and Truth* (Washington, DC: Catholic University of America Press, 1991), 1-5.

[131] Finnis, *Moral Absolutes*, 31-57.

[132] Finnis, *Nuclear Deterrence, Morality and Realism*, 297-319.

[133] Finnis, *Natural Law and Natural Rights*, 100-29.

[134] Finnis, *Moral Absolutes*, 60-63.

[135] See George, *Defence of the Natural Law*, 92-101.

[136] Since Finnis does not ultimately adopt the qualifier innocent, for sound reasons, to be explained in chapter five, the reader should not think that the omission of the qualifier is unintended at this juncture. See Finnis, *Nuclear Deterrence, Morality and Realism,* 297-319; Germain Grisez, "Towards a Consistent Natural Law Ethics of Killing," *American Journal of Jurisprudence* 15 (1970): 64-97.

[137] See Finnis, *Nuclear Deterrence, Morality and Realism,* 297-319, on detailed arguments as to why it is always wrong to intentionally kill another human being. These arguments apply the ten criteria of practical reasonableness to the intrinsic good of human life.

[138] See Joseph Boyle, "An Absolute Rule Approach," in *A Companion to Bioethics*, eds. Helga Kuhse and Peter Singer (Malden: Blackwell, 1998), 72-79.

[139] Jean Porter, "Basic Goods and the Human Good," *Thomist* 47 (1993): 27-49.

[140] Porter, "Basic Goods," 37-38.

[141] Porter, "Basic Goods," 35-36.

[142] Grisez, Finnis and Boyle, "Practical Principles," 108-9.

[143] See Gerard V. Bradley and Robert P. George, "The New Natural Law Theory: A Reply to Jean Porter," *American Journal of Jurisprudence* 39 (1994): 303-15.

[144] Bradley and George, "New Natural Law," 303-15.

[145] James M. DuBois, commenting on an earlier draft of this chapter.

[146] Finnis, *Fundamentals of Ethics*, 70-78.

[147] I adapted this line of argumentation to support Finnis from insights gleaned from Alan Gerwith, *Reason and Morality* (Chicago: Chicago University Press, 1978), 46-51, and from Berys Gaut "The Structure of Practical Reason," in *Ethics and Practical Reason*, eds. Garrett Cullity and Berys Gaunt (Oxford: Clarendon Press, 1997), 161-88.

[148] Example derived from Robert George, "Recent Criticism of Natural Law Theory," *University of Chicago Law Review* 55 (1988): 1390-91.

[149] Lloyd L. Weinreb, *Natural Law and Justice* (Cambridge: Harvard University Press, 1987); Russell Hittinger, *A Critique of the New Natural Law Theory* (Notre Dame: University of Notre Dame Press, 1987).

[150] Weinreb, *Natural Law and Justice,* 109-113.

[151] Hittinger, *Critique of the New Natural Law Theory,* 44-45.

[152] George, "Natural Law and Human Nature," in *Natural Law Theory: Contemporary Essays*, ed. Robert P. George (Oxford: Clarendon Press, 1992), 31-41.

[153] Mark C. Murphy, "Self-Evidence, Human Nature, and Natural Law," *American Catholic Philosophical Quarterly* 69 (1995): 471-84.

[154] See Finnis, "Scepticism, Self-Refutation, and the Good of Truth," in *Law, Morality, and Society*, eds. Paul Hacker and Joseph Raz (Oxford: Clarendon Press, 1977), 247-67.

[155] See also the following for an excellent small book arguing for possibility of self evidency in practical reasoning: Renford Bambrough, *Moral Scepticism and Moral Knowledge* (London: Routledge, 1981).

[156] Garth L. Hallett, *Greater Good: The Case for Proportionalism* (Washington, DC: Georgetown University Press, 1995), 20-29; Robert McKim and Peter Simpson, "On the Alleged Incoherence of Consequentialism," *New Scholasticism* 62 (1988): 349-52. See also David Luban, "Incommensurable Values, Rational Choice, and Moral Absolutes," *Cleveland State Law Review* 38 (1990): 65-83; Matthew H. Kramer, "How Not to Oppugn Consequentialism," *Philosophical Quarterly* 64 (1996): 213-20, the latter arguing that the Socratic choice to suffer wrong can be perfectly well expressed in consequentialist terms!

[157] Hallett, *Greater Good,* 20-21.

[158] McKim and Simpson, "Alleged Incoherence," 350.

[159] Porter, "Basic Goods," 39-42; Hittinger, *Critique of the New Natural Law Theory,* 74-79; Russell Pannier, "Finnis and the Commensurability of Goods," *New Scholasticism* 61 (1987): 427-39; R. George Wright, "Does Free Speech Jurisprudence Rest on a Mistake? Implications of the Commensurability Debate," *Loyola of Los Angeles Law Review* 23 (1990): 763-90.

[160] Pannier, "Finnis and the Commensurability of Goods," 443-44.

[161] Wright, "Does Free Speech Jurisprudence Rest on a Mistake", 72-73.

[162] Joseph Boyle and John Finnis, "Incoherence and Consequentialism (or Proportionalism) – A Rejoinder," *American Catholic Philosophical Quarterly* 64 (1990): 271-77.

[163] Boyle and Finnis, "Incoherence and Consequentialism," 273-74.

[164] See John Finnis, "Intention and Side-Effects," *in Liability and Responsibility*, eds. R. G. Frey and Christopher W. Morris (Cambridge: Cambridge University Press, 1992), 32-64.

[165] See Finnis, *Natural Law and Natural Rights*, 106-9.

[166] Hittinger, *Critique, passim*; Henry Veatch, "Review of Natural Law and Natural Rights," *American Journal of Jurisprudence* 26 (1981): 247-59; Henry Veatch, "Natural Law and the Is-Ought Question (reprint from 1981)," *in Swimming Against the Current in Contemporary Philosophy* (Washington, DC: Catholic University of America Press, 1990), 293-311; George W. Constable, "A Criticism of 'Practical Principles, Moral truth, and Ultimate Ends'," *American Journal of Jurisprudence* 34 (1987): 19-22; Ralph MacInery, *Ethica Thomistica;* Vernon J. Bourke, "Review of John Finnis' Natural Law and Natural Rights," *American Journal of Jurisprudence* 24 (1981): 243-47. The most notable target of this line of critique is the fallacious nature of the naturalistic fallacy. It states that nature contains within it a normative anthropology—ethics is discovered in nature which itself contains the 'normative directedness'.

[167] See Finnis's "Practical Reasoning, Human Goods and the End of Man," 23-36.

[168] See Germain Grisez, "Natural Law and Natural Inclinations: Some Comments and Clarifications," *New Scholasticism* 61 (1987): 307-20;

Germain Grisez, "The Structures of Practical Reason: Some Comments and Clarifications," *Thomist* 52 (1988): 269-91.

[169] Finnis, *Natural Law and Natural Rights*, 34.

[170] George, *Defence of the Natural Law*, 83-91.

[171] George, *Defence of the Natural Law*, 83-91.

Chapter Five

Natural Law and the Ethics of Self-Killing

Introduction

In the previous chapter, I have argued for a defence of a natural law approach as a credible and sustainable foundation for ethical theory. I argued both negatively and then positively. Negatively, I argued that critical systemic weaknesses in both consequentialist and deontological approaches to ethical theory render such theories fundamentally flawed in their structural underpinnings. I argued that the task for natural law was to incorporate some of the valid insights afforded by those theories whilst overcoming major weaknesses. Positively, I argued that the natural law approach of John Finnis provided ethical theory with a credible foundationalism rooted in the notion of basic incommensurable human goods. I specifically argued that such a foundation gave a solid basis for a reasoned defence of the notion that there are indeed certain concrete exceptionless moral norms that can be said to exist as 'moral roadblocks', in order to prevent the performance of certain kinds of action that would damage or impede the status of the basic human goods.

Building on groundwork of the previous chapter, this chapter seeks to work out the implications of this framework of basic human goods as it pertains to the concrete problem of intentional killing, whether of self or another. In particular, this chapter will seek to justify a number of concepts that will serve to support the existence of a concrete exceptionless moral norm, namely, that it is always a serious moral wrong to intentionally act to kill a human being (whether self or another), regardless of a further appeal to consequences or motive.

Worth of Human Life

Life as a Basic Human Good

In the preceding chapter, human life was classified by John Finnis as a basic human good. As such, its status was described as being self-evident.[1] The recognition of the status of the good is not, as such, derived from some more foundational descriptive premise such that we can, say, prove its status by means of a syllogism, where the goodness of life is introduced as some kind of middle term (e.g., P1 human beings tend to preserve their lives; P2 life is good; C therefore, human beings ought to preserve their lives).[2]

As an intelligible human good, capable of being valued for its own sake (*per se*), and not merely instrumentally (as a means to some further end), life is a good that is not capable of being deduced or derived from the recognition of other prior goods.[3] In grasping the intrinsic worth of human life, a person is able to transparently understand that it is a basic good not only for that person but also for all persons who are of our kind—a basic human good.[4]

Due to the operation of practical reason itself as a basic human good, this 'architectonic' good directs the exercise of fully reasoned choice relating to the array of basic human goods (and other, non-basic, instrumental or auxiliary goods).[5] Following from our grasp of human life as a basic incommensurable good, it cannot be practically reasonable both to affirm that (a) 'human life is a basic human good', and (b) that 'human life *qua* human life can be intentionally acted against to its destruction'. If life is a basic human good, to seek to directly attack that good is to misunderstand its basic status as the kind of human good that it is.[6]

It follows that in making a choice that seeks to act against the good of human life, the agent is making a practically unreasonable choice, practically unreasonable because the choice instantiates a stunting of the reflexive good of practical reasonableness itself (in its various requirements, e.g., the Pauline Principle 'do not do evil that good may come of it'), and thus represents a failure to deliberate practically in a fully reasonable way concerning the impact of the choice made (and executed) on the basic human goods (the primary constituents of human flourishing).[7]

If life is truly such a basic human good, then a choice to seek to treat it *merely* as an instrumentally valuable good would be to unreasonably discount its worth, and would therefore represent an act of unreasonable (hence wrongful) choice. A morally right choice needs to respect all the criteria of practical reasonableness in the making and execution of a choice if that choice is to pass muster in the 'practical reasonableness stakes'.[8]

Of course, human life does have a certain instrumental quality as well, since it is utilised in the pursuance of all other goods. Participation in all other goods is dependent on the person's continuing participation in that basic good. What is important to grasp here, however, is not that life cannot have an important instrumental dimension, for we need to engage this good in the pursuit of all projects, but that in seeking to utilise it instrumentally it ought to be respected in and through its own valuational status as a good of basic incommensurable worth, and, thus, should not be directly acted against.[9]

Having stated that the good of human life is a basic self-evident good for human persons, does that mean that analysis must end there? In brief, no. The self-evidence of the basic human good *qua* good does not mean that dialectical reasoning cannot be engaged in to *indirectly support* the practical reasonableness of respecting the good of human life in the deliberative choices that persons make concerning their actions.[10] It is to the use of such dialectical reasoning, supportive of the status of human life as such a basic human good, that I now turn to consider.

Only Personal Life?

In chapter two, several challenges were posed regarding the status of the good of human life. Human life itself is often perceived only as an instrumental good at the service of the person. It is said that human life, as such, is not a basic human good, and is merely a necessary means utilised in the promotion of other goods. When human life itself fails to live up to our expected requirements, it can ultimately be dispensed with. Merely being a living member of the species, *Homo sapiens*, is considered to offer no valid ground for ascribing to all humans an 'inviolability' that protects them from being intentionally killed.[11]

Lying behind such accounts are forms of threshold sufficiency criteria used to establish whether or not individual human beings are able to qualify as human persons. On one side of the threshold is considered to be a human life worthy of being valued since it instantiates feature(s) X...Z. A human Life with feature(s) X...Z is alone considered worthwhile, since it instantiates that which is sufficient to attribute real value to human existence. Thus, there are effectively two primary categories of human life to be identified: 'personal life' manifesting feature(s) X...Z, and 'non-personal life' that is incapable of manifesting feature(s) X...Z. Human life is valued as long as it is capable of instantiating the feature(s) sufficient to constitute personal life. Mere non-personal life (not worth living and thus not worthy of full protection from intentional killing) is thus heavily contrasted with personal life (worth living and thus alone worthy of full protection from intentional killing).

Jonathan Glover, James Rachels, Ronald Dworkin, Peter Singer, Helga Kuhse, and John Harris all subscribe to the notion that what is truly valued is not human life as such but personal life, life that is capable of manifesting the sufficient feature(s) X...Z—rationality, self-awareness, consciousness, etc., or some composite thereof.[12] They therefore identify certain attributes that alone are sufficient to warrant the classification of being a person. The voice of John Locke can be seen to echo strongly in such approaches, for he defined a person as "a thinking intelligent being that has reason and reflection and can consider itself as itself."[13]

In the conclusions reached by the above-mentioned authors, all would argue that patients suffering from advanced forms of senility, or the permanently comatose, cannot be regarded as persons, and will not therefore be classified as being possessed of lives truly worth living. Since they are not properly capable of being categorised as persons, they cannot be accorded the same protections that we ascribe to those we do identify as persons.[14]

The principle difficulty with such theories of the worth of human life, however, stems from *an inadequate justification* upon which to make such a determination that an individual human life Y *must contain* those sufficient feature(s) X…Z in order to qualify for the status of being regarded by others as a 'person'.[15]

With regard to non-philosophical usage, people in general do not make a distinction between attributions of the status 'person' and attributions of the status 'human being'. Basic patterns of usage point not to the widespread understanding of being a person as actually having 'self-awareness … X …Z' but rather to a widespread understanding that being a person is treated synonymously with *being a particular kind of being* (by virtue of his or her membership in that distinct class of being). 'Y is a human being', and not, say, a horse or a cat, is interchangeable with 'Y is a person', since 'Y is recognisably one of us'.[16]

This assertion of an interchangeable understanding between 'person' and 'human being', is bourn out by the prevailing definitions offered by the *Oxford English Dictionary*, where the noun 'person' is viewed as referring to (i) an individual human being, and (ii) human beings distinguished from other things, especially lower animals. Of course it is right to be wary of dictionary definitions. They are clearly not definitive. Nevertheless, I think that the patterns of usage witnessed by the *OED* are supportive evidence for the proposition that people generally do not use 'person' and 'human being' to refer to *differences in kind* between 'human persons' and 'human non-persons', such that the former are entitled to have their lives regarded as worthy of being fully protected by negative prohibitions whilst the latter are not.[17]

Consider further a common reaction to patients suffering from advanced senility, or to patients in a permanent vegetative state. Often we will say that the patient is in a profoundly damaged/disabled condition, or that a patient's quality of life is at a minimum, and so on. Often we will be deeply disturbed by the gap that exists between the condition of the patient and his or her flourishing as a human being. No one (except the perverted) would want to be placed in such a condition. Human life is very imperfectly manifested in such a condition.[18] Yet, it simply does not follow that we would generally seek to infer from this debilitated state of being that the patient has ceased to be a person and has therefore undergone *such a change in kind* that we now regard the patient as a 'non-person'.[19]

Our *ready ability* to identify with 'human non-persons' in a way that we do not seem able to identify with 'non-human non-persons' seems to offer additional testimony as to why we continue to view such 'human non-persons' as persons *simpliciter* despite their profoundly damaged state of being.[20] This ready ability to make such identification helps to make sense of the observation that people can and do seek to defend and promote human life without seeking an explanation for protecting or preserving human life in those who are profoundly damaged *beyond an appeal to that good itself* (i.e., when asked to explain actions such as continuing to feed a severely demented Alzheimer's patient).[21] As such a basic good, an indispensable constituent of our being, human life itself is capable of providing an adequate explanation for rendering actions of this kind properly intelligible to us in a way that actions of this kind can not be explained for 'non-human non-persons'.[22]

Still, it can be argued that the above account is simply the product of muddled conventional thinking, conventional thinking spurred on by the impact of understandable but ultimately irrational sentiment concerning the state of patients in those kinds of condition.[23] There is, however, good philosophical reason to affirm that those pre-philosophical apprehensions that we have concerning the uses of the term 'person' and 'human being', are indeed sound. This can be achieved by positing a credible account of what it is to be a human person by virtue of being a member of the species, *Homo sapiens*. It explains why our basic identification with profoundly damaged 'human non-persons' is not merely a product of convention, sympathy, or compassion, but is ultimately ontological in nature.[24]

Aquinas quoted and affirmed the definition of what it is to be a person, as stated by Boethius. A person is "an individual substance of a rational nature."[25] The definition offered by Boethius is inherently more satisfactory than the definition offered by John Locke, for it is able to account for our understanding of what can be termed our 'species solidarity'—a solidarity that points against the classification or treatment of profoundly damaged human beings as sub-personal (*semihominem*) and whose lives are consequently judged to be of less worth than the rest of us.[26]

Rather than focusing on the idea that the *individual must be actually rational* (conscious, self-aware, etc.) in order to be thought of as a person (as with John Locke), this definition clearly points to a second basic understanding of what it is to be a person.[27] A person is an *individual who is a member of a class of being characterised by those attributes*. When we reflect on the nature of our species *Homo sapiens,* it is clear that our species is a kind that is rational, self-aware, and so on. This holds true even if some members of that species are incapable of rational thought, lack self-awareness, and so on.[28]

Jenny Teichman supports this central line of argumentation when she states that "the idea that a creature can have a rational nature without being rational … does not appear to me to be any more intrinsically problematic than the idea that all cattle are mammals—even the bulls."[29] Teichman, therefore, challenges the idea that the way in which we classify our own kind ought to be treated any differently from the way we classify other things. Does a dog cease to be classified as a dog when it has lost its bark? Does a pail cease to be classified as a pail when it is no longer capable of holding water due a large hole on its bottom? If not, why should the very senile or the permanently comatose be classified as non-persons even if they are deeply defective with respect to an exercisable capacity for rational thought or a capacity for self-awareness?[30]

We can therefore credibly argue that 'non-persons' in a state of severe impairment are still fully members of the same species to which we all belong. The very senile or permanently comatose do not become members of a different species. Through their 'natural kind' they still speak to us as members of the same species via a common shared human nature and continue to make many of the same moral claims upon us, for example, a right not to be intentionally killed by other persons in acts of non-consensual euthanasia. [31]

When Aristotle stated that we are by nature 'rational animals', he was not making a statement particular to those fully functional members of the human species at the height of their faculties. He was, rather, defining the essential universal nature of the species that we are *qua* species.[32] He was pointing out what the nature of being a member of the human species entails simply by being a recognisable member of that species. It is a credible principle of reasoning to state that by virtue of the basic kind of being a thing is, the archetypal characteristics of that kind can be ascribed to any member of that kind, *even though not every member of that kind, may, as a matter of fact, actually manifest those archetypal characteristics.*[33] Therefore, it can be stated that all members of our species can justifiably be said to participate and share in the rightful protection offered to the archetypal members of our species because of what they essentially are, *irrespective of the particular circumstances of any given member.*[34]

Why then should being profoundly damaged detract from the moral status of certain human beings if they are by virtue of their nature as fully human as the most fully flourishing members of our species? Such damage does not render them a member of a different species, for differences between humans concerning levels of intelligence, levels of consciousness, levels of coherence or incoherence in thoughts, etc. *are all questions of degree and not of kind.*[35] It is not a question of a decline in, or non-presence of, an ability that is capable of rendering a *substantial change* in the nature of a human being. Rather, it is only the event of death itself that is capable of bringing about a substantial change in the kind of thing that we are. It is death that brings about a fundamental ontological change in status, for a corpse is no *longer an individual with a human kind of nature.*[36]

By virtue of the status of being a member of the human species, then, that status can indeed be said to be one of being a person *simpliciter*. All persons are entitled to the same basic types of immunity from intentional killing as are accorded the archetypal mature members of the species. It can, in consequence, never be morally justified to intentionally kill human beings on the ground that individual lives are judged to be insufficiently worthwhile in order to qualify for the kinds of protection that Rachels, Dworkin, Singer, Kuhse, and Harris would reserve only for humans who are actually capable of individually exercising those attributes of our kind.

Better off Dead?

Central to the claims of supporters of suicide, and assisted suicide, is the claim that we can justifiably argue that it makes sense to say that a person would be 'better off dead' rather than continuing to live, say, a life of severely diminished quality. Such value judgements, it is said, are comparatively sound.[37] Yet, how is it possible for death to benefit the person who dies? Death destroys the person. How can we produce a benefit, therefore, if we destroy the self, the potential beneficiary?

One of the commonest lines of argumentation made here is termed the 'deprivation account'. Key exponents include Thomas Nagel, Harry Silverstein, and Fred Feldman.[38] The argument advanced basically trades on a parallel question concerning death, arguing that a person can be *posthumously harmed* by his or her future loss, even though death means that the person is no longer actually in existence to experience it.[39] For example, suppose Shakespeare's life would have included more literary achievement if he had lived for a few more years. Because literary achievement is a good, Shakespeare can be said to have had a less good life overall than he would have had if he had lived longer. Living a less good life is a harm to the person. By excluding those future possible achievements, then, Shakespeare's death can be said to be a harm to him, for it prevented a life that would have been better than it was.[40]

Trading on this parallel, it is then argued that death can be a benefit in a comparison of future possible lives. Suppose a person's life would go on containing severe suffering and pain. That person would be better off having a shorter life than having a life of stretched out misery. Since living a better life is a benefit, it is said that living the shorter life, here, is a benefit, since it is the better life. By interfering with the infliction of evils, the person's death can therefore be said to be a genuine benefit to him or her, since it prevents a worse life being lived.[41]

By engaging in such comparisons of future lives, the conclusion is reached by deprivation theorists that death is only an evil for the person if the future lost is one that offers better prospects for the person than death itself. Death itself is typically conceived of as the destruction of the self; the non-existence of the self; the non-state of non-being.[42]

How can we respond to this assessment that death can be said to benefit a patient when the patient's future prospects in life seem so grim? The non-state that death brings in its wake is seen as being preferable to the continuance of life. Yet are persons who make and act upon such calculations objectively justified in opting for death? Can it truly be a rational act for a person to choose the destruction of self over the continuation of self, even a self racked by the severe impositions of pain and suffering?[43]

Philip Devine attempts to criticise the logicality of a decision to self-kill by stating what he considers to be the obscurity of what we can know about death.[44] He argues that if rational choice requires that a person know what he or she is choosing (a leap in the dark not sufficing), then it cannot be rationally possible to intentionally choose death because of the "opaqueness of death."[45] As Devine says, " ... a precondition of rational choice is that one knows *what* one is choosing, either by experience or by the testimony of others who have experienced it or something very like it."[46] Death cannot be rationally commensurated against, for we do not know what we are comparing life to. Thus, contrary to the argument posited by Ronald Dworkin, James Rachels, and Peter Singer, in chapter two, life cannot simply be judged an overall evil and acted against by intentionally embracing death, for the 'overall evil of life' cannot be rationally traded in for the 'opaqueness of death'. For Devine, choosing death is simply akin to leaping into the bowels of radical uncertainty that cannot function as a useful ground for objective rational choice.[47]

Whilst I agree with Devine's conclusion that intentionally opting for death is ultimately an unreasonable act, I think his reasoning for supporting that conclusion lacks credibility, since the epistemic premise of his argument here is faulty. Firstly, it can be stated that even if death really is shrouded in mystery, it is sometimes possible to make rational decisions without our knowing exactly what we are choosing. Consider a quiz programme in which the contestant is asked to take a fixed prize of cash or a mystery gift. The participant opts for the mystery gift. This risk seems perfectly reasonable.[48] Can this not function as an analogy for a patient faced with the prospect of suffering and pain who opts for the 'mystery' of death?

Secondly, I crucially do not think that the mystery option is the actual choice placed before us, for I think that we can have sufficient relevant knowledge about death to understand important implications of the choice being opted for. Unlike Devine, I think that the unreasonableness of opting for death arises precisely because we do know enough about what is being chosen to make it an objectively irrational choice.[49]

What we can know about death is that it results in the destruction of the self. There will no longer be a human being in existence. There will be no carrier of value or disvalue. There will be no subject in existence that is capable of bearing any of the kinds of predication typical of living human beings. Death is an event that results in the non-being of the human person that was.[50] Unlike Devine, I would argue that an intention to bring about this non-state, given the relevant (if incomplete) knowledge we have about it, points to the incoherence behind the idea that death can really be said to be a benefit for the person who is dead, as argued for by contemporary deprivation authors.[51]

When we assert that a person is harmed or benefited by a state, this requires that there is *actually a subject in existence* who is capable of being the bearer of the value or disvalue. If a person must actually exist in order to be

183

the subject bearer of harms and benefits that happen, then how can there be said to be a subject who is capable of being benefited posthumously by his or her death? This line of argumentation against deprivation accounts (that death can be a benefit) is convincingly argued for by John Donnelly and J.L.A. Garcia. If a person succeeds in killing himself or herself, there can be no betterment ascribed to the person. For Donnelly, it is muddled to argue that a person can be said to be posthumously benefited or harmed if the person must first be destroyed as a prerequisite for the benefit.[52]

The irrationality of thinking that death can be a benefit for a person is further addressed by Garcia.[53] If it is good to be without pain, as indeed it is under most circumstances, this presupposes the existence of the subject in order to instantiate that good (any good). If a person can be 'better off dead', then the continued existence of the person must continue after death. Yet no one on the basis of reason alone can justifiably claim that death can allow for the continuation of the person *qua* person. To realise goods and to minimise evils requires the presence of that single constant, a live human being, who can possibly make sense of such value statements. For Garcia, therefore, it is quite illicit to jump from the evaluation of means to minimise, or be free from, the evils of suffering and pain, to the conclusion that the destruction of the subject itself can make a person in any meaningful sense better off. Consequently, all that can reasonably be done is to *seek to benefit persons in their present lives*, that is to improve as best we can the extent of their flourishing within the framework of humanitarian means available at our disposal.[54]

Contrary to Donnelly and Garcia, Nagel argues that there are plausible exceptions that render such accounts sensible to us, notwithstanding the destruction of the subject. For example, Nagel argues that a person can be harmed posthumously by having his or her reputation harmed, and can therefore be said to be posthumously benefited by having his or her reputation restored. When all is said and done, therefore, it seems that we can reasonably talk of 'benefiting the dead'.[55]

In reply, it can be stated that there are other plausible explanations of what is meant by the dead 'being subjected' to harms and benefits that do not presuppose that the dead can actually be said to experience those harms or benefits. Thus, to take Nagel's example concerning posthumous reputation, we can plausibly state that it is the *reputation of a former person* that is harmed, say, by an act of slander, and not a person as such.[56] Similarly we can say that the reputation of a former person is benefited by nice things being said about the former person. The living seek to protect their reputations because they, whilst alive, identify with them and realise that *the reputations* they identify with are capable of being posthumously harmed or benefited. Such an unforced account of the notion of posthumous reputation, and similar ways of speaking, means that we can indeed decline to withdraw the charge of incoherence behind the idea that a person who has 'ceased to be' can truly be said to be harmed or benefited.[57]

If the above arguments are sound, (i) that we can have enough relevant knowledge of what death would entail, and (ii) that the dead cannot really be said to be harmed or benefited, then I think they severely undermine the contemporary deprivation accounts of death.

Contrary to those accounts, I would argue that it is death *per se* that is really the objective evil for us, not because it deprives us of a prospective future of overall good judged better than the alternative of non-being. It cannot be about harm to a former person who has ceased to exist, for no person actually suffers from the subsequent non-participation. Rather, death in itself is an evil to us because it ontologically destroys the current existent subject—it is the ultimate in metaphysical lightening strikes.[58] The evil of death is truly an ontological evil bourn by the person who already exists, independently of calculations about better or worse possible lives. Such an evil need not be consciously experienced in order to be an evil *for the kind of being* a human person is. Death is an evil because of the *change in kind* it brings about, a change that is destructive of the type of entity that we essentially are. Anything, whether caused naturally or caused by human intervention (intentional or unintentional) that drastically interferes in the process of maintaining the person in existence is an objective evil for the person. What is crucially at stake here, and is dialectically supportive of the self-evidency of the basic good of human life, is that death is a radical interference with the current life process of the kind of being that we are. In consequence, death itself can be credibly thought of as a 'primitive evil' for all persons, regardless of the extent to which they are currently or prospectively capable of participating in a full array of the goods of life.[59]

Concerning willed human actions, it is justifiable to state that any intentional rejection of human life itself cannot therefore be warranted since it is an expression of an ultimate disvalue for the subject, namely, the destruction of the present person; a radical ontological Rubicon that we cannot begin to objectively weigh against the travails of life in a rational manner. This is, I think, a key insight that flows from Immanuel Kant's opposition to suicide referred to in the history chapter. To deal with the sources of disvalue (pain, suffering, etc.) we seek to irrationally destroy the person, the very source and condition of all human possibility. Michael Wreen expresses well this valid Kantian insight when he states that suicide is "... the repudiation, the ontological repudiation of our very humanity ... a repudiation that is metaphysically possible only for humanity."[60]

Quality of Life Assessment

A common link is drawn between a patient's right to refuse treatment and the right of a patient to assess the quality of his or her own life. Such a right, it is claimed, is tantamount to an assessment of the worth of life, such that a patient with a low life quality can commit suicide, be assisted in that goal, or be euthanised.[61] Here, I would argue, that this train of thought posits a mistaken frame of reference for the moral evaluation of the duties we have towards the preservation of human life. It carries plausibility, firstly, because it trades partly on the looseness or 'open texture' of language, and secondly, because it expands upon an appropriate sphere of decision making in which patients are indeed intimately involved in the assessment of the burdens and benefits of treatment.[62]

No reasonable person would say that a life of less complete, less perfect, human flourishing is better than a life of more complete, more prefect, human flourishing.[63] A life endowed with more flourishing, that realises more profusion in various horizons of possibility, is a fuller life than a life that is impaired in its ability to flourish. In that sense there can be said to be more 'quality', a greater instantiation of good, in the former than the latter.[64] But it is an illicit move to go from that sense of flourishing and its diminishment, to the conclusion that a life is not worth living, for there is quite simply no critical threshold that can be crossed, such that a diminishment in flourishing ceases to instantiate any inherent good genuinely worth preserving.[65]

An appeal can be made (and usually is) to various forms of consequentialism to justify the conclusion that certain lives are not worth living. But this, for reasons already mentioned in chapter three, is incoherent. Consequentialism purports to offer an answer by posing a common denominator to reckon with these factors, but the complexity of human value, most significantly the incommensurability of certain goods, defies all such levelling attempts.[66]

W.D. Ross, Charles Fried, Ronald Dworkin, and other proponents of mixed consequentialist systems, simply propose *prima facie* duties without explaining exactly what it is about the nature of the process of human reasoning that determines the strength of certain values, such that the duty to respect them is overridden in some situations, but not in others.[67] Perhaps an appeal to convention may provide some sort of guide. However, this just retreats into a form of subjectivity taking comfort in fact that a practice may be widely spread. This will not do when we consider the course of human history that has thrown up radically evil forms of convention, e.g., eugenics, mass killing, etc.[68]

Again, if a life is judged not worth living, what is it about death that is supposed to be judged objectively commensurable to staying alive? How is it calculated? Perhaps intuition can attempt to supply an answer. However, a thoroughgoing appeal to intuition here simply negates the ability we have to use practical reason to inform our decision making and guide our choices. But this will not do, for it is tantamount to saying that in the very situations where human reason is most crucially needed it is of no use to us! In reality, such a thoroughgoing appeal to intuition readily degenerates into a form of *a posteriori* rationalisation to justify choices already opted for on the basis of sub-rational emotion.[69]

Whilst use of language sometimes leads us to suspect that lives are often evaluated in terms of their overall worth, we should nevertheless be very suspicious of attempting to extrapolate from statements that (i) 'doing X is a valuable part of A's life and that A's life is diminished by not being able to do X', to (ii) 'A's life is no longer worth living and it is therefore right to intentionally end it because A cannot do X'. Such inferences only seem plausible because there is a shift in the correct locus of evaluation, especially in the framework of medical decision making, from the *worthwhileness of certain treatments* to the *worthwhileness of certain lives*.[70]

The correct question to be focused upon, contra Ronald Dworkin, Helga Kuhse, and John Harris, should be whether a proposed treatment for a patient would be worthwhile; not whether a patient's life would be worthwhile. The distinction between the worthwhileness of certain treatments and the worthwhileness of certain lives is no mere semantic ploy, for it legitimately seeks to address what the scope of decision making concerning the preservation of life and health should be. In doing so, it provides for a *sphere of delimitation* where patient choice concerning treatment can reasonably be made.[71]

The responsibility for safeguarding and promoting the good of health lies primarily with the patient and not with the medical profession. That patient assessment should be centred squarely on the impact of proposed treatments, however, is not tantamount to endorsing the idea that we can truly judge the worth of our own lives. The capacity to choose crucially brings with it *the responsibility* of making choices that do in fact serve to promote rather than undermine the ends of integral human flourishing. Given the diversity of choices that are consistent with human flourishing, there will often be considerable leeway in a patient's deliberation. Yet, leeway does not endorse license, and there are limits on the shaping of reasonable choice concerning the refusal or withdrawal of treatments.[72]

The non-consequentialist framework being espoused here is not one of naïve vitalism, for in many cases it is indeed licit to withhold or withdraw life-preserving treatment.[73] More precisely, there cannot be said to be a duty to undergo a treatment that is not worthwhile (offering no reasonable hope of benefit to the patient), or that is considered medically futile.[74] Without offering any exclusive listing of factors, Germain Grisez and Joseph Boyle helpfully list several factors that would offer reasonable grounds for justifying the withdrawal or non-provision of a medical treatment: a risky or experimental treatment; avoidance of significant further pain or trauma associated with treatment; the impact that a treatment may have on the patient's participation in activities or experiences the patient values; conflicts with deep-seated moral or religious principles to which the patient is committed to; a treatment psychologically repelling or repugnant to the patient; compelling burdens on family or finances.[75]

Such a framework for decision making can indeed be abused and can result in the refusal of treatments that would seem to offer considerable benefits to patients without significant burden being attached to them. This will come as no surprise, and indeed can result in decisions that are directly suicidal in nature. However, the question that needs to be faced here is that there need be no essential incompatibility between, one the one hand, placing severe restraints on interference with the persistent choice of patients, even though they are intentionally suicidal, and yet, on the other, still uphold the respect due to the good of human life.[76]

It is a 'brute fact' that interference would be visited with all manner of difficulty, not least the fact that successful treatment usually requires the active co-operation of the patient. The problems that would be visited by enforcing treatments against the vehement will of a patient would be immense. Effects on the morale of the patient, family, and professions would be considerable. One only has to consider the impact of force feeding against a person's will to see the traumatic means that may have to be resorted to. Further than that, the imposition of such an overt act of countermanding a patient's decision, would serve only to undermine the already pressed reputation of the medical profession in the eyes of the public, suspicious of paternalistic interventionism by physicians, and with it, a concomitant perception of disregard for the dignity of the individual patient.[77]

For those reasons then, the general decision not to overrule a patient's suicidal intent to end life by refusal or withdrawal of treatment, other than by means of, say, persuasion, will sometimes happen. Yet, this does not amount to a policy of condoning the aiding and abetting of a suicide. Rather, it represents a principled decision to intentionally act for a good objective, the common good of patients, and the community generally. This good objective being acted for may practically permit the consequence of resultant death as an unintended yet fair side effect of a good intention. This is a sensible and principled way of responding to the reality, particularly in the context of medicine, that in order to prevent the execution, even of a serious wrong, there is only so much that can reasonably be done to protect patients from the consequences of their own wrongful decisions.

As a final caveat to this section, it should be noted that nothing that I have said above grants recognition, even by the back door, of a 'right to die', that is, a right to intentionally commit 'passive' suicide or euthanasia. There is not, nor can there be, any such moral right. Doctors and nurses who do not physically prevent a persistent suicidal choice need not condone nor approve of the choice, since they may be acting for the sake of other tangible goods in not physically interfering.[78] Of course some doctors and nurses may condone, or even encourage and share in, such an object. They ought not to do so, and in doing so betray not only the authentic value response to the basic human goods of life and health, but also the appropriate value response to the goods of beneficence and non-malevolence that are appropriate teleological ends of their respective professions.[79]

Personal Autonomy

In chapter two, we saw lines of argumentation posited designed to recognise a right to self-determination that can justify the personal choice to commit suicide or to be assisted in committing suicide. The value of personal autonomy played an important part in underpinning a right to self-determination regarding the making of such choices. Here, I am concerned to evaluate the claim that personal autonomy is such a constitutive moral value, that its can furnish reasoned grounds to justify the conclusion that it is sometimes right to intentionally act against the basic good of human life.

Kantian Legacy

As was discussed in chapter three, D.A.J. Richards is a contemporary philosopher who purports to derive the constitutive value of personal autonomy from the work of Immanuel Kant.[80] Richards states that Kant was a rationalist, and that his interpretation of autonomy consequently needs to be updated in the light of modern insights into psychology, recognising the importance of desires, emotions, etc.[81] Yet, does Richards really offer us an interpretation of personal autonomy that has any real claim to be described as authentically Kantian?

Here, I think, Richards is being disingenuous in claiming such an intellectual pedigree. What Richards effectively does is to abolish Kant's central use of what can usefully be described as a rationally guided 'moral autonomy'.[82] He replaces this with a conception of personal autonomy that owes more to the tradition of J.S. Mill that to any substantive Kantian conception. The end product is to uphold the paramount nature of the will, untethered to any set of objective moral principles that govern the will. The human will becomes directed, not through an appeal to rationality à la Kant, but by an appeal to what amounts to the endorsement of a thoroughgoing appeal to subjectivism.[83]

Kant appealed to the Categorical Imperative because he thought that the structure of abstract reason itself could furnish necessary categories to constitute a moral law to guide choice. For Kant, the autonomy of a rational being was subject to the laws of morality. Autonomy is only actualised through a life of duty.[84] What Richards essentially does is to abolish Kant's rationale for the autonomous will and effectively substitute it with Kant's heteronomous will, a will subject to the 'slave of the passions'. The result is that the human will is freed from any essential constraints, and persons are therefore 'liberated' to set their own ends according to their own heteronomous wants and desires.[85]

I would agree with Richards's divergence from Kant, to the extent that Kant was misguided in thinking that an appeal to bare abstract rationality could provide the necessary foundations for guiding worthwhile human choices.[86] However, what Richards further proposes is a jump from one error (a non-teleological rationalistic formalism) to another (subjectivism). He proposes that we should effectively give up any pretence to apprehend the ends of human choice cognitively.[87]

My concern here is not to decry the conception of autonomy as such. The label points to important aspects of the moral life. Rather, my concern is precisely one of seeking to examine the foundations upon which an adequate conception of (personal) autonomy can be founded, foundations that Kant's emphasis on (moral) autonomy (albeit flawed), rightly suggests cannot be understood by an abandonment of the will to the vagaries of wants and desires.[88]

Consider, for example, the idea of personal autonomy posited by Joel Feinberg.[89] Feinberg, in my view, does a good job of listing many qualities of autonomy that are important conditions for proper human flourishing. I can agree that there is indeed an important sense in which we are (*part*) authors in the shaping of our lives. [90] However, my problem with Feinberg, and with other accounts of personal autonomy, is precisely one of what I perceive to be a failure to place crucial limitations on an appeal to this value, a failure that itself manifests an axiological confusion over the status of this value when viewed within a wider teleological framework of reference.[91]

The value of autonomy lies in the fact that it is through our choices that we are able to reflectively promote our own flourishing as human beings (and that of those around us). The capacity to choose brings with it the responsibility of making not just any choice, but choices that do in fact promote, rather than undermine, human flourishing. What is needed is a concept of *reason governed autonomy* (i.e., capacity to choose directed by the operation of the good of practical reason).[92]

All the authors referred to in chapter three, who are keenly supportive of the good of personal autonomy, deny the ability of reason to apprehend a teleological framework for establishing the good life. No determinate ends can be demonstrated for the underwriting of morality. The common denominator here, consequently, is an underlying scepticism concerning the fonts of human value.[93] They reject the possibility that practical reason, operating on the insights of human nature, can indeed apprehend an array of goods that are genuinely fulfilling for the human person. By abolishing the relevance of pursuing the inherent worthwhileness of certain determinate goods (having also abolished Kantian categoricals), the result is a collapse into the diversity of 'self-creationism'.[94] Abolish the relevance of such basic human goods and we do indeed become Pico della Mirandola's beings seeking to carve out our own definition of human form, in our own image. One set of plans, goals, desires, etc. becomes as good as any other.[95] Having freed the will, having become Prometheus unbound, current thinking on personal autonomy readily concludes that the power to live or die, as determined by self-assessment, can indeed be an appropriate manifestation of personally autonomous choice.[96]

Qualified Value of Personal Autonomy

There is an alternative to understanding the possibilities and limits of autonomy found in a natural law conception of human persons and what fulfils them. Such a conception resists the mutation of autonomy into the doctrine of the 'paramountcy of the will'.[97] The framework of basic human goods needs be engaged, and in doing so the excessive voluntarism that lurks behind many contemporary accounts of personal autonomy can be set in high relief.[98] Since chapter three has dealt with the systematics underpinning this method of ethics, I shall not repeat them here. Suffice it to state that it does indeed offer objective grounds for claiming that there are authentic ends towards which all constitutive choices made should be informed and guided by. An adequate conception of our autonomy will see it, as always and everywhere (trans-historically, trans-culturally) tethered to the realisation of those primary human goods.[99]

A measure of genuine freedom for deliberative choice relating to our participation in those goods, is indispensable to morality. Further, our character formation and integrity depend on the recognition of such a prerequisite. If we are to lead a moral life, we must have a measure of freedom which brings with it the possibility of choosing wrong. Without the possibility of choosing wrong, we cannot in any meaningful sense be said to make constitutive choices about ourselves at all. Without it we would be essentially non-moral beings, incapable of acting rightly or wrongly. Equally, a will overcome by passion and compulsion would rob us of this necessary measure of freedom.[100]

Autonomy, then, can be said to afford the person with an operational sphere of freedom to make constitutive choices regarding ourselves; what we stand for, and what we will become.[101] Yet, this does not equate to the proposition that autonomy, as such, can therefore claim to have the status of a basic human good. Rather, it can be said to be a necessary prerequisite, a conditional possibility, that facilitates the instantiation of *practically reasonable deliberation* in our decision making regarding the adoption of different courses of action. Promoting human flourishing cannot be achieved by the capacity for choice in itself, but rather, can only result from the making of constitutive choices that actually manifest *reasoned deliberation,* as with a will subject to the governance of criteria of practical reasonableness.[102]

Joseph Raz, in his *Morality of Freedom*, argues that personal autonomy is actually an intrinsic good because it is perfective of the human person, to be who, and what, they are.[103] He does not seek to ground the good of autonomy in an anti-perfectionism derived from scepticism about objectivity in ethics.[104] His account of autonomy is therefore refreshing in that regard. He argues that particular actions, autonomously made, may indeed be valueless, degrading, or wicked, but out of respect for the person *qua* person, we must respect the right of the person, even to make destructive choices.[105]

Raz does a significant job in pointing to the importance of stressing *personal integrity and responsibility* in human conduct. To abdicate from such responsibility is indeed to lead a life of impoverishment, a life lacking in wellness of being. However, here, in line with Robert George, I think that his judgement concerning the *intrinsic status* of the good of personal autonomy is misplaced. If any deliberative choice is a direct manifestation of the intrinsic good of personal autonomy, then he seems to be committed to the proposition that even gravely wicked deliberative choices do in fact positively engage the intrinsic good of autonomy, and as such can therefore be said to manifest intrinsic value. If that is the case, then how can he claim that some exercises of autonomous choice can truly be said to be valueless?[106]

There is an important sense, in the thrust of what Raz states, in which respect for persons does centre round the exercise of constitutive choices, even degrading or valueless choices.[107] However, respect for persons, in my view, is crucially tethered to the radical potential of the human being as to *what could be* realised in and through autonomous choices made, not the exercise of autonomous choice *per se*. By making such an argument it is possible to agree with Raz about the truly valueless nature of some choices, without being committed to the idea that we are disrespecting persons by seeking to limit certain manifestations of autonomous choice. The intrinsic aspect of value that Raz touches upon, adequately framed, is not one of autonomous choice, but rather one of judging the product of autonomous choices with reference to standards of reasonableness.[108]

Autonomy, more adequately perceived, represents our human capacity to realise and participate in a whole array of basic goods, as well as other utility goods in their service. This is especially so for the reflexive goods of friendship, harmony, conscience, and religion, briefly discussed in chapter three, goods that depend on exercise of choice as a condition for their actualisation. In the fields of human endeavour, therefore, choice can be exercised in all manner of fulfilling ways. Choice gives rise to all manner of instantiations of creative human possibility. When autonomy is, however, viewed as a *per se* end, it becomes analogous to a rudderless ship on the open sea, listless, without any sails, without any captain.[109]

Given the legitimate plurality of lifestyles and life choices that are consistent with human flourishing, many choices are properly consistent with human well-being. As such, they merit respect. In consequence, it is essential to be heavily circumspect in proposing restrictions on a person's exercise of autonomous choice. Still, an exercise of autonomy truly merits respect only when it is exercised in accordance with (or is at least compatible with) a framework of reasonableness. For example, X's decision to assist in the suicide of Y could be an exercise of personal autonomy, yet it does not merit respect, since it illicitly attacks a moral norm that protects basic human goods. Certain autonomous choices are immoral because they represent an unreasonable attack on the status of particular basic human goods. This is especially the case when the decision seriously harms a person (self or other), e.g., a decision to duel to the death, to sell oneself into slavery, to assist in suicide, and so on.[110] Claims centred on an appeal to personal autonomy are, in other words, only really worthy of being respected in light of the reasonableness of the autonomous choice itself.[111]

If the principle of the basic good of human life is accepted, as I have argued above, its implications for the right to die should be patent. We cannot subvert the order of goodness and uphold the good of autonomy above its own warranted status. If it is immoral to intentionally kill (self or other), as I have argued above, then the capacity for autonomous action is being misdirected and misused, and as such can have *no necessary* claim on persons to be respected as a choice.

Rational Suicide Revisited

Returning back to a brief reconsideration of the notion of 'rational suicide', in light of our discussion concerning the value of personal autonomy, the muddled nature of the notion should be apparent. Even if suicide were 'instrumentally rational' in relation to the given goal of death, the question still becomes one of the reasonableness of the very end of the choice itself. Whilst I do not doubt that some patients can choose to kill themselves, and may do so by using reason in a kind of technical effectiveness fashion to justify a proposed adoption of means, the key question is still the reasonableness of intending death as a legitimate goal.

Once we climb beyond the Humean legacy that conceives of reason purely in terms of hypothetical imperatives 'if you seek X then Y' and understand reason in terms of a teleological relationship to important constitutive ends, the action becomes objectively unreasonable precisely as it is viewed in relation to its attack on the constituents of human flourishing. The action can be seen to contradict the very nature of the goods that render intelligible the exercise of human choice. Thus, the claim that suicide can be a truly reasonable act can be set aside when viewed in its wider context that considers the very ends of human flourishing.

The serious consideration of such a choice itself manifests a sign of unreasonableness no doubt often resulting from severe depression, or other forms of psychological disturbance. More than that, however, the degree to which a person can be exercising a genuine capacity for autonomous decision making, in such a situation, is also very suspect, due to the influence of many other forms of pressure falling short of a clinical state.[112] The degrees to which pain, feelings of worthlessness, guilt, and isolation may radically compromise deliberative choice, are all terribly underestimated. This is evidenced by the fact that when these problems are addressed and substantially ameliorated, often in a hospice environment, patients do not in fact seek to kill themselves or seek the aid of others in doing so.[113] Suicide and assisted suicide are usually not the last acts of the defiant autonomous will in the face of adversity, as assisted suicide proponents would lead us to believe. Rather, they are all too often pitiful pleas for help, for love and commitment, on the part of others.[114] The true objects of our concern, as with any medical problem, ought to be the minimisation of burdens and the creation of suitable environments in which to achieve this. Creative endeavours, utilised on behalf of suffering patients, ought to be precisely directed at the reduction/relief of burdens, not at the intentional killing of the patient whose capacities to think clearly are already under considerable strain, and who may understandably be lured to a seemingly attractive but false solution to remove those burdens.

Double Effect Reasoning

In chapter two, we saw a variety of attacks on the use of double effect reasoning to resolve conflicts between actions that entail the causation of both good and evil in their performance. Such reasoning is required in order to provide for the justification of an action where moral absolutes are seen to clash with one another. Without double effect reasoning, two possible courses are left open; either we embrace some notion of the pre-moral weighing of goods, or we accept the absolutes but are driven to posit a heavily restricted scope for action, whereby only actions having good foreseeable effects can be performed. Contrary to the criticisms made against double effect reasoning, I argue that a sustainable defence of this manner of reasoning can be indeed be provided, thereby credibly supporting the *via media* double effect reasoning offers between the Scylla of laxism associated with consequentialist modes of thought and the Charybdis of unnecessary rigorism that would arise without an appeal to something like the criteria of double effect reasoning.

A Good or Indifferent Object?

The first criterion of double effect reasoning, that the object of an act be good or indifferent, is denied by forms of argument stating that there are no essential 'moral objects' of an action. As argued by Jonathan Bennett, it is said not to be possible to 'isolate' the object of an action from questions of consequence.[115] The structural assessment of an action cannot be viewed this way. Objects, by the operation of what is called the 'accordion effect', are elided into the desirability of outcomes.[116] Actions are appropriately described in terms of the resultant state-of-affairs generated by what an agent certainly or foreseeably knows will flow from a given action. It consists of a possible state-of-affairs to realise, a plan to bring about that state-of-affairs, and a series of performances to bring about the desired overall result.[117] Right actions are those whose predicted consequences will generate a balance of good over evil.

In reply, it can be stated that much of the rejection of the notion of 'object' stems from a misunderstanding of the correct locus of human action itself in a teleology of authentic human ends. Such misunderstanding is fuelled by the influence of a Kantian formalism that has been unable to reply satisfactorily to the question of what gives an act its basic degree of specificity. It is no accident that Kantianism contributed directly to a rejection of the analysis of an action in terms of the traditional determinants of analysis—object, end, and circumstances.[118] That rejection was further completed by a thoroughgoing consequentialist turn that denied that there can be a teleology of the basic constituents of human flourishing that can provide the 'primary sources' or 'building blocks' of goodness that can meaningfully ground basic act descriptions.[119]

By rejecting Kantian and consequentialist modes of thought, for the reasons expressed in chapter three, we can, in my view, only intelligibly ground a theory of action by starting from a conception of the intelligible sources of goodness. As Eric D'Arcy recognises, there is a vocabulary of moral 'case terms' or 'kinds of action' that are linked directly to the recurrent and important events that relate to the basic ends of human flourishing.[120]

These case terms have an important dependency on the trajectories of human well-being, and as such, cannot be endlessly re-fashioned.[121] A teleological basis for the moral assessment of action has a much greater explanatory power for defining and setting limits on the description of an action, precisely because it takes seriously the tethering of an action to the status of distinguishable and specifiable goods.

Here, we can appeal to the Aristotelian use of genus and species, to help determine the relevant classification and assessment of an action by virtue of an examination of the goals that are intelligibly worthwhile for us to pursue (given the nature we have).[122] Kantian and consequentialist based ethics are unable to arrive at a satisfactory set of specifiable moral case terms, precisely because they are not rooted in the trajectories of human flourishing. As medicine, for example, uses case terms to name different species of disease, so too, we can apply a taxonomy of species to inform the use of an array of moral case terms. By understanding the status of the basic incommensurable good of human life, we can arrive at the specification of case terms that guide action in conformity (or disorder) with that end. It is no 'accident' that we have developed basic moral case terms precisely around the forms of human conduct that seek to attack or damage basic aspects of integral human flourishing. Thus, the goods that inform the use of moral case terms such as murder, suicide, rape, theft, etc., render such act descriptions meaningful, by virtue of the distinguishable goods they are associated with.

Moving on to consider G.E.M. Anscombe's analytical distinction between intentional behaviour (rendered intelligible by reason of discerning its immediate goal that can incorporate various sub-actions), and the motive of the agent in so intending to behave, we can say that the 'object' of an action represents the 'what' element of an action, and motive represents the 'why' or 'end' element of an action (for the sake of which the intelligible object to be performed is being considered).[123] Stated in classical terms, the 'what' element to be performed is designated the *finis operis* and the 'why' element is designated the *finis operantis*.[124]

In addition to those two elements, there is the further element of circumstance in which an action takes place, the element of circumstance pertaining to such questions as how? where? when? who?, etc[125]

Utilising those three structural elements of an action, it is justifiable to state, as with the first criterion of double effect reasoning, that an action can indeed be considered bad by reason of its primary intended object. Such an action cannot be performed since there is a basic marker of deprivation present, a bad proximate choice of means that cannot be rendered neutral or good (or otherwise cancelled out or negated) by a further appeal to the elements of motive or circumstance. Crucially, an action cannot be rendered good when it is deprived of its first and primary source of goodness since it gives the proposed action its basic character formation—the kind of action it is essentially constituted to be.[126]

Turning to the case of suicide, in an act of suicide there is usually an immediate primary object in view—the cessation of the agent's own life. This is what the agent chooses to perform as a means to a further end. As a chosen form of behaviour that immediate object is necessarily intended. The object is usually chosen with a view to the end of terminating pain and suffering, in circumstances where they are not being presently relieved. To seek to 're-describe' the action as, say, 'mercy induced death', is really to mistakenly ignore the grounded way in which proposed actions are concretely specifiable and capable of further analysis in terms of their component elements. Those elements closely tie the characterisation of human actions to a meaningful frame of reference that align act-descriptions to the goods that ultimately render intelligible all purposeful human behaviour.

We need not doubt, in the case of many suicides, that the motivation in seeking to intentionally elect for the adoption of such means is a good one. However, it is vital to realise that a good motive cannot render the act a good one, since it cannot change the basic deprivation present in the first and primary source of goodness of the act—the object—that gives the present action being proposed its intelligibility as a species of willed human behaviour. Such acts, are, so to speak, structurally disordered, since they seek to intentionally harm a basic constituent of human flourishing in order to pursue the cause of some further good. In the case of suicide, it would be tantamount to stating that we can intentionally attack the basic good of human life itself for the sake of relief of suffering.

People, in my view, seek to act against a basic good because there may be said to be something of a 'short circuiting' present in the manner of their reasoning. Patients faced with circumstances that place such pressure on their reason are often understandably deeply confused about priorities of value (and, with appropriate qualification pertaining to circumstances, the family, and servants of care, also). Yet, no matter how seemingly compelling the circumstances, this basic deprivation, whose primary proposed objective is an attack on the good of human life, cannot be transformed into a morally acceptable species of deliberately chosen behaviour.

To be sure, lest my analysis seem unduly harsh, questions of blameworthiness may be mitigated or lessened, even to the point of non-culpability, by an analysis of the end and circumstances of an action, but the act itself will not undergo a fundamental 'transformation of species' into something qualitatively different as a result. To do so by re-description, based on an appeal to those other elements of an action, serves only to shroud or conceal, not change, the real character of the kind of action actually being proposed for execution.

Intention/Foresight

Turning now to a consideration of the second criterion of double effect reasoning, we saw in chapter two that the relevancy of this criterion was rejected on the basis that it was dependent on an invalid epistemological division between the notion of intention and the notion of foresight.

Before proceeding to the defence of this criterion of double effect, that only the good can be intended, it is necessary to start with an admission. Authors such as Joseph Boyle and Thomas Sullivan, who have defended intention/foresight, do seem to appeal to the distinction as if it were based on just such an epistemological division in the practical reasoning of the agent.[127] As G.E.M. Anscombe has demonstrated, however, this epistemic view lacks credibility where the effects of an action are certain, or virtually certain, to the knowledge of the agent.[128]

Here, however, I would state that this ground is not the correct one for arguing for the justification of a division between intended and foreseeable side-effects. The appropriate distinction is a *volitional* one not an *epistemic* one. This distinction is, *prima facie*, supported by the use of ordinary language. For example, it is raining outside and I have a hole in my shoe. My foot gets wet as a result. Whilst *I knew* that my foot would get wet, it is plainly odd to say that *I intended* that my foot would get wet even though I knew with certainty that it would occur.[129]

John Finnis argues that ordinary language is supportive of the distinction between intention and foresight. He mentions the example of a person who stutters in a society that is not tolerant of speech impairments. It would be strange indeed to say that the person who stutters intended to give offence to people, even though it is certain that some offence would inevitably be taken.[130]

It would, therefore, seem that ordinary language at least is capable of grasping that there is something *volitionally* different in intending and having foreknowledge of an occurrence, even if that occurrence is certain to follow. This would suggest that those who dismiss intention versus foresight may indeed be too quick in reaching such a conclusion.

The intention/foresight distinction can be set in higher relief when we consider the common kinds of pre-philosophical apprehension that we have concerning the infliction of harm upon others. I find Thomas Cavanaugh's work highly illuminating here. He convincingly argues that intention/foresight does not rest on the primacy of knowledge, but rather, on the anatomy of the will.[131] Using a spatial metaphor, to intend evil as an end is to embrace it most deeply within our person. To intend an evil means is still to closely embrace evil within the disposition of the will, since means are the necessary vehicles chosen in order to achieve ends. It is only in permitting effects that lie outside the immediate trajectory of the will relating to a choice of end or means that it becomes possible to accept the negative results that may ensue. Here, there can be said to be sufficient distance between the direction of the will and resulting effects to allow us to permit the causation of evil as a result of our action.[132]

This can be further explained in terms of an intensity metaphor. To will something evil as an end is to will evil with the greatest degree of intensity possible. To will something evil as a means is of a more moderate intensity since it is not chosen in and of itself. To will something as a side-effect is to engage the will with the least degree of intensity. Thus, to will death as a side-effect does not mobilise the will in sufficient depth, since the resultant evil, so to speak, can be said to 'stand around' the will's central direction relating to the adoption of an end or a means.[133]

The degrees of willing result from the extent to which an agent's volition is embracing evil. The importance of moral psychology cannot be ignored as the will is a faculty of the mind that acts as a *mediatrix* between knowledge and the command of other faculties to produce action.[134] It does not follow, therefore, that the knowledge of the agent can provide sufficient grounds for rejecting the relevance of the intention/foresight distinction. Other more plausible grounds can be substituted. To the extent that critics of intention/foresight have concentrated on an epistemic foundation, their criticisms are off target. Moreover, such a volitional ground for drawing the distinction would fit in well with the traditional categorisation of crime concerning homicide.[135]

The basic *mens rea* for homicide is understood to be an intent on the part of the agent to cause the death of another.[136] Here I would suggest that Cavanaugh's distinction captures the condemnation of killing as an end or as a means. Both involve an unacceptable direction of the will contrary to the duty to respect human life. However, this need not be the case when assessing culpability for a side-effect, providing that its causation was not directly willed as an evil. Such for example, may well be the case of a nurse administering a high dose of morphine as a necessary means to achieve the good of relieving pain, even if it certainly foreshortens life.[137] She need not will the hastening of death as an essential part of her adopted means.

That death can be said to 'stand around' the direction of the will in such a case can be further illustrated by a thought experiment. Imagine a situation in which additional medicine could be provided that would counteract the negative effects of the morphine and may actually increase the patient's life-span. The nurse who truly wills only the pain relief could reasonably provide such additional treatment, since her will is not directed against the good of human life. There would be no contradiction for her to adopt both courses of action simultaneously. This cannot be said of the nurse whose will is essentially contra life since she cannot simultaneously will both the hastening of death and the preservation of the patient's life.[138]

There remains one further point to be considered here, namely, James Rachels' argument concerning the lack of a plausible distinction between extrinsically identical acts and interior dispositions of the will. He, moreover, argued that even if the distinction could be made, it would be of no practical import. Underlying Rachel's critique is basically the attitude that an agent possesses an array of mental states and those states can simply be manipulated by an instant change of thought pattern.

Intentions are indeed forms of mental state, but they are not mere states of mind that can be 'selected' or 'de-selected' at the drop of a pen. The very nature of an extensional action, from the beginning, and during its performance, depends upon the object that is willed. Intention does not amount to 'fixing' vision in one direction and simply 'keeping one's mind' off the others.[139]

Often we can indeed determine what the willed object of an action actually was by looking at the evidence, by asking a series of pertinent questions concerning the observed action and its circumstances. For example, what did the physician do to minimise or lessen the side-effects of his action?

Was a less damaging solution available? Did the physician take other counter measures available to help offset the causation of the bad effects?, and so on.[140]

Whilst I would agree with Rachels that we are indeed blind with respect to the ability to directly view the heart of another person, he significantly overlooks the question of evidential inference as to a person's disposition. Whilst I would accept that there is some scope for ambiguity concerning, for example, doses of pain medication administered to relieve pain and suffering, *no such ambiguity* is entailed by a deliberate act of prescribing a lethal dose of pain medication to a patient in order to assist the taking of life. From this *actus reus* it is reasonable to infer that the intent of the provider was precisely to render the patient dead by aiding and abetting an act of suicide. The fact that there is ambiguity in one set of circumstances is no argument for dismissing the lack of ambiguity in another.[141] Moreover, even in the case of relieving pain there will clearly be cases where a bad intent can be inferred. Such, for example, may well be the administration of a high dose of pain medication sufficient to induce respiratory failure without any significant justificatory correlation to the patient's previous treatment pattern or underlying stage of pathology.[142]

Causation

The third criterion of double effect reasoning is designed to place limits on what can be claimed in the name of intention with reference to the order of physical causality. The order of physical causality is relevant because it places tangible side-constraints on our toleration of the generation or production of evil in the world.[143] Intentions are not to be regarded as 'free floating' entities able to stamp themselves on causes at will, but rather, must be viewed as being closely *tethered* to the casual means by which we seek to extensionally shape and interact with the world.[144] If the good effect of an action is properly intended, then, as a necessary (not sufficient) sign of the probity of that intention (given our practical knowledge of structures of causal change), it is reasonable to insist that the good effect of the action ought to be causally prior to (or at least be concomitantly simultaneous with) the bad effect.

Causality then has an important role to play in the assessment of the morality of an action. Causal changes in the word that proceed from the actions of an agent, particularly those that bring about the death of a person, so to speak, cry out for explanation. If a causal change that results in death *cannot be reconciled* with a credible placement in the chain of causation then the action should not be performed. Yet, attention to causal ordering, whilst necessary, *is not sufficient* to guarantee the correct directness of an action. Thus, for example, if claims to having a good intention can be discounted due to other factors, e.g., the breach of other compelling and restraining duties, appeals to an otherwise plausible chain of causality *simply cannot* vitiate those other defects.

For double effect reasoning, what matters in assessing responsibility for causation, is the *manner and order* in which a cause was brought about, not simply the *brute fact of causal happening.* The crucial focus should not be placed on the mere presence or absence of a cause, but on an examination of the placement of the good and bad effects flowing from an action into a causal sequence *assessed in the light of a consideration of prior duties.*

Does a nurse who turns off the respirator of a non-competent patient, considered futile treatment, really stand in the same relationship to a patient as a son who turns off his mother's respirator in order to acquire a large inheritance?[145] Clearly, in both cases the causal onset of death quickly results. However, I would argue that any apportionment of responsibility via the patient's death differs radically in the two cases. It does not follow because action X and Y share a certain extrinsic causal result that X and Y is essentially equivalent. Such a manoeuvre is crudely consequentialist in outlook, and gives no scope whatsoever to non-consequentialist factors that govern an action, most significantly, the good intention of the agent corroborated by a credible causal sequence of events.

In the case of the nurse who turns off the respirator, there need only be intent to comply with professional responsibility regarding an advanced directive requesting the withdrawal of treatment or a medical judgement concerning the non-provision or withdrawal of futile treatment. Death need not be intended. A good intention here can indeed be supported by causal sequencing, since the bad effect does not causally precede the good effect but is concomitant with it. The son's case differs radically. There is no morally good or indifferent object. In such a case, the son takes upon himself responsibility for the causation of death, notwithstanding a plea that he is bringing about the same sequencing of causal change in the world. Such corroboration is *necessary but not sufficient* to justify the morality of his action. Other significations of context crucially contra-indicate the licitness of his action. Crucially, he cannot assume responsibility for the execution of medical instructions, as he has no such authority.

Responsibility for Side Effects

The last criterion of double effect reasoning, concerning proportionality, is criticised on the ground that it is a thinly disguised attempt to smuggle in consequentialist methodology by the back door.[146] However, a more detailed examination of the fourth criterion reveals the crucially limited and qualified way in which consequences are relevant to moral decision making; a relevance that makes no attempt to pretend that the real diversity of goods involved can be reduced to the level of an appeal to any kind of common denominator. Instead, there is an appeal to other morally relevant considerations that can be brought to bear in seeking to limit the causation of bad effects that will ensue from the pursuance of the good. The fourth criterion can be said to represent an attempt to summarily capture the different facets of a duty not to be manifestly (negligently/recklessly) unfair, in considering a proposed action, to the reasonably apprehended interests of self and/or others (framed in the context of prior commitments; commitments that may be general or may be limited, say, to a particular profession or role).[147]

The following can be listed as non-exhaustive but relevant specifications of this duty: if the agent is going to cause a serious evil effect, there needs to be a serious reason accorded to justify it. A trivial reason will not suffice. Secondly, if the evil effect would most likely happen anyway, in the course of events, the case for licitness becomes stronger. Thirdly, the causation of the proposed evil ought to be a last resort. If there was a less destructive means of achieving the good effect, it should be elected (again out of attention to the need to be fair viz. the impact that the bad effects will have on self or upon others).[148]

These features function as plausible agent centred side-constraints that serve to limit the scope of the ensuing bad effects of an action. The causation of death, for example, always requires a serious justificatory reason.[149] An example will help make this apparent. Consider a driver who speeds along a city road at 120mph. She seeks to experience the thrill of fast driving. The car strikes a pedestrian crossing the road. The pedestrian is killed. She pleads in her defence that she did not intend to kill anyone. This may well be true. However, there is a death caused by the action of the driver. Moreover, she had the power to prevent death by driving carefully at moderate speed. The thrill of fast driving cannot stand in any fair correspondence to the potential risk posed to human life. It was foreseeable that such an event could occur. Notwithstanding the lack of intent to kill, the driver's conduct was blameworthy.

The state of mind of the agent is a wider concept than intent, and blameworthiness attaches to human conduct of a reckless or negligent nature. By not fairly scrutinising the potential consequences of her action, the driver assumed responsibility for her state of recklessness. There was a disregard for the safety of others, a general duty incumbent on motorists. To classify an action as a side-effect *does not* entail the conclusion that a side effect is automatically permitted, since it was not intended.[150] In consequence, the scope of duty relating to the preservation of human life (regard for the safety of others) cannot be equivalenced to the emotional rush of fast driving. The side-effect is *manifestly unfair.*

By the use of such argumentation, I think it reasonable to conclude that the kinds of assessment of consequence being proposed here in consideration of the fourth criterion of double effect reasoning *does not begin* to serve the needs of consequentialist methodology. The criterion simply represents a final striving to offset the grosser forms of unfairly causing evil in the world, in a fashion that makes no pretence to being an adequate, complete, or otherwise self standing (and sufficient) criterion, for doing so.

All Acts and Some Omissions

Finally, under this section, let us briefly address the question of act and omission in moral analysis. As we saw in chapter two, Michael Tooley, Judith Lichtenberg, and others, argue that if we can establish equivalence between acts and omissions, that distinction is always going to be irrelevant to moral decision making concerning killing and letting die (and by implication to double effect reasoning generally, since it really represents the broader frame of reference in which discussions of killing and letting die take place).[151]

Such a conclusion, however, would be far too hasty. Looking at the sets of cases they both discuss, I would have no difficulty in classifying both Tooley's and Lichtenberg's contrasting pairs as *moral equivalents in the contexts given.* All the agents are, in the circumstances, equally culpable. Yet, this equivalence cannot be sustained apart from a consideration of the specific prior negative and positive duties at stake.

There are negative duties relating to the good of human life; it is wrong to intentionally act against such a basic good. To intentionally act against such a basic good is always unreasonable, since it denies the intrinsic nature of the good. Secondly, there are positive duties relating to the good of human life. Such would be a duty of ready rescue. To fail to act on those positive duties *can render* an omission morally equivalent. The good of life can be attacked by act or omission.[152]

Yet, in the absence of a prior duty, there is simply no moral or legal requirement incumbent on the agent. If acts and omissions are to be judged as moral equivalents, this can only flow from an analysis of the initial prior duties, not independently of them.[153] What Tooley's and Lichtenberg's analysis points to here, is the importance of taking omissions as well as acts *seriously* in evaluating moral conduct. It rejects simplistic reductionism and complacency by thinking that an omission is always permissible since it is not a cause in the conventional sense of 'doing something'. We can most assuredly intend to kill by both forms of deed. However, it is crucially misguided to think that the equivalency of act and omission in some sets of circumstance entails that they must always be regarded as equivalent. All such comparisons have to be judged by a prior analysis of the incumbent duty and the failure manifested by the agent in acting or refraining from acting.

In arguing that acts and omissions are *not always symmetrical*, consider the following: a physician ought not to intentionally kill his or her patient by injecting into the veins of the patient a lethal poison in order to hasten death. This is an exceptionless or perfect negative moral duty incumbent on the physician. The same cannot be said for the imperfect moral duty to positively preserve life. This is imperfect because it *may sometimes yield* to the contingencies of circumstance. If a physician, judging a medical treatment to be futile because it will not significantly lengthen a patient's life, omits the treatment, it is simply misguided to state that the physician wilfully hastens the death of the patient in a manner that can be equivalenced to the breach of a perfect moral obligation not to intentionally kill. Some omissions may be the moral equivalents of deliberate action *but not all omissions are*, and we must differentiate between the two in the light of an analysis of a failure to fulfil the nature of the prior duties that are incumbent.[154] We should, in consequence, be cautious of falling into the opposite error of claiming too much in the name of omission in order to overcompensate for the unjustified neglect that failure to act by omission has sometimes received in past moral analysis.

Casuistry and Double Effect

It is now appropriate to point out the implications of my interpretation of double effect reasoning for some hard cases on suicide. Consider first the case of Socrates. Can Socrates be said to have intentionally committed suicide by the manner of his own death? Could his actual death not give witness to the notion, notwithstanding an opposition to suicide in the *Phaedo*, that intentional self-killing was justified, at least in those circumstances?

Such a case is argued by Roger G. Frey and Isidor F. Stone.[155] Judge Reinhardt, in his notable opinion in the US Federal case of *Compassion in Dying v. Washington*, also makes this point.[156] They argue that by drinking the hemlock, Socrates intended that his death be the proximate means of implementing the death penalty passed by the Athenian Court. As such, his death must be classified as an intentional suicide regardless of the underlying motive for which the act of taking the hemlock was undertaken.

However, such an analysis, notwithstanding its initial plausibility, can be made the subject of a convincing counter-argument, given a more detailed and exacting understanding of the nature of his act in administering poison to his body. It can be argued that he was intent on bearing witness to the importance of obedience to the law of the state, for the sake of the common good. His end was therefore a good one. He would not flee thus causing potential scandal.[157] Secondly, it can be argued that the act of self-ministering the poison, as a means to that end, need not be interpreted as an act of intentional self-killing. Certainly the act of self-ministration was intended, but this need not be thought of as equivalent to intentional self-killing by lethal means.[158] He could have intended only to perform the requirement of the law that he administer the prescribed dose of poison to himself. [159] It is important to distinguish, as has already been stressed in this chapter, between questions of knowledge and the scope of an agent's intent. Certainly Socrates had knowledge, a foresight, that the self-ministration of the poison would most likely kill him. However, this is a separate question from what was, strictly speaking, intended. As such, it can be argued that his death need not have been intended and could thus be regarded as a *side-effect of the good objective of his action* (an act simultaneously instantiating a legally authorised sentence with the concomitant bad side effect of inducing death).

Another common case discussed in the literature is the death of Captain Oates. Oates left the shelter of the exploration camp and wandered out into the bitterly cold weather of the Antarctic. He could not survive long in those conditions.[160] Was this a case of suicide, albeit one motivated by altruism?

On the basis of the contextual evidence, it seems that there is a case for arguing that the action of Oates *need not* be classified as a suicide. As we have stated, actions can be *identical in extrinsic appearances* and yet have a different moral character. There is, I think, a possible reasonable description of his intentional action that need not be classified as one of pursuing the objective of intending his own death in order to pursue an altruistic end. In this context, Oates *could reasonably* have intended the object of preserving the means of life support for other members of the exploration party, in conditions of scarcity, and in conditions where his own ill health would place a greater burden on those resources. His objective *need not* have entailed the intentional destruction of his own life, but rather tolerated this bad effect as a side-effect of his intentional object (preserving important life sustaining supplies for the rest of the members of the party).

It is important here not to confuse the fact that a bad effect is foreseen as being certain with the conclusion that it is therefore *necessarily* intended. Corroboration of this is supplied by the causal order of his behaviour. The action of placing himself outside the shelter and away from being 'rescued' by the other members of the party significantly preceded the causal onset of death. However, even if his death was not intended, did his action not entail an 'immoral risk' to his own life? Even if this were conceded, his action ought not to be classed as one of suicide, for suicide, strictly speaking, requires an intention to destroy one's own life. Here we should recognise another moral case term for acts of this nature, say, *reckless self endangerment*, that can be considered morally wrong, in addition to intentional acts of suicide. This seems plausible. Nevertheless, there is good reason to think that Oates' action here would not fall under any such case term. He could reasonably point to the serious reason of furthering the chances of the survival of several lives to justify the bad effect. Secondly, his death was indeed likely to happen anyway given his poor state of health, and this can add to the strength of his reasoning in permitting the bad side effect. Finally, given the context, it is not unreasonable to assume that the other members of the party would attempt to dissuade or even prevent him from embarking on such a course of action if he did not depart from the shelter. Since no lesser means would be available to preserve the supplies (if he were present, presumably, the other explorers would insist on sharing supplies with him), it seems reasonable to think that his acceptance of the bad side-effect of his own death, did function as a last resort.

Consider now the case of a soldier who launches himself or herself on top of a grenade in order to minimise the explosion of the grenade that, left unmuffled, could reasonably be expected to have killed the lives of several comrades in the field.[161] Is this necessarily a case of intending suicide as a means to pursuing an altruistic motive? Here, I think that the action need not reasonably be construed as one of intending suicide. The object of the soldier's action could reasonably be described as the immediate and proximate one of protecting the lives of fellow soldiers. The soldier need only have intended that in acting to minimise the blast, the lives of others would be protected. Again, even if death were seen as being certain, this does not mean that the bad effect of the action was necessarily intended.

Such an account can be supported by an appeal to the causal sequencing of events. The bad effect of the soldier's death did not precede the good effect. Rather, the bad effect was concomitant with the good effect. Finally, there is good reason to think that the final criterion of double effect reasoning can justify the permission of the bad effect here since it is undertaken for sufficiently serious reasons (saving several lives), and, given the circumstances of such a short time in which to act, offers a credible ground for claiming to be a last resort.

A more perplexing case of difficulty is the case of a soldier captured behind enemy lines and is fearful of passing on vital intelligence information to the enemy under torture.[162] Could a soldier who sought to take a lethal pill in such circumstances not be said to have intentionally ended his or her life as the means of pursuing the good effect? All systems of ethics inevitably generate hard cases that arise at the margins of the application of its principles. Here, however, I cannot see how the objective of this soldier could be construed as anything other than an act of suicide in order to pursue an altruistic motive of preventing the risk to other lives. The death of this soldier is the *necessary causal antecedent* to the good being pursued. His or her death is a necessary preceding condition for securing his or her silence. It will not do to claim that, strictly speaking, death was not the intended objective of the action, but only one of seeking to render him or her impervious to the influence of torture. The causal order of achieving the good of silence is procured precisely by the prior destruction of his or her bodily life by the consumption of a lethal means. As already stated, intentions cannot be divorced from the order of causality in the physical world and be viewed as some sort of free floating entity capable of stamping themselves upon the order of physical causality at will. Here the order of causal sequencing points to the intention of utilising a lethal means to bring about death in order to achieve the good effect of silence in order to protect the lives of others.

Here, licit means would require, for example, escape, lack of communicativeness, or dissimulation. Lest my judgement seem unduly harsh, it is important to point out that I do not think that a soldier who committed suicide in such circumstances need incur blameworthy culpability as a result of the suicide. The *pressures and fear would be immense*, and might well be sufficient to overcome the will of many soldiers placed in such an appalling predicament. Nevertheless, such pressures should not mistakenly tempt us into engaging in a re-classification of the nature of the action being undertaken, for actions should not be reclassified on the basis of coercion, or any other from of pressure brought to bear, for those are second order questions to be addressed once the nature of the intended action itself has been identified.

A Consistent Ethic of Killing?

The final issue to be addressed, in conclusion to this chapter, is the criticism made by Margaret Battin, Richard Norman, and others, that the 'sanctity of life' tradition is one hampered by inconsistency in its ethical outlook concerning certain justifications for killing. Some forms of intentional killing do seem to be permitted and others do not.[163]

Innocence is commonly referred to as the denominator quality that can justify the intentional killing of some persons, in some situations, but not others. Classic cases of this have been considered to be actions of self-defence and capital punishment. Here, I must confess to finding the criticism made of appeals to innocence penetrating. I am at a loss as to what the *lack of the quality of innocence* could possibly amount to, such that it can be said to wipe out or discount the inherent worth of the good of human life. An intentional act of killing, of its nature, must necessarily entail a direct attack on the nature of this good. I frankly concur with the criticism that the 'sanctity of life' tradition has been inconsistent in the formation of some of its justifications for the actions of self-defence and capital punishment, for I do not think it reasonable to argue that human life is a good that can be intentionally acted against, whether as a means or as an end. The good of human life does not cease to lose its status as a basic human good by virtue of a loss of innocence. No fundamental ontological transformation takes place in the being of the person. Contrary to a stated position of Aquinas, for example, a murder does not become ontologically demoted to the status of a 'beast', a *semi-hominem*.

There ought to be consistency in the ethics of intentional killing across the board. The logic of our prior analysis points to the recognition of an exceptionless moral norm of the kind that *all intentional killing* of human beings, without further qualification, should be considered illicit, and not simply the intentional killing of the innocent. A genuine and credible consistency, therefore, can be achieved in a natural law ethics of killing, via the acceptance of a moral norm that prohibits all intentional killing of human beings *simpliciter*. This is the justifiable response that ought to follow from an analysis of Battin's and Norman's critiques of consistency in the sanctity of life tradition, not any possible expansion in the class of intentional killings, based on an appeal to yet other suspect qualities, to embrace yet further intentional acts of killing (e.g., acts of suicide, assisted suicide, and euthanasia).

Does this mean that I am committed to a rigorist position that human life itself can never be fatally impacted as a result of some of our actions? No. The whole point of double effect reasoning was to provide a credible framework for the analysis of actions that bring about both good and bad effects. Here, I would point to the analysis of intentional killing in the light of double effect reasoning to see what manner of actions can be reconciled with the causation of death.

Turning to the question of self defence, by the use of double effect reasoning, as classically recognised by Aquinas, it is possible to use lethal force in order to justify an act of self-defence, without thereby intending the death of an aggressor. The good of human life is still reasonably respected in its intrinsic worth, for it is not intentionally attacked. It is therefore entirely possible to consistently defend actions of self-defence without conceding that they should necessarily be viewed as cases of intending to kill. Self-defence need not be thought of as a case of intending to kill a non-innocent aggressor, but rather, can correctly be viewed as one of using required force in order to repel the immediacy of the aggression.[164]

In comparison, capital punishment is inherently more difficult to reconcile with double effect reasoning and the norm not to intentionally kill. If the intentional objective in capital punishment were, say, one of pre-emptive societal self-defence with a view to preventing subsequent acts of killing *by that particular criminal*, based on credible evidence, then perhaps death could be considered concomitant with the good effect being pursued, according to the third criterion of double effect reasoning. Yet, such a justification could not begin to account for the many forms of capital punishment that have been historically justified. The plausibility of capital punishment *in a limited number of cases*, on such a ground, cannot be construed as a blanket endorsement of the practice.

Moreover, there is an additional source of potential injustice that would be difficult to skirt around in the circumstances of contemporary Western society, even on that limited ground. It would seem to be immoral to intentionally pursue the good of societal protection via capital punishment where other lesser means were available to achieve the same objective, for it would not then be undertaken as a last resort. This is part of the fourth criterion of double effect reasoning. Whilst such an act may not, strictly speaking, be an intended killing, it nevertheless would seem to entail the causation of an *unfair side-effect* that needlessly damages the good of human life, since lesser means of protecting society from the future acts of the criminal would be available (e.g., prison sentencing, including life sentencing).

A common form of justification proposed for capital punishment cannot be reconciled with a duty not to intentionally kill, namely, the killing of a criminal for the sake of deterrence. If a human life was taken in order to deter another person from undertaking a crime, then death would indeed be the intended means of seeking to bring about the good effect of influencing people to desist from committing crimes. Deterrence, if it is to be welcomed, can only be indirectly 'hoped for' as the unintended side-effect of an action already justified in its central moral determinants.

Finally, what of the argument derived from retribution? Can it not be said that in executing a criminal the act is one whose intended objective is punishment, not killing?[165] Unfortunately, space prevents a detailed elaboration of this point. It must suffice to state here that that such an interpretation lacks plausibility as a description of the action when we consider that the means of inflicting punishment necessarily proceed through the antecedent causation of death itself in order to realise the good of retribution.

The good of retribution is not antecedent to, or concomitant with, the bad effect of death. Death is prior in the causal chain of events. 'But for' the prior death of the criminal, retribution cannot be achieved. The good effect is brought about by means of the bad effect. In the light of my analysis, therefore, it is ultimately disingenuous to claim that capital punishment is capable of being justified as a side-effect of pursuing the good object of retribution, since death, in that case, is being intentionally willed as the antecedent of the good.

By further developing such an approach to analysis, only touched upon in this section, it is indeed possible to respond to the charge of inconsistency in killing by accepting the validity of the criticism, were death is intentionally sought, thus striving to overcoming it. In particular, the norm against all intentional human killing, combined with a credible account of double effect reasoning, is capable of effectively responding to this consistency criticism in a plausible and sustained way.

Notes to Chapter Five

[1] John Finnis, *Natural Law and Natural Rights*. Corr. ed. (Oxford: Clarendon Press, 1982), 61-69, 85-87.

[2] For more discussion on the idea of self-evidence and the significance of non-derivability see Joseph Boyle, "Natural Law and the Ethics of Traditions," in *Natural Law Theory*, ed. Robert P. George (Oxford: Clarendon Press, 1992), 3-30. See also Montague Brown, *The Quest for Moral Foundations* (Washington, DC: Georgetown University Press, 1996), 92-97.

[3] Boyle, "Natural Law," 3-12. See also Mark C. Murphy, "Self-Evidence, Human Nature, and Natural Law," *American Catholic Philosophical Quarterly* 69 (1995): 471-84.

[4] John Finnis, *Fundamentals of Ethics* (Washington, DC: Georgetown University Press, 1983), 50-53.

[5] Finnis, *Natural Law and Natural Rights*, 126-67.

[6] On the consistent implications of not intentionally attacking this good see Gerard V. Bradley, "No Intentional Killing Whatsoever: The Case of Capital

Punishment," in *Natural Law and Moral Inquiry*, ed. Robert P. George (Washington, DC: Georgetown University Press, 1998), 155-73; Joseph Boyle, "An Absolute Rule Approach," in *A Companion to Bioethics*, eds. Helga Kuhse and Peter Singer (Oxford: Blackwell, 1998), 72-79.

[7] Joseph Boyle, "Reverence for Life and Bioethics," in *Linking the Human Life Issues*," ed. Russell Hittinger (Chicago: Regnery, 1986), 105-13.

[8] Finnis, *Natural Law and Natural Rights*, 118-25.

[9] On clarification surrounding the instrumental uses of the good of human life compatible with respect for that good see the discussion by Joseph Boyle in his "Sanctity of life and Suicide: Tensions and Developments within Common Morality," in *Suicide and Euthanasia: Historical and Contemporary Themes*, ed. Baruch Brody (Dordrecht; Boston: Kluwer Academic, 1989), 221-50.

[10] Robert P. George, "Recent Criticism of Natural Law Theory," *University of Chicago Law Review* 55 (1988): 1390-92.

[11] Peter Singer, "Life's Uncertain Voyage," in *Metaphysics and Morality: Essays in Honour of J.J.C. Smart,* eds. P. Pettit, R. Sylvan and J. Norman (Oxford: Blackwells, 1987), 154-72; Peter Singer and Helga Kuhse, "More on Euthanasia," *The Monist* 76 (1993): 158-74.

[12] Jonathan Glover, *Causing Death and Saving Lives* (London: Penguin, 1977), 51-53, 158-62, 192-94; James Rachels, *The End of Life* (New York: Oxford University Press, 1986), 26, 60-77; Peter Singer, *Practical Ethics*. 2nd ed. (New York: Cambridge University Press, 1993), ch. 7., esp. 184-86; Ronald Dworkin, *Life's Dominion* (London: Harper Collins, 1993), 68-101; Helga Kuhse, *The Sanctity of Life Doctrine in Medicine: A Critique* (Oxford: Clarendon Press, 1987), 198-220; John Harris, *Value of Life* (London: Routledge & Kegan Paul, 1985), 87-110.

[13] John Locke, *Essay Concerning Human Understanding* (London: Dent, 1961), 280. For a good discussion of problems associated with Locke's theory of the person specifically centred on questions of consciousness and identity see Bert Gordijn, "The Troublesome Concept of the Person," *Theoretical Medicine and Bioethics* 20 (1999): 347-59.

[14] See Gilbert C. Meilaender, "Terra es animata: On Having a Life," *Hastings Center Report* 23 (1993): 25-32; J.P. Moreland, "Humanness, Personhood, and the Right to Die," *Faith and Philosophy* 12 (1995): 95-112; Jens Saugstad "Abortion: The Relevance of Personhood: A Critique of Dworkin," *Zeitschrift fur philosophische Forschung* 49 (1995): 571-83.

[15] See Patrick Lee "Human Beings are Animals," in *Natural Law and Moral Inquiry*, ed. Robert P. George, 135-51; Tim Chappell, "In Defence of Speciesism," in *Human Lives: Critical Essays on Consequentialist Bioethics,* eds. David S. Oderberg and Jacqueline A. Laing (New York: St. Martin's Press,1997), 96-108; Michael Wreen, "My Kind of Person," *Between the Species* 2 (1986): 23-8; Wreen, "In Defense of Speciesism," *Ethics and Animals* 5 (1984): 47-60.

[16] Jenny Teichman, *Social Ethics* (Oxford: Blackwells, 1996), 29-36.

[17] For a discussion of the *Oxford English Dictionary* definition see Jenny Teichman, "The Definition of Person," *Philosophy* 60 (1985): 175-85. For discussion see also Luke Gormally, "Definitions of Personhood," *Catholic Medical Quarterly* 44 (1993): 7-12.

[18] Luke Gormally, "Non-Persons, Human Dignity and Justice," in *The Dependent Elderly: Autonomy, Justice, and Quality of Care*, ed. Luke Gormally (New York: Cambridge University Press, 1992), 81-88.

[19] John Finnis, "Persons and their Associations," *Proceedings of the Aristotelian Society* 63 (1989): 267-74; Gormally "Definitions," 7-12.

[20] John Finnis, "Misunderstanding the Case Against Euthanasia," in *Euthanasia Examined: Ethical, Clinical and Legal Perspectives*, ed. John Keown (Cambridge: Cambridge University Press, 1995), 68-70; "Persons," 267-74.

[21] Boyle, "Sanctity of Life," 236-40.

[22] Boyle, "Sanctity of Life," 236-40; Wreen, "In Defense of Speciesism," 51-54.

[23] See for example Singer & Kuhse, "Euthanasia," 171-73.

[24] Brian Scarlett, "The Moral Uniqueness of the Human Animal," in *Human Lives: Critical Essays on Consequentialist Bioethics,* eds. David S. Oderberg and Jacqueline A. Laing, 78-95. See also Lawrence Becker, "Human Being: The Boundaries of the Concept," *Philosophy and Public Affairs* 4 (1975): 334-59.

[25] See G.E.M. Anscombe and Peter Geach, *The Three Philosophers* (Oxford: Blackwell, 1973), 7, who mention Aquinas quotation of Boethius's, *Contra Eutychen*, 13.

[26] Philip E. Devine, *The Ethics of Homicide* (Ithaca: Cornell University Press, 1978), 51-57.

[27] As Finnis states in "Abortion, Natural Law, and Public Reason," in *Natural Law and Public Reason,* eds. Robert George and Christopher Wolfe (Washington, DC: Georgetown University Press, 2000), 91, "… each living human being possesses, actually and not merely potentially, the *radical capacity* to reason, laugh, love, repent, and choose as this unique, personal individual … the unique, individual, organic functioning of the organism that comes into existence as a new substance at the conception of the human being and subsists until his or her death, whether ninety minutes, ninety days, or ninety years later; a capacity, individuality, and personhood that subsists as real and precious even while its operations come and go with many changing factors such as immaturity, injury, sleep, and senility."

[28] Scarlett, "Moral Uniqueness," 91-92. See also Timothy Chappell, "Reductionism about Persons; and What Matters," *Proceedings of the Aristotelian Society* 98 (1998): 41-57.

[29] Teichman, "Definition," 180-81.

[30] Scarlett, "Moral Uniqueness," 91-92.

[31] John Finnis, "The Value of the Human Person," *Twentieth Century (Australia)* 27 (1972): 126-37; "The Consistent Ethic: A Philosophical Critique," in *Consistent Ethic of Life*, ed. Thomas G. Fuchtmann (Kansas City: Sheed and Ward, 1988), 140-81.

[32] John Haldane, "Biothics and the Philosophy of the Human Body," in *Issues for a Catholic Bioethic* (London: Linacre Centre, 1999), 77-89.

[33] Devine, *Ethics of Homicide*, 51-57.

[34] John Finnis, "The 'Value of Human Life' and 'the Right to Death': Some Reflections on Cruzan and Ronald Dworkin," *Southern Illinois University Law Journal* 17 (1993): 559-71; "A Philosophical Case Against Euthanasia," in *Euthanasia Examined: Ethical, Clinical and Legal Perspectives*, ed. John Keown, 23-35.

[35] Teichman, *Social Ethics*, 39.

[36] On substantial changes in kind see Mary Rousseau, "Elements of a Thomistic Philosophy of Death," *Thomist* 43 (1979): 581-602; Armand

Maurer, "Descartes and Aquinas on the Unity of the Human Being: Revisited," *American Catholic Philosophical Quarterly* 67 (1993): 497-511.

[37] See for example John Harris, "Euthanasia and the Value of Life," in *Euthanasia Examined: Ethical, Clinical and Legal Perspectives*, ed. John Keown, 6-20; Dan Brock, "Medical Decisions at the End of Life," in *A Companion to Bioethics*, eds. Helga Kuhse and Peter Singer, 231-41; Margaret Battin, *The Least Worst Death* (New York: Oxford University Press, 1994).

[38] Thomas Nagel, "Death," in *Applied Ethics*, ed. Peter Singer (Oxford: Oxford University Press, 1986), 9-18; Harry Silverstein, "The Evil of Death," *Journal of Philosophy* 77 (1980): 401-24; Fred Feldman, "Some Puzzles about the Evil of Death," *Philosophical Review* C2 (1991): 205-27.

[39] See George Pitcher, "The Misfortunes of the Dead," *American Philosophical Quarterly* 21 (1984): 183-88.

[40] See F.M. Kamm, *Morality, Mortality: Death and Whom to Save form It* (Oxford: Oxford University Press, 1993), 13-22.

[41] Kamm, *Morality*, 13-22; Kamm, Why is Death Bad and Worse than Prenatal Non-existence?" *Pacific Philosophical Quarterly* 69 (1988): 161-64.

[42] Anthony L. Brueckner and John Martin Fischer, "Why is Death Bad?" *Philosophical Studies* 50 (1986): 213-21; Roderick Chisholm, "Coming into Being and Passing Away: Can the Metaphysician Help," in *Language, Metaphysics, and Death*, ed. John Donnelly (New York: Fordham University Press, 1978), 13-24.

[43] See J.C. Murphy, "Rationality and the Fear of Death," *Monist* 59 (1976): 187-203; Robert Kastenbaum, "Suicide as the Preferred Way of Death," in *Suicidology: Contemporary Developments*, ed. Edwin S. Shneidman (New York: Grune & Stratton, 1976), 425-41.

[44] Devine, *Ethics of Homicide*, 23-31.

[45] Devine, *Ethics of Homicide*, 26.

[46] Devine, *Ethics of Homicide*, 24 (his emphasis).

[47] Devine, *Ethics of Homicide*, 23-31.

[48] This line of thought was made as a written comment upon an earlier draft of this chapter by James M. Dubois.

[49] See Michael Wreen, "The Logical Opaqueness of Death," *Bioethics* 1 (1987): 366-71; "Importune Death a While," *Public Affairs Quarterly* 17 (1996): 153-62.

[50] Even from a Christian perspective informed by Thomism, the human being, the self, ceases to exist, even though the soul may survive the destruction of the body. For detailed analysis of the soul as substantial form see David Braine, *The Human Person: Animal and Spirit* (Notre Dame: University of Notre Dame Press, 1992), 480-511.

[51] Kamm, *Mortality, Morality*, 20-21.

[52] John Donnelly, "Suicide and Rationality," in *Language, Metaphysics, and Death*, ed. John Donnelly, 96-100.

[53] J. L. A. Garcia, "Are Some People Better Off Dead? A Reflection," *Logos* 2 (1999): 68-81; "Better Off Dead?" *APA Newsletter on Philosophy and Medicine* 1 (1993): 85-88.

[54] Garcia, "Are Some People," 70-72. See also John M. Dolan, "Judging Someone Better Off Dead," *Logos* 2 (1999): 48-67.

[55] Nagel, "Death," 9-18. See also a similar line of argument taken by Joel Feinberg in his *Harm to Others* (Oxford: Oxford University Press, 1984): 79-95.

[56] Ernest Partridge, "Postumous Interests and Postumous Respect," *Ethics* 91 (1981): 243-64.

[57] Partridge, "Postumous," 245-51. See also Don Marquis, "Harming the Dead," *Ethics* 95 (1985): 159-61; Mary Mothersill, "Death," in *Moral Problems: A Collection of Philosophical Essays*, ed. James Rachels (New York: Harper & Row, 1971), 380-85.

[58] Michael Wreen, "The Definition of Euthanasia," *Philosophy and Phenomenological Research* 48 (1988): 637-53; "Passing the Bottle," *Philosophia* 16 (1986): 427-44; "Defining Death," *Public Affairs Quarterly* 8 (1987): 87-99.

[59] For further elaboration of this axiological point see Timothy Chappell, *Understanding Human Goods: A Theory of Ethics* (Edinburgh: Edinburgh University Press, 1998), chs. 3 & 4.

[60] Wreen, "Importune Death," 159.

[61] James Rachels, "Killing, Letting Die, and the Value of Life," in his *Can Ethics Provide Answers? And Other Essays in Moral Philosophy* (Lanham: Rowman and Littlefield, 1997), 69-79; Peter Singer, "Is the Sanctity of Life Ethic Terminally Ill?" *Bioethics* 9 (1995): 327-42; Helga Kuhse and Peter Singer, "Prolonging Dying is the Same as Prolonging Living," *Journal of Medical Ethics* 17 (1991): 205-6; John Harris, *The Value of Life* (London: Routledge & Kegan Paul, 1985); Dan Brock, "Euthanasia," in *Arguing Euthanasia*, ed. Johnathan D. Moreno (New York: Simon & Schuster, 1995), 196-210; Lofty L. Basta and Carole Post, *A Graceful Exit: Life and Death on Your Own Terms* (New York: Plenum Press, 1996); Michael D. Bayles, "The Value of Life," in *Health Care Ethics*, eds. Donald Van de Veer and Tom Regan (Philadelphia: Temple University Press, 1987), 265-89.

[62] Peter Sandoe, "Quality of Life," *Ethical Theory and Moral Practice* 2 (1999): 11-23.

[63] For a valid uses of those comparative terms see Andrew F. Reeve, "Incommensurability and Basic Values," *Journal of Value Inquiry* 4 (1997): 545-52.

[64] Reeve, "Incommensurability," 545-48.

[65] Finnis, "Value of Human Life," 559-71; Finnis, "Philosophical Case Against," 23-35.

[66] David S. Oderberg, *Applied Ethics* (Oxford: Blackwells, 2000), 60-70

[67] Robert P. George, *In Defense of Natural Law* (Oxford: Clarendon Press, 1999), 192-98; Finnis, *Fundamentals of Ethics*, ch. 2.

[68] Richard Sherlock, "Euthanasia," in his *Preserving Life: Public Policy and the Life Not Worth Living* (Chicago: Loyola University Press, 1987), 117-39. See also Lisa Sowle Cahill, "Sanctity of Life, Quality of Life, and Social Justice," *Theological Studies* 48 (1987): 105-23; William E. May, "What Makes a Human Being to be a Being of Moral Worth?" *Thomist* 40 (1976): 416-43.

[69] Kant classically saw the danger inherent in such an approach when he confronted the Scottish School centred on the emotion of sympathy. For discussion of the possible roles for intuition in moral judgement.

[70] See Per Sundstrom, "Peter Singer and Lives Not Worth Living," *Journal of Medical Ethics* 21 (1995): 35-38; Daniel P. Sulmasy, "Death and Human Dignity," *Linacre Quarterly* 61 (1994): 27-36; Robert A. Destro, "Quality-of-life Ethics and Constitutional Jurisprudence: The Demise of Natural Rights and Equal Protection for the Disabled and Incompetent," *Journal of Contemporary Health Law and Policy* 2 (1986): 71-130; Wesley J. Smith, "Our Discardable People," *Human Life Review* 24 (1998): 78-87.

[71] See Luke Gormally, "Against Voluntary Euthanasia," in *Principles of Health Care Ethics*, ed. Raanan Gillon (London: John Wiley, 1993), 763-74; *Euthanasia, Clinical Practice and the Law*, ed. Luke Gormally (London: Linacre Centre, 1994), 119-24; G. Kevin Donovan, "Decisions at the End of Life," *Christian Bioethics* 3 (1997): 188-203.

[72] For elaboration on the idea of a legitimate sphere of leeway for end of life decision making see Edward W. Keyserlingk, The Quality of Life and Death," in *Quality of Life: The New Medical Dilemma* (New York: Paulist Press, 1990): 35-53; Paul Ramsey, *The Patient as Person* (New Haven: Yale University Press, 1970), 113-64; Brian Johnstone, "Sanctity of Life and Quality of Life," *Linacre Quarterly* 52 (1985): 258-70; Arthur Dyck, "An Alternative to an Ethic of Euthanasia," in *To Live and to Die: When Why and How?*, ed. R. H. Williams (New York: Springer-Verlag, 1973), 107-11; Cynthia B. Cohn, "Quality of Life and the Analogy with the Nazis," *Journal of Medicine and Philosophy* 8 (1983): 113-35.

[73] On vitalism see Morton Beckner "Vitalism," in *The Encyclopedia of Philosophy*, ed. Paul Edwards (New York: Macmillan, 1967), 253-56.

[74] See especially the work of Edmund D. Pellegrino: "Decisions to Withdraw Life-Sustaining Treatment: A Moral Algorithm," *Journal of the American Medical Association* 283(8) (Feb. 2000): 1065-67; "Patient and Physician Autonomy: Conflicting Rights and Obligations in the Physician-Patient Relationship," *Journal of Contemporary Health Law and Policy* 10 (1994): 47-68; "Doctors Must not Kill," *Journal of Clinical Ethics* 3 (1992): 95-102; "The Place of Intention in the Moral Assessment of Assisted suicide and Active Euthanasia," in *Intending Death: The Ethics of Assisted Suicide and Euthanasia*, ed. Tom Beauchamp (Upper Saddle River: Prentice Hall, 1996), 163-83.

[75] Germain Grisez and Joseph Boyle, *Life and Death with Liberty and Justice: A Contribution to the Euthanasia Debate* (Notre Dame: University of Notre Dame Press, 1979), 414-19.

[76] John Finnis, Bland: Crossing the Rubicon?" *Law Quarterly Review* 109 (1993): 329-37. See also Luke Gormally, "Walton, Davies, Boyd and the Legalisation of Euthanasia," in *Euthanasia Examined*, ed. John Keown, 113-38.

[77] Joseph Boyle, "The American Debate on Artificial Nutrition and Hydration," in *The Dependent Elderly*, ed. Luke Gormally, 38-46.

[78] Pellegrino, "Doctors Must Not Kill," 95-102.

[79] See Lance Simmons, "On Not Destroying the Health of One's Patients," in *Human Lives*, ed. David Oderberg, 144-60; Ezekiel J. Emanuel, "What is the Great Benefit of Legalizing Euthanasia or Physician-Assisted Suicide?" *Ethics* 109 (1999): 629-42.

[80] David A. J. Richards, "Autonomy and Rights," *Ethics* 92 (1981): 3-20; Richards, *Sex Drugs, Death and the Law* (New Jersey: Rowman & Littlefield, 1982), 59-62.

[81] David A.J. Richards "Kantian Ethics and the Harm Principle," *Columbia Law Review* 87 (1987): 457-71.

[82] See Ray Lanfear, "Moral Autonomy and Reason," *Journal of Value Inquiry* 20 (1986): 183-93.

[83] Janet E. Smith, "The Pre-eminence of Autonomy in Bioethics," in *Human Lives*, ed. David Oderberg, 182-95.

[84] See Barbara Secker, "The Appearance of Kant's Deontology in Contemporary Kantianism: Concepts of Patient Autonomy in Bioethics," *Journal of Medicine and Philosophy* 24 (1999): 43-66.

[85] See Hadley Arkes, "'Autonomy' and the 'Quality of Life': The Dismantling of Moral Terms," *Issues in Law and Medicine* 2 (1997): 421-33; S. H. Furness, "Medical Ethics, Kant and Mortality," in *Principles of Health Care Ethics*, ed. Raanon Gillon, 159-71; Nigel M. de S. Cameron, "Autonomy and the Right to Die," in *Dignity and Dying*, eds. John F. Kilner, Arlene B. Miller and Edmund D. Pellegrino (Grand Rapids: Eerdmans, 1996): 23-33.

[86] Finnis, *Fundamentals of Ethics*, 120-34.

[87] The function of reason in Richards system essentially becomes one based purely on hypothetical imperatives. In a hypothetical imperative, the relationship is one of means to conditional ends. It can be expressed in the

following form 'if X then Y'. In itself, such an imperative tells us nothing about the rightness or wrongness of the willed ends in themselves. It simply states that if the agent wishes to pursue the desired end then effectiveness and efficiency in the choice of means should also be willed. See further D.D. Raphael, *Moral Philosophy* (Oxford: Oxford University Press, 1981), 14-15, 55.

[88] Teichman, *Social Ethics*, 68-70.

[89] Joel Feinberg, *Harm to Self*, 27-51; Feinberg, "Autonomy," in *The Inner Citadel: Essays on Individual Autonomy*, ed. John Christman (New York: Oxford University Press, 1989), 27-49.

[90] In Feinberg's case, the influence informing his conception of personal autonomy is correctly identified as J.S. Mill, not Kant. See Smith, "Pre-eminence," 182-88.

[91] John Finnis, "On the Practical Meaning of Secularism," *Notre Dame Law Review* 3 (1998): 491-516.

[92] Robert P. George, *Making Men Moral* (New York: Clarendon Press, 1993), 176-82; "Moral Autonomy", 183-93.

[93] See the extended discussion of this point in John Finnis, "Scepticism, Self-Refutation, and the Good of Truth," in *Law, Morality, and Society*, eds. Paul Hacker and Joseph Raz (Oxford: Clarendon Press, 1977), 247-67.

[94] Martin Rhonheimer, *Natural Law and Practical Reason* (New York: Fordham University Press, 2000) 182-84, 195-97.

[95] Rhonheimer, *Natural Law*, 195-97.

[96] Leon Kass, "Is There a Right to Die?" *Hastings Center Report* 23 (1993): 34-43; Daniel Callahan, "When Self-Determination Runs Amok," *Hasting Center Report* 22 (1992): 52-55.

[97] Ronheimer, *Natural Law*, 182-84.

[98] Smith, "Pre-eminence," 182-95.

[99] Finnis, *Natural Law*, 100-3.

[100] See Germain Grisez and Olaf Tollefsen, *Free Choice: A Self-Referential Argument* (Notre Dame: University of Notre Dame Press, 1976), ch 1.

[101] John Finnis and Anthony Fischer, "Theology and the Four Principles," in *Principles of Health Care Ethics*, ed. Raanon Gillon, 31-44.

[102] George, *Making Men Moral*, 180-82; Boyle and Grisez, *Life and Death*, 248-57.

[103] Joseph Raz, *The Morality of Freedom* (Oxford: Clarendon Press, 1986), chs. 14 & 15.

[104] On this point see Patrick Neal, "Perfectionism with a Liberal Face? Nervous Liberals and Raz's Political Theory," *Social Theory and Practice* 20 (1994): 25-58.

[105] Raz, *Morality of Freedom*, 370-99.

[106] George, *Making Men Moral*, 161-88.

[107] See John Finnis, "Legal Enforcement of 'Duties to Oneself': Kant v. the Neo-Kantians," *Columbia Law Review* 87 (1987): 433-56.

[108] George, *Making Men Moral*, 161-88; Finnis, "Legal Enforcement," 433-39.

[109] Robert George, "Liberty Under the Moral Law," *Heythrop Journal* 34 (1993): 175-82.

[110] Grisez and Boyle, *Life and Death*, 125-27.

[111] Luke Gormally, "Euthanasia: Some Points in a Philosophical Polemic," *Linacre Quarterly* 57 (1990): 14-25.

[112] See for example E.H. Cassem, "Depressive Disorders in the Medically Ill," *Psychosomatics* 36 (1995): S2-S10. Hendin and Klerman note that while terminally ill patients may experience thoughts of suicide, it is usually the result of a depression that is transitory in nature. The norm would seem to be that the overwhelming majority of terminally ill patients resist death and fight for life until the end. See H. Hendin and G. Klerman, "Physician-Assisted Suicide: The Dangers of Legalization," *American Journal of Psychiatry* 150 (1993): 143-45.

[113] Edmund Pellegrino, "The Place of Intention in the Moral Assessment of Assisted Suicide and Active Euthanasia," in *Intending Death*, ed. Tom Beauchamp (New Jersey: Prentice Hall, 1995), 163-83, 172-74.

[114] Larson and Amundsen, *A Different Death*, 248-52.

[115] See further his analysis in *The Act Itself* (New York: Clarendon Press, 1995).

[116] Arthur R. Miller, "Acts and Consequences: Squeezing the Accordion," *Metaphilosophy* 18 (1987): 200-7.

[117.] John Finnis, "The Act of the Person," in *Persona Verità, e Morale: Atti del Congresso Internazionale di Teologia Morale*, ed. Aurelio Ansaldo (Roma: Citta Nuova Editrice, 1987), 165.

[118] See further Rocco J. Gennaro, "The Relevance of Intentions in Morality and Euthanasia," *International Philosophical Quarterly* 36 (1996): 217-27; James G. Hanink, "Some Light on Double Effect," *Analysis* 35 (1975): 147-51; J. L. A. Garcia, "Double Effect," in *Encyclopedia of Bioethics*, ed. Warren Thomas Reich. Rev. ed. (New York: Simon & Schuster Macmillan, 1995), 636-41.

[119] John Finnis, "Object and Intention in Moral Judgements According to St. Thomas Aquinas," in *Finalité intentionnalité: doctrine Thomiste et perspectives modernes*, ed. J. Follon and J. McEvoy (Paris: Librairie Philosophique J. Vrin/Leuven: Éditions Peeters, 1992), 127-48.

[120] Eric D'Arcy, *Human Acts* (Oxford: Clarendon Press, 1963), 24.

[121] D'Arcy, 21, 24.

[122] D'Arcy, 26-28.

[123] G.E.M. Anscombe, *Intention.* 2nd ed. (Oxford: Blackwell, 1963), 37-40.

[124] D. Gallagher, "Aquinas on Moral Action: Interior and Exterior Acts," *Proceedings of the American Catholic Philosophical Association* 64 (1990): 118-29. See also Ralph McInerny, *Ethica Thomistica.* 2nd ed. (Washington, DC: Catholic University of America Press, 1996), ch. 4.

[125] Janet E. Smith, *Humanae Vitae: A Generation Later* (Washington, DC: Catholic University of America Press, 1991), 215-20. See also T. Mullady, "The Moral Act," *Ethics & Medics* 19 (1994): 1-2.

[126] Smith, *Humanae Vitae*, 215-20.

[127] See for example Joseph Boyle, "Who is Entitled to Double-Effect?" *Journal of Medicine and Philosophy* 16 (1991): 475-94; "Further Thoughts on Double Effect: Some Preliminary Responses," *Journal of Medicine and Philosophy* 16 (1991): 565-70; "On Killing and Letting Die," *New Scholasticism* 51 (1977): 433-52; Joseph Boyle and Thomas D. Sullivan, "The Diffusiveness of Intention Principle," *Philosophical Studies* 31 (1977): 357-60.

[128] G.E.M. Anscombe, "Action, Intention, and Double Effect," *Proceedings of the American Catholic Philosophical Association* 56 (1982): 12-25.

[129] An example suggested by reading Manuel G. Velasquez, "Defining Suicide," *Issues in Law & Medicine* 3 (1987): 37-51.

[130] John Finnis, "Intention and Side-Effects," in *Liability and Responsibility: Essays in Law and Morals*, eds. R.G. Frey and Christopher Morris (Cambridge: Cambridge University Press, 1991), 32-64, 46.

[131] See Thomas A. Cavanaugh, "Act Evaluation, Willing and Double Effect," *Proceedings of the American Catholic Philosophical Association* 72 (1998): 243-53; "Double Effect and the Ethical Significance of Distinct Volitional States," *Christian Bioethics* 3 (1997): 131-41; "The Intended/Foreseen Distinction's Ethical Relevance," *Philosophical Papers* 25 (1996): 179-88. See also J.L.A. Garcia "Intentions in Medical Ethics," in *Human Lives: Critical Essays on Consequentialist Bioethics,* eds. David S. Oderberg and Jacqueline A. Laing, 161-81.

[132] Garcia, *Intention in Medical Ethics*, 172-73.

[133] Cavanaugh, *Act Evaluation*, 249.

[134] Cavanaugh, *Double Effect and the Ethical Significance of Distinct Volitional States*, 137-39. See also Thomas Nagel, *The View From Nowhere* (New York: Oxford University Press, 1986), 179. According to Nagel it is of the nature of evil that it should repel us.

[135] See Finnis, *Intention and Side-Effects*, 32-64.

[136] See Finnis, "On the Practical Meaning of Secularism," 511.

[137] Daniel P. Sulmasy, "Killing and Allowing to Die: Another Look," *Journal of Law, Medicine and Ethics* 26 (1998): 55-63. See also Robert Barry and James E. Maher, "Indirectly Intended Life-Shortening Analgesia: Clarifying the Principles," 6 *Issues in Law & Medicine* 6 (1990): 117-51.

[138] Garcia, *Intention in Medical Ethics*, 175.

[139] See David S. Oderberg, *Moral Theory* (Oxford: Blackwells, 2000), 105-10.

[140] Oderberg, *Moral Theory*, 105-10.

[141] See Kevin P. Quinn, "Assisted Suicide and Equal Protection: In Defense of the Distinction Between Killing and Letting Die," *Issues in Law and Medicine* 13 (1997): 145-67.

[142] See Stephen R. Latham, "Aquinas and Morphine: Notes on Double Effect at the End of Life," *DePaul Journal of Health Care Law* 1 (1997): 625-44.

[143] Philip Devine, "The Principle of Double Effect," *American Journal of Jurisprudence* 19 (1974): 44-60.

[144] Hanink, "Some Light on Double Effect," 147-51; Robert Barry, "Stones and Streetcars: A Clarification of the Doctrine of the Double Effect," *Irish Theological Quarterly* 1-2 (1981): 127-36.

[145] See chapter three.

[146] Robert P. George, "A Problem for Natural Law Theory: Does the Incommensurability Thesis Imperil Common Sense Moral Judgments?" *American Journal of Jurisprudence* 37 (1992): 345-89.

[147] On fairness see Finnis "Intention and Side Effects," 32-64.

[148] Suzanne M. Uniacke, "The Doctrine of Double Effect," *Thomist* 48 (1984): 188-218; J.L.A Garcia, "Intentions and Wrongdoings," *American Catholic Philosophical Quarterly* 69 (1995): 605-17; E.T. Hannigan, "Is It Ever Lawful to Advise the Lesser of Two Evils?" *Gregorianum* 30 (1949): 104-29; Christopher Kaczor, "Double-Effect Reasoning from Jean Pierre Gury to Peter Knauer," *Theological Studies* 59 (1998): 297-316.

[149] On non-criminal responsibility in tort law see Finnis, "Intention in Tort Law," in *Philosophical Foundations of Tort Law*, ed. David G. Owen (New York: Clarendon Press, 1995), 229-46.

[150] New York law for example maintains that responsibility for suicide can result due to recklessness. See J.A. Alesandro, "Physician-Assisted Suicide and New York State Law," *Albany Law Review* 57 (1994): 819-915.

[151] See the discussion of Tooley and Lichtenberg in chapter three.

[152] See Joseph Boyle, "Sanctity of Life," 221-47. He convincingly argues why the inherent dignity of human life provides sufficient reason why one should not intentionally kill an innocent person.

[153] Harvey Green, "Refraining and Responsibility," *Tulane Studies in Philosophy* 28 (1979): 103-13.

[154] Thomas A. Cavanaugh, "Currently Accepted Practices That Are Known to Lead to Death, and PAS: Is There an Ethically Relevant Difference?" *Cambridge Quarterly of Healthcare Ethics* 4 (1998): 375-81.

[155] R .G. Frey, "Did Socrates Commit Suicide," *Philosophy* 53 (1978): 106-8 [reprinted in *Suicide: The Philosophical Issues*, eds. Margaret P. Battin and David J. Mayo (New York: St.Martin's Press, 1980), 35-47]; Isidor F. Stone, *The Trial of Socrates* (Boston: Little, Brown & Co., 1988), 194-5. See also R. A. Duff, "Socratic Suicide," *Proceedings of the Aristotelian Society* 83 (1983): 48-56.

[156] *Compassion in Dying v. Washington* 79 F.3d (9th Circ. 1996), 807. Here Judge Reinhardt draws upon the work of Alfred Alvarez. See his *Savage God*, 59.

[157] See John E. Peterman and William Paterson, "The Socratic Suicide," in *New Essays on Socrates*, ed. Eugene Kelly (Lanham: University Press of America, 1984), 3-15.

[158] Michael Smith "Did Socrates Kill Himself," *Philospohy* 55 (1980): 253-4; Richard E. Walton, "Socrates' Alleged Suicide," *Journal of Value Inquiry* 14 (1980): 287-99.

[159] Smith "Socrates," 253-4.

[160] Suzanne Stern-Gillet, "The Rhetoric of Suicide," *Philosophy and Rhetoric* 20 (1987): 160-70.

[161] Robert Martin, "Suicide and Self-Sacrifice," in *Suicide: The Philosophical Issues*, eds. Margaret P. Battin and David J. Mayo (New York: St. Martin's Press, 1980), 48-68.

[162] Uniacke, "Doctrine of Double Effect," 188-218.

[163] Nicholas Denyer, "Is Anything Absolutely Wrong?" in Human Lives: Critical Essays on Consequentialist Bioethics, eds. David S. Oderberg and Jacqueline A. Laing, 39-57.

[164] Alfred Wilder, "The Meaning and Place of the Principle of Double Effect in St. Thomas Aquinas," in *Sanctus Thomas De Aquino Doctor Hodiernae Humanitatis,* ed. Leo Elders (Rome: Pontificia Accademia di S. Thommaso, 1995), 571-80; Daniel F. Montaldi, "A Defense of St. Thomas and the Principle of Double Effect," *Journal of Religious Ethics* 14 (1986): 296-332.

[165] Finnis thinks that some justification can be taken from restoring the order of fairness that was disrupted. See his *Fundamentals of Ethics*, 118. However, I fail to see how this is not achieved by the means of acting intentionally against life itself as the means of restoring the order of fairness.

Chapter Six

Natural Law, State Intervention and the

Common Good

Introduction

In the preceding chapter, I have put forward what I take to be a credible and sustained defence of the concrete exceptionless moral norm that it is always a serious moral wrong to intentionally act to kill a human being (whether self or another), regardless of a further appeal to consequences or motive. Such intentional killing, it was argued, is necessarily entailed by acts of suicide, assisted suicide, and voluntary euthanasia. As of yet, however, crucial questions centring on the interface between morality, politics, and jurisprudence, concerning the imposition of coercive legal sanctions, still need to be addressed. Put simply, actions of suicide, assisted suicide or euthanasia may be considered immoral, but should they be subject to legal prohibition on that count? Why are they not questions to be resolved according to the conscience of the individual? If the condition of immorality alone is not considered sufficient for legal prohibition, what further justifications might be needed to subject certain kinds of immoral action to the force of legal sanction?

The first part of this chapter will initially proceed with a critical assessment of the arguments of anti-perfectionists (H. Tristram Engelhardt; John Rawls) that it is not the business of the state to enforce deep or substantive conceptions of what constitutes the 'moral life', upon its citizens. The state does not enjoy any such grand foundation for its authority. Rather, the state is based on inherently weaker notions of the limited goals that the state can serve to pursue and promote, especially in contemporary conditions of diverse pluralism. A related anti-perfectionist notion, put forward by Ronald

Dworkin, is then addressed, concerning the requirement that the state treat its citizens with equal concern and respect. Dworkin argues that an adequate understanding of this notion will provide a solid basis for denying the state paternalistic authority to enforce on its citizens a substantive theory of the good life.

This part of the chapter will then proceed to critically assess the idea that liberal notions of the state need not be founded on an anti-perfectionism, but rather, can seek to defend liberal goals on the basis of its own thicker notion of human flourishing, constituted by key liberal values—nothing less than a liberal perfectionism to ground limits on the authority of the state to enforce certain kinds of norm on its citizens (Joseph Raz; William A. Galston).[1]

In the next part, I then turn to the positive task of working out the implications of the natural law for co-ordinating public life together, centred on its perfectionist understanding of human flourishing and the role it envisions for the state in promoting that flourishing via its idea of the common good. It is argued that its conception of the person in society, centred on the common good, provides a solid framework for assessing both the justification for, as well as the limits on, the role of the state to use its power to legally enforce certain (appropriately qualified) forms of moral standard.

Finally, the concluding part of this chapter examines the relevance of slippery slope reasoning to understanding the impact that the legalisation of assisted suicide or euthanasia may have on the common good of society. In short, it seeks to assess whether such a prudential form of reasoning can, of itself, still provide sufficient justification to persuade those who would not otherwise ban those practices from tolerating their subsequent legalisation.

State Authority and the Limits of Secular Reasoning

Anti-Perfectionism

H. Tristam Engelhardt and John Rawls, as we saw in chapter two, seek to limit the reach of state power by restraining the authority of the state to endorse and support a substantive (perfectionist) theory of the good. Such claims have a heritage directly derived from the political philosophy of J.S. Mill.[2] In the face of considerable disagreement concerning what a good life might actually consist in, and the fractious nature of the power of reason to demonstrate the veracity of its conclusions to others, states need to be neutral in the pursuit of what they can seek to impose upon people.[3]

Engelhardt proposes a retreat to a minimalist state concerned with the very basic conditions of peaceful toleration of one another; a toleration made possible by the imposition of minimalist demands and maximum permissiveness.[4] Further co-operation and restriction on action was considered possible only by additional agreement, or by a consensual sharing of a substantive theory of the good in various non-state associations and communities.[5]

Rawls conceived of the reach of the state being limited by appeals to his idea of restricted 'public reason', eschewing substantive or metaphysical doctrines in order to build up circles of overlapping consensus, and in doing so, preserve a strong role for negative liberty, as well as providing some role for positive liberty built on thin goods, that can serve as common conditions for the promotion of many different and diverse ends.[6]

Having endorsed the concept of state neutrality concerning different visions of the good, that the state has no role to play in making men and women moral, no role in 'perfecting' persons, our authors make further appeal to variations of J.S. Mill's harm principle. The *only ground* for restricting a person's exercise of liberty is the one of restricting harms that are essentially other regarding and cannot command consent (in Engelhardt's case by consent based on the principle of permissiveness, or in Rawls's case, by virtue of public reason further reflected in his notions of legitimacy and reciprocity).[7]

Although many significant details separate their respective accounts of the authority of the state to regulate and control the affairs of its citizens, they nevertheless have a strong bond of similarity, viewed more expansively, based on a scepticism concerning an appeal to any deep or substantive forms of reason, as a basis for state intervention. In consequence, they have a commitment in practice to high degrees of toleration of a variety of deep and opposing ways of life, based on the idea that interference must be limited for the sake of a minimum glue of cohesiveness. Where Engelhardt and Rawls do essentially differ is on *questions of degree* as to how serious the fissure in our capacity for shared ethical reasoning actually is. For Engelhardt, that fissure is near complete, and any contentful non-procedural reasoning is necessarily entirely partisan.[8] For Rawls, there is a limited form of contentful public reason that can serve as an overarching umbrella, and can be reciprocally appealed to in the regulation of public life together.[9]

Engelhardt and Rawls are not simply speaking to those who share their essential respective outlooks on public life, but are seeking to convince 'perfectionists', those who have a thick theory of the good (of what fulfils persons), that they should indeed, for the sake of preserving legitimacy, follow them down their respective paths. [10] Having argued in chapter three that the foundations of morality are indeed perfectionist, the key question to be addressed here is whether a perfectionist need be drawn into accepting either argument for high degrees of permissiveness in order to justify the legitimacy of paternalistic state intervention?[11]

Engelhardt's Procedural Morality

Turning firstly to Engelhardt, it seems that the plausibility of his case depends on the conclusion that the only real alternative left in Western societies, due to failures of rationality, are declines into anarchy, or authoritarianism, or acceptance of the principle of permission, with all that it entails.[12] For Engelhardt, the latter is justifiable and the other alternatives not. Yet, we are entitled to ask, what is the basis of the justification offered for appealing to the latter rather than the former two options (assuming that they are the only alternatives)?

Engelhardt needs to demonstrate to the perfectionist that there are indeed convincing grounds for embracing his option. Yet, if we are really to take his claim concerning the power of human reason seriously, to the conclusion he thinks warranted, there would be nothing much to say on the matter to others not of his mind frame, on his own project of permission.[13] What can the status of those initial propositions concerning permission possibly be? For Engelhardt, non-formal reason is necessarily partisan in outlook. Yet, if it is truly partisan in the way he thinks, then what is to prevent the acceptability of other partisan appeals to deeply authoritarian structures of governance, or anarchy? Why is his alternative *any better* if we are indeed sceptical of the possibilities of moral knowledge (and what constitutes human flourishing) in the way he thinks?[14]

When we start to look at the foundations of his contentless procedural project, however, we can in fact discern a smuggling in of contentful substantial forms of reasoning, thus undermining his claim that we can in fact create a contentless foundation for moral deliberation, as an alternative to 'discredited' contentful moralities.[15] Consider the foundational principle of permission itself. This is dependent on a whole array of substantive baggage concerning reasoned apprehension as to *what it is to be a person.* Persons engage in complex processes of *deliberation, negotiation, and agreement.* The whole edifice of his contractualism is built upon the assumptions of contact theory *as a paradigm for normative human behaviour and conduct.*[16] Any one with a vague knowledge of the development of mercantilism in the West will know the controversial normative assumptions upon which 'free' exchange has been premised. These are not mere 'innocent assumptions' that can be treated as 'light matter', and are manifestly not simply the product of the purely formal operations of reason, and are therefore heavily pregnant with initial substantive content.

Engelhardt repeatedly states that his secular morality is purely procedural. It has "inescapable rules but no content."[17] Here, he seems to want it both ways, to have a contentless, yet contentful, morality. However, he cannot. If it were genuinely contentless, then it would be an empty framework incapable of generating the crucial normative premises that he needs. If he did introduce substantive initial content, he would be begging his own question concerning the supposed failure of all traditional moralities to justify heavy substantive starting points.[18]

Crucial assumptions of what it is to be a human person and what fulfils a human person must substantively stand somewhere. He seeks to say both that non-formal reason is necessarily partisan, and yet his own substantive assumptions crucially need a non-partisan underpinning that must be more than merely formal if the perfectionist (or any other person who doesn't share his partisanship) is going to be reasonably convinced by him to support such a project.[19]

In the previous edition of his text, he appealed to the key positive value of autonomy, a notion with deep substantive normative baggage.[20] Yet, the move to re-label it as the principle of permission, in the second edition, cannot render it merely 'formal' as a starting point, for it presupposes a very controversial and contested view of the human person. Calling it the principle of permission rather than the value of autonomy, changes the label used, but not the central contested issue at stake.[21]

Consider this question further with reference to his discussion of infanticide. It becomes more and more evident as we learn what Engelhardt's "purely procedural morality" actually entails.[22] He, as with an array of other thinkers, states that infants are non-persons. Persons must have the exercisable deliberative capacities for negotiation and agreement.[23] Yet, we are entitled to ask, why are those the determinate characteristics for personhood that grant immunity from intentional killing, and not others? Is an appeal to the species protection principle unreasonable? Why should we reasonably follow him in the attribution of those characteristics as being constitutive of personhood? The answer, on his own prior terms, is that we need not, for we can state that he stresses certain characteristics of the person to the exclusion of others, thus trading on deep content. If we contest Engelhardt's foundationalism based on the operative principle of permission, and with it, his view of the human person, we need not concede the conclusions he seeks to derive from it.[24]

Consider further the question of assisted suicide. For Engelhardt, this is largely dependent on the principle of permission and further agreement. Since it is unlikely those persons will give up the right to control the manner and timing of their own deaths, they retain that right (subject to other contractual duties that may need to be discharged first).[25] Yet, why should we be convinced by the appeal to the principle of permission, given the view of the person upon which it is predicated? A perfectionist will not be convinced, since the appeal begs the earlier, more foundational question, of what it is to be a person, that Engelhardt's answer itself presupposes.

Questions of what constitute a harm to the human person cannot be answered without grounding content as to what it is to be a human person. We are entitled to say that an interpretation of harm will itself be based on the presuppositions of what it is to be a person, what the authentic interests at stake really are, and how we should respond to them, e.g., whether or not paternalistic intervention may be required to prevent or limit that harm for the sake of the common good.[26]

Rawls's Public Reason

Engelhardt's project was premised on the assumption that the key principle of permission, and the minimal authority it would grant to the state, in conditions of diverse pluralism, would avoid recourse to anarchy or authoritarianism. However, is this really the choice facing Western society?[27] I suspect that Engelhardt really offers a false set of alternatives, and that this false set is in fact challenged by John Rawls's notion of overlapping circles of consensus. Alliances and webs of stability can be formed by appeals to 'public reason' that do not require the near complete abandonment of the public square to the forces of maximum permissiveness.[28]

Rawls does a valuable task in expanding the range of political conceptions available to modern debate beyond the minimalist state. Here, I partially agree with Rawls that the public square, in a number of ways, does indeed depend on alliances, consensus building, and some forms of compromise based on toleration.[29] However, my chief problem with his account is the anti-perfectionist nature of his limitation on what constitutes a valid reason for being part of that public sphere.[30]

Rawls is concerned to protect a diversity of conceptions of the good he thinks compatible with a thin theory of reason called 'public reason'. This is the only form of reason fit to inform the resolution of public controversy. It is said to form a principled ground for denying the imposition of 'doctrine' on citizens.[31] Yet, his claim to be neutral, as derived from his conception of public reason, is dependent on the sustainability of this restricted ground for limiting appeals to what is reasonable.[32] In this respect, it shares the same burden as his earlier claim in the *Theory of Justice* that basic human rationality will produce anti-perfectionist outcomes, eschewing thick theories of the good.[33]

His *Theory of Justice*, however, rested on an unjustifiable premise, for it proposed that we must recognise only principles of justice that would be adopted in the original position behind a veil of ignorance.[34] Yet, there is no good reason to assume, as Rawls did, that proper deliberation need be hampered by such a constraint.[35] Perfectionists may justifiably claim that if their positions really are true and demonstrable, then they should be entitled to act upon them and not be so constrained by an unsubstantiated procedural device that simply loads the dice in favour of the desirability of anti-perfectionist outcomes.[36]

Turning now to his *Political Liberalism,* there is also a crucial and unsubstantiated loading of the dice, namely, that it is illegitimate to propose for public consideration, principles or values judged true and supported by substantial reasoning (e.g., reasons capable of public articulation, accessible to all by virtue of the capacities we have for practical and theoretical reason).[37] Perfectionists who propose them cannot reasonably be expected to sever the chains of their reasoning into the emaciated form of reasoning that would result from the operation of Rawls's methodological guillotine. The result is not one of neutrality at all, but one of discounting other theories of the good from their own reflective consideration of what is good for society to pursue and promote.[38]

Rawls's notions of legitimacy and reciprocity are conditioned by his view of what constitutes a reasonable citizen in his methodology of political constructivism. Yet, he needs to state precisely why reasonable citizenship cannot entail putting forward propositions for consideration in public life that appeal to reasoned evidence truly claimed to be accessible to all.[39]

Rawls's version of accessible reason is plausible only to those who share his assumptions of partial scepticism concerning deeper substantive reasoning. Yet, for the perfectionist, this cannot be coherent, for the reasonable simply cannot be divided up that way into 'thin public' and 'thick private'. If there are good reasons to conclude that a course of action should be followed, accessible to others, perfectionists will not, so to speak, mutilate the source of that reason, for to do so would rob it of its framework of meaningfulness.[40]

For those reasons then, Rawls cannot expect those not of his bent to concur with him in limiting claims to what is a reason for action to the standard set by his own partial scepticism, albeit a scepticism shared by many others. Those perfectionists who think that there is truth in practical reason accessible to all, will have firm grounds for rejecting his idea of what constitutes the 'publicly reasonable', and with it, what public life can commit itself to in terms of grounds for state intervention.[41]

There are many reasonable differences which arise in public life and which reflect legitimate differences in commitment. But in relation to some matters, for example the protection of human life itself, the perfectionist will indeed claim that there are right answers that are true and accessible to all, notwithstanding the fact of disagreement.[42] How can such differences be accounted for? Here we can only point to the fact that where reason is operative there can be mistakes, and such mistakes are inevitably part of what G.E.M. Anscombe terms the 'twistiness' of human thought (exacerbated by a cultural fog that denies the possibility of any certainty in moral knowledge).[43] Contra Rawls, what the perfectionist need not do is abandon appeals to the substantive operation of reason, and in doing so hand over public life to the deep quagmire of scepticism.[44]

In Rawls's quest to provide for the conditions of public life, he essentially seeks to construct a society that is manifestly not neutral, between competing versions of the good. Rawls is engaged in a parameter setting exercise that is unreasonable due to the restrictive sense of reason he wishes to legitimise in the public arena. In consequence, it is not an arena of earnest inquiry, but one that seeks to clip the wings of other deeper appeals to reason, appeals with which liberalism itself ultimately disagrees.[45]

Once it is conceded that wider appeals to reason must contribute to an understanding of problems, these wider appeals must inevitably effect what constitutes a reasonable ordering of values and principles. Public reasoning inevitably becomes a less restrictive and more open-ended source of inquiry. When all is said and done, reason that is based upon 'substantive doctrine' must be granted its rightful place in the public arena, and cannot be methodologically discounted or side-stepped.[46]

Applying this point to the question of assisted suicide, Rawls, a signatory to the *Philosphers' Brief,* thinks that public reason must justify the conclusion that there is a right to assisted suicide for those who are terminally ill, suffering, and who are competent.[47] Yet, the point of reasoned contestation is one of why the values must reasonably be resolved the way he thinks? Curiously, he seems to think that the value of human life in any intrinsic sense is 'doctrinal', and hence excluded as 'unreasonable', but the value of personal autonomy is entirely within the scope of 'public reason'.[48]

Contrary to Rawls, we can say that what constitutes a harm worth preventing, will itself be determined by the stance taken on the nature of what values are truly at stake. It seems that what really counts as a publicly accessible reason, of what is doctrinal and what is not, is left to the judgement of Rawls and like-minded thinkers. It is tempting indeed to conclude that the phrase 'public reason' often functions as a euphemism for liberal premises. Yet it *need not*, if Rawls accepts that the concept of public reason should encompass appeals to substantive reasoning more generally. When public reason is opened up to this wider sense, the fact of pluralism is taken seriously. It is addressed in a way that is not unduly dismissive of a tradition like natural law that does claim accessibility and persuasiveness in seeking to influence the ordering of public policy towards a reconciliation of competing values that is *legitimate, fair, and reciprocal*, because it seeks to demonstrate the justification for the values it proclaims by credible argumentation under the full and frank scrutiny of the public eye.[49]

Equal Worth and Respect

As we saw in chapter two, Ronald Dworkin argued for the existence of a moral right to do a moral wrong.[50] The argument is essentially one of stating that interfering with profound questions of meaning does not respect persons in their equal worth.[51] To prevent a person from exercising a choice for death, in conditions of considerable pain and suffering, is said to represent an unwarranted devaluing of the life of that person, even if it was considered to be a morally unjustifiable rejection of the value of human life. Rights act as trumps over impositions of what is best for that individual, framed around the notion of respecting the equal worth of others.[52]

The strength of this argument depends upon accepting the notion that in imposing certain constraints on an individual's exercise of choice, those state impositions *necessarily manifest* a disrespect for persons (that an individual is treated as lacking in equality of worth).[53] However, it is far from obvious that legislative concern for the moral environment of citizens is indicative of disrespect and even contempt. Such legislation can manifest a profound respect for the equal worth and dignity of all persons by protecting people from acts judged truly unworthy and harmful, e.g., acts of assistance in procuring the suicide of another.[54]

Whilst some conduct is condemned as unworthy, it does not follow that this is equivalent to the proposition that any human person is less worthy than any other human person.[55] The paternalism involved in a decision to legally intervene and prevent assistance in suicide can be reconciled with a profound sense of commitment to equal worth and dignity. It seems far too stretched a claim to make that seeking to structure legislation in a way that offers reasonable grounds for furthering what is objectively fulfilling of persons, necessarily manifests a disrespect for the person *qua* person, and not just the unworthiness of certain choices themselves.[56]

The state cannot remain neutral to such questions, for certain forms of choice are indeed seriously morally wrong and need not command our respect. In consequence, there cannot be a *moral right to do a wrong*.[57] What there can be, perhaps, is a legal duty to refrain from coercive interference in the exercise of certain moral wrongs (of toleration) since it may be judged that interference with the exercise of certain choices would unjustifiably prejudice other interests of society in pursuing and protecting the common good.[58]

For the sake of upholding some goods, and necessary freedoms to pursue those goods, it may be that many bad choices may need to be tolerated, subject only to forms of non-coercive disapprobation (e.g., community censure). The coercive force of the law, as Dworkin never tires of pointing out, is a blunt power that needs to be used sparingly and wisely.[59] Thus, for example, there is a duty to refrain from interfering coercively, in most circumstances, with acts of lying. However, even here, the state has an interest in threatening the coercive use of force in some situations where the service of important goods demands truthfulness. Thus, it is not permissible to intentionally lie in court, or to intentionally lie and pervert the course of justice.

The state should be circumspect in its use of coercive power. Law does not have the capacity to change the hearts and minds of persons who think that they are being denied equal worth.[60] A person's choices should not be lightly overruled. Yet, if Dworkin thinks that apprehensions of unworthiness concerning profundity of meaning are key, then this would surely count against all manner of 'unwarranted' intervention, e.g., the imposition of taxes on those who think that taxation is an affront to their respectful consideration by the state (for the maintenance of their own wealth is of deep and profound meaning to them). Apprehensions of unworthiness cannot therefore be a realistic foundation for such an appeal, for it demands far too much in the face of any claim on the part of the state to intervene in the protection and promotion of key values.[61] Of course, Dworkin may have a different apprehension of what judgements are properly respectful and what judgements are not. But such claims really do look decidedly untenable unless they are indeed based on a consideration of *what exercises of choice are truly judged worthy of being respected.*[62] It can thus be stated that certain judgements as to the worthlessness of certain choices do not require a denial of the equal worth of persons who always retain a radical dignity, at times in spite of their apprehension of their own self-worth.[63]

Perfectionist Liberalism

Liberals such as Joseph Raz and William Galston, challenge the premises of Rawls's *Political Liberalism*, and other forms of anti-perfectionism.[64] They argue that it is necessary to focus on a substantive theory of the good, the key values that are truly constitutive of human well-being, in a foundational way.[65] Those values are perfectionist, since they are what makes life fulfilling and rewarding. Crucially, they discount the possibility of founding political structures neutrally.[66] Those values must be embraced as part of a comprehensive theory of the good. Such a key value is the value of personal autonomy, considered genuinely basic and of great worth. It cannot be adequately protected by default to supposed neutrality or impartiality. If an authentic array of plurality is to be preserved, it requires a central perfectionist defence.[67]

Joel Feinberg considers the value of personal autonomy to be supported by an analogy with the sovereignty of the state and a right not to be interfered with. As a state loses its sovereignty with breaches of its territory, so too an individual's sovereignty is lost when coercive impositions are made.[68] Yet such a negative delimitation, for the perfectionist liberal, is inadequate, for it fails to genuinely value constitutive autonomy as a positive value in its own right, a value that can justify some paternalistic measures that actually enhance the value of personal autonomy for the individual, and society, in the longer term.[69]

With perfectionist liberalism, therefore, we see a clear appeal to constitutive values that should furnish the grounds for shaping public policy and the framing of laws. What is refreshing in those accounts of liberalism is the need to embrace and found state concerns on what is necessary for the promotion of human well-being. Only by embracing and promoting such values can we begin to legitimise the exercise of state power in a way that credibly respects the nature of persons.[70] Liberal perfectionist accounts, therefore, have structural similarities with accounts of natural law theory, at least to the extent that they seek to promote a contentful theory of what it is to flourish as a human person.[71] Such questions are the central concern of society and the state. They reject the claim that important civil liberties will necessarily be jeopardised by state action that stands for the promotion of human well-being, and is not derived from anti-perfectionism. State action cannot be neutrally based. Human reason is able to grasp the importance and significance of human well-being.[72] Where they differentiate themselves from natural law assessments of what constitutes well-being, is in their concern that natural law theory fails to fully appreciate the value of personal autonomy as an important aspect of human well-being.[73]

Here, I would admit that natural law theory has indeed historically paid a lack of attention to the legitimate concern of anti-perfectionists and liberal perfectionists in understanding and protecting the importance of certain human liberties (e.g., freedom of religious worship).[74] I would agree that concerns flowing from personal autonomy can be legitimate in many respects, and many restrictions cannot be justified against its appeal. The law is often a blunt instrument to control human behaviour. Appeals to it must indeed be carefully circumscribed, undertaken as a last resort, and only embarked upon where significant interests are at stake. There are indeed authentic ranges of plural forms of life. There is no one form of good living.[75]

Where I think liberal perfectionism goes astray, however, is in its over emphasis on the stress of the value of personal autonomy at the expense of an adequate recognition of other important values. Properly circumscribed, autonomy is an important good, worthy or respect and promotion. However, it is not a basic human good. It is, rather, an important instrumental good.[76] As such, it is sometimes reasonable to intentionally limit the exercise of this good in order to promote and protect basic human goods constitutive of the human person. Such a basic good is the good of human life itself, a good where it is not reasonable to seek to intentionally act against it for the sake of the promotion of other goods, including personal autonomy. It is in relation to the protection of such a good, that the paths of liberal perfectionism and natural law perfectionism may significantly diverge.[77]

Here I am not arguing that perfectionist liberalism is necessarily committed to supporting the need for a policy of a right to suicide or assisted suicide. They may, for example, find slippery slope arguments convincing enough to justify a policy of circumscribing an exercise of autonomy due to the need to ensure the protection of people who are frail and vulnerable from societal pressures.[78] I address this important issue later in the chapter. What does concern me, however, is that the strongest argument for the preservation of human life is deprived of its central constitutive role, due to an over concentration on the good of personal autonomy at the expense of a proper focus on the strength of other crucial goods.[79]

The Common Good

Community, Friendship, and Justice

For John Finnis, community is constituted from the shared objectives of those who comprise it. The good of the community is forged from the good of each and every individual member of the community.[80] This understanding of community does not render Finnis's conception of the community essentially one marked by individualism, as some may allege, for amongst the basic human goods of each and every member of the community is the good of friendship (*societas*).[81] Friendship is not simply an instrumental good for the sake of which other goods can be pursued. It is a basic good in and of itself, necessarily inter-personal.[82] It is the more expansive good of which the good of justice itself is a part—rendering to each person his or her due. Friendship, therefore, can be said to be instantiated and promoted in every just act, and damaged by every act of injustice.[83]

It is due to the basis upon which friendship and justice are intrinsic aspects of human flourishing, that a direct attack upon those goods can never be justified for the sake of the common good.[84] Where there is injustice, notwithstanding appearances to the contrary, every member of the community can be said to be harmed by the failure to recognise and act upon the requirements of justice.[85] In every intentional killing, for example, there is a genuine harm rendered against the entire community, due to the *incivility* of the act as an attack on human life itself, an indispensable requirement upon which civil community is itself founded.[86] In all acts of injustice, each and every member of the community is exposed to an act of harm that lacks genuine concern for the promotion of true civil community with one another.[87]

The basic human goods, and the ways in which they can be pursued, are only fully realisable in a community ordered in an open and expansive way towards embracing the goods of friendship and justice. To be able to practically realise these goods, people need to co-operate to create conditions conducive to the preservation and promotion of important goods, including a myriad of worthwhile projects compatible with them. The individual cannot flourish apart from, or in isolation from, this vitally important social dimension to human fulfilment.[88] The neglect of this important social dimension to the human person can indeed be said to be an impoverishment prevalent in liberal philosophy that perpetrates a false sense of 'being left alone'.[89]

If individuals are to flourish, then community too must reflect the conditions that allow the basic human goods to flourish. To the extent that the state (a body that derives its coercive and regulatory authority from the central task of furthering the common good) does not promote these goods, it undermines those goods, and in doing so undermines the shared well-being of the community (ultimately calling into question the very rationale for its authority).[90]

Common Good not Greater Good

John Finnis defines the common good as: "a set of conditions which enables the members of a community to attain for themselves reasonable objectives, or to realise reasonably for themselves the value(s), for the sake of which they have reason to collaborate with each other (positively and/or negatively) in a community."[91] The common good is not a mere aggregation of overall interests, or the sum of individual interests à la utilitarianism.[92] It is not simply some grand exercise in cost benefit analysis (although, to be sure, a certain appropriately qualified sphere for such calculations is needed as a subordinate question of pursuing *legitimate goals* effectively and efficiently, e.g., building a bridge or a motorway). Rather, what is signified here by the common good is importantly delimited and structured by what is judged to be conducive to promoting the genuine good of each and every member of the community respected in their radical dignity and equal worth.[93]

According to Finnis, every individual has a responsibility to regard the common good in acts of choice. It is one of the criteria of practical reasonableness. Thus, it is always wrong to choose in ways that violate the basic goods of others (thus attacking their equal worth and dignity).[94] The basic constituents of human flourishing need to be respected, especially by those who have responsible decision-making capacity in the co-ordination of community life together by the setting of policy and law. Friendship and justice are goods that need to underpin all co-ordination decisions, further informed and moderated by all the requirements of reasonableness, in the framing of choices.[95] Those in authority have a special responsibility with regard to the common good. The whole object of just authority, justly executed, is to preserve and advance the common good over those whom (and for the sake of which) authority is exercised. The decisions of those in authority are justified precisely to the extent that they are made for the common good.[96] Decisions need to respect the basic goods of flourishing and seek to *create a framework of conditions* that promote those goods. To the extent that decisions made are clearly contrary to the common good (e.g., a failure to respect the basic constituents of flourishing for *each and every* person), they can be said to examples of unjustifiable and unwarranted exercises of power.[97]

Spheres of the Common Good

The common good is a multi-faceted good that importantly refers both to the commonality of basic human goods and to the mutual shaping of choices concerning those goods.[98] Those goods are properly actualised in community with others. Thus the common good requires a due regard for the framing of conditions to serve and promote the basic goods of human flourishing, conditions that need to be co-ordinated, and that instantiate the requirement that we act reasonably towards one another in shaping the choices that we make.[99] The need to recognise the well-being of others, mitigates against any false sense of isolationism or retreat from responsibility that results in a denial of those crucial aspects of mutual concern.[100]

All basic human goods can be participated in, and actions co-ordinated inter-personally without the intervention *per se* of state political structures. The principle of subsidiarity (from the Latin *subsidium*, meaning help) is important here when we consider the level of appropriate decision making concerning 'spheres' of the common good.[101] It is all to easy to adopt centralising tendencies, where power and decision making get absorbed into higher levels of co-ordination, leaving subsidiary societies weakened.[102] Families, associations, and other forms of co-operative endeavour, require a proper recognition of their specific common goods, informed by their own legitimate (though more narrowly circumscribed) goals.[103]

Concern for the principle of subsidiarity clearly implies that actions of the state, in pursuing the sphere of co-ordination that constitutes the political common good, cannot be directed against the legitimate goals of other spheres of the common good. State action in the service of the common good is reserved for the reasonable conditions it alone can seek to help promote; conditions that cannot be, or have manifestly failed to be, achieved by other narrower spheres of the common good, e.g., families, neighbourhoods, and associations.[104]

Limits on Pluralism?

The political common good is uniquely concerned to promote further harmonising conditions that would otherwise only be very imperfectly met, without the use of state sanction and control, by other spheres of the common good.[105] Crucially, there needs to be recognition that individuals will have many reasonable objectives, for the sake of which, worthwhile choices can be made. There are innumerable worthwhile life plans that can be chosen that reflect a myriad of possibility.[106] State action is grossly unjust when the legitimate scope for plurality in society is unduly curtailed or thwarted. Such restrictions do not serve to secure, promote, or otherwise enhance, the common good.[107]

Yet, if there is an authentic array of plurality, the promotion of the common good cannot be regarded as the creation of a set of conditions to promote whatever choices persons may want to choose, by whatever means they deem fit.[108] Rather, the common good is served by the framing of a set of *reasonable conditions* for responsible civil life together.[109] This might, as has already been stated, require some toleration of unreasonable choices for the sake of the common good, but it certainly does not render illegitimate the use of all coercive paternalistic intervention in the control of some unworthy choices.[110] The justification of paternalistic authority relates primarily to the control of unreasonable choices that are particularly undermining because they manifest serious distortions of the conditions necessary for the mutual co-ordination of common life together.[111]

Moral Ecology?

Will an appeal to the ecology of a society not encourage fears that the state has potential for all manner of personal invasions of liberty? Is it not simply an endorsement of law as a blunt instrument in the service of heavy handed paternalism?[112] Can the use of legal coercion really be deployed for the sake of promoting virtue and suppressing vice in the name of the common good?

The idea of the common good can be traced back to the thought of Aristotle.[113] For Aristotle, the polity, through its regulatory function of law making, could use coercive force to further virtue and discourage vice in those lacking the requisite prudence to conduct themselves virtuously.[114] Aristotle thought that the use of force could suppress vice, and in doing so create conditions whereby the 'average' citizen could better respond to the calling of the virtuous life.[115]

The influence of Aristotle is clearly reflected in Aquinas's understanding of the relationship between law and the service of the common good.[116] Aquinas argued in the *De Regno*, that the king who wishes to fulfil his duty to lead people to virtue, must, as far as possible, help people lead virtuous lives. The King, via his coercive power, should restrain wickedness and seek to promote virtuous action.[117] In the *Summa Theologiae*, Aquinas argued that human law can justifiably permit some vices since law must to some extent reflect the condition of the people, and therefore not seek the impossible in furthering the common good.[118]

From what has been stated above, it may seem that Aristotle and Aquinas have missed an important fundamental point, namely, that coercing people to conform to do the right thing does not make them morally better. It does nothing more that lead to conformity in external signs of behaviour. It does not make people genuinely virtuous, but simply restrains certain external conduct. Law cannot lead to the conversion of a person's heart. Law, therefore, cannot *make* a person virtuous.[119]

I agree with this criticism to the extent it appears that Aristotle and Aquinas do, at times, seem to speak of the law as having the main goal of leading people directly into the 'open arms' of virtue. It cannot. Law, in its enforcement, can only lead to external constraint on the outward manifestations of human behaviour. Additionally, it is important to point out that forms of life style compatible with authentic forms of human flourishing *are rather more diverse* than they would have recognised.[120] Nevertheless, there is, I think, an important dimension to Aristotle's and Aquinas's normative jurisprudence that has significant validity.

Given the tendency of people to react on the basis of passion and desire, law can be utilised in a *limited and circumscribed* way to calm such disruptions, placing restraints on the stronger temptations to unfriendly and uncivil conduct.[121] Its concern here is to place restrictions on the path of temptation to deeply harmful and destructive choices. A particularly strong focus here would be to restrain the activities of those who seek to tempt or facilitate others into the making of harmful and destructive choices.[122]

Implications for Suicide and Assisted Suicide

A state that wishes to promote and foster respect for the good of human life needs to restrain the action of those who would commit contra-life acts of intentional killing. It may not lead to a conversion of heart, but that need not be its directly intended goal. Prevention of a significant harm to the common good can provide reasonable justification for considering coercive prohibition.

Reflecting on the requirements of the common good and the use of legal coercion, I would argue that the act of suicide, whilst nevertheless immoral, ought not to be subjected to criminal sanction. Punishment is grossly unwarranted in cases where the burden of punishment is borne by the family, and where suicide is often undertaken in conditions of severe distress and disturbance of the mind. Law must be tempered to conditions properly appreciative of where its powers to control and influence are efficacious. Mercy and compassion, not punishment, ought to inform our understanding of the actions of the suicide and those who have attempted suicide.

Cases of active assisted suicide and active euthanasia are of a different order. No person can have a sanctioned right to attack the good of human life in others, without undermining the foundations of *civil/friendly* community (no form of violence of this kind is a peaceful and respectful act, whether it is consented to or not). The duty not to intentionally kill is basic to a proper understanding of civilised life in society with others. Such a willingness to help is wrongful, since it renders the act more probable by a willingness to assist. A person who intentionally assists in the suicide of another denies the basic worth of the life so ended. Further, such an act communicates the supremely uncivil message that some lives are indeed not worth living. Such is an unfair signal to others that their lives in an impaired condition may also be unworthy of living. The state has a paramount responsibility to prevent this form of conduct. Were it to tolerate it, it would be engaged in an act of *uncivil abandonment* towards those who reasonably look to political community to foster and promote the co-ordination of supportive conditions needed for responsible social life together.

What of cases of assisted suicide or euthanasia undertaken by the omission or withdrawal of treatment? Here, I would argue that the shaping of the law needs to focus on the preservation of reasonable choices, and this may entail the toleration of a sphere of activity of unreasonable choice, for the sake of not unduly impinging on reasonable choice. Thus, toleration of an extensive right to withdraw treatment can be for the sake of the common good, since over interference and disregard for a considerable discretion on the part of the patient in the decision making process, may result in many bad side-effects. Toleration, here, is required, precisely because many acts of withdrawal of treatment are compatible with an intention to be free of the burden's of a treatment, and not of life itself. For the sake of respecting those reasonable choices, some degree of necessary toleration of unreasonable choices is required. The same cannot be said for positive acts of assisted suicide or euthanasia. Here the intent is always intimately tied to the goal of ending life itself. Such acts cannot be tolerated, for the act of toleration here would be one that grants legitimacy to the idea that civil community can condone the negation of the life of one of its members by the intentionally destructive act of another.

Slippery Slope Arguments

Prudence and Policy

I have argued above that the protection of the good of human life is foundational to the idea of the common good. To the extent that the good is undermined by intentional acts of killing, the flourishing environment of that society is weakened. The foundation for legitimacy of state authority is the promotion and protection of the common good.[123] In considering what implications a state instituted policy of assisted suicide or euthanasia may have on the common good, it is necessary to prudentially consider what further implications such policies might bring in their wake. Further considerations of this kind need to be examined because it may still be possible to identify good reasons for those who do not accept the main argument posed in this chapter, to still oppose the legalisation of those practices, on the basis of such prudential deliberation.

Policy makers in the United Kingdom found such slippery slope forms of argumentation to be sufficiently compelling for that country to uphold its existing laws that prohibit the practices of assisted suicide or voluntary euthanasia. Such arguments cannot therefore be dismissed as the last desperate attempt of a sanctity of life ethic to impose its imperatives onto the free deliberations of contemporary pluralistic society.[124] An adequate consideration of the common good of society requires such considerations to be factored in, and they may be found convincing by those who, as a matter of principle, do not oppose the idea of assisted suicide or voluntary euthanasia.[125] Whilst I do not expect that any one slippery slope argument, considered singly, will bear enough weight to convert many others to abandon their policy of advocacy, I would argue that their cumulative weight, when taken together, can indeed offer serious reasoned grounds for doing so.[126]

Forms of Slippery Slope

According to David Lamb, three basic forms of slippery slope argumentation can be identified. There are two logical forms, and one empirical form.[127] The first logical form states that if no significant conceptual difference between Y and Z can be identified that has any real import, the justification used to support Y will also entail a justification for Z. If Y is deemed unacceptable in practice, then Z should also be considered unacceptable, since the two cannot be reasonably distinguished. The second logical form is a variation of the first, whereby it is considered that X and Z may be significantly different, but that there is no significant difference between X and Y and in consequence, via the acceptance of intermediary steps, the acceptance of Z will eventually be reached. The empirical form of the slippery slope states that in accepting Y, due to the vagaries of psychological, cultural and social factors, this will result in the eventual acceptance of Z.[128]

Whilst I would readily concede at the outset that slippery slope arguments are based on projections, and therefore are prone to the complexities of considering what might reasonably happen, they cannot be avoided on that count.[129] There are of course occasions when slippery slope arguments are indeed abused, simply to entrench the position of the existing status quo, and any change becomes associated with an appeal to 'sliding down the slippery slope'. However, as Sissela Bok wisely points out, their abuse *in some settings* does not therefore justify a blanket rejection of their use *in other more appropriate settings*.[130] This is a process of reasoned discernment. She concludes that the assisted suicide/euthanasia context is just such an appropriate setting. Any attempt to formulate public policy here must take seriously not only what is immediately envisaged by the creation of present policy, but also must prudently assess what further implications may be plausibly risked from the creation of that initial policy.[131]

Weak Conceptual Road Blocks

In the argumentation of those who support the legalisation of physician assisted suicide, there is an attempt to point to the clear conceptual difference between a policy of assisted suicide and forms of euthanasia. Since they advocate that a clear conceptual ground for differentiation exists, it is argued that there is no need to embark upon a slippery slope at all, providing adequate safeguards are in place to protect the consensual nature of the choice being made, and an appropriately narrow class of beneficiaries can be established.[132]

The *Philosophers' Brief* makes such assurances central to reassuring the Supreme Court of the *modesty and practicality* of its proposal for the legalisation of physician assisted suicide.[133] R.G. Frey similarly make the point that conceptual differentiation and appropriate safeguards can allay fears that a policy of legalisation will not bring about a spree of extension resulting in unacceptable practices.[134]

Can the claim that a policy that legitimises physician assisted suicide be adequately differentiated from a policy that also legitimates the practice of voluntary euthanasia? In the introduction to the book, I pointed out that the definitional distinction between the two centred around the question of who performed the last act of administering the fatal means. In physician assisted suicide, the last act is said to be performed by the patient, not the physician. In the model statute drafted by Charles Baron, and in the legislation enacted in the State of Oregon, the ministration of the lethal means is clearly stated to be performed by the patient and not the physician, or any other third party.[135] Such a distinction has legal significance by virtue of being enacted. However, the key question to be addressed is whether or not it is rational in the sense that it can be justified as a clear line that can serve as a benchmark between acts of assisted suicide and acts of voluntary euthanasia. There is good reason to think that it cannot. Many supporters and opponents of physician assisted suicide alike view its enactment as being but one step on the path to a fuller embracement of voluntary euthanasia itself. There is good reason to view this as a logical extension of the rationale inherent in the right of assistance to suicide itself.[136]

What moral significance differentiates an act of assistance from the direct ministration of the lethal means by the physician? It cannot be a question of intent, for morality and the law have historically considered aiding and abetting an act as the intentional adoption of a common enterprise.[137] Consider a person who plans a robbery, with the actual execution of the robbery carried out by a third party. The planner may be nowhere near the physical execution of the act. Such an appeal cannot exonerate the planner. If we do not readily seek to exonerate people intimately tied to the sharing of a common enterprise, why should we make such a distinction in the case of physician assisted suicide? The distinction carries no weight in other cases across a broad spectrum of human action. For this reason I think that an appeal to who performs the last act in a common shared enterprise is an illusionary distinction that cannot be given the force that is required of it. It is quite simply an irrelevant distinction that cannot plausibly separate the physician who prescribes the lethal dose of medication from shared responsibility in the final outcome of the common enterprise.[138] If it is not considered blameworthy for a physician to prescribe a lethal dose of medication to a patient for self-ministration , it is surely not blameworthy for the physician himself or herself to directly administer such a dose into the mouth or veins of a patient too weak to undertake the final act of the common enterprise. In consequence, the acceptance of Y, due to the making of a distinction that does not carry with it any significant moral import, entails the consequence that Z should also be viewed as an acceptable practice.[139]

That such a distinction cannot be reasonably maintained can be further demonstrated by the values that inform appeals to assisted suicide in the first place. These values centre around the alleviation of pain and suffering, and respect for the personal autonomy of the patient to determine whether or not life ceases to be a good worth pursuing.[140] This leads directly into a consideration of the second form of logical argument. Once X is viewed in the context of the wider values that are driving the advocacy of the practice, those values supply the necessary intermediate steps necessary to similarly legitimate the licitness of practice Z. In such a context, it is bizarre to say that patient A can be the beneficiary of suicide because he or she is able to execute the final act, but patient B who may be physically incapable of doing so cannot be the beneficiary. Again, the entailment, when viewed against the backdrop of the wider principles informing the debate, carries with it a justification for the legitimacy of voluntary euthanasia.[141]

The question of intermediate steps from the acceptance of X to the entailment of Z, can be further illustrated by the grey area that exists regarding when assistance can be said to end, and when direct ministration by a third party begins. Would a physician who, in contravention of the Oregon law, placed the lethal prescription in the hand of the patient, be punished for his or her failure to see the significance difference between placing the prescription by the patient's bedside and into the patient's hand? Would a physician who placed the prescription into the mouth of the patient too weak to perform the final act be punished? I think that such answers would be negative, for prosecutors and juries alike will singularly fail to grasp that the line drawn cannot bear the burden of gravity that is required of it. Thus, by a series of practically indistinguishable steps, the eventual conclusion would indeed be reached that the practice of voluntary euthanasia is also justifiable.[142]

Empirical Erosion of Boundaries

In addition to the logical forms of slippery slope argument that point towards the acceptance of voluntary euthanasia as well as assisted suicide, there are good reasons to think that the nexus of entailment would be further strengthened by the empirical form of slippery slope argument. The driving motivations for a policy of physician assisted suicide are increasing based on a framework of quality of life judgements allied to the exercise of personal autonomy.[143] Given the ascendancy of those values in wider society, can a law that seeks to maintain the threshold of assisted suicide remain immune from those pressures for very long? In the Netherlands, for example, according to an official 1990 government report, assisted suicide formed only a small proportion of the wider species of euthanasia practices. Only 400 (0.3%) of all deaths were classified as acts of assisted suicide. The figure for active euthanasia was 2300 deaths (1.8%).[144] That they form only a comparatively small proportion is significant, because the wider consideration of values points towards the need for a wider frame of methods required to deal and compensate for a wide range of psychological dispositions amongst patients who may have different preferences for how they may wish to die.[145] Should a final act of mercy be denied those patients who from one reason or another find it more difficult to execute the last act themselves? Again, once the question of assisted suicide is viewed against the backdrop of those values that fuel the movement towards assisted suicide, the values themselves point to the licitness of further practices designed to achieve the same objectives. Patients should not be discriminated against because they have additional psychological as well as possible physical obstacles to overcome in the execution of the final act.

A Possible Objection

A common objection raised against slippery slope forms of reasoning here is that the line of defence concerning assisted suicide is no more or less unreasonable than the existing status quo of 'letting die' versus 'killing'.[146] If the law can live with one practical set of compromises, it can live with another without fear of decent into the frightening spectre of Nazism.[147]

Whilst I would concede that appeals to worst case scenarios are often used to disguise exaggerated claims, I think that the limited appeal to the potential implications I am making is well short of such a 'doomsday prediction'. Further, I think that proponents of assisted suicide are, at best, implicitly committed to rather more than they propose, and that their line of demarcation is a poor substitute for the existing line of demarcation between the toleration of certain passive suicides, out of concern to advance genuine patient interests, and the illicitness of active forms of killing advanced by the ministration of a lethal dose of medication (whose only plausible immediate objective is to render the patient dead). Such a distinction can be clearly grasped, since it falls squarely within the corpus of traditional moral and legal reflection that an act of homicide is always entailed by the deployment of such means.[148] There is no ambiguity entailed by actions of this nature. Thus, notwithstanding the fact that some passive suicides may indeed be tolerated for the sake of protecting valid patient concerns, such toleration cannot be translated into acceptance of a class of active acts that have no claim to instantiate a legitimate means, since they entail an intentional use of lethal force.[149] Defending this traditional line is, therefore, based upon grounds that have substantial import, and as such provide the best means available of averting any trend towards other practices, such as voluntary euthanasia, that are deemed unacceptable to the promotion and service of the common good.[150]

Classes of Beneficiary

Of course the best means of avoiding what I have just said is to accept the case for voluntary euthanasia, as, say, practised in the Netherlands, and thus undercut the argument made thus far.[151] Yet, the acceptance of voluntary euthanasia brings with it other slippery slope considerations concerning classes of beneficiary. Let us accept for the purposes of argument that, for some individuals at least, a genuine act of consent to voluntary euthanasia is possible. To what categories of individual should this be applied to? Here, I think the question becomes one of justifying the discrimination of classes involved. If the grounds for classification seem unfairly arbitrary, then it is reasonable to suppose that pressure from excluded groups will proceed by analogy to ever wider degrees of incorporation.[152]

An initial objection to this line of reasoning can be met. It is sometimes objected that in, say, speeding legislation, a line is drawn somewhere that is generally adhered to, even though there are no clear grounds for establishing maximum speed limits at 50 or 70 mph. Lines can be drawn and adhered to even though the rationale for drawing the line where it is lacks a compelling reason. Similarly, we set an age for voting at 18, yet there are no compelling grounds for setting the age at 18 rather than 17 or 19 years of age. Why should voluntary euthanasia be any different?[153]

With reference to the question of speed limits, I would point out that no significant discrimination of classes is being employed. The limitation applies to motorists generally. Whether black or white, male or female, rich or poor, all are constrained to the same degree and share the benefits and burdens of such a policy accordingly. Does a lower speed limit not discriminate against fast drivers? Perhaps it does. However, that is surely a trivial imposition for the sake of co-ordinating speed policy generally for the sake of the common good. What of the second example concerning voting? Here I would point out that whilst a significant human right is being temporarily restricted, there are good grounds for doing so. In establishing a minimum age for voting, the state cannot be expected to inquire into the competency of each and every individual to vote. A general age is settled upon that seems to encompass the need of some degree of maturation sufficient to enter into a participation in democratic politics. Such a temporary restriction on the young cannot be seen as singling out particular classes of the population generally, for the key aspect of maturation is focused upon as having general presumptive application.

Making these points, therefore, does not advance the case for voluntary euthanasia, for they have to offer good grounds for seeking to enumerate and establish classes of beneficiaries that are not going to be perceived as being unfairly discriminatory in relation to other classes of potential beneficiaries.[154] Here, the burden is one of creating sub-sets of a population of patients who may be singled out for special treatment. If the values are narrowly construed in the identification of beneficiaries, they may well turn out to be considered inherently question-begging in the light of the predominant concerns that motivate patients towards advocacy of a right to voluntary euthanasia in the first place.[155]

Here, I think that the second form of logical slippery slope conjoins with the empirical slippery slope creating a potentially wide application for voluntary euthanasia than most of its advocates would not seek to endorse or support. As such, there are good reasons for not embarking on a policy that seeks to legitimate the practice of voluntary euthanasia in the first place for any potential class of beneficiary.

Terminal Illness?

A common stipulation made is that the class of beneficiary should be restricted to the terminally ill, who experience unbearable pain, and who have only six or less months to live.[156] Yet, why should the potential class be restricted in this fashion? Consider the case of Titus, a patient who is chronically sick and who may have two or three years to live in a condition he finds intolerable. He experiences frequent bouts of pain and seeks to end his life. If he has a right to determine his own conception of life, and what those burdens mean to him, then why should he be denied the benefit of such a merciful release? Why should he be paternalistically protected from his settled will that his life is no longer considered worth living? The qualification that a person be terminally ill seems to exclude him unreasonably from that key benefit. It is simply far from being clear or well founded that the status of being 'terminally ill' carries with it any real significance in terms of status.[157]

Intolerable Pain?

What of the position that a patient should be experiencing intolerable pain? Pain is of course a great debilitation when it overcomes a persons sense of control and dignity.[158] Yet, the question must be faced, why should pain be the sole grounds for limiting the potential class of beneficiary. The broader category of 'suffering' brings with it a much wider class of concern that patients commonly experience. Consider the case of Berth, a woman who learns she has ALS. She has a horror of losing self control, and seeks to end her life before she is reduced to the state that the disease will bring in its wake. Why should she be denied the ability to control the manner and timing of her death with the support of medical assistance?

Again, when we focus upon the values and motivations that inform the movement towards active forms of assistance in death, the frontiers of limitation break down, because the values at stake do not point neatly to a small discrete class of potential beneficiary. [159] On the contrary, they point to the self-determination of the patient to decide for himself or herself what the conditions of intolerability are. Such has been the experience in the Netherlands where the criteria for euthanasia *are no longer* limited to the terminally ill or those suffering unbearable pain.[160] There is good reason to think that the values informing the move to assisted suicide and voluntary euthanasia will lead to the creation of ever broader classes of beneficiaries, *not the narrow discrete classes* currently being proposed in the debate in the Untied States, for they do not offer any convincing rationale for the limitations being stipulated.[161]

Free and Uncoerced Choice?

Another common stipulation in proposals for assisted suicide or voluntary euthanasia is that the choice be one that is made freely and without undue compulsion.[162] I have no doubt that in some cases at least, patients can make 'instrumentally rational' choices to end their lives in terms of the settled values that they have.[163] But how can we adequately limit the potential class of beneficiary to those whose choice is genuinely free and unpressurized? The choice to commit suicide is not simply any old choice, but is one that is irrevocable, and that ends the very life of the patient. The gravity of the choice should surely entail that the choice is made in *conditions of maximum suitability*.[164] Yet, many ominous forms of pressure exist in societies that do not have an adequate framework of pain management and hospice care in place to offer dignified and caring alternatives to the option of assisted suicide or voluntary euthanasia.[165] There are many millions of citizens in the United States who do not have health insurance, and who are dependent on the graces of overstretched charity care to meet needs. Can such a situation possibly be one that is conducive to ensuring that the choice of many patients opting for assisted suicide or voluntary euthanasia be genuinely free?[166]

Here, I find that the conclusions of the *New York Task Force* to be quite compelling as evidence against the proposition that a set of procedures to ensure free and voluntary consent can possibly offer a satisfactory set of safeguards against external forms of pressure.[167] Consider, for example, a patient who is near poor, frail, without health insurance, and afraid of being a burden. Can we be assured that counselling procedures and treatment for depression can adequately provide the necessary protection against those kinds of pressure? Despite all the emphasis on respecting a patient's right to determine whether to go on living or not, the freedom to make such a choice will, for many, be undertaken in conditions that are far from being optimific.[168] A state policy must adequately address *not merely the possibility* that some cases of active assistance in death may be freely and voluntary undertaken, but must consider its duty to adequately protect all members of society, especially the frail and vulnerable, from those kinds of pressure.[169]

Non-Voluntary or Involuntary Euthanasia?

Considering whether the practice of voluntary euthanasia will be limited to the realm of the consensual, it is argued that a clear and distinctive line separates voluntary euthanasia from questions of non-voluntary or involuntary euthanasia. However, such a line must be viewed within the context of the increasing influence of quality of life judgements. Physicians are not mere instruments and are influenced by the wider framework of values that impinge upon society generally. If such debilitated forms of human existence are seen to be undignified, and are no longer seen to instantiate any quality of life worth preserving, is it mere speculation to suggest that physicians may, on their own initiative, act to relieve a patient of that indignity? Should such a patient be deprived of the benefit of merciful release, simply because he or she is no longer competent, or perhaps is too afraid to give the necessary consent? Given such a chain of reasoning, it seems far from improbable that some physicians may indeed seek to act out of concern to relieve such patients of the perceived 'burden of continuing existence'.[170]

That such an argument is not mere speculation can again be illustrated with reference to the practice of euthanasia in the Netherlands. In an official 1990 government report, it was conceded that 1000 (or 27%) of actively induced deaths, were performed on patients who did not or were incapable of granting their consent.[171] Despite the formation of guidelines that euthanasia should only be practised on those giving consent to the procedure, many cases of euthanasia were non-voluntary, and in some cases were involuntary. This tendency, I think, clearly illustrates that the motive of mercy killing in order to end the perceived low quality of patients' lives is capable of taking on an *independent force of its own*, and as such does not seem to be readily curtailed by the creation of guidelines that stress the voluntary nature of the choice being made.

Of course it can be argued that that is the state of play in the Netherlands and cannot simply be compared with the prevailing situation in the United States. Yet, I find such a line of retort naïve in light of the wider consideration of the social and cultural dynamics that are similarly present in the United States. The same kinds of consideration would affect the decisions of physicians in the United States as well as the Netherlands.

Ethos of the Medical Profession
A final question that emerges in slippery slope considerations is whether or not a society should be tempted in the first place to place such a power to actively procure death into the hands of physicians. The safest way of avoiding risks of power transference here is precisely one of upholding the traditional ethos of the medical profession and the reinforcement of that traditional ethos by a defence of the existing law that prohibits the active procurement of a patient's death by means of assisted suicide or voluntary euthanasia.[172] This prohibition is at least as old as, and is most famously formulated in, the Hippocratic Oath. It is also upheld in the current code of the American Medical Association.

The medical profession historically prohibited assisted suicide and euthanasia because the end that medical practice properly serves—the promotion of human health—would indeed be radically undermined should the physician engage in the ministration of lethal drugs or advice to patients. Only if the means used serve a professionally appropriate end, can medical practice insulate itself from a descent into forms of practice that are truly at odds with the vocation of the physician as healer and servant of care.

Once it becomes acceptable to act in a way that actively intends the death of the patient, it is no mere foolish speculation to envisage the significant expansion of the circumstances in which the death of a patient can be actively procured, whether consensual or not. It is not necessary to appeal to any Orwellian nightmare to substantiate this, but rather, it is possible to appeal to the evidence of the Netherlands, a society that has already practised assisted suicide and euthanasia for over twenty years, to illustrate those kinds of concerns.[173]

Notes to Chapter Six

[1] Especially personal autonomy. As John Kekes states in his *Against Liberalism* (Ithaca: Cornell University Press, 1997), 15, "Although pluralism, freedom, rights, equality, and distributive justice are the basic values of liberalism, it must be explained why liberals attach such great importance to them. ... [personal autonomy] is the true core of liberalism, the inner citadel for whose protection all the liberal battles are waged."

[2] See Will Kymlicka, "Liberal Individualism and Liberal Neutrality," in *Communitarianism and Individualism*, eds. Shlomo Avineri and Avner De-Shalit (New York: Oxford University Press, 1992), 165-85. See also Joseph Raz, "Liberalism, Skepticism and Democracy," *Iowa Law Review* 74 (1989): 761-86.

[3] William R. Lund, "Egalitarian Liberalism and Social Pathology: A Defense of Public Neutrality," *Social Theory and Practice* 3 (1997): 449-78; Roger Paden, "Democracy and Liberal Neutrality," *Contemporary Philosophy* 14 (1992): 17-20.

[4] H. Tristram Engelhardt, *The Foundations of Bioethics*. 2nd ed. (New York: Oxford University Press, 1996), 67-84.

[5] See his "Privacy and Limited Democracy: The Moral Centrality of Persons," *Social Philosophy and Policy* 17 (2000): 120-40.

[6] John Rawls, *Political Liberalism* (New York: Columbia University Press, 1996), 131-67.

[7] See Engelhardt, *Foundations of Bioethics*, 114-5, 118-20, 124-8; Rawls, *Political Liberalism*, 190-200. For a good discussion of the development of the harm principle see John D. Hodson, *The Ethics of Legal Coercion* (Boston: D. Reidel, 1983), 34-42.

[8] Engelhardt, *Foundations of Bioethics*, 40-64.

[9] See his earlier discussion of the notion of overlapping consensus in "The Idea of Overlapping Consensus," *Oxford Journal of Legal Studies* 7 (1987): 232-64.

[10] See Joseph Boyle, "Radical Moral Disagreement in Contemporary Health Care," *Journal of Medicine and Philosophy* 19 (1994): 184-200.

[11] On the general idea of perfectionism as a general platform for critiquing anti-perfectionist foundationalism, see Steven Wall, *Liberalism, Perfectionism, and Restraint* (New York: Cambridge University Press, 1998), 7-24. See also Joseph Raz, "Facing Diversity: The Case of Epistemic Abstinence," *Philosophy and Public Affairs* 3 (1990): 3-46.

[12] Engelhardt, *Foundations of Bioethics*, 3-16, 67-69.

[13] Soren Holm "Secular Morality and its Limits," *Medicine, Healthcare and Philosophy* 1 (1998): 75-77.

[14] Michael Wreen, "Nihilism, Relativism, and Engelhardt," *Theoretical Medicine and Bioethics* 19 (1998): 73-88. See also Thomas J. Bole, "Faulting Engelhardt's Libertarianism by Default," *Southwest Philosophy Review* 15 (1999): 169-76.

[15] Kevin Wm. Wildes, "Engelhardt's Communitarian Ethics: The Hidden Assumptions," in *Reading Engelhardt,* eds. B.P. Minogue, G. Palmer-Fernandez, and J.E. Reagan (Dordrecht: Kluwer, 1997), 77-93.

[16] Soren Holm "Secular Morality," 75-77; and his "The Peaceable Pluralistic Society and the Question of Persons," *Journal of Medicine and Philosophy* 13 (1988): 379-86.

[17] Engelhardt, *Foundations of Bioethics*, 69.

[18] Wreen, "Nihilism, Relativism, and Engelhardt," 80-82.

[19] James L. Nelson, "Everything Includes Itself in Power: Power and Coherence in Engelhardt's 'Foundations of Bioethics'," in *Reading Engelhardt*, 15-29. See also Vincent Bourguet, "Miseries of Ethical Formalism," *Revue Thomiste* 99 (1999): 307-30.

[20] Originally published in 1986. See Klaus Hartmann, "The Foundations of Bioethics," *Journal of the British Society for Phenomenology* 20 (1989): 166-69.

[21] Hartmann, "Foundations," 166-69; Holm, "Peaceable Pluralistic Society," 379-86.

[22] Gary E. Jones, "Engelhardt on the Abortion and Euthanasia of Defective Infants," *Linacre Quarterly* 50 (1983): 172-81.

[23] Engelhardt, *Foundations of Bioethics*, 135-54. See also his earlier chapter "Some Persons are Humans, Some Humans are Persons, and the World is What We Persons Make of It," in *Philosophical Medical Ethics: Its Nature and Significance*, eds. Stuart F. Spicker and H. Tristram Engelhardt (Boston: D. Reidel, 1977), 183-94.

[24] See J.C. Moskop "Persons, Property or Both? Engelhardt on the Moral Status of Young Children," in *Reading Engelhardt*, 163-74.

[25] Engelhardt, *Foundations of Bioethics*, 340-54. See also his "The Foundations of Bioethics: Liberty and Life with Moral Diversity," *Reason Papers* 22 (1997): 101-8.

[26] Boyle, "Radical Moral Disagreement," 193-9. See also Vinit Haksar, *Equality, Liberty, and Perfectionism* (New York: Oxford University Press, 1979), 193-235.

[27] See Tom L. Beauchamp, "Engelhardt's Foundations," *Reason Papers* 22 (1997): 96-100.

[28] See Michael Pakaluk, "The Liberalism of John Rawls: A Brief Exposition," in *Liberalism at the Crossroads*, eds. Christopher Wolfe and John Hittinger (Landham: Rowman and Littlefield, 1994), 1-18; Kent Greenawalt, "On Public Reason," *Chicago-Kent Law Review* 69 (1994): 669-89.

271

[29] As does Peter F. Lake. See his "Liberalism Within the Limits of the Reasonable Alone: Developments of John Rawls' Political Philosophy, its Political Positivism, and the Limits on its Applicability," *Vermont Law Review* 19 (1995):603-42.

[30] Russell Hittinger , "John Rawls, 'Political Liberalism'," *Review of Metaphysics* 3 (1994): 585-602.

[31] Rawls, *Political Liberalism*, 212-27.

[32] Robert George and Chrstopher Wolfe, " Natural Law and Public Reason," in *Natural Law and Public Reason*, eds. Robert George and Christopher Wolfe (Washington, DC: Georgetown University Press, 2000), 51-58.

[33] Pakaluk, "Liberalism of John Rawls," 12-18.

[34] John Finnis, "On the Practical Meaning of Secularism," *Notre Dame Law Review* 73 (1998): 506-9. See also Gary C. Leedes, "Rawls's Excessively Secular Political Conception," *University of Richmond Law Review* 27 (1993): 1083-93, arguing that Rawl's anti-perfectionsim is tantamount to being constructed on an exclusionary perspective against religious viewpoints.

[35] John Finnis, "Legal Enforcement of 'Duties to Oneself': Kant v. Neo-Kantians," *Columbia Law Review* 87 (1987), 433-7; Robert George, "Public Reason and Political Conflict: Abortion and Homosexuality," *Yale Law Journal* 106 (1997): 2475-95.

[36] Joseph Raz, *Ethics in the Public Domain: Essays in the Morality of Law and Politics* (New York: Clarendon Press, 1994), 60-81.

[37] George and Wolf "Natural Law and Public Reason," 53-58. As George points out in "Public Reason and Political Conflict," 2502, "A sound principle of public reason for a deliberative democracy would indeed require citizens and policymakers to justify their political advocacy and action by appeal to principles of justice and other moral principles accessible to their fellow citizens by virtue of their "common human reason." It would, however, exclude no reasonable view in advance of its dialectical consideration "on the merits" in public debate. Nor would it exclude religious views as such. What it would exclude, rather, as grounds of public policymaking generally, are appeals to sheer authority (religious or otherwise) or to "secret knowledge," or the putative truths revealed only to an elite (or the elect) and not available, in principle, to rational persons as such. A sound principle of public reason would, in short, be very wide. Its goal would be the "perfectionist" one of

settling law and public policy in accordance with what is true as a matter of justice, human rights, and political morality generally."

[38] John Finnis, "Abortion, Natural Law, and Public Reason," in *Natural Law and Public Reason*, eds. Robert George and Christopher Wolfe, 76-84.

[39] Finnis, "Abortion, Natural Law, and Public Reason," 76-84; Paul J. Weithman, "Citizenship and Public Reason," in *Natural Law and Public Reason*, eds. Robert George and Christopher Wolfe, 154-62.

[40] Weithman, "Citizenship and Public Reason," 154-62; George and Wolf, "Natural Law and Public Reason," 53-58.

[41] Robert George, *Defense of the Natural Law* (New York: Clarendon Press, 1999), ch. 7.

[42] Boyle, "Radical Moral Disagreement," 193-99. See also Raz, *Ethics in the Public Domain,* 60-81.

[43] G.E.M. Anscombe, "War and Murder," in *Nuclear Weapons: A Catholic Response*, ed. Walter Stein (New York, NY: Sheed and Ward, 1962), 60.

[44] Michael J. White makes a strong claim that a deeply rooted kind of scepticism drives
 the anti-perfectionist's insistence that only certain kinds of questions can be raised in the public square. See his *Partisan or Neutral? The Futility of Public Political Theory* (Lanham: Rowman and Littlefield, 1997), 17-28.

[45] See Michael J. Sandel, "Political Liberalism," *Harvard Law Review* 107 (1994), 1765-94; *Democracy's Discontent: America in Search of a Public Philosophy* (Cambridge: Harvard University Press, 1996), 26-54; Heidi M. Hurd, "The Levitation of Liberalism," *Yale Law Journal* 105 (1995): 795-824. Their idea of what constitutes a public reason is similar in key ways to the one defended by John Finnis and Robert George, who reject Rawls's restrictions on public reason. For Sandel, promotion of 'civic virtue' is necessary because the exercise of liberty itself requires people to have the responsible virtues necessary for self-government in crucial areas of life. For Sandel, reasoned public deliberation on such questions as abortion and assisted suicide is essential in order to bring republican civic virtues to bear on how those questions should be resolved. For Sandel, the question is centrally one of whether the purported right in question helps make people good citizens or not. However, whilst there is much of value in what Sandel argues in seeking to cultivate and develop a virtuous citizenry, my concern is one of why Sandel thinks that civic republicanism can provide sufficient warrant to claim to be

the legitimate framework for the foundation for political and legal action as such. Whilst such values may be more readily accessible in terms of a historical tradition and have a significant role to play in public life, those values are themselves derived from a tradition of natural rights. Such civic values, in my view, crucially need such a reasoned foundation if they are to be accorded anything more that the status of being virtues of a tradition that happens to be part of historical American culture. The weakness in Sandel's position is that the reasonableness of the civic virtues themselves need to be accorded a trans-cultural and trans-historical dimension that is more than simply a pragmatic *modus vivendi*. Sandel seems reluctant to further underpin his republican virtues in something other than a broad understanding of political traits that happen to be shared by a particular tradition. So untethered, Sandel's republican virtues can indeed result in the notion of the common good being positively furthered as a result of a moral pact legitimising the practise of assisted suicide—a deliberative exercise of the self-governed. Yet, in terms of a natural law comprehension of the constituents of human flourishing, and the role of the state in fostering and promoting the common good, such an agreement *cannot be conceded* without attacking the centrality of meaning as to what it is that the common good is necessarily there to protect, foster, and promote.

[46] See Miriam Galston, "Rawlsian Dualism and the Autonomy of Political Thought," *Columbia Law Review* 94 (1994): 1842-59.

[47] Ronald Dworkin *et al.*, "Assisted Suicide: The Philosophers' Brief," *New York Review of Books* (27 Mar 1997): 41-47.

[48] Rawls, *Political Liberalism*, 243-4.

[49] George and Wolfe, "Natural Law and Public Reason," 53-62; Hittinger, "John Rawls," 585-602.

[50] See the discussion in chapter three. See also his *Taking Rights Seriously* (Cambridge: Harvard University Press, 1977), 177-81.

[51] Patrick Neal, "Dworkin on the Foundations of Liberal Equality," *Legal Theory* 2 (1995): 205-26.

[52] Ronald Dworkin, *Life's Dominion* (London: Harper Collins, 1993), ch. 7.

[53] Finnis, "Kant v. Neo-Kantians,", 433-7; Christopher Wolfe, "Ronald Dworkin," in *Liberalism at the Crossroads*, ed. Christopher Wolfe and John Hittinger, 29-40.

[54] See Basil Mitchell, *Law, Morality, and Religion in a Secular Society* (New York: Oxford University Press, 1967), 70-86; Hodson, *The Ethics of Legal Coercion,* 43-52; David Lyons, *Ethics and the Rule of Law* (New York: Cambridge University Press, 1984), 170-89. See also John H. Kultgen, *Autonomy and Intervention: Parentalism in the Caring Life* (New York: Oxford University Press, 1995), 28-34.

[55] As Augustine of Hippo classically stated *"cum dilectione hominum et odio vitiorum* (with love for mankind and hatred of sins)" in *Rule of St. Augustine* (Westminster: Newman Press, 1956). On the importance of dignity and worth in lawmaking see further Joseph Boyle, "A Catholic Perspective on Morality and the Law," *Journal of Law and Religion* 1 (1983): 227-40.

[56] John Finnis, "Rights and Equality of Concern and Respect," in *Morality, Harm and the Law,* ed. Gerald Dworkin (Boulder: Westview Press, 1994), 43-45; Robert George, *Making Men Moral* (New York: Oxford University Press, 1993), 71-82.

[57] John Finnis, "Liberalism and Natural Law Theory," *Mercer Law Review* 45 (1994): 687-704; William A Galston, "On the Alleged Right to do Wrong," *Ethics* 93 (1983): 320-24.

[58] Finnis, *Natural Law and Natural Rights*, 260-64; "Is Natural Law Theory Compatible With Limited Government," in *Natural Law, Liberalism and Morality*, ed. Robert George (Oxford: Clarendon Press, 1996), 1-26.

[59] Neal, "Dworkin," 205-9. See also discussion in J.W. Harris, *Legal Philosophies.* 2nd ed. (London: Butterworths, 1997), ch. 10; Brian Bix, *Jurisprudence* (London: Sweet and Maxwell, 1999), ch. 15.

[60] John Locke classically recognised this inability to directly change hearts and minds in his first *Letter on Toleration.* See also Eric D'Arcy, *Conscience and its Right to Freedom* (New York: Sheed and Ward, 1961). This topic, of limits on authority, is discussed further *infra* under the conception of the common good.

[61] John Finnis, Law, Morality, and Sexual Orientation," *Notre Dame Law Review* 69 (1994): 1049-76.

[62] Finnis "Kant v. Neo-Kantians," 437-40.

[63] Finnis "Kant v. Neo-Kantians," 437-40; "Practical Meaning of Secularism," 502-9.

⁶⁴ Joseph Raz, "Liberalism, Autonomy, and the Politics of Neutral Concern," *Midwest Studies in Philosophy* 7 (1982): 89-120; *The Morality of Freedom* (Oxford: Clarendon Press, 1986); *Ethics in the Public Domain.* On William A. Galston, see his *Liberal Purposes: Goods, Virtues, and Diversity in the Liberal State* (New York: Cambridge University Press, 1992); "Pluralism and Social Unity," *Ethics* 99 (1989): 711-26; "Two Concepts of Liberalism," *Ethics* 105 (1995): 516-34. See also Albert W. Dzur, "Function, Convention, and Policy: William Galston and the Redefinition of Liberal Purposes," *Public Affairs Quarterly* 12 (1998): 101-17; Stephen Wall, *Liberalism, Perfectionism and Restraint*, chs. 6 & 7.

⁶⁵ Jeremy Waldron, "Autonomy and Perfectionism in Raz's Morality of Freedom," *Southern California Law Review* 62 (1989): 1127-38. See also David McCabe, "Private Lives and Public Virtues: The Idea of a Liberal Community," *Canadian Journal of Philosophy* 28 (1998): 557-85. Karl Hostetler, "Towards a Perfectionist Response to Ethical Conflict," *Studies in Philosophy and Education* 17 (1998): 295-302.

⁶⁶ See Patrick Neal, "Perfectionism with a Liberal Face? Nervous Liberals and Raz's Political Theory," *Social Theory and Practice* 20 (1994): 25-58.

⁶⁷ Galston, *Liberal Purposes,* 140-64; George Sher, *Beyond Neutrality: Perfectionism and Politics* (New York: Cambridge University Press, 1997), 89-96.

⁶⁸ See discussion in chapter three of this work.

⁶⁹ Galston, *Liberal Purposes,* 165-90; Sher, *Beyond Neutrality,* 72-104; Wall, *Liberalism,* 7-26.

⁷⁰ See Vinit Haksar, *Equality, Liberty, and Perfectionism,* for an earlier defence of the need to ground our public philosophy on human well being. He argues that the idea that all human beings have the right to equal respect and consideration cannot be satisfactorily answered except by a perfectionist turn. For a more spirited defence of the notion of perfectionism centred on the civic virtues, see William M. Sullivan, *Reconstructing Public Philosophy* (Berkeley: University of California Press, 1982).

⁷¹ Haksar, *Equality, Liberty,* 65-99; Sher, *Beyond Neutrality,* 199-240.

⁷² See William M. Sullivan, "Bringing the Good Back In," in *Liberalism and the Good,* eds. R. Bruce Douglas, Gerald M. Mara, and Henry S. Richardson (New York: Routledge, 1990), 148-66.

[73] Raz, *Morality of Freedom*, 369-400; Wall, *Liberalism*, 162-82.

[74] George, *Defence of the Natural Law*, 127-38.

[75] Robert George, "Moralistic Liberalism and Legal Moralism," *Michigan Law Review* 88 (1990): 1415-29; John Finnis, "Is Natural Law Theory Compatible With Limited Government?" in *Natural Law, Liberalism, and Morality*, ed. Robert George. (Oxford: Clarendon Press, 1996), 1-26.

[76] George, *Making Men Moral*, 161-88.

[77] George, *Making Men Moral*, 161-88; John Finnis, "The Consistent Ethic: A Philosophical Critique," in *Consistent Ethic of Life*, ed. Thomas G. Fuechtmann. (Kansas City: Sheed and Ward, 1988), 140-81.

[78] Joram Graf Haber, "Should Physicians Assist the Reaper?" *Cambridge Quarterly of Healthcare Ethics* 5 (1996): 44-50.

[79] John Finnis, "A Philosophical Case Against Euthanasia.," in *Euthanasia Examined: Ethical, Clinical and Legal Perspectives*, ed. John Keown (Cambridge: Cambridge University Press, 1995), 23-35; "The 'Value of Human Life' and 'the Right to Death': Some Reflections on Cruzan and Ronald Dworkin," *Southern Illinois University Law Journal* 17 (1993): 559-71.

[80] Finnis, *NaturalLaw and Natural Rights*, 134-60.

[81] I am thinking here of authors writing from a robust communitarian perspective who stress more the notion of a socially relational self.

[82] Finnis, *Natural Law and Natural Rights*, 141-48.

[83] See his *Aquinas* (Oxford: Oxford University Press, 1998), 111-17, 118-23.

[84] On an excellent review and discussion of the intimate association between friendship and justice in community, of civic friendship, drawing on the thought of Jacques Maritain, see James V. Schall, *Maritain: Philosopher in Society* (Landham: Rowman and Littlefield, 1998), ch. 8.

[85] Finnis, *Natural Law and Natural Rights*, 141-44; *Aquinas*, 118-23.

[86] Finnis, *Aquinas*, 141-43. See also his "Public Good: The Specifically Political Common Good in Aquinas," in *Natural Law and Moral Inquiry*, ed.

Robert P. George (Washington, DC: Georgetown University Press, 1998), 174-209.

[87] Finnis, *Fundamentals of Ethics*, 127-24; "The Consistent Ethic," 140-81.

[88] As Maritain states in "The Conquest of Freedom," in *The Education of Man: The Educational Philosophy of Jacques Maritain*, ed. Donald Gallagher (Garden City: Doubleday, 1962), 172-73, "If the person has the opportunity of being treated as a person in social life ... it is first of all due to the development of law and to instututions of law. *But it is also and indispensably due* to the development of civic friendship, with the confidence and mutual devotion it implies on the part of those who carry it out ... [the proper direction in which the state should be headed and] towards which true political emancipation tends in the inauguration of the fraternal city."

[89] John Finnis, "Liberalism and Natural Law Theory," *Mercer Law Review* 45 (1994): 687-704.

[90] Philip E. Devine, *Natural Law Ethics* (Westport: Greenwood, 2000), 138-39.

[91] Finnis, *Natural Law and Natural Rights*, 155. His definition is broadly compatible with other definitions of the common good. See for example, John XXIII, *Mater et Magistra*, 84 "[the common good] embraces the sum total of those conditions of social living, whereby men are enabled more fully and more readily to achieve their own perfection." See also David Hollenbach, *Claims in Conflict: Retrieving and Renewing the Catholic Human Rights Tradition* (New York: Paulist Press, 1979), 64, defining common good as a "set of social conditions which facilitate the realization of personal goods by individuals."

[92] This has always been a central claim of the 'common good tradition' closely associated with natural law theory. As Thomas Gilby states in his *Between Community and Society* (New York: Longmans, Green, 1953), 89-90, the common good is taken to "... mean what all share in whether they be taken singly or all together....The common good, then, may belong either to the group and its members *en masse*, or directly and personally to each individual comprised."

[93] See Henry B. Veatch, *Human Rights: Fact or Fancy?* (Baton Rouge: LSU Press, 1985), 124-34.

[94] Finnis, "Is Natural Law Theory Compatible With Limited Government," in *Natural Law, Liberalism, and Morality*, ed. Robert George (Oxford: Clarendon Press, 1996), 1-26.

[95] Robert George, "Individual Rights, Collective Interests, Public Law, and American Politics," *Law and Philosophy* 8 (1989): 245-61. George criticises an influential liberal conception of individual rights and collective interests that insufficiently addresses the shared participatory notion of the common good, differentiating it from the mere strategic pursuit of collective interests often associated with the use of the phrase 'public good'. See also Michael A. Smith, "Common Advantage and Common Good," *Laval Theologique et Philosophique* 51 (1995): 111-25. Smith draws upon the Aristotelian-Thomistic tradition to address the question of the common good and how it is differentiated from the collective pursuit of individual private advantage.

[96] Iniobong Udoidem, *Authority and the Common Good in Social and Political Philosophy* (Lanham: University Press of America, 1988), 3-15.

[97] John Finnis, "Unjust Laws in a Democratic Society: Some Philosophical and Theological Reflections," *Notre Dame Law Review* 71 (1996): 595-604; "The Authority of Law in the Predicament of Contemporary Social Theory," *Notre Dame Journal of Law, Ethics and Public Policy* 1 (1994): 115-37.

[98] Devine, *Natural Law Ethics*, 138-39.

[99] Finnis, *Natural Law and Natural Rights*, 141-56.

[100] Louis Dupre, "Common Good and Open Society," in *Catholicism and Liberalism*, eds. R. Bruce Douglass and David Hollenbach (Cambridge: Cambridge University Press, 1994), 172-95.

[101] See Finnis's on *Aquinas*, 237 it is "… unjust for more extensive associations to assume functions which can be performed efficiently by individuals or by less extensive associations." See also *Natural Law and Natural Rights*, 146, 159.

[102] Jean Bethke Elshtain, "Catholic Social Thought, the City, and Liberal America," in *Catholicism and Liberalism*, eds. R. Bruce Douglass and David Hollenbach , 151-71.

[103] Finnis, *Aquinas*, 222-28.

[104] The common good of the political community has important elements which are not really shared with any other community, for example, the

restoration of justice by punishment of those who have offended against reasonably posited laws. See Leo J. Elders, "Common Good as Goal and Governing Principle of Social Life: Interpretations and Meaning," in *Principles of Catholic Social Teaching* (Milwaukee: Marquette University Press, 1998), 103-17,188-90. See also B.J. Diggs, "The Common Good as Reason for Political Action," *Ethics* 83 (1973): 283-293.

[105] See John Haldane, "The Individual, The State, and the Common Good," *Social Philosophy and Policy* 13 (1996): 59-79.

[106] Here I am basically in agreement with Joseph Raz. See his *Morality of Freedom*, 395-98.

[107] George, *Defence of the Natural Law*, 133, 229-36.

[108] See Aldo Tassi, "Anarchism, Autonomy, and the Common Good," *International Philosophical Quarterly* 17 (1977): 273-83.

[109] Finnis, *Natural Law and Natural Rights*, 219-23, 26-4.

[110] Peter Redpath, "Private Morality and Public Enforcement," in *Freedom, Virtue, and the Common Good*, eds. Curtis L. Hancock and Anthony O. Simon. (Notre Dame: American Maritain Association, 1995), 332-41.

[111] George, *Making Men Moral*, 71-82.

[112] See Keith Lovin, "The Moral End of Law," *Southwest Philosophical Studies* 5 (1980): 11-17.

[113] See Aristotle, *Nicomachean Ethics* in *The Basic Works of Aristotle*, ed. Richard McKeon, trans. W. D. Ross (New York: Random House, 1941), 1094b, "Every state is a community of some kind, and every community is established with a view to some good."

[114] See Aristotle, *Nicomachean Ethics,* 1179b.

[115] See Aristotle, *Nicomachean Ethics,* 1180a.

[116] Richard A. Crofts, "The Common Good in the Political Theory of Thomas Aquinas," *Thomist* 37 (1973): 155-73.

[117] Aquinas, *On Kingship*, trans. Gerald B. Phelan (Toronto: Pontifical Institute of Mediaeval Studies, 1949), I 15/16. There, Aquinas stresses that it is the goal of the authority of the king to directly lead his people to virtue "… in

line with the pursuit of heavenly blessedness ... [and therefore to] ... prescribe whatever things lead to such blessedness and forbid, as far as possible, the contraries of those things."

[118] S.T. I-II, q. 95, a.1; q. 96, a. 2. For Aquinas, it was sometimes necessary to tolerate vices in a society where their non-toleration would lead to greater damage to the common good. However, Aquinas does not depart from the essential Aristotelian premise that the positive law can and should be used, where practicable, to lead people towards virtue. The limits of enforcement are not based on supposed moral rights not to be coerced against choosing vice but what is possible given the conditions prevalent in a given society. For commentary, see M. Cathleen Kaveny, "Toward a Thomistic Perspective on Abortion and the Law in Contemporary America," *Thomist* 55 (1991): 343-96.

[119] See Heta Häyry, "Legal Paternalism and Legal Moralism," *Ratio Juris* 4 (1991): 202-18; *Ratio Juris* 5 (1992): 191-201.

[120] A point stressed by Robert George. See his *Making Men Moral*, 42-47.

[121] See Lovin, "Moral End of Law,"11-17. See also M. Cathleen Kaveny, "The Limits of Ordinary Virtue: The Limits of the Criminal Law," in *Choosing Life: A Dialogue on Evangelium Vitae*, eds. Kevin Wm. Wildes and Alan C. Mitchell (Washington, DC: Gergetown University Press, 1997), 132-49.

[122] Hence the need to control, for example, the activities of drug traffickers who seek to lure others into states of dependency (a form of moral suicide?). By analogy, those who would tempt, encourage, or assist the sick or weak to commit suicide.

[123] Udoidem, *Authority and the Common Good*, 3-15.

[124] See Margaret Otlowski, *Voluntary Euthanasia and the Common Law* (Oxford: Clarendon Press, 1997), ch. 1-2, for a detailed examination of the status of the debate in the United Kingdom and how slippery slope concerns about control were found convincing by the House of Lords.

[125] See Charles J. Dougherty, "The Common Good, Terminal Illness, and Euthanasia," *Issues in Law and Medicine* 9 (1993): 151-65. Whilst slippery slope arguments do appeal to the impact of consequences resulting from a change in policy, from the point of view of natural law ethics, they can be viewed as *making matters worse*, of causing additional damage to the common good, in addition to the harm imposed upon the common good by permitting private intentional killing, in and of itself.

[126] Dougherty, "Common Good," 160-61.

[127] David Lamb, *Down the Slippery Slope: Arguing in Applied Ethics* (London: Croom Helm, 1984), 1-19; "Down the Slippery Slope," in *Explorations in Medicine*, ed. David Lamb (Aldershot: Gower, 1987), 199-222. See also Frederick Schauer, "Slippery Slopes," *Harvard Law Review* 99 (1985): 361-83; Jeffrey P. Whitman, "The Many Guises of the Slippery Slope Argument," *Social Theory and Practice* 20 (1994): 85-97.

[128] For an excellent account of the use of the a combined or full blown account of the different kinds of slippery slope to argue against the legalisation of physician assisted suicide, due to the onset of a duty to die, see Griffin Trotter, "Assisted Suicide and the Duty to Die," *Journal of Clinical Ethics* 11 (2000): 260-71.

[129] See Gary Colwell, "Slippery Slopes, Moral Slides and Human Nature," *Informal Logic* 17 (1995): 43-66. See also W. H. Nielsen, "The Slippery Slope Argument Against the Legalization of Voluntary Euthanasia," *Journal of Social Philosophy* 18 (1999): 12-27.

[130] Sissela Bok, "Euthanasia," and "Physician Assisted Suicide," in Gerald Dworkin, R. G. Frey, and Sissela Bok, *Euthanasia and Physician-Assisted-Suicide* (New York: Cambridge University Press, 1998), 107-27, 128-39.

[131] Sissela Bok, "Physician Assisted Suicide," 128-39.

[132] Helga Kuhse, "Why Killing Is Not Always Worse—and Is Sometimes Better—Than Letting Die," *Cambridge Quarterly of Healthcare Ethics* 4 (1998): 371-74; Franklin G. Miller, Timothy E. Quill, and Howard Brody, "Regulating Physician Assisted Death," *New England Journal of Medicine* 331 (1994): 119-23.

[133] Ronald Dworkin *et al.* "The Philosophers' Brief," *New York Review of Books* (Mar. 27 1997): 41-47.

[134] R.G. Frey, "The Fear of a Slippery Slope," in Gerald Dworkin R. G. Frey, and Sissela Bok, *Euthanasia and Physician-Assisted-Suicide*, 43-63.

[135] Charles H. Baron *et al.* "A Model State Act to Authorize and Regulate Physician-Assisted Suicide," [reprinted] in *Last Rights: Assisted Suicide and Euthanasia Debated*, ed. Michael M. Uhlmann (Washington, DC: Ethics and Public Policy Center, 1998), 551-76. See also Simon M. Canick, "Constitutional Aspects of Physician-Assisted Suicide After Lee v. Oregon," *American Journal of Law and Medicine* 23 (1997): 69-96.

[136] Nielsen, "The Slippery Slope Argument," 13-17; John D. Arras, "The Right to Die on the Slippery Slope," *Social Theory and Practice* 8 (1982): 285-328.

[137] Alexander M. Capron, "Legalizing Physician-Aided Death," *Cambridge Quarterly of Healthcare Ethics* 5 (1996): 10-23; "The Right to Die: Progress and Peril," *Euthanasia Review* 2 (1987): 41-59.

[138] Yale Kamisar, "Physician-Assisted Suicide: The Last Bridge to Active Voluntary Euthanasia," in *Euthanasia Examined: Ethical, Clinical and Legal Perspectives*, ed. John Keown (Cambridge: Cambridge University Press, 1995), 225-60. See also Rocco J. Gennaro, "The Relevance of Intentions in Morality and Euthanasia," *International Philosophical Quarterly* 36 (1996): 217-27.

[139] Kamisar, "Physician-Assisted Suicide," 230-36.

[140] See Ronald Dworkin *et al.* "The Philosophers' Brief," 41-47. See also Catherine L. Bjorck, "Physician-Assisted Suicide: Whose Life is it Anyway?" *Saint Mary University Law Review* 47 (1994):371-97.

[141] On the spread of practices from physician assisted suicide to voluntary euthanasia, see John Finnis, "The Fifth Annual Fritz B. Burns Lecture: Euthanasia, Morality, and the Law," Loyola of Los Angeles Law Review 30 (1997): 1473-87; John D Arras, "Physician-Assisted Suicide: A Tragic View," *Journal of Contemporary Health Law and Policy* 13 (1997): 361-89.

[142] Philip E. Devine, *The Ethics of Homicide* (Ithaca: Cornell University Press, 1978), 184-48; Robert George, "Death, be not Proud," *National Review* 47 (1995): 49-50.

[143] See Ronald Dworkin, *Life's Dominion: An Argument About Abortion, Euthanasia and Individual Freedom* (London: Harper Collins, 1993), ch. 8.

[144] For discussion of the statistics see, John Keown, "Further Reflections on Euthanasia in The Netherlands in the Light of The Remmelink Report and The Van Der Maas Survey," in *Euthanasia, Clinical Practice and the Law*, ed. Luke Gormally (London: Linacre Centre, 1994), 222-7.

[145] See John Keown, "The Law and Practice of Euthanasia in the Netherlands," *The Law Quarterly Review* 108 (1992) 51-78. See also Herbert Hendin, "The Slippery Slope: The Dutch Example," *Duquesne Law Review* 35 (1996): 427-42, and his book *Seduced By Death: Doctors Patient, and the Dutch Cure* (New York: W. W. Norton & Co, 1997); Richard Fenigsen, "The Report of the

Dutch Governmental Committee on Euthanasia," *Issues in Law and Medicine* 7 (1991): 339-44.

[146] See Howard Brody, "Causing, Intending, and Assisting Death," *Journal of Clinical Ethics* 4 (1993): 112-17.

[147] Kuhse, "Why Killing Is Not Always Worse," 271-74; Gerald Dworkin, "Public Policy and Assisted Suicide," in Dworkin, Frey and Bok, *Euthanasia and Physician-Assisted Suicide*, 64-80.Cf. John Woods, "Slippery Slopes and Collapsing Taboos," *Argumentation* 14 (2000), 107-34.

[148] See Thomas Anthony Cavanaugh, "Currently Accepted Practices That Are Known to Lead to Death, and PAS: Is There an Ethically Relevant Difference?" *Cambridge Quarterly of Healthcare Ethics* 4 (1998): 375-81.

[149] See Edmund E. Pellegrino, "The Place of Intention in the Moral Assessment of Assisted Suicide and Active Euthanasia," in *Intending Death: The Ethics of Assisted Suicide and Euthanasia*, ed. Tom L. Beauchamp (Englewood Cliffs: Prentice Hall, 1995), 163-83.

[150] Daniel Callahan, "When Self-Determination Runs Amok," *Hastings Center Report* 22 (1992): 52-55.

[151] Margaret P. Battin, "Voluntary Euthanasia and the Risks of Abuse: Can We Learn Anything From the Netherlands," *Law, Medicine and Health Care* 20 (1992): 133-43.

[152] Raymond J. Devettere, "Slippery Slopes and Moral Reasoning," *Journal of Clinical Ethics* 3 (1992): 297-301.

[153] G. Steven Neeley, "The Constitutional Right to Suicide. The Quality of Life and the Slippery Slope: An Explicit Reply to Lingering Concerns," *Akron Law Review* 29 (1994): 53-81; Battin, "Voluntary Euthanasia," 138-42.

[154] Yale Kamisar, "Against Assisted Suicide—Even in a Very Limited Form," *University of Detroit Mercy Law Review* 72 (1995): 739-45.

[155] Kamisar, "Against Assisted Suicide," 739-45.

[156] See Baron, "Model State Act," 557-58. The original restriction to the terminally ill was argued for earlier by Glanville Williams in his *The Sanctity of Life and the Criminal Law* (New York: A. Knopf, 1972).

[157] Dougherty, "Common Good," 155-58.

[158] Matthew E. Conolly, "Alternative to Euthanasia: Pain Management," *Issues in Law and Medicine* 4 (1989): 497-507.

[159] See the discussion on the expansion of classes due to relief of suffering concerns in Martin Gunderson and David J. Mayo, "Altruism and Physician Assisted Death," *Journal of Medicine and Philosophy* 18 (1993): 281-95.

[160] On the desire of physicians to respond to the suffering of patients as a motive for directly assisting with death, see Herbert Hendin, "Seduced by Death: Doctors, Patients, and the Dutch Cure," *Issues in Law and Medicine* 10 (1994): 123-68.

[161] Arras, "Physician-Assisted Suicide," 369-70. See also Scott FitzGibbon and Kwan Kew Lai, "The Model Physician-Assisted Suicide Act and the Jurisprudence of Death," *Issues in Law and Medicine* 13 (1997): 173-216.

[162] Dan Brock, "Voluntary Active Euthanasia," *Hastings Center Report* 22 (1992): 10-22.

[163] Daniel Callahan, "Self-Extinction-The Morality of the Helping Hand," in *Physician-Assisted Suicide*, ed. Robert Weir (Bloomington: Indiana University Press, 1997), 69-84.

[164] Trotter, "Assisted Suicide," 263-8; Ira R. Byock, "Physician-Assisted Suicide is Not and Acceptable Practice," in *Physician-Assisted Suicide*, ed. Robert Weir, 107-18.

[165] Trotter, "Assisted Suicide," 263-8; Greg A. Sachs *et al.* "Good Care of Dying Patients: The Alternative to Physician-Assisted Suicide and Euthanasia," *Journal of the American Geriatrics Society* 43 (1995): 553-62.

[166] M. Cathleen Kaveny, "Managed Care, Assisted Suicide, and Vulnerable Populations," *Notre Dame Law Review* 73 (1998): 1275-310; Daniel P. Sulmasy, "Managed Care and Managed Death," *Archives of Internal Medicine* 155 (1995): 133-6; Susan M. Wolf, "Physician-Assisted Suicide in the Context of Managed Care," *Duquesne Law Review* 35 (1996): 455-79.

[167] New York State Task Force, *When Death is Sought: Assisted Suicide and Euthanasia in the Medical Context* (New York: New York State Task Force, 1994), 117-48.

[168] For critiques of assisted suicide by advocates for those with disabilities, see Stephen L. Mikochik, "Assisted Suicide and Disabled People," 46 *DePaul*

Law Review 46 (1997): 987-1002, and Paul Steven Miller, "The Impact of Assisted Suicide on Persons with Disabilities—Is it a Right Without Freedom?" 9 *Issues in Law & Medicine* 9 (1993): 47-61.

[169] New York Task Force, *When Death Is Sought*, 125.

[170] Trotter, "Assisted Suicide," 265-6.

[171] Peter J.P. Tak, *Euthanasia in the Netherlands* (Leipzig: Leipziger, 1997).

[172] On physician, virtue, and euthanasia, see for example, Grant R. Gillett, "Learning to Do No Harm," *Journal of Medicine and Philosophy* 18 (1993) 253-68.

[173] In June 1996, the AMA House of Delegates reaffirmed its continued opposition to assisted suicide and to euthanasia. See American Medical Association, *Physician Assisted Suicide*, Report 59.

Chapter Seven

Natural Law, Judicial Review and the Legalisation of

Assisted Suicide in the United States

Introduction

In the preceding chapter, analysis of the implications of a natural law ethics for political and jurisprudential issues concerning suicide and assisted suicide, was general in scope. It was not tied to an analysis of the constitutional conditions of any particular polity. In this chapter, I will seek to concretise some of those insights via an assessment of relevant aspects of the constitutional framework of the United States, pertaining to moves to legalise assisted suicide. Proceeding initially to clarify some questions concerning the relationship between natural law and positive law, I will then explore some questions of judicial interpretation relevant to understanding the meaning and scope of the 14th Amendment of the US Constitution, especially the amendment's Due Process Clause. Our analysis will culminate in a review and analysis of two significant constitutional judgements of the Supreme Court, decided in 1997, that directly centre on the legal status of assisted suicide—*Washington v. Glucksberg* and *Vacco v. Quill*.

Natural Law and Positive Law

Status of Unjust Laws

A traditional question for natural law concerns the relationship between principles of natural law and the positive law of a given country.[1] Certain natural lawyers, such as Charles E. Rice, William Bentley Ball, and Raymond Begin, view the natural law as having a residual plenary authority that judges may appeal to in striking down a particular positive law that offends against the basic foundations of the natural law.[2] Appealing to Aquinas, they state that a law that offends against the natural law is not, properly speaking, a law, but is rather, a perversion of the law.[3]

Whilst I concur with their stress on the need to assess the wisdom of particular positive laws against the normative framework of the natural law, to deny the validity of a duly enacted positive law (precisely as posited law) seems to needlessly set into play a conflict with the common and conventional understanding of law as it pertains to certain 'rules of recognition' that can be said to grant the positive law of a given state the status of a duly enacted and authorised law.[4]

I am not arguing that laws of any given state may not be unjust, clearly they can, as assessed by the standards of the natural law.[5] Grossly unjust laws need not bind the conscience of an individual to be obedient to them (although one may prudentially seek to accommodate them for the sake of preserving the common good, e.g., upholding the general good of respect for the rule of law itself).[6] Rather, drawing on an insight from H.L.A. Hart, what I am stating is that there can be such a thing as a recognised law that is unjust, but that may nevertheless be considered a validly constituted law.[7] The *validity of a positive law* can be viewed as a distinguishable question from the morality or wisdom of a given law. If a law is unjust, it is better to speak of it in terms of its injustice and not deny its status as a validly (though wrongfully) posited law.[8]

It may seem that I am proposing something of a separation of natural law from positive law, such that there is no necessary connection. Such a conclusion would be mistaken. What I am precisely stating is that the natural law itself provides *normative grounds* for assessing the *content* of the positive law of a polity, and as such is the standard for assessment as to whether or not particular positive laws are *pro bono* or not.[9] Moreover, there are good grounds for pointing out that, via an examination of the ideals and aspirations that actually inform any empirical polity, many concrete expressions of natural law may actually be found in the constitutional fabric. With regard to the United States Constitution, as Russell Hittinger points out, it is possible to discern the disparate influence of many tenets of natural law, albeit expressed through the language of natural rights and the language of the Anglo-American common law tradition.[10]

Constitutional Foundations

There can be many forms of government, and many constitutional arrangements that may create duly authorised positive laws that are broadly compatible with the approach of natural law. Natural law itself contains no particular determination as to whether a constitution should be written or not, whether a constitution should be federal or unitary, or whether judges have residual plenary authority to appeal to a 'higher law', and so on.[11] Several forms and permutations need not conflict with the general function of law itself to promote and serve the political common good of a society. Within the context of the United States polity, therefore, there is *no contradiction* in saying, on the one hand, that a law is valid according to the rules of recognition of that polity, and on the other, that a given law is unjust and should be changed to something more in keeping with the constituents of human flourishing, *by the given method of change* the United States polity itself authorises.[12]

With those remarks in mind concerning the relationship between natural law and positive law, what is the source of constitutional legitimacy in the United States? The United States Constitution is the foundational political and legal charter upon which the governance of that polity was constituted.[13] The Constitution was drafted by several framers, and was duly enacted by the authority of state ratifiers meeting in conventions. As such, a new *groundnorm* was established that became the subsequent benchmark of legitimacy. The Federal government, the governments of the states, and the Supreme Court, have as much legitimate authority as was granted to them by virtue of that foundational charter.[14]

It follows that this foundational document, as amended, has the full force of being the ultimate positive law of the land to which all powers are subject. Of course, I am simplifying matters here, but in virtue of that constitutional settlement, legislation can be said to be *ultra vires* when it seeks to impose burdens or restrictions that are not warranted by the powers reserved to legislative bodies. Similarly, judicial judgement can be said to be *ultra vires* when it exceeds the scope of its authority to interpret and enforce the text of the Constitution. The Constitution then provides the benchmark for judging the legitimacy of actions by the different branches of government, including the rulings of the judiciary.[15]

Constitutional Interpretation

Need for Judicial Review

Turning now to consider the question of what the Constitution itself actually stands for, some examination of approaches to judicial interpretation cannot be avoided. No provisions exist in the Constitution for creating guidelines as to how the judicial task of interpretation should be performed. Additionally, the Constitution is a document that is often somewhat vague or general in its language. It is far from being transparent in terms of the scope and extent of some of its key provisions.[16] It is not my intention to exhaustively analyse competing schools of constitutional interpretation. Rather, I will confine myself to discuss a few concerns centred on the notion that the more methods of interpretation depart from any substantive connection to the text itself, and proceed *sui generis*, the more such methods will invite charges of engaging in an illegitimate usurpation of judicial power vis-à-vis the legislative branches of government and the democratic deliberation of the people.[17] Respect for the *rule of law* (an important condition of the common good) may be put at risk when judges are seen to resolve cases upon the basis of their own moral and political views, views that appear to have little or no cognisable basis in the text of the Constitution.[18]

Originalism

There has been an Originalist movement in recent years led by Justice Scalia and Robert Bork, to focus on questions of the original intent of the framers and ratifiers of the Constitution, and subsequent amendments.[19] Their concern has been one of the legitimacy of the authority of judges themselves to engage in what they consider to be a *de facto* usurpation of power from the legislative branches of federal and state legislators—effectively creating a plenary judicial law making power.[20] Scalia and Bork argue that the judiciary should not be concerned to impose its own values upon questions of interpretation, but should endeavour to put into effect the original meaning of the Constitution.[21]

I think that Scalia and Bork are correct to emphasis that respect for the judicial function is weakened when sweeping attempts are made to judicially legislate in a manner that unduly divorces questions of interpretation from the history and traditions of that society. This creates a reformatory agenda that constantly pits itself against the contrary tendencies of the legislative branches of government.[22] Where major controversies are in question, and where the Constitution itself is either silent or very indeterminate, an appeal to judicial authority is inept at deciding what the normative outcome of such debates ought to be.[23]

It is one thing to ensure that respect for democratic process and popular participation are protected in order to preserve the operation of democratic processes themselves from being forestalled or undermined by the operation of majoritarianism. It is quite another to think that appeals to the judiciary should determine the question of controverted outcomes that have nothing to do with the fairness of the processes of democratic decision making itself. There is no reason to think that the deliberations of nine justices of the Supreme Court exercising such a power will reach better outcomes that the outcomes reached by a body of deliberative legislators or the initiative of citizens. Of course, legislators and citizens may well make bad decisions, often some grossly bad decisions, but so too can justices of the Supreme Court.[24] The question is whose decisions, good or bad, should be determinate in terms of the parameters set by the Constitution?

Notwithstanding my basic agreement with Scalia's and Bork's pleas for judicial restraint, however, I think that the strategy of interpretation presented by originalism, is ultimately unrealistic and unduly limiting. The discernment process of establishing the original intent of the Constitution is painfully difficult and fraught with imprecision, due to the fact that legislation is often the result of compromise between a variety of disparate viewpoints. Contrary and divergent justifications for legislation can often be impossible to reconcile.[25] Moreover, at face value, originalism seems to deny the possibility that it is legitimate for a judicial body to proceed *narrowly and cautiously by analogy* in an incremental expansion of the interpretation of the Constitution, in light of changing circumstances dictated by new and unforeseen events.[26] A Supreme Court can, without usurping the authority of other branches of government, proceed by a process of circumspect adaptation of the existing law closely aligned to prior authority.

Moderate Interpretivism

The position I am advocating, in comparison to originalism, can be designated one of moderate or restrained interpretivism. A leading proponent of this general perspective is Michael Perry, who stresses the need for a more incremental and circumspect development in interpretation, respectful of the democratic branches of government.[27] It may be objected at this point that such an interpretivist strategy may be too weak to have allowed the Supreme Count to have made any significant watershed decisions, for example, its famous ruling in the case of *Brown v. the Board of Education*, abolishing the infamous Jim Crow statutes.[28] However, such a conclusion would be unwarranted. The passage of the Fourteenth Amendment was designed to recognise the notion of equality between all men (and subsequently women) in the eyes of states' authority. The Supreme Count could rightly have proceeded by tight analogical reasoning, on the implications of equality, to reach the conclusion that people are not treated equally when they are grossly discriminated against in terms of access to the benefits of public provision.[29] It could reasonably have overturned its earlier decision in *Plessy v. Ferguson* as being both naïve and misguided in its belief that respect for equality could possibly be achieved by policies that endorse the notion of separate but equal treatment.[30]

Due respect for restrained interpretation does not, therefore, result in a blanket endorsement of the status quo. Current practices may indeed breach Constitutional standards, when those standards are cognised with fidelity to the mischief they were considered to remedy in the first place (with due restrained extension to time and circumstance).[31]

Radical Interpretivism

Advocacy of 'moderate interpretivism' can be contrasted with schemes of radical or transformative interpretivism. Radical interpretivism seeks to unify and systematise the *collage of the historical Constitution* by abstracting values into an overarching schema for reform.[32] Such projects of grand synthesis are often motivated by appeals to the value of liberty or personal autonomy as the master value by which standards and provisions of the Constitution are to be judged.[33] Such an interpretative approach can be seen in the work of Ronald Dworkin and D.A.J. Richards.[34]

For Dworkin, interpretation is a process of creating an integrity out of the morass of particular rules and standards.[35] Law as integrity seeks to identify and draw out the underlying principles at stake in constitutional interpretation. In the context of the United States, Dworkin sees liberty, or personal autonomy, functioning as the underlying principle that best explains the evolving will of that society, and provides the central constitutional linchpin for the adjudicative processes to order and structure the 'unfolding narrative' around.[36] Hercules, Dworkin's heroic judge, seeks to interpret the Constitution in the light of the weight accorded to those underlying principles.

Dworkin's judge is not concerned simply to adopt an incremental approach to interpreting the Constitution, but rather, can actively seek to promote and advance underlying abstract principles. An activist judiciary is crucially required in order to knit the various constitutional provisions together into a meta-narrative.[37]

Richards's form of interpretation also stresses the transformative vision of judicial interpretation, by stressing the need for judges to discern the underlying values at stake and seek to advance them.[38] For Richards, those values are almost entirely the values supported by anti-perfectionist accounts of liberalism. The state should be neutral with reference to any particular vision of the good life. The state should not seek to burden its citizens with forms of paternalistic intervention that coerce them into abstaining from acts that individuals perceive to be good for them. Only concerns of significant harm to others can form a legitimate basis for government control. For Richards, this is the underlying framework that should inform contemporary constitutional interpretation, since it is those values that are reflective of the 'living Constitution' of the United States.[39]

Although Dworkin and Richards differ on particular questions as to how far liberty should be extended when compared to the claim of other values and principles, they share a common front with regard to the need for an activist judiciary to protect this unfolding settlement from the encroachment of legislative intervention on the part of federal or state legislatures.

My critique of this kind of transformative approach to interpretation is influenced by the work of John Hart Ely.[40] According to Ely, the founders created the Constitution in order to protect democratic structures of government so that substantive political values could be fairly derived through ordinary political institutions. When indeterminate or open-textured provisions of the Constitution are in question, the judiciary should be content to ascertain that fair and democratic government processes have been followed in the creation of those laws.[41]

Laws, even foundational laws, are not the outcome of *grand strategies of philosophical design,* but of compromise struck by the operation of the political processes of law making. Such is the preserve of the legislative branches of government, not judges. By engaging in abstract forms of synthesising, an activist judiciary is in danger of disenfranchising those deliberative bodies from seeking to work out political settlements that engage the democratic will of the people. Judicial fiat undermines the legitimate expectations of those who do not share the vision of discernment found convincing on the part of an activist judiciary, and who do not see in its exercise of power any foundation in the agreed constitutional text.[42]

Exercises in a restrained and incremental judicial extension or curtailment of existing rights and practices are unlikely to lead to widespread charges of undermining constitutional legitimacy. Sweeping constitutional changes imposed by a judiciary, changes that are deeply controversial, are of a different order of magnitude. It is one thing for a citizenry to accept an unpalatable law when it is the result of democratic deliberation, quite another when it is the result of imposition by a judicial body that proceeds on the basis of its own 'free floating' narrative interpretation of the Constitution to refashion the political landscape.[43] The more that the citizenry of a country comes to view processes of judicial review as merely an extension of raw political decision making, the less faith they will have in the ability of the judiciary to uphold the rule of law impartially, and the Constitution itself will be undermined. Justice White, in the case of *Bowers v. Hardwick,* aptly summed up the implications of this line of critique: "The [Supreme] Court is most vulnerable and comes nearest to illegitimacy when it deals with judge-made constitutional law having little or no cognisable roots in the language or design of the Constitution." In doing so, "the Judiciary takes to itself further authority to govern the country without express constitutional authority."[44]

Fears that deliberative democratic process may result in a distortion of the goals of an authentic common good, can be met by pointing out that it is not bizarre or flying in the face of reality to think that such bodies *are no less or more capable* of settling on the truth of a matter, in the subsequent shaping of laws, than the deliberations of a body of judges.[45] Moreover, those branches of government have the clear authority, by virtue of the Tenth Amendment, to substantiate the legitimacy of their claim to be the appropriate bodies authorised to make such determinations, for: "The powers not delegated to the United States by the Constitution, nor prohibited by it to the States, are reserved to the States respectively, or to the People."[46]

Fourteenth Amendment

Due Process: Purely Procedural?

Gerard Bradley, Robert Bork, and Raoul Berger argue that the intent of the ratifiers in passing the Due Process Clause of the Fourteenth Amendment was essentially one of recognising the need to protect people from the arbitrary actions of states that would deprive them of "life, liberty, or property, without due process of law."[47] They argue that there are documented grounds for asserting that this provision of the Fourteenth Amendment was intended to be a purely procedural protection, not a charter to invalidate states' laws on the basis of the substantive content of duly enacted laws.[48] Certainly, no one could claim that the amendment was not designed to grant procedural protections. However, for the following reasons stated by Michael Perry, I think that such an interpretation is too narrow.[49]

Perry argues that this narrow interpretation of the amendment is flawed, since the historical sources appealed to are far from being uniform, and can reasonably accommodate the view that some substantive protection was also envisaged. Perry further points to the necessity of reading the text of the amendment in its completeness in order to discern the broader extent of its envisaged scope. For example, immediately preceding the Due Process Clause is the following: "No State shall make or enforce any law which shall abridge the privileges or immunities of citizens of the United States." Perry argues that it would be odd to treat this Privileges Clause as entirely separate from the Due Process Clause following it.[50]

The implausibility of arguing that no substantial protection was envisaged by the Due Process Clause can also be demonstrated by the following powerful counter-factual. Even a fair procedural trial would not save from constitutional protection a perverse law that made it a criminal offence to take a perfectly harmless afternoon walk in a public park, in short, to exercise many of the traditional rights and privileges that are part and parcel of the history of a people who inherited the English common law; a tradition that crucially viewed an array of concrete and specific rights as part of the patrimony of its citizens.[51]

Substantive Due Process

For those above reasons, then, I think the Fourteenth Amendment has direct relevance to questions of substance. Does this mean that the amendment can therefore be interpreted as a general power granted to the Supreme Court to strike down an array of state laws on the basis of an appeal to general abstract notions of liberty or personal autonomy?[52] Not according to the rulings of the Supreme Court itself, in *Palko v. Connecticut* and *Moore v. City of East Cleveland.* In the first case, liberties were deemed to be fundamental to "ordered liberty," only if they were considered so essential that "neither liberty or justice would exist if they were sacrificed."[53] The means of specifying fundamental liberties was given further clarification in the second case, whereby they would be judged with reference to those held to be "deeply rooted in this Nation's history and tradition."[54] In the second case, no new test was being proposed. Rather, what was being proposed was a refinement of how the notion of what constituted ordered liberty should be further specified.[55]

The question of whether "neither liberty or justice would exist" is not to be conceived of as a free-floating abstraction, but rather, is to be assessed through the prism of deeply rooted history and tradition. History and tradition, not judicial grand synthesising, is the crucial benchmark for determining whether a particular liberty is such that ordered liberty can scarcely exist were it prohibited or eliminated.[56] Ordered liberty, therefore, is not an 'independent path' for the creation of a new liberty right, when the deeply rooted history and tradition of the American People have accorded the specific liberty little or no protection or recognition. As Chief Justice Rehnquist and Justice Scalia stated in *Michael H. v. Gerald D.*, courts considering substantive due process claims ought to "... refer to the most specific level at which a relevant tradition protecting, or denying protection to, the asserted right can be identified."[57]

Radical or transformative theories of interpretation stress the appeal to abstract principles as the basis for systematising the Constitution. Liberty, in particular, takes on such a transformative role because it is seen as the 'architectonic' value that makes sense out of the prevailing concerns of contemporary political life. Yet, such appeals tend to ignore the complexities of historical patterns of evolution and growth that have informed the shape of the political landscape, patterns that are far from being uniform in endorsing abstract appeals to liberty as a trumping value when key conflicts emerge with other values.

The key problem in engaging in such a form of interpretation is the profound one that it claims a power that runs contrary to a people's expectations that are widely understood to be framed in terms of deeply rooted historical rights and privileges. Courts surely come closest to perceptions of acting illegitimately when they proceed to render decisions that overturn the laws of states that have strongly rooted historical credentials; laws that seek to balance questions of liberty with other conflicting interests of the states in preserving and promoting the common good.[58]

History and Tradition Test

There are many liberties protected by the Due Process Clause that have had a rooted historical connectedness. The legitimacy of those rulings is underscored by a careful attention to the *specific rights and privileges* that tradition and history have sought to protect and promote. Moreover, the relevant history and tradition is not simply one of reference to isolated pockets of practice that may have a local history and tradition in an individual state, but must be judged with reference to the wider history and tradition of the United States itself.[59]

Consider by way of illustration two cases that are legitimate outcomes of an examination of specific rights and privileges that have a clear place in the history and tradition of the American People, and are, so rooted, compatible with the notion of ordered liberty. In the early part of the last century, the Supreme Court in *Meyer v. Nebraska* struck down a law of the State of Nebraska that banned children from learning a foreign language in public schools.[60] Such a liberty was considered to be unreasonably infringed upon, since it was widely recognised that students had a right to acquire knowledge, and that parents had a right to direct the upbringing of their children.[61]

Here, the identification of basic rights was predicated on the Court's recognition that certain *personal relationships* are so critical to how that society has historically ordered itself, that they are entitled to a high level of protection from government interference.[62] The same consideration of the nature of historically protected relationships was appealed to in the case of *Griswold v. Connecticut.*[63] In that case, the Supreme Court relied upon the specific historical recognition of the marital relationship in order to invalidate a Connecticut State law that prohibited a physician from giving a married couple information and advice about contraceptive practices.[64] Here, the right appealed to was not an abstract right to be left alone generally, but rather, it was one of seeking to protect the notion of intimacy within the nature of the historically recognised marital relationship. There was no suggestion that a free-floating general overarching privacy or liberty right was being recognised.[65]

Again, the limiting factor in those cases was the historically significant nature of certain relationships. Unfortunately, departure from such a constrained approach to interpretation can be traced to the Supreme Court case of *Eisenstadt v. Baird.*[66] In this case, the Court relied upon Griswold, a case based on the intimacy of the marital relationship, to strike down a state law that made it a criminal offence to distribute contraceptives to unmarried persons. Here the Court proclaimed a general right to contraception regardless of specific context.[67]

How was such a right linked to the question of deeply rooted historically protected relationships? The Court effectively created such a right without inquiring into whether history and tradition had recognised the validity of such a generally protected relationship.[68] If the question of 'ordered liberty' is severed from historical and traditional roots, how are such rights to be determined? So unconstrained, the standard quickly becomes one of what the judiciary themselves think the answer should be, justified by their own abstract frame of reference.

Having created a new liberty right in *Eisenstadt v. Baird*, the Supreme Court seemingly gave some credence to something of a radical or transformative approach to constitutional interpretation.[69] The ruling in that case provided precedent for future cases to proceed with the creation of new privacy or liberty rights unconstrained by the need for tethered historical justification.

Of course judicial bodies are not uniform, and contrary tendencies do emerge. In the case of *Bowers v. Hardwick*, for example, the Supreme Court upheld a Georgia statute that prohibited acts of sodomy. The justification here was largely one based on the lack of historical protection afforded to the nature of such an intimate relationship. [70] The "Party of Principle" approach may prefer to treat such a ruling as an aberration of the enlightened reasoning contained in *Eisenstadt v. Baird*.[71] However, that case represented something of an attempt to recognise a lesson from the Court's experience with its ruling in *Roe v. Wade*, that the rulings of the Court are most controversial, and invite charges of illegitimacy when they proceed on the basis of granting protection to certain practices that have a long pattern of historical prohibition, prohibitions that had been considered quite compatible with the notion of ordered liberty.[72]

Fourteenth Amendment and Assisted Suicide

Suicide

Unlike the widespread adoption of many branches of the English common law, e.g., contract and tort, the American colonies did not generally adopt the punishment of suicide. Massachusetts did, however, punish suicide with forfeiture of property and proscribed church burial rites until the practice fell into desuetude and was abolished in 1823. Whilst the states of New York and Oregon did not punish a suicide, they did hold it to be a grave wrong involving moral turpitude.[73] All statutes or common law interpretations punishing suicide have since been repealed or struck down. As the crime of suicide was abolished, or never applied, so too criminal sanctions for attempted suicide were either never applied or repealed.[74]

As Thomas Marzen *et al.* point out, it would be a quite erroneous conclusion to draw that the lack of legal sanction implied approval or a recognition of the creation of a 'right' to commit suicide, much less a right to receive assistance in committing suicide. Rather, it seems that punishment was rejected as being unsuitable, since it effectively punished the family of the suicide and did not really function as a deterrent. Removal of criminal sanction was motivated by a prevailing sense of the need for compassion, prompted by a growing body of psychological literature that pointed to a pronounced diminishment of responsibility on the part of the suicide; to be regarded more as victim than 'culprit'.[75]

Assisted Suicide

It does not follow (logically or practically) that if punishment for suicide (or attempted suicide) is not appropriate, punishment for acts of assisted suicide cannot be appropriate. There is reason to invoke the effectiveness of the use of the criminal law in the latter, due to the actions of third parties who would face penalty of law and would influence the actions of many citizens who desire to be law abiding and not beak the law. As the fact that some persons break the law and steal the property of others is no argument for abandoning the enforcement of theft laws, so the fact that some physicians may break the law, and in doing so extract some public sympathy, is no reason to abandon the law in this area either.[76]

Notwithstanding the efforts of the *Hemlock Society*, the *Euthanasia Society of America*, *Compassion in Dying*, and various other reform movements since the 1920's to gain legal acceptance of assisted suicide, all but four states criminally proscribe assistance in procuring suicide either by statute or by common law.[77] In the states of Ohio, Virginia, Utah, and Wyoming, the law is somewhat indeterminate (though this *does not* necessarily imply any condonation). Only one state, Oregon, has positively sanctioned the right to assistance in suicide, at the time of writing. In the other states, despite ballot and legislative initiatives (e.g., Washington, California, and Michigan), assistance in suicide is regarded as a felony, a species of homicide, and is punishable with imprisonment.[78]

As statutes increasingly replaced and codified the common law, derived from England, assisted suicide was classified as a crime in most of the American states. By the time of the ratification of the Fourteenth Amendment in 1868, nine states had adopted statutes explicitly criminalising assisted suicide. The *Field Code*, a codification project that influenced legislative changes in the 19th century, contained a specific criminal prohibition against assisted suicide.[79]

Euthanasia

Laws against the practice of euthanasia are more straightforward. Euthanasia is a form of intentional homicide undertaken for a motive of mercy. Whether by common law or by statute, it is considered a species of murder.[80] Courts and legislatures alike have historically refused to treat questions of consent or motives of mercy as a valid defence to such intentional acts of killing. At best, such considerations have been taken into account as part of the sentencing process, when mitigating circumstances are addressed. In no state has voluntary active euthanasia ever been sanctioned.[81] Constitutional history therefore provides remarkably little support for a right to assisted suicide or to voluntary euthanasia, and without such support, the Supreme Court, as stated in *Bowers v. Hardwick,* ought to be very reluctant to "... take a more expansive view of our authority to discover new fundamental rights imbedded in the Due Process Clause."[82]

Withdrawal of Treatment

The state of the question concerning the possibility of assisted suicide or euthanasia by omission is more complex. Here I shall simply note the following significant observation concerning the historical development of United States law. The right to be free from unwanted bodily invasion was recognised in 1914 in the case of *Schloendorff v. New York Hospital.* In this case, the leading authority on right of refusal, Justice Cardozo, stated that "every human being of adult years and sound mind has a right to determine what shall be done with his [her] own body."[83] Such a right has been repeatedly recognised in subsequent case law.[84]

In the case of *Karen Anne Quinlan,* the court concluded that where a patient was in such a profoundly disabilitated condition, and where there was medical support to sustain that life, there could be a decision to withdraw life support.[85] This line of argumentation found in *Quinlan* was defended in the cases of *Superintendent of Belchertown State School v. Saikewicz,*[86] *Brophy v. New England Sinai Hospital,*[87] and in the Supreme Court case of *Cruzan v. Director, Missouri Health Department.*[88]

The point that I wish to stress here (instantiated further in various states' living will legislation and the Federal *Self-Determination Act of 1990*)[89] is that this line of authority, *in and of itself,* should not be interpreted to imply a recognition of the legitimacy of assisted suicide or euthanasia, by omission. This line of authority does not affirm a 'right to die'.[90] Rather, such authorities cumulatively recognise a right to be free from unwanted bodily invasions, and do not affirm that *the manner and timing of death* as such can be determined by the individual patient. Certainly such legal measures *can be utilised* to pursue an overtly suicidal objective. Yet, that point, at best, can only support the conclusion that in enacting legal measures to protect patients from the *burden of disproportionate means*, the law inevitably expresses toleration of practices that fall within the necessarily broad scope needed to protect that interest (due discretion as to the circumstantial needs of individual patients as to what constitutes undue burdensomeness).[91]

It would have been a gross act of judicial law making had the Supreme Court, in *Cruzan*, invalidated laws that prohibited assisted suicide, since common law and the deliberations of many state legislatures have recognised a crucial distinction between protecting that traditional right (freedom from burdensome treatment), and creating what would amount to the institutionalisation of a right to aid and abet the killing of a patient. However, it did not. Instead, the Supreme Court recognised the common law right to be free from *unwanted invasions of the body*, nothing more and nothing less (extended to the judgement of a surrogate decision maker with appropriate evidentiary requirements). Of course it recognised that in advancing the legitimate interests of many patients to be free from unwelcome burdens, such latitude may sometimes be deployed for suicidal purposes. Yet, this unintended side-effect of protecting an important and long recognised common law right was considered justified in order to protect the legitimate interest of patients. It did not amount to an endorsement of suicide, much less of assisted suicide, where the intent of the patient and the physician *must be* precisely one of procuring the death of the patient.

Having looked at the history and tradition of the specific liberty interest being appealed to by proponents of assisted suicide and voluntary euthanasia, there is no substantive evidence to suggest that assisted suicide, or voluntary euthanasia, are liberty rights that have deep roots in the history and tradition of the American people. The common law had condemned the private use of lethal force by individuals (apart form self-defence), and this extended to the practice of assisted suicide.[92] The bulk of the states have had a long historical tradition of prohibiting those practices. Consent, especially, has never been seen as a legitimate ground for engaging in, or assisting in, acts of intentional killing. Just as state laws have protected individuals from, say, selling themselves willingly into slavery or engaging in duels to settle disputes, so states have traditionally been charged with protecting human persons from consensual acts of intentional killing.[93]

Casey Mystery Passage?

The abortion cases are appealed to by some advocates as authority for recognising a liberty right or interest in determining the manner and timing of death. In particular the famous mystery passage in *Planned Parenthood of Southeastern Pennsylvania v. Casey* is appealed to (see the discussion of the *Philosophers' Brief* in chapter three).[94] This passage was cited in the context of justifying the termination of the life of a foetus not accorded the status of being a person. As the context in Casey makes clear, however, such a passage was not intended to be used as a justification for taking the lives of legally recognised natural persons, whether consented to, or not. It is not therefore an appropriate part of the relevant history and tradition of the specific liberties being considered.[95]

Disregard for relevant historical context is even more apparent when such a passage is itself directly contradicted by the Supreme Court in the case of *Cruzan*. Acts of assisted suicide were *clearly distinguished* from the specific liberty of being free from burdensome invasions of the body. This precedent is clear and direct and cannot be side-stepped by the appeal to an authority that is both isolated in terms of the unique and bizarre particularities of the abortion question, and is most certainly not directly in point as a precedent for determining questions of killing between legally recognised natural persons.[96]

Disregard for relevant context is at its most acute when the mystery passage in *Casey* is treated as a free-floating abstraction. The passage is an *obiter dictum*, an utterance way beyond the scope of the problem being addressed in *Casey*.[97] It is a very loose passage, that, if taken seriously, would justify the most radically laxist of conclusions. It could, for example, be used to support the right of any person to assistance in suicide, or voluntary euthanasia in any circumstance the person happened to see fit, whether healthy or ill.[98] It would support the practice of any intimate act or relationship judged by the person to express his or her own meaning of existence, no matter how degrading, providing there was ostensive consent. Such would not be a charter for any notion of 'ordered liberty', but would be one of promoting unrestrained licence in the most libertarian manner.[99]

A Question for State Discretion?

Is the historical record, therefore, simply one of permitting state legislators to resolve those specific liberty questions for themselves, in ways they see fit? Could they not tolerate, or even promote, assisted suicide if they thought it appropriate? Such a judgement would be mistaken, however, for it is not compatible with the relevant deeply rooted history and tradition that a state has constitutional discretion to abrogate its responsibility to protect the lives of its citizens by legalising acts of assisted suicide or voluntary euthanasia, no matter how narrowly posited the purported right may be drafted.[100] States have a paramount interest in protecting the lives of its citizens, by prohibiting the intentional private lethal use of force (except for reasonable force used in questions pertaining to self-defence). *There is no more foundational immunity inherent in the tradition of Common law and the history and tradition of the American people than the protection of the lives of citizens from the private use of lethal force.* The risks entailed by potential slippery slopes (documented in chapter five) strongly highlight the power and wisdom of protecting this foundational immunity, such that no state can be permitted to abrogate such protection, regardless of democratic deliberation (short of successful constitutional amendment). Can we doubt, for example, that the Supreme Court would strike down a state statute that permitted duelling, or other lethal consensual assaults? No. The same rationale applies to assisted suicide or voluntary euthanasia. Questions of mercy and compassion should be directed to support the means for improving the condition of patients and their care, not directed to efforts seeking to legitimate the intentional private use of lethal force to terminate life. Consent has never been regarded as a grounds for justifying the procurement of the death of one citizen by another, notwithstanding questions of motive, and its abandonment strikes at the heart *of the traditional privileges and immunities* that the American nation has stood for and is covenanted to protect.

Analysis of Assisted Suicide Cases

Washington v. Glucksberg

Turning now to a consideration of the Supreme Court rulings directly concerned with the constitutional legitimacy of assisted suicide, in *Washington v. Glucksberg*, the majority opinion adopted a more moderate and constrained jurisprudential approach than it had previously demonstrated in some of its earlier substantive due process rulings.[101] In contrast to the earlier *en blanc* ruling of the Ninth Circuit, whose majority opinion relied heavily on the mystery passage in *Casey*, (itself following the interpretation of the district court judge's earlier ruling that found *Casey* "highly instructive"), the majority opinion, written by Chief Justice Rehnquist, discounted its precedential value when considering the question of the *specific liberty* of assisted suicide. Liberty was to be assessed with reference to the history and tradition of the nation concerning the specific liberty right or interest being claimed, not by *obiter dicta* issued in other cases.[102]

Unlike the opinion of Judge Reinhardt, writing for the majority in the Ninth Circuit (known for his expansive approach to constitutional interpretation), the analysis of the history and tradition contained in the Supreme Court majority opinion was well grounded. The same cannot be said for Reinhardt's opinion.[103] In his review of the relevant history and tradition,

Reinhardt arbitrarily discounted the importance of the common law inheritance of the nation and the long enactments of many states laws, in favour of undue attention to the citation of literary suicides, the misreading of ancient philosophical sources, and the misconstrual of non-religious grounds for opposing suicide .[104]

On the basis of the recognised test for substantive due process review upon which the recognition of a liberty right to assisted suicide ought to be founded, there were no significant grounds for granting recognition to such a right.[105] The central justification offered for the invalidation of the State of Washington's criminal statute prohibiting assisted suicide was therefore constitutionally groundless.[106] Assisted suicide statutes were properly compatible with the notion of ordered liberty (notwithstanding appeals to consent and the condition of patients faced with considerable pain and suffering), since they were traditionally recognised as advancing important state interests in seeking to preserve the immunity of citizens from the dangers of legitimising such acts of killing.

In addition to a paramount interest in preserving the lives of its citizens, the Supreme Court majority opinion also found persuasive the evidence of slippery slope arguments to the effect that more that the lives of a few terminally ill patients experiencing pain could be placed at risk, no matter how narrow and circumscribed the scope of such legislation was intended to be. They recognised that if a law was enacted creating a right to assisted suicide for a particular class of patients, such as the terminally ill, it would be very difficult to restrict the availability of assisted suicide only to those within that class. Additionally, it would be very difficult to restrict the availability of assisted suicide to free and voluntary choices, due to many invidious social pressures that may come into play, influencing the judgement of the poor, the elderly, and the vulnerable.[107]

However, despite several praiseworthy aspects of the Court's ruling in this case that upheld the State of Washington's criminal law statute against assisted suicide, the Supreme Court majority was mistaken in one crucial respect. Here, the Supreme Court effectively said that whilst a state legislature was permitted to uphold such laws, *they need not do so*. On such a basis, the State of Oregon's assisted suicide statute was validated, since the Supreme Court had effectively ruled that whilst laws outlawing assisted suicide were valid, so too were laws that legalised the practice.[108] This was a wrongful conclusion to draw, because it failed to follow through with the logic of its own analysis concerning history and tradition, as well as the risks posed by potential slides down the slippery slope.

As I have pointed out earlier in this chapter, the immunity and protection of citizens from the lethal use of private force should not be regarded as a discretionary matter for enforcement. States ought to be constitutionally obliged to accord such protection by the use of the criminal law, for only the use of criminal sanction can claim to be of sufficient weight to uphold and protect the nature of the life interest at stake. There are clear and compelling grounds for denying the legitimacy of any state to enact assisted suicide legislation, for in doing so, there is a failure to adequately protect the life of citizens who are undisputedly persons, and must therefore be accorded such immunity, an immunity that cannot be waived.[109] Protection from the private use of lethal force should have been regarded as constitutional bedrock, and thus providing the necessary grounds for invalidating the Oregon statute permitting the legalisation of assisted suicide.

Vacco v. Quill

Turning now to an analysis of the second case, *Vacco v. Quill,* the matter at stake concerned the interpretation of the Equal Protection Clause of the Fourteenth Amendment.[110] The clause states that no state should " … deny to any person within its jurisdiction the equal protection of the laws."[111] Are terminally ill patients who prefer death by means of assisted suicide being unjustly discriminated against by the refusal of states to permit physicians to assist them with the termination of their own lives? Does the distinction drawn between withdrawal of treatment and assisted suicide pass muster in terms of the rational basis test required by the Equal Protection Clause?

In the opinion of Judge Miner, writing for a three judge panel, the Second Circuit Court of Appeal found that patients were being discriminated against in the dying process, by being unreasonably denied the support of active assistance in hastening their own deaths.[112] Whilst that court rightly rejected assisted suicide on the grounds of a liberty right under the Due Process Clause, it found an equivalent basis for establishing such a right under the auspices of the Equal Protection Clause. No convincing rational basis existed for drawing a distinction between the withdrawal of life support and the provision of lethal means in assisted suicide. Since the withdrawal of life support materially contributed to the death of the patient, there was no practical significance in accepting, on the one hand, the withdrawal of support, and on the other, rejecting the positive provision of means to achieve the same practical outcome—the death of the patient.[113]

The credibility of such an interpretation, however, was based on a misconstrual of the *rational basis* upon which other existing rights concerning the withdrawal or termination of treatment were predicated. Those rights did not support a 'right to die' amounting to the authorisation of a right to determine the *manner and timing* of death.

There is an important rational discrimination posited between the *right to be free from unwanted bodily invasion*, on the one hand, compatible with an assessment of the burdens of treatment, and a *right to be rendered dead*, on the other. There is compelling authority to support this distinction in reason, and in the tradition of common law pertaining to battery.[114] There are, therefore, no adequate grounds for inferring discriminatory lack of equal protection, for the same right, *to be free from unwelcomed bodily invasion*, is of general application and is not discriminatory between classes of patient. The Second Circuit seriously misframed the nature of the right being recognised in its analysis of withdrawal of treatment cases.[115]

The right to refuse life-sustaining treatment, is a negative right only, not a positive right. It is the negative right not to be subject to treatment, especially treatment that is burdensome and that does not seem to afford the patient any reasonable hope of benefit. It is clear from many court rulings on the subject, not least the Supreme Court's own ruling in *Cruzan*, that there is a recognised negative right to be free from unwanted treatment, not a general right to determine the manner and timing of death, which may encompass both positive and negative means to achieve that objective.[116]

The ruling of the Second Circuit was therefore a ruling that lacked a justifiable grounding. That judgement was rightly overturned in the majority ruling of the Supreme Court. Here the Supreme Court upheld the rationality of the discrimination between withdrawal or termination of life support and the right to actively procure death with the assistance of a physician. Again, Chief Justice Rehnquist, wrote for the majority. New York's distinction between the right to refuse life-sustaining medical treatment and suicide, survived rational basis review because it was based on sound legal analysis pertaining to questions of intent. The distinction between refusing care and assisting suicide was clearly justified on grounds of intent. "The law has long used actors' intent or purposes to distinguish between two acts that may have the same result."[117] Thus, the common law of homicide distinguishes " ... between a person who knows that another person will be killed as the result of his conduct and a person who acts with the specific purpose of taking another's life."[118] A physician who withdraws care pursuant to an express patient request, need only intend to respect the wishes of the patient and need not intend to kill. In contrast, a doctor assisting a suicide must necessarily and primarily intend that the patient be killed.

Concurrences in the Two Cases

Ronald Dworkin, in his analysis of the Supreme Court rulings, states that some comfort for future judicial innovation can be taken from the separate concurrences issued in both cases. A right to some form of active assistance in suicide in all states might yet be recognised by a future revisitation of the issue by the Supreme Court.[119] Justices O'Connor, Ginsberg, and Breyer issued a concurrence that seems to leave open the possibility that the Supreme Court may be prepared to revisit the question at a later date.[120] This might occur on the basis of a future action that focuses on cases of competent terminally ill patients, enduring considerable pain or intolerable suffering, that can not be adequately addressed or relieved by alternative methods of treatment.[121]

Separate concurrences were also filed by Justice Souter and by Justice Stevens. Justice Souter attacked the basis of the majority opinion on the grounds of its express declaration to limit substantive due process analysis to specific liberties recognised in history and tradition in favour of a broader, more expansive, interpretation of the Constitution. A broader interpretation could yet determine that some instances of assisted suicide provision may be justified, once the implications of a liberty interest are unpacked in the light of innovation by the states.[122]

Justice Stevens focused his concurrence on a critique of justifying the distinction between refusing treatment and actively assisting a suicide, on the basis of intent. If the consequences of withdrawal and active assistance are essentially the same, then the two actions are basically equivalent. Both physicians may intend the same result. A physician who terminally sedates a patient is merely complying with the wishes of the patient in order to hasten death. So too, may a physician who complies with a patient's request for a lethal dose of medication.[123]

Critique of the Concurrences

Notwithstanding the observations contained in the concurrences, and the potential window of opportunity they might seem to present to proponents of the legalisation of assisted suicide, all those possible grounds for possible future revisitation can be convincingly met.

Turning, firstly, to Justice Souter's critique of the limitation placed on due process review by the majority opinion. As I have already argued, history and tradition has been affirmed in numerous Supreme Court cases as the legitimate ground upon which to assess substantive due process claims. Only such a restriction in interpretation can prevent the Supreme Court turning into a *de facto* body exercising an untethered power to refashion the constitutional landscape under its own self-referential guidance as to what might be meant by the abstract concept of liberty.

Rather than risk disregarding the deeply rooted history and traditions of the nation, as the Court had proceeded to do in its earlier abortion rulings, and at some cost to its perceived legitimacy, the majority opinion rightly reaffirmed the importance of specific historical analysis in this area of constitutional law, setting aside the direct relevance of abstract discussions about the "right to define one's own concept of existence, of meaning, of the universe, and of the mystery of human life."[124] A clear specific long-standing tradition, running contrary to the toleration or acceptance of the practices of assisted suicide or euthanasia, cannot be traded in for a general frame of reference drawing heavily upon the highly controversial abortion rulings. They are manifestly not precedents for the proposition that it is legitimate for one natural person to intentionally kill another natural person on the grounds of consent or relief of suffering.

Turning to the problem raised by Justice Stevens concerning equal protection requirements, the argument for a distinction between cases of withdrawal or non-provision of treatment, and cases of assistance in suicide, do indeed pass constitutional muster, since they are rational in justification, based as they are on differences of intent.[125] Justice Stevens may not accept this point, due to his Benthamite consequentialist action analysis, but there is a compelling case for the relevance and validity of the distinction supported by the common law, the creation of criminal codes, and by ordinary human experience.

As I have argued in detail in chapter three of this monograph, the intentional object of an action is of a different moral and legal character from the foreseeable but unintended consequences of an action. Suffice it here to make the following remarks.[126] Intentions are central to the analysis of action and to questions of responsibility pertaining to action. They are central to questions of criminal responsibility concerning homicide. For example, the law recognises important distinctions between degrees of murder and manslaughter based on whether or not the action was done intentionally, with knowledge but not intention, recklessly, or negligently. The importance of intentionality to the analysis of criminal conduct has been confirmed by the Supreme Court on many occasions, and by the decisions of many state supreme courts. It is as relevant to questions of assisted suicide as it is to any other case of homicidal action between natural persons.

Justice Stevens can only reach his conclusion concerning equivalence between distinct kinds of action by focusing on the consequences of the action rather than focusing on the intentional objective of the action, for an action may look similar or even identical in terms of result but be profoundly different in kind. Yet we need not follow his consequentialist turn. We can justifiably state that in cases of the withdrawal or non-provision of treatment, patients can decline care for many sound reasons that need not imply an intention to kill, e.g., the specific intention of the patient and physician alike may be to avoid the continuing burdens of treatment. Whilst there can sometimes be questions of ambiguity attached to decisions to withdraw or withhold treatment, decisions that can sometimes be taken in order to pursue suicidal objectives, many cases are clearly reconcilable with a good intent on the part of both patient and physician. No such decision *need of necessity imply* that either the patient or the physician has an intent to kill, even if it is certainly foreseeable that the onset of death may quickly result.

Such, however, is not the case with an action of assisted suicide. No good intent can ever be rendered compatible with an action of this kind. In such an action there is necessarily an intent to prescribe a lethal dose of medication to a patient in order to procure the taking of the life of that patient. Assistance in killing is the intended objective. From this *actus reus* it is always reasonable to conclude that the intent of the physician was precisely to render the patient dead, by aiding and abetting the suicide.

Turning, finally, to the concurrence of Justices O'Connor, Ginsberg, and

Breyer, it can indeed be recognised that they are right to empathise with the plight of those who are faced with the unenviable prospect of dying in conditions of considerable pain. There is indeed a legitimate interest in patients being free from unbearable pain. Patients understandably have a great fear of abandonment to pain and the lack of its adequate management. With regard to focusing attention on such questions, the assisted suicide movement has brought about some good in its wake, for it has forced policy makers to address the neglect of many patients who are not sufficiently cared for in terms of provision of an adequate array of options for treatment and support.

Yet, notwithstanding the legitimacy of such interests, how can such interests be used to support the conclusion that human life, impaired as it is, can justly be intentionally acted against? Human life cannot be traded in for the legitimate interest of pain relief, for such a judgement *has no plausible basis* for principled restraint or limitation. What then of a right to be free from intolerable suffering other than pain? Need the patient be terminally ill? Slippery slope considerations, discussed in chapter five, come rushing to the foreground.

It is one thing for federal and state legislatures to work towards supporting the expectations of patients to receive the best palliative care measures possible, and to work towards the provision of other measures designed to support that humanitarian goal, but it is quite another to argue that it is an interest that can be used to trump the interest of the state in preserving human life from intentional attack. History and tradition clearly do not furnish grounds for justifying the intentional private use of lethal force to pursue the motive of pain relief. To seek to rule a law unconstitutional that bans assisted suicide, *on the ground of provision of pain relief,* would be tantamount to an overt act of judicial law making.

Rather than legalise assisted suicide, as such, in order to promote better pain management, it is argued that the threat of criminal prosecution could simply be lifted from all physician actions ostensibly undertaken in order to alleviate pain. Could a blanket immunity from criminal prosecution not be granted for all forms of palliative care authorised by a physician?[127]

Here, I would argue that initiatives for better pain management techniques for the care of patients should not result in the restructuring of existing criminal law provisions, but rather, attention should be focused on attempts to *alleviate crucial misperceptions as to what the scope of the existing criminal law actually prohibits.*

The most acute concern is over the potential criminal liability of physicians in the treatment of pain via possible life shortening medications. Physicians consistently express fear of potential criminal liability for possible practices of 'over-prescription'. Yet, such a fear is not founded upon any reasonable basis. To date, there have been no successful criminal prosecutions in the United States, of physicians using analgesics to control the use of pain.[128] Physicians are therefore unduly fearful of the perceived risks involved in pursuing the legitimate objective of seeking to relieve the pain of their patients, even if death is hastened as a result.

The criminal law test is one of 'beyond reasonable doubt'. Prosecutors are very well aware of this high evidential standard, and it needs *to be more effectively communicated* to physicians in alleviating their misplaced perceptions of exposure to potential criminal liability for adequate pain management. The correct emphasis here ought to be one of education and the promotion of cultural change in the perception of health professionals. Providing there is *a plausible medical justification* for the prescription and administration of a drug, no prosecution for 'over prescription' is remotely probable. The fear of prosecution, therefore, is not well grounded if a physician has any *plausible basis* for prescribing pain medication for the treatment of a patient.

Old habitual fears die hard, hence the *pressing need* for the education and training of physicians to be aware of the latitude afforded to them in the treatment of pain. If the restoration of health, can no longer be achieved, the physician is obliged to do all that is proper and necessary to relieve pain, even if the measures taken may incidentally shorten life.

Efforts should go into education and training, not the granting of blanket immunity from prosecution. Such a blanket immunity is not warranted, for the criminal law should seek to promote a *via media* between unwarranted fear of 'over-prescription' on the one hand, with the need for reasonable outer boundaries of constraint on the practices of physicians, on the other. The criminal law must retain the right to prosecute flagrant breaches of medical practice, such that no reasonable physician could plausibly have authorised the prescription of such pain medication, in those clinical circumstances, unless there was indeed a primary intent to hasten the death of the patient. Again, it must be stressed that no physician can view this restrained appeal to criminal sanction as an excuse for undertreating pain, for such a threshold will be high and would only be crossed by flagrant breaches of professional practice standards. Yet, without such a boundary, the law would indeed grant a virtual licence to physicians to practice assisted suicide without any potential for criminal liability. The aim of the criminal law in protecting human life from intentional killing, and the duty of the medical profession to adequately relieve the pain of patients, *need not jarringly conflict*, and can indeed be viewed as capable of mutual accommodation.

Notes to Chapter Seven

[1] Aquinas raises this key question when discussing the relationship between natural law and human law. See ST I-II q. 95, a. 1. The natural law is the ultimate source of normativity for the positive law of any society. See Robert J. Hendle, "St. Thomas Aquinas and American Law," in *Thomistic Papers II*, eds. Leonard A. Kennedy and Jack C. Marler (Houston: University of St. Thomas, 1986), 59-84.

[2] Charles E Rice, "Some Reasons for a Restoration of Natural Law Jurisprudence," *Wake Forest Law Review* 24 (1989): 539-71; "The Problem of Unjust Laws," *Catholic Lawyer* 26 (1981): 278-85; William Bentley Ball, "Natural Law and the Power of the Courts," *Catholic Social Science Review* 1 (1996): 14-20; Raymond Francis Begin, *Natural Law and Positive Law* (Washington, DC: Catholic University Press, 1959). See also G. Ambrosetti, "Christian Natural Law," *American Journal of Jurisprudence* 16 (1971): 290-

301; Russell Kirk, "Natural Law and the Constitution of the United States," *Notre Dame Law Review* 69 (1994): 1035-47.

[3] See Rice, "The Problem of Unjust Laws," 278-85.

[4] The phrase 'rule of recognition' is borrowed from H.L.A. Hart. See his *The Concept of Law*, 2nd ed. (New York: Oxford, 1994), 89-96.

[5] For an detailed discussion of this matter of obligation and injustice see Robert J. Araujo, "Thomas Aquinas: Prudence, Justice, and the Law," *Loyola Law Review* 40 (1995): 897-921.

[6] Araujo, "Thomas Aquinas," 906-13. See also Robert George, "Natural Law and Civil Rights: From Jefferson's 'Letter to Henry Lee' to Martin Luther King's 'Letter from Birmingham Jail'," *Catholic University Law Review* 43 (1993): 143-57; John Finnis, "Unjust Laws in a Democratic Society: Some Philosophical and Theological Reflections," *Notre Dame Law Review* 71 (1996): 595-604.

[7] On the thesis that alternative interpretative strands, on the status of a positive law, arise from the body of Aquinas's work, see Daniel A. Degnan, "Two Models of Positive Law in Aquinas: A Study of the Relationship of Positive Law and Natural Law," *Thomist* 46 (1982): 1-32.

[8] Robert George, "*Natural Law and Positive Law,*" in *The Autonomy of Law*, ed. Robert George (Oxford: Clarendon Press, 1996), 321-34.

[9] John Finnis, "The Truth in Legal Positivism," in *The Autonomy of Law*, ed. Robert George, 195-214.

[10] For various examples of the relevance of the natural law tradition via the prism of natural rights language, see Russell Hittinger, "Liberalism and the American Natural Law Tradition," *Wake Forest Law Review* 25 (1990): 429-99. See also Charles S. Desmond, "Natural Law and the American Constitution," *Fordham Law Review* 22 (1953): 235-45.

[11] See Christopher Wolfe, "Judicial Review," in *Natural Law and Contemporary Public Policy*, ed. David F. Forte (Washington, DC: Georgetown University Press, 1998), 157-89

[12] Wolf, "Judicial Review," 173-83. See also Russell Hittinger, "Natural Law in the Positive Law: A Legislative or Adjudicative Issue?" *Review of Politics* 55 (1993): 5-34.

[13] Hadley Arkes, *Beyond the Constitution* (Princeton: Princeton University Press, 1990), 1-28.

[14] Arkes, *Constitution*, 1-28.

[15] Gerald V. Bradley, "Moral Truth, the Common Good, and Judicial Review," in *Catholicism, Liberalism, and Communitarianism*, eds. Kenneth L. Grasso and Gerald V. Bradley (Lanham: Rowman & Littlefield, 1995), 115-32.

[16] James B. Thayer, "The Origin and Scope of the American Doctrine of Constitutional Law," in *Constitutional Law and its Interpretation*, eds. Jules L. Coleman and Anthony Sebok (New York: Garland, 1994), 1-28.

[17] On the uneasy division between questions of 'judicial interpretation' and 'judicial law making', see generally Peter H. Irons, *Brennan vs. Rehnquist: The Battle for the Constitution* (New York: A. Knopf, 1994). Brennan represents the more radical interpretivist standpoint, and Rehnquist, a more constrained textual based perspective.

[18] See Francis Canavan, *The Pluralist Game: Pluralism, Liberalism, and the Moral Conscience* (Lanham: Rowman & Littlefield, 1995), 51-61. See also *The Rise of Modern Judicial Review: from Constitutional Interpretation to Judge-Made Law* (New York: Basic Books, 1986).

[19] Antonin Scalia, *A Matter of Interpretation: Federal Courts and the Law* (Princeton: Princeton University Press, 1997); "Originalism: The Lesser Evil," *University of Cincinnati Law Review* 57 (1989): 849-65; Robert H. Bork, *The Tempting of America: the Political Seduction of the Law* (New York: Free Press, 1990); *Slouching Towards Gomorrah: Modern Liberalism and American Decline* (New York: Regan Books, 1996).

[20] Gregory Bassham, *Original Intent and the Constitution: A Philosophical Study* (Savage: Rowman and Littlefield, 1992), 17-38.

[21] Scalia, "Originalism," 852-54; Bork, Tempting of America, 143-60. See also Kathleen A. Brady, "Putting Faith Back Into Constitutional Scholarship: A Defense of Originalism," *Catholic Lawyer* 36 (1995): 137-201.

[22] Brady, "Putting Faith," 137-42.

[23] Brady, "Putting Faith," 181-84.

[24] See John Hart Ely, *Democracy and Distrust: A Theory of Judicial Review* (Cambridge: Harvard University Press, 1980), 87-88.

[25] Bassham, *Original Intent,* 91-108.

[26] See Sanford Levinson, "The Operational Irrelevance of Originalism," in *Liberty Under Law,* ed. Kenneth L. Grasso and Cecilia Rodriguez (Lanham: University Press of America, 1997), 113-28.

[27] Michael J. Perry, *The Constitution in the Courts: Law or Politics?* (New York: Oxford University Press, 1994), 15-27; *Morality, Politics, and Law: A Bicentennial Essay* (New York: Oxford University Press, 1988), 121-78.

[28] See for example, Laurence H. Tribe and Michael C. Dorf, *On Reading the Constitution* (Cambridge: Harvard University Press, 1991), ch. 2, who argue for the necessity of judicial activism to resolve fundamental civil rights questions. See also Earl M. Maltz, "Brown v. Board of Education," in *Constitutional Stupidities, Constitutional Tragedies*, eds. William N. Eskridge and Sanford Levinson (New York: New York University, 1998), 207-16.

[29] On the need for restraint and one the importance of tight analogical reasoning in judicial interpretation, see Christopher Wolfe, *How to Read the Constitution: Originalism, Constitutional Interpretation, and Judicial Power* (Lanham: Rowman and Littlefield, 1996), 85-106. See also Cass R. Sunstein, *Legal Reasoning and Political Conflict* (New York: Oxford University Press, 1996), 171-82.

[30] Perry, *Constitution in the Courts*, 136-60.

[31] See Sunstein, "Analogical Reasoning," in *Legal Reasoning*, 62-100.

[32] William Gangi, *Saving the Constitution from the Courts* (Norman: University of Oklahoma Press, 1995), 170-226.

[33] Wolfe, *How to Read the Constitution,* 107-24.

[34] Ronald Dworkin, *Law's Empire* (London: Fontana, 1986); *Freedom's Law: The Moral Reading of the American Constitution* (Cambridge: Harvard University Press, 1996); David A.J. Richards, *The Moral Criticism of Law* (Encino: California Dickenson, 1977); *Toleration and the Constitution* (New York: Oxford University Press, 1986).

[35] Dworkin *Law's Empire,* 227-28, 245-58.

[36] Dworkin *Law's Empire,* 228-58; *Freedom's Law,* 72-116, 130-46.

[37] Stephen Guest, *Ronald Dworkin* (Stanford: Stanford University Press, 1991), 46-59.

[38] Richards, *Toleration*, 46-66.

[39] Richards, *Toleration*, 231-54.

[40] Ely, *Democracy and Distrust,* 34-67. See also his *On Constitutional Ground* (Princeton: Princeton University Press, 1996).

[41] Ely, *Democracy and Distrust*, 34-67.

[42] Wolfe, *How to Read the Constitution*, 3-26.

[43] Christopher Wolfe, *Judicial Activism: Bulwark of Freedom or Precarious Security?* Rev. ed. (Lanham: Rowman & Littlefield, 1997), 47-68.

[44] *Bowers v. Hardwick*, 478 U.S. 186, 194 (1986).

[45] Wolfe, *Judicial Activism,* 99-110.

[46] Quoted in *Readings in the Philosophy of Law*, eds. John Arthur and William H. Shaw. 3rd ed. (Upper Saddle River, NJ: 2001), 665.

[47] Quoted in Arthur and Shaw, *Readings*, 665.

[48] Gerald V. Bradley, "Remaking the Constitution: A Critical Reexamination of the Bowers v. Hardwick Dissent," *Wake Forest Law Review* 25 (1990): 501-46; Bork, *Tempting of America*, 36-49; Raoul Berger, *Government by Judiciary: The Transformation of the Fourteenth Amendment* (Cambridge: Harvard University Press, 1977), 1934, "Whether one can determine 'precisely' what due process meant, however, is not nearly so important as the fact that one thing quite plainly it did not mean, in either 1789 or 1866; it did not comprehend judicial power to override legislation on substantive or policy grounds."

[49] Perry, *The Constitution in the Courts*, 161-90.

[50] Perry, *The Constitution in the Courts*, 161-90. See also Michael K. Curtis "The Fourteenth Amendment and the Bill of Rights," *Connecticut Law Review* 14 (1982): 237-306.

[51] Here we can indeed observe an occasion whereby some facets of natural law theory have application to the Constitution via the idea of justice protecting

and preserving traditional privileges and immunities commonly recognised, and dis likely therefore not to have confined itself to purely procedural questions of due process. See further A. J. Reck, "Natural Law and the Constitution," *Review of Metaphysics* 42 (1989): 483-511; William E. Nelson, "The Role of History in Interpreting the Fourteenth Amendment," *Loyola of Los Angeles Law Review* 25 (1992): 1177-85.

[52] *Pace* the work of Ronald Dworkin, D.A.J. Richards and Laurence Tribe, discussed *supra.*

[53] *Palko v. Connecticut,* 302 U.S. 319 (1937), 325-26.

[54] *Moore v. City of E. Cleveland,* 431 U.S. (1977), 503.

[55] For an overview on this general line of interpretation, see John E. Nowak and Ronald D. Rotunda, *Constitutional Law,* 5th ed. (St. Paul: West, 1995), ch. 11. See also Melvin I. Urofsky, "Justifying Assisted Suicide: Comments on the Ongoing Debate," *Notre Dame Journal of Law, Ethics & Public Policy* 14 (2000): 893-906.

[56] As Case Sunstein argues, it is very much to the point of interpreting a substantive due process claimas to whether an existing and time-honoured convention, described at the appropriate level of generality, is violated by the proposed practice. See his *One Case at a Time: Judicial Minimalism on the Supreme Court* (Cambridge: Harvard University Press, 1999), 98-104.

[57] *Michael H. v. Gerald D.,* 491 U.S. 110 (1989), 127. Also, as Chief Justice Rehnquist states in Glucksberg, we "have always been reluctant to expand the concept of substantive due process because guideposts for responsible decision-making in this uncharted area are scarce and open-ended. ... By extending constitutional protection to an asserted right or liberty interest, we, to a great extent, place the matter outside the arena of public debate and legislative action. We must therefore exercise the utmost care whenever we are asked to break new ground in this field, ... *lest the liberty protected by the Due Process Clause be subtly transformed into the policy preferences of the members of this Court.* (My emphasis), *Washington v. Glucksberg,* 521 U.S. 702 (1997), 720.

[58] See Bradley "Moral Truth, the Common Good, and Judicial Review," 115-32.

[59] Nowak and Rotunda, *Constitutional Law,* ch. 11.

[60] *Meyer v. Nebraska,* 262 U.S. 390 (1923).

[61] Hadley Arkes, *First Things: An Inquiry into the First Principles of Morals and Justice* (Princeton: Princeton University Press, 1986), 345-47.

[62] Bradley, "Remaking the Constitution," 533-41.

[63] *Griswold v. Connecticut*, 381 U.S. 479 (1965).

[64] J. Stuart. Showalter, *The Law of Hospital and Health Care Administration: Cases and Materials* (Ann Arbor: Health Administration Press, 1993), 124-26.

[65] John Finnis, "Law, Morality, and 'Sexual Orientation," 1075-76.

[66] *Eisenstadt v. Baird*, 405 U.S. 438 (1972).

[67] Bradley, "Remaking the Constitution," 533-41. See also Robert George and Gerald Bradley, "Marriage and the Liberal Imagination," *Georgetown Law Journal* 84 (1995): 301-20.

[68] John T. Noonan, *A Private Choice: Abortion in America in the Seventies* (New York: Free Press, 1979), 21.

[69] Ronald Dworkin, "Sex, Death and the Courts," *New York Review of Books* (Aug. 8 1996), 44.

[70] *Bowers v. Hardwick*, 478 U.S. 186 (1986).

[71] See, for example, Mark John Kappelhoff "Bowers v. Hardwick: Is There a Right to Privacy," *American University Law Review* 37 (1988): 487-511; Brett J. Williamson, "The Constitutional Privacy Doctrine After Bowers v. Hardwick," *Southern California Law Review* 62 (1989): 1927-1929.

[72] Bork, *The Tempting of America*, 116-26.

[73] Norman St. John-Stevas, *Life, Death and the Law* (New York: Meridian, 1964), 241-46.

[74] Keith Burgess-Jackson, "The Legal Status of Suicide in Early America: A Comparison With the English Experience," *Wayne Law Review* 29 (1982): 57-87.

[75] Thomas J. Marzen *et al.*, "Suicide: A Constitutional Right?," *Duquesne Law Review* 24 (1985): 98-105.

[76] See James Bopp and R. E. Coleson, "The Constitutional Case Against Permitting Physician Assisted Suicide for Competent Adults With Terminal Conditions," *Issues in Law and Medicine* 11 (1995): 253-68; Russell Hittinger, "Private Uses of Lethal Force: The Case of Assisted Suicide," *Loyola Law Review* 43 (1997): 151-78.

[77] See Table of jurisdictions in Jennifer M. Scherer and Rita J. Simon, *Euthanasia and the Right to Die: A Comparative View* (Lanham: Rowman & Littlefield Publishers, 1999), 41-46. See also Simon M. Canick, "Constitutional Aspects of Physician-Assisted Suicide after Lee v. Oregon," *American Journal of Law and Medicine* 23 (1997): 69-96.

[78] Jonathan R. Rosenn, "The Constitutionality of Statutes Prohibiting and Permitting Physician-Assisted Suicide," *University of Miami Law Review* 51 (1997); 876-79.

[79] Marzen *et al.*, "Suicide: A Constitutional Right?," 76-77.

[80] See Wayne R. LaFave and Austin W. Scott, *Criminal Law*. 2nd (St. Paul: West, 1986), sec. 3.5.

[81] Rosenn, "Constitutionality," 876-79.

[82] Justice White in *Bowers v. Hardwick*, 194-95.

[83] *Schloendorff v. New York Hospital,* 211 N.Y. 125 (1914), 129.

[84] See Barry R. Furrow *et al.*, Health Law, 3rd ed. (St. Paul: Westlaw, 1997), 1059-94.

[85] *Karen Anne Quinlan,* 70 N.J. 10 (1976).

[86] 370 N.E.2d 417 (1977).

[87] 497 N.E. 2d 626 (1986).

[88] 110 S.Ct. 2841 (1990).

[89] *Patient Self Determination Act*, 42 U.S.C. Section 1395 cc(a)(1) et. seq., 1990.

[90] John Finnis, "The 'Value of Human Life' and 'the Right to Death': Some Reflections on Cruzan and Ronald Dworkin," *Southern Illinois University Law Journal* 17 (1993): 559-571.

[91] Germain Grisez and Joseph M. Boyle, *Life and Death with Liberty and Justice: A Contribution to the Euthanasia Debate* (Notre Dame, IN: University of Notre Dame Press, 1979), 414-19. See also C. Ann Potter, "Will the 'Right To Die' Become a License To Kill? The Growth Of Euthanasia In America," *Journal of Legislation* 19 (1993): 31-62.

[92] Hittinger, "Private Use," 170-74.

[93] See generally, George J. Annas, "The Bell Tolls for a Right to Suicide," in *Regulating How We Die: The Ethical, Medical, and Legal Issues Surrounding Physician-Assisted Suicide*, ed. Linda L. Emanuel. (Cambridge: Harvard University Press, 1998), 203-33.

[94] *Planned Parenthood v. Casey*, 505 U.S. 833 (1992), 851.

[95] Michael B. Hickey, "Reading the Mystery Passage Narrowly: A Legal, Ethical and Practical Argument against Physician Assisted Suicide," *Notre Dame Journal of Law, Ethics and Public Policy* 12 (1998): 567-603.

[96] Hickey, "Mystery Passage," 571-73

[97] See James M. Dubois, "Physician-Assisted Suicide and Public Virtue: A Reply to the Liberty Thesis of 'The Philosophers' Brief," *Issues in Law and Medicine* 15 (1999): 159-79. See also Richard E. Coleson, "The Glucksberg and Quill Amicus Curiae Briefs," *Issues in Law and Medicine* 13 (1997): 20-23.

[98] Dubois, "Physician-Assisted Suicide," 162-63.

[99] Dubois, "Physician-Assisted Suicide," 162-63.

[100] Hittinger, "Private Use," 170-74.

[101] *Washington v. Glucksberg*, 521 U.S. 702 (1997).

[102] *Washington v. Glucksberg*, 521U.S. (1997), 708.

[103] See *Compassion in Dying v. Washington*, 79 F.3d 790 (9th Cir. 1996) (en banc).

[104] See Darrel W. Amundsen, "The Significance of Inaccurate History in Legal Considerations of Physician-Assisted Suicide," in *Physician-Assisted Suicide*, ed. Robert F. Weir (Bloomington: Indiana University Press, 1997), 3-32;

Dwight G. Duncan and Peter Lubin, "The Use and Abuse of History in Compassion In Dying," *Harvard Journal of Law and Public Policy* 20 (1996): 175-214.

[105] *Washington v. Glucksberg*, 521 U.S. (1997), 708.

[106] Dan Crone, "Assisted Suicide and the U.S. Court of Appeals for the Ninth Circuit: A Philosophical Examination of the Majority Opinion in Compassion in Dying v. Washington," *University of San Francisco Law Review* 31 (1997): 399-432.

[107] *Washington v. Glucksberg*, 521 U.S. (1997), 704.

[108] See Patrick M. Curran "Regulating Death: Oregon's Death With Dignity Act and the Legalization of Physician-Assisted Suicide," *Georgetown Law Journal* 86 (1998): 725-49.

[109] The grave doubts expressed by the Court concerning constraints on potential slippery slopes should have reinforced the unconstitutional nature of tolerating all such practices by any State of the Union. It is quite simply an *unjustifiable constitutional risk* to the traditional protections and immunities accorded to the American People to think that any state law that permits assisted suicide for some class of patients, such as the terminally ill, will not evolve within time to permit the euthanasia of other patients, even those who are not competent. Such risk taking should not be tolerated for it, in itself, exposes that traditional protection to a process of progressive, piece by piece weakening. Here, the Court should have taken rather more seriously the claims of voluntary euthanasia advocates who believe that once they acquire support for a right to assisted suicide for some terminally ill patients, it will be far easier for them to push the frontiers forward and claim support for a broader, more encompassing set of euthanasia laws.

[110] *Vacco v. Quill*, 521 U.S. 793 (1997).

[111] Quoted in Arthur and Shaw, *Readings in the Philosophy of Law*, 665.

[112] *Quill v. Vacco*, 80 F.3d 716 (2d Cir. 1996).

[113] *Quill v. Vacco,* F. 3d., 729.

[114] See Craig Paterson, "On "Killing" versus "Letting Die" in Clinical Practice: Mere Sophistry with Words?" *Journal of Nursing Law* 6 (2000): 25-44.

[115] Susan R. Martyn and Henry J. Bourguignon, "Physician-Assisted Suicide: The Lethal Flaws of the Ninth and Second Circuit Decisions," *California Law Review* 85 (1997): 371-426; Kathleen McGowan, "Physician Assisted Suicide: A Constitutional Right?" *Catholic Lawyer* 37 (1997): 245-58.

[116] Paterson, "On "Killing" versus "Letting Die", 25-44.

[117] *Vacco v. Quill*, 521 U.S. (1997), 802.

[118] *Vacco v. Quill*, 521 U.S. (1997), 802, referring to *Morissette v. United States*, 342 U.S. 246 (1952).

[119] Ronald Dworkin, "Assisted Suicide: What the Court Really Said," *New York Review of Books* (Sept. 25 1997), 40-4.

[120] *Washington v. Glucksberg*, 521 U.S. (1997), 737.

[121] *Washington v. Glucksberg*, 521 U.S. (1997), 737.

[122] *Washington v. Glucksberg*, 521 U.S. (1997), 769.

[123] *Washington v. Glucksberg*, 521 U.S. (1997), 750-51.

[124] *Planned Parenthood v. Casey*, 505 U.S. (1992), 851.

[125] This distinction crucially runs throughout the Anglo-American legal system and is therefore generally regarded as bedrock for the framing of criminal law. See Wayne R. LaFave and Austin W. Scott, *Criminal Law*, 2nd ed. (St. Paul: West, 1986), sec. 3.5.

[126] See John Finnis's critique of the *Philosophers' Brief* in "On the Practical Meaning of Secularism," 511, on the grounds that the authors side-step the crucial distinction between foreseen and intended killings, resulting in a "... very poor fit with reality, law, and professional ethics."

[127] Tonya Eippert, "A Proposal to Recognize a Legal Obligation on Physicians to Provide Adequate Medication to Alleviate Pain," *Journal of Law and Health* 12 (1998): 381-405; Donald G. Casswell, "Rejecting Criminal Liability for Life Shortening Palliative Care," *Journal of Contemporary Health Law and Policy* 6 (1990): 127-44.

[128] See for example Ann Alpers, "Criminal Act or Palliative Care? Prosecutions Involving the Care of the Dying," *Journal of Law, Medicine and Ethics* 26 (1998): 308-31.

Chapter Eight

Conclusion

From the outset of the book, it has been stressed that the framework used here for engaging important moral and legal concerns arising from the practices of suicide, assisted suicide, and euthanasia, would be a natural law based ethics. Such an approach to ethical discourse has not been prominent in 'main stream' ethical discourse due to the widespread suspicion that natural law merely serves to operate as a kind of 'cloaking device', shrouding what really amounts to an attempt to impose 'divine imperatives' on otherwise liberated secular society. Dispense with the legitimacy of privileged appeals to religion or thick appeals to metaphysical constructs, it is said, and the case for a natural law ethics starts to look decidedly threadbare.

In response to this prevalent point of view, I set about the task of seeking to justify a natural law based ethics whose fundamental structure is not derived either from appeals to religion or from deep substantive metaphysical constructs. Such a task, I have argued, is vital if natural law ethics is going to be able to provide publicly accessible reasons to justify its normative conclusions in a way that critically engages, and can therefore make a positive contribution towards, the state of contemporary dialogue.

I have argued, in the body of the work, that a viable and sustainable approach to natural law ethics can be seen in the work of John M. Finnis and other collaborators. Crucial to the rehabilitation of a natural law based approach to ethics has been the way in which a philosopher such as Finnis has been able to effectively respond to key criticisms made of natural law theory, especially to criticisms made by philosophers based in the Anglo-American analytical tradition. His approach to natural law ethics, in terms of its structural underpinnings, is not derived either from the truths of revealed religion or from a robust metaphysics.

Unlike some contemporary natural law accounts that continue to derive

329

natural law theory from the presuppositions of a robust metaphysics (e.g., Russell Hittinger), Finnis argues for the importance of self-evident (underived) basic human goods that are directly accessible to the operation of our practical human reason. Such starting points are not derived from speculative reasoning, but are rather constituted by the appeal of primary intelligible goods that make direct normative appeals to our practical mode of knowing.

In his analysis of what constitutes practical human reason, and how it structurally operates, Finnis is able to challenge another key difficulty strongly associated with the tradition of natural law inquiry—the ready perception that a natural law ethics has to be based on a thoroughgoing appeal to naturalism. Unlike many historical and contemporary accounts of natural law, a major strength of Finnis's approach is that he does not seek to side-step or by-pass the significance of the is/ought distinction by arguing that we can actually seek to deduce a normative conclusion from a factual premise about human nature. Normative conclusions can only be derived from prior normative premises and these must have non-reducible starting points directly apprehended by practical insight.

In seeking to approach the investigation of suicide, assisted suicide, and euthanasia from the perspective of nature law, it was necessary firstly to engage in historical inquiry in order to explore the array of ideas used in support of traditional moral and legal prohibitions against these acts. Secondly, it was necessary to trace historical and contemporary ideas that would lend support to those practices, at least in certain qualified circumstances.

In the light of my analysis of historical justifications for prohibition, I concluded that there are several 'natural law' appeals made that cannot function as publicly accessible grounds for restricting those practices. Firstly, there is the appeal made to God's dominion. Such a ground is dependent on the privileged claims of faith, and as such cannot provide a naturally accessible reason to place restrictions on the activities of those who do not share such a faith based ground.

Secondly, another key idea that has firm roots in the natural law tradition, the immortality of the soul, is sometimes used to justify an opposition to suicide. However, it too cannot pass muster in the justification stakes. Even if it was conceded, for the purposes of argument, that the human soul was rationally demonstrated to be immortal (in some significant contentful sense), this idea cannot (independently of implicit religious belief) tell us whether it can be right or wrong to intentionally hasten our departure by means of self-inflicted lethal means.

Having conceded that these two notions, clearly associated with the natural law tradition of inquiry, cannot function as publicly accessible reasons, and cannot therefore serve as grounds to justify restrictions on personal freedom, critics further raise several positive arguments in favour of a strong penumbra of individual choice (concerning self-killing and many other areas of human conduct). Such ideas, especially in contemporary analysis, are strongly influenced by consequentialist and *prima facie* based deontological approaches.

Firstly, there is the critique that the good of human life is not an inviolable good such that it cannot be commensurated against when it is placed in direct conflict with other pressing values, for example, pain and suffering. It is argued that the quality of 'personal life' is what is really to be valued, not mere biological or physiological life.

Secondly, it is also stressed that the good of self-determination, grounded in personal autonomy, is such that it would be wrong to interfere with a person's choices, where the decision is primarily self-regarding and the person is competent and aware of the consequences of his or her decision.

Thirdly, they challenge an important part of natural law ethics, which is its support for double effect reasoning. If such reasoning were not viable as part of an account of action theory, for example, the meaningfulness of the distinction between intention and foresight, it would render natural law's support for the existence of concrete moral absolutes impossibly rigorist.

In response to each of these major criticisms, I have argued that natural law ethics contains within it the resources to respond in a credible and sustained way. Firstly, it was often stated in the tradition that human life can not be intentionally acted against, because to do so would run contrary to the natural human inclination to preserve life. Albeit expressed in naturalistic terms, such a response does point in the direction of a non-naturalistic response that captures, so to speak, the significance and status of the good of human life. Our capacity for practical human reason, the measure of the good and bad, the right and wrong, is able to grasp the direct intrinsic normative appeal of the good of human life. In so doing, we also grasp the ways in which choices can be made that are compatible with respect for the status and significance of this good (as properly apprehended). Such apprehension, juxtaposed with the failure of consequentialist methodology to provide plausible criteria for value commensuration, lends credence to the claim of natural law ethics that certain kinds of action are respectful of the intrinsic appeal of the good of human life, as well as and why certain kinds of action are not compatible with respect for that good.

Amongst the basic human goods is that of practical reasonableness itself, a good that generates modes of responsibility or criteria of practical reasonableness that direct the making of our choices. These criteria place limits on our action; limits that ought to be respected if we are truly concerned with reasonably responding to the primary appeal of such basic human goods as indispensable components of what constitutes the integral human fulfilment of the human person.

Secondly, with respect to the good of self-determination grounded in personal autonomy, this is an important but non-basic (auxiliary or facilitative) good which, adequately perceived, represents a necessary condition of possibility to realise and participate in the whole array of basic goods and other supportive goods in their service. This is especially so for the reflexive goods of friendship, harmony, conscience, and religion—goods that depend on the exercise of choice as a prerequisite for their actualisation in our lives. Choice, in short, gives rise to all manner of instantiations of human possibility in many different fields of human endeavour. Yet, it does not follow from this that we should conclude that all autonomous choices need, of necessity, command our respect or even toleration. The capacity is there for the purpose of leading a (more or less) reasonable life, shaping a virtuous character, promoting our integral human fulfilment in and through the practically reasonable choices that we make. If a proposed choice fails to be practically reasonable, and directly attacks or unfairly damages one of the basic constituents of human flourishing (e.g., the good of human life), then the choice can be considered wrongful and not worthy of any necessary claim to command our respect or our toleration for the nature of that choice.

Thirdly, with reference to double effect reasoning (so crucial to the traditional distinction drawn between killing and letting die), I have argued that it is indeed capable of sustained defence against the major criticisms posed against it. I sought to explain and clarify, in turn, each of the four necessary and sufficient conditions of this approach to practical decision making in conflict situations between basic human goods. (More specifically, the negative and positive duties those goods give rise to as mediated through the 'architectonic' good of practical reasonableness). In particular, I focused on the second condition concerning intention and foresight and have argued how that condition can be defended by shifting the focus of interpretation away from an epistemological basis to a volitional basis centred on an anatomy of the human will. Volitional analysis is able to explain how markedly different levels of our 'entanglement with evil' result from the intentional willing of evil (as and end or as a means) rather than merely permitting or tolerating a certain amount of evil as a collateral side effect of an otherwise good action.

Finally, it is important to realise that natural law ethics is not just concerned with a narrow analysis of morality in any overly constrictive interpretation of what constitutes the 'moral domain'. As an approach to ethics, it is also fundamentally concerned with wider questions of how individual decisions impact the common good of a society. Persons are not regarded as 'little islands' unto themselves. In short, a natural law based approach has political and jurisprudential implications for how we order society. For natural law ethics, there is a necessary connection between the conduct of individuals and the wider moral ecology or environment of a society. Contrary to the argumentation of H.Tistram Engelhardt and John Rawls concerning the role of limits on the state in promoting a substantive notion of a mutual, shared, common good, I have argued that natural law has a reasonable and publicly accessible corpus of principles to draw upon, that can justify the legitimacy of certain powers of the state to promote 'conditions' conducive to pursuing this good for the genuine interest of all its members.

An important part of the state's role in promoting the common good is protecting due respectfulness for the commonality of the basic human goods, especially the good of human life itself (including an authentic array of diversity of choice in society compatible with respectfulness for those goods). A natural law approach has within it the necessary resources needed to justify significant restrictions on individual human conduct, particularly forms of conduct that are deemed to be especially destructive or undermining of the framework of protecting and promoting that common good. Contrary to those who would argue that the toleration of intentional killing would not be particularly undermining of the common good, I have argued that such an action is deeply destructive of the common good, for it openly propagates and encourages the 'supremely uncivil idea' that it is permissible to assist in the intentional killing of another human person on the basis of a bold 'quality of life assessment'—an assessment that is ultimately predicated on the notion that certain human lives are no longer deemed worthy of living. Such an idea strikes at the very heart of what the common good stands for, since it is built on the bedrock of due respect for the basic constituents of human flourishing, and cannot be furthered by open disregard for those elements, including the promotion of laws and policies conducive to, rather than undermining of, those goods.

Even if the idea of the intrinsic good of human life is not found sufficiently convincing, by some, to justify the use of the coercive apparatus of the state to dissuade physicians and others from assisting in deliberate acts of assisted suicide and euthanasia, I have argued that there are also good prudential grounds flowing from slippery slope kinds of reasoning to provide sufficient warrant to justify maintaining and enforcing legal prohibitions on those kinds of acts.

As a concluding caveat, with reference to the winds of prevailing political change blowing in the contemporary United States, I can only state that time will tell whether or not individual state legislators and citizens will be convinced by the kinds of argument contained in this book, such that they will seek to resist legislative proposals for legalising physician assisted suicide in the different states. The ball is now, so to speak, in their hands, due to the 1997 Supreme Court rulings in *Washington v. Glucksberg*, and *Vacco v. Quill*.

My concern in the book has been to render as credible a case as possible, based on natural law ethics, as to why such legislative initiatives can and should be resisted for the sake of the common good of society. This common good, built on promoting and respecting the authentic flourishing of each and every person, is foundational to a sensible and restrained interpretation of the United States Constitution.

As I have argued, state legislators and citizens should not abrogate the responsibility of protecting the lives of fellow citizens by legalising acts of assisted suicide or voluntary euthanasia, no matter how narrowly drafted the purported right may be. States have a paramount interest in protecting the lives of their citizens, by prohibiting the intentional lethal use of force (except for reasonable proportionate force used in questions pertaining to matters of self-defence). The risks entailed by potential slippery slope argumentation also strongly underline the power and wisdom of protecting this key state interest, such that no state ought to abrogate itself from maintaining and enforcing legal prohibitions against practices that would attack or undermine it.

Bibliography

Ackrill, J.L. *Aristotle.* Oxford: Clarendon Press, 1981.

Adams, E.M. *Ethical Naturalism and the Modern World-View.* Westport, CT: Greenwood, 1973.

Aiken, William. "The Quality of Life." In *Quality of Life: The New Medical Dilemma,* edited by James J. Walter and Thomas A. Shannon, 17-25. New York: Paulist Press, 1990.

Alesandro, J.A. "Physician-Assisted Suicide and New York State Law." *Albany Law Review* 57 (1994): 819-915.

Alpers, Ann. "Criminal Act or Palliative Care? Prosecutions Involving the Care of the Dying." *Journal of Law, Medicine and Ethics* 26 (1998): 308-31.

Alvarez, Alfred. Literature in the Nineteenth and Twentieth Centuries." In *Handbook for the Study of Suicide,* ed. Seymour Perlin, 31-60. New York: Oxford University Press, 1975.

————. *Savage God: A Study of Suicide.* New York: Random House, 1972.

Ambrosetti, G. "Christian Natural Law." *American Journal of Jurisprudence* 16 (1971): 290-301.

American Medical Association. Physician Assisted Suicide. Report 59.

Amstutz, Jakob. "Philosophers on Death." *Essence* 2 (1978): 129-38.

Amundsen, Darrel. W. *Medicine, Society, and Faith in the Ancient and Medieval Worlds.* Baltimore, MD: Johns Hopkins Press, 1996.

————. "Suicide and Early Christian Values." In *Suicide and Euthanasia: Historical and Contemporary Themes,* edited by Baruch A. Brody, 77-154. Dordrecht and Boston: Kluwer, 1989

Annas, George J. "The Bell Tolls for a Right to Suicide." In *Regulating How We Die: The Ethical, Medical, and Legal Issues Surrounding Physician-Assisted Suicide,* edited by Linda L. Emanuel. Cambridge, MA: Harvard University Press, 1998.

Anscombe, G. E. M. "Action, Intention, and Double Effect." *Proceedings of the American Catholic Philosophical Association* 56 (1982): 12-25.

———. "Brute Facts." In her *Ethics, Religion and Politics*, vol. III, 22-5. Oxford: Blackwell, 1981.

———. "War and Murder." In her *Ethics, Religion and Politics*, vol. III, 51-64. Oxford: Blackwell, 1981.

———. "Modern Moral Philosophy." [reprinted from 1958] In *Virtue Ethics*, edited by Roger Crisp and Michael Slote, 26-44. Oxford: Oxford University Press, 1997.

———. *Intention.* 2nd ed. Oxford: Blackwell, 1963.

———, and Peter Geach, *The Three Philosophers*. Oxford: Blackwell, 1973.

Aquinas, Thomas. On Kingship, translated by Gerald B. Phelan. Toronto: Pontifical Institute of Mediaeval Studies, 1949.

———. *Summa Theologica*, translated by the English Dominican Fathers. New York: Benziger, 1948.

Araujo, Robert J. "Thomas Aquinas: Prudence, Justice, and the Law." *Loyola Law Review* 40 (1995): 897-921.

Aristotle. *Nicomachean Ethics. The Basic Works of Aristotle*, edited by Richard McKeon & translated by W. D. Ross. New York: Random House, 1941.

Arkes, Hadley. "'Autonomy' and the 'Quality of Life': The Dismantling of Moral Terms." *Issues in Law and Medicine* 2 (1997): 421-33.

———. *Beyond the Constitution*. Princeton, NJ: Princeton University Press, 1990.

———. *First Things: An Inquiry into the First Principles of Morals and Justice*. Princeton: Princeton University Press, 1986.

Armstrong, R. A. *Primary and Secondary Precepts in Thomistic Natural Law Thinking.* The Hague: Martinus Nijhoff, 1966.

Arras, John D. "Physician-Assisted Suicide: A Tragic View." *Journal of Contemporary Health Law and Policy* 13 (1997): 361-89.

————. "The Right to Die on the Slippery Slope." *Social Theory and Practice* 8 (1982): 285-328.

Arthur, John, and William H. Shaw, eds. *Readings in the Philosophy of Law.* 3rd ed. Upper Saddle River, NJ: 2001.

Ashley, Benedict M. *Living the Truth in Love.* New York: Alba House, 1996.

————. "What is the End of the Human Person? The Vision of God and Integral Human Fulfilment." In *Moral Truth and Moral Tradition: Essays in Peter Geach and Elizabeth Anscombe*, edited by Luke Gormally, 68-96. Dublin: Four Courts, 1994.

Ashmore, R. "Aquinas and Ethical Naturalism." *New Scholasticism* 49 (1975): 76-86.

Asselin, Don T. "A Weakness in the "Standard Argument" for Natural Immortality." In *Freedom, Virtue, and the Common Good*, edited by Curtis L. Hancock and Anthony O. Simon, 17-27. Notre Dame, IN: American Maritain Association, 1995.

Atkinson, Gary M. "History of Catholic Teaching on Prolonging Life." In *Moral Responsibility in Prolonging Life Decisions,* edited by Donald G. McCarthy and Albert Moraczewski, 95-115. St. Louis,MO: Pope John Center, 1981.

Atwell, John. "Ross and Prima Facie Duties." *Ethics* 88 (1978): 240-49.

Augustine of Hippo. *City of God*, translated by H. Bettenson. London: Penguin, 1972.

Ayer, A.J. *Hume.* Oxford: Oxford University Press, 1980.

Ball, William Bentley. "Natural Law and the Power of the Courts." *Catholic Social Science Review* 1 (1996): 14-20.

Bambrough, Renford. *Moral Scepticism and Moral Knowledge.* London: Routledge, 1981.

Barden, Garrett. "Defending Self-Defence." *Irish Philosophical Journal* 1 (1984): 25-35.

Baron, Marcia. "On the Alleged Repugnance of Acting from Duty." *The Journal of Philosophy* 81 (1984): 179-219.

Barry, Robert. *Breaking the Thread of Life.* New Brunswick, NJ: Transaction Pub., 1994.

———. "The Catholic Condemnation of Rational Suicide." In *Contemporary Perspectives on Rational Suicide*, edited by James L. Werth, 29-35. Philadelphia: Brunner/Mazel, 1999.

———. "The Development of the Roman Catholic Teaching on Suicide." *Notre Dame Journal of Law, Ethics and Public Policy* 9 (1995): 449-501.

———. "Stones and Streetcars: A Clarification of the Doctrine of the Double Effect." *Irish Theological Quarterly* 1-2 (1981): 127-36.

———, and James E. Maher, "Indirectly Intended Life-Shortening Analgesia: Clarifying the Principles." 6 *Issues in Law & Medicine* 6 (1990): 117-51.

Bassham, Gregory. *Original Intent and the Constitution: A Philosophical Study.* Savage, MD: Rowman and Littlefield, 1992.

Basta, Lofty L., and Carole Post, *A Graceful Exit: Life and Death on Your Own Terms.* New York: Plenum Press, 1996.

Battaglia, Anthony. *Toward a Reformulation of Natural Law.* New York: Seabury Press, 1981.

Battin, Margaret P. "Ethical Issues in Physician-Assisted-Suicide." In *Last Rights: Assisted Suicide and Euthanasia Debated,* edited by Michael M. Uhlmann. Washington, DC: Ethics and Public Policy Center, 1998.

———. *Ethical Issues in Suicide.* Englewood Cliffs, NJ: Prentice-Hall, 1995.

———. *The Least Worse Death.* New York: Oxford University Press, 1994.

———. "Voluntary Euthanasia and the Risks of Abuse: Can We Learn Anything From the Netherlands." *Law, Medicine and Health Care* 20 (1992): 133-43.

———, and David J. Mayo, eds. *Suicide: The Philosophical Issues.* New York: St. Martin's Press, 1980.

Bayles, Michael D. "The Value of Life." In *Health Care Ethics*, edited by Donald Van de Veer and Tom Regan. Philadelphia,PA: Temple University Press, 1987.

Beauchamp, Tom L. "Engelhardt's Foundations." *Reason Papers* 22 (1997): 96-100.

————. "Suicide." In *Matters of Life and Death: New Introductory Essays in Moral Philosophy*, edited by Tom Regan. New York: McGraw-Hill, 1994.

————. "An Analysis of Hume's Essay 'On Suicide'." *Review of Metaphysics* 30 (1976): 73-95.

————. "The Justification of Physician-Assisted Deaths." *Indiana Law Review* 29 (1996): 1173-1200.

————, and Arnold Davidson , "The Definition of Euthanasia." *Journal of Medicine and Philosophy* 4 (1979): 294-312.

————, and James F. Childress, *Principles of Biomedical Ethics.* 4th ed. New York: Oxford University Press, 1994.

Becker, Lawrence. "Human Being: The Boundaries of the Concept." *Philosophy and Public Affairs* 4 (1975): 334-59.

Beckner, Morton. "Vitalism." In *The Encyclopedia of Philosophy*, edited by Paul Edwards, 253-56. New York: Macmillan, 1967.

Bedau, Hugo. "The Right to Life." *Monist* 52 (1968): 550-72.

Begin, Raymond Francis. *Natural Law and Positive Law.* Washington, DC: Catholic University Press, 1959.

Bennett, Jonathan. *The Act Itself.* Oxford: Oxford University Press, 1995.

————. "Morality and Consequences." In *Tanner Lectures on Human Values,* vol. 2, edited by S. M. McMurrin, 47-116. Salt Lake City: University of Utah, 1981.

————. "Whatever the Consequences." In *Ethics*, edited by J. J. Thompson and Gerald Dworkin, 211-36. New York: Harper and Row, 1968.

Bentham, Jeremy. *An Introduction to the Principles of Morals and Legislation. Utilitariarism*, edited by Mary Warnock. London: Fontana, 1979.

Berger, Arthur S., and Joyce Berger, eds. *To Die or Not to Die: Cross-Disciplinary, Cultural and Legal Perspectives on the Right to Choose Death.* New York, NY: Praeger, 1990.

Berger, Raoul. *Government by Judiciary: The Transformation of the Fourteenth Amendment.* Cambridge, MA: Harvard University Press, 1977.

Billings, J. Andrew, and Susan D. Block, "Slow Euthanasia." *Journal of Palliative Care* 32 (1996): 21-22.

Bix, Brian. *Jurisprudence: Theory and Context*. London: Sweet and Maxwell, 1999.

Bjorck, Catherine L. "Physician-Assisted Suicide: Whose Life is it Anyway?" *Saint Mary University Law Review* 47 (1994):371-97.

Blázquez, Niceto. "The Churches Traditional Moral Teaching on Suicide." In *Suicide and the Right to Die*, edited by Jacques Pohier and Dietmar Mieth, 63-74. Edinburgh: T. & T. Clark, 1985.

Bok, Sissela. "Euthanasia." In Gerald Dworkin, R. G. Frey, and Sissela Bok, *Euthanasia and Physician-Assisted-Suicide*, 107-27. New York: Cambridge University Press, 1998.

Bole, Thomas J. "Faulting Engelhardt's Libertarianism by Default." *Southwest Philosophy Review* 15 (1999): 169-76.

Bopp, James, and R. E. Coleson. "The Constitutional Case Against Permitting Physician Assisted Suicide for Competent Adults With Terminal Conditions." *Issues in Law and Medicine* 11 (1995): 253-68.

Bork, Robert H. *Slouching Towards Gomorrah: Modern Liberalism and American Decline*. New York: Regan Books, 1996.

———. *The Tempting of America: the Political Seduction of the Law*. New York: Free Press, 1990.

Bourguet, Vincent. "Miseries of Ethical Formalism." *Revue Thomiste* 99 (1999): 307-30.

Bourke, Vernon J. "Review of John Finnis' 'Natural Law and Natural Rights'." *American Journal of Jurisprudence* 24 (1981): 243-47.

———. *Ethics*. New York: MacMillan, 1966.

Boyle, Joseph. "An Absolute Rule Approach." In *A Companion to Bioethics*, edited by Helga Kuhse and Peter Singer, 72-79. Malden, MA: Blackwell, 1998.

———. "The American Debate on Artificial Nutrition and Hydration." In *The Dependent Elderly*, edited by Luke Gormally. New York: Cambridge University Press, 1992.

————. "Radical Moral Disagreement in Contemporary Health Care." *Journal of Medicine and Philosophy* 19 (1994): 184-200.

————. "Natural Law and the Ethics of Traditions." In *Natural Law Theory*, edited by Robert P. George, 3-30. Oxford: Clarendon Press, 1992.

————. "Who is Entitled to Double-Effect?" *Journal of Medicine and Philosophy* 16 (1991): 475-94.

————. "Further Thoughts on Double Effect: Some Preliminary Responses." *Journal of Medicine and Philosophy* 16 (1991): 565-70

————. "Sanctity of life and Suicide: Tensions and Developments within Common Morality." In *Suicide and Euthanasia: Historical and Contemporary Themes*, edited by Baruch Brody, 221-50. Dordrecht and Boston: Kluwer, 1989.

————. "Reverence for Life and Bioethics." In *Linking the Human Life Issues* edited by Russell Hittinger. Chicago, IL: Regnery, 1986.

————. "A Catholic Perspective on Morality and the Law." *Journal of Law and Religion* 1 (1983): 227-40.

————. Towards Understanding the Principle of Double Effect." *Ethics* 90 (1980): 527-38.

————. "*Praeter Intentionem* in Aquinas." *The Thomist* 42 (1978): 649-65.

————. "On Killing and Letting Die." *New Scholasticism* 51 (1977): 433-52.

————, and John Finnis. "Incoherence and Consequentialism (or Proportionalism) – A Rejoinder." *American Catholic Philosophical Quarterly* 64 (1990): 271-77.

————, and Thomas D. Sullivan. "The Diffusiveness of Intention Principle." *Philosophical Studies* 31 (1977): 357-60.

Bradley, Gerard V. "No Intentional Killing Whatsoever: The Case of Capital Punishment." In *Natural Law and Moral Inquiry*, edited by Robert P. George, 155-73. Washington, DC: Georgetown University Press, 1998.

————. "Remaking the Constitution: A Critical Reexamination of the Bowers v. Hardwick Dissent." *Wake Forest Law Review* 25 (1990): 501-46.

————, and Robert P. George, "The New Natural Law Theory: A Reply to Jean Porter." *American Journal of Jurisprudence* 39 (1994): 303-315.

Brady, Kathleen A. "Putting Faith Back Into Constitutional Scholarship: A Defense of Originalism." *Catholic Lawyer* 36 (1995): 137-201.

Braine, David. *The Human Person: Animal and Spirit.* Notre Dame: University of Notre Dame Press, 1992.

Brandt, Richard B. *Morality, Utilitarianism and Rights.* Cambridge: Cambridge University Press, 1992.

―――. "The Rationality of Suicide." In *Suicide: The Philosophical Issues,* edited by Margaret Battin and David Mayo, 117-32. New York: St. Martin's Press, 1980.

―――. "The Morality and Legality of Suicide." In *A Handbook for the Study of Suicide,* edited by Seymour Perlin. New York: Oxford University Press, 1975.

―――. "Toward a Credible Form of Utilitarianism." In *Contemporary Utilitarianism,* edited by Michael Bayles. Garden City, NY: Doubleday, 1968.

Bratman, Michael. *Intention, Plans and Practical Reason.* Cambridge, MA: Harvard University Press, 1987.

Brock, Dan W. "A Critique of Three Objections to Physician-Assisted Suicide." *Ethics* 109 (1999): 519-54.

―――. "Medical Decisions at the End of Life." In *A Companion to Bioethics*, edited by Helga Kuhse and Peter Singer, 231-41. Malden, MA: Blackwell, 1998.

―――. "Physician-Assisted Suicide is Sometimes Morally Justified." In *Physician-Assisted Suicide*, edited by Robert Weir, 86-103. Bloomington, IN: Indiana University Press, 1997.

―――. "Euthanasia." In *Arguing Euthanasia*, edited by Jonathan D. Moreno, 196-210. New York: Simon & Schuster, 1995.

―――. *Life and Death: Philosophical Essays in Biomedical Ethics.* New York: Cambridge University Press, 1993.

―――. "Voluntary Active Euthanasia." *Hastings Center Report* 22 (1992): 10-22.

————. "The Value of Prolonging Human Life." *Philosophical Studies* 50 (1986): 401-28.

————. "Recent Work in Utilitarianism." *American Philosophical Quarterly* 10 (1973): 241-76.

Brody, Baruch A., ed. *Suicide and Euthanasia: Historical and Contemporary Themes*. Dordrecht and Boston: Kluwer, 1989.

Brody, Howard. "Causing, Intending and Assisting Death." *Journal of Clinical Ethics* 4 (1993): 112-25.

————. "Assisted Death—A Compassionate Response to Medical Failure." *New England Journal of Medicine* 327 (1992): 1384-88.

Brown, Montague. T*he Quest for Moral Foundations*. Washington, DC: Georgetown University Press, 1996.

Brueckner, Anthony L., and John Martin Fischer, "Why is Death Bad?" *Philosophical Studies* 50 (1986): 213-21.

Burgess-Jackson, Keith. "The Legal Status of Suicide in Early America: A Comparison With the English Experience." *Wayne Law Review* 29 (1982): 57-87.

Burt, Donald X. "To Kill or Let Live: Augustine on Killing the Innocent." *Proceedings of the American Catholic Philosophical Association* 58 (1984): 112-19.

Burton, Robert. *Anatomy of Melancholy*. 3 vols. Oxford: Clarendon Press, 1989-94.

Cahill, Lisa Sowle. "Sanctity of Life, Quality of Life, and Social Justice." *Theological Studies* 48 (1987): 105-23.

Callahan, Daniel. "When Self-Determination Runs Amok." *Hasting Center Report* 22 (1992): 52-55.

Cameron, Nigel M. de S. "Autonomy and the Right to Die." In *Dignity and Dying*, edited by John F. Kilner, Arlene B. Miller and Edmund D. Pellegrino. Grand Rapids, MI: Eerdmans, 1996.

Campbell, Robert, and Diane Collinson. *Ending Lives*. Oxford: Blackwell, 1988.

Canavan, Francis. *The Pluralist Game: Pluralism, Liberalism, and the Moral Conscience.* Lanham, MD: Rowman & Littlefield, 1995.

————. *The Rise of Modern Judicial Review: from Constitutional Interpretation to Judge-Made Law.* New York: Basic Books, 1986.

Canick, Simon M. "Constitutional Aspects of Physician-Assisted Suicide after Lee v. Oregon." *American Journal of Law and Medicine* 23 (1997): 69-96.

Capron, Alexander M. "Legalizing Physician-Aided Death." *Cambridge Quarterly of Healthcare Ethics* 5 (1996): 10-23.

————. "The Right to Die: Progress and Peril." *Euthanasia Review* 2 (1987): 41-59.

Carrick, Paul. *Medical Ethics in Antiquity: Philosophical Perspectives on Abortion and Euthanasia.* Dordrecht and Boston: D. Reidel, 1985.

Cassem, E. H. "Depressive Disorders in the Medically Ill." *Psychosomatics* 36 (1995): S2-S10.

Casswell, Donald G. "Rejecting Criminal Liability for Life Shortening Palliative Care." *Journal of Contemporary Health Law and Policy* 6 (1990): 127-44.

Cavanaugh, Thomas A. "Act Evaluation, Willing and Double Effect." *Proceedings of the American Catholic Philosophical Association* 72 (1998): 243-53.

————. "Currently Accepted Practices That Are Known to Lead to Death, and PAS: Is There an Ethically Relevant Difference?" *Cambridge Quarterly of Healthcare Ethics* 4 (1998): 375-81.

————. "Double Effect and the Ethical Significance of Distinct Volitional States." *Christian Bioethics* 3 (1997): 131-41.

————. "The Intended/Foreseen Distinction's Ethical Relevance." *Philosophical Papers* 25 (1996): 179-88.

Chappell, Tim. *Understanding Human Goods: A Theory of Ethics.* Edinburgh: Edinburgh University Press, 1998.

————. "Reductionism about Persons; and What Matters." *Proceedings of the Aristotelian Society* 98 (1998): 41-57.

————. "In Defence of Speciesism." In *Human Lives: Critical Essays on Consequentialist Bioethics,* edited by David S. Oderberg and Jacqueline A. Laing, 96-108. New York: St. Martin's Press,1997.

Charlesworth, Max. *Bioethics in a Liberal Society.* Cambridge: Cambridge University Press, 1993.

Chisholm, Roderick. "Coming into Being and Passing Away: Can the Metaphysician Help." In *Language, Metaphysics, and Death*, edited by John Donnelly. New York: Fordham University Press, 1978.

————. "The Structure of Intention." *Journal of Philosophy* 67 (1970): 636-52.

Choron, Jacques. *Suicide.* New York: Charles Scribner, 1972.

————. "Death as a Motive of Philosophic Thought." In *Essays in Self-Destruction*, edited by Edwin S. Shneidman, 59-77. New York: Science House, 1967.

————. *Death and Western Thought.* London: Macmillan, 1963.

Christman, John. *The Inner Citadel: Essays on Individual Autonomy.* New York: Oxford University Press, 1989.

Cohn, Cynthia B. "Quality of Life and the Analogy with the Nazis." *Journal of Medicine and Philosophy* 8 (1983): 113-35.

Coleman, Jules L., and Anthony Sebok, eds. *Constitutional Law and its Interpretation.* New York: Garland, 1994.

Coleson, Richard E. "The Glucksberg and Quill Amicus Curiae Briefs." *Issues in Law and Medicine* 13 (1997): 20-23.

Colwell, Gary. "Slippery Slopes, Moral Slides and Human Nature." *Informal Logic* 17 (1995): 43-66.

Conolly, Matthew E. "Alternative to Euthanasia: Pain Management." *Issues in Law and Medicine* 4 (1989): 497-507.

Constable, George W. "A Criticism of 'Practical Principles, Moral truth, and Ultimate Ends'." *American Journal of Jurisprudence* 34 (1987): 19-22.

Cooper, John M. "Greek Philosophers on Suicide and Euthanasia." In *Suicide and Euthanasia: Historical and Contemporary Themes,* edited by Baruch A. Brody, 9-38. Dordrecht and Boston: Kluwer, 1989.

Copenhaver, Brian P., and Charles B. Schmitt, *Renaissance Philosophy*. Oxford: Oxford University Press, 1992.

Copleston, Frederick. *Aquinas*. London: Penguin Books, 1955.

Covell, Charles. *The Defence of Natural Law*. New York: St Martin's Press, 1992.

Crisp, Roger, and Michael Slote. *Virtue Ethics*. Oxford: Oxford University Press, 1997.

Crocker, Lester G. "The Discussion of Suicide in the Eighteenth Century." *Journal of the History of Ideas* 13 (1952): 47-72.

Crawford, J. M. B., and J. F. Quinn. *The Christian Foundations of Criminal Responsibility*. Lewiston: Edwin Mellen, 1991.

Crofts, Richard A. "The Common Good in the Political Theory of Thomas Aquinas." *Thomist* 37 (1973): 155-73.

Crone, Dan. "Assisted Suicide and the U.S. Court of Appeals for the Ninth Circuit: A Philosophical Examination of the Majority Opinion in Compassion in Dying v. Washington." *University of San Francisco Law Review* 31 (1997): 399-432.

Curran, Charles. "Respect for Life: Theoretical and Practical Implications." In C. Curran, *Issues in Sexual and Medical Ethics*, 198-226. Notre Dame: Notre Dame University Press, 1977.

Curran, Patrick M. "Regulating Death: Oregon's Death With Dignity Act and the Legalization of Physician-Assisted Suicide." *Georgetown Law Journal* 86 (1998): 725-49.

Curtis, Michael K. "The Fourteenth Amendment and the Bill of Rights." *Connecticut Law Review* 14 (1982): 237-306.

Dancy, Jonathan. "An Ethic of Prima Facie Duties." In *A Companion to Ethics*. Oxford: Blackwell, 1991.

D'Arcy, Eric. *Human Acts: An Essay in Their Moral Evaluation*. Oxford: Clarendon Press, 1963.

———. *Conscience and its Right to Freedom*. New York: Sheed and Ward, 1961.

Darwall, Stephen. "Kantian Practical Reason Defended." *Ethics* 96 (1985): 89-99.

―――. *Impartial Reason.* Ithaca, NY: Cornell University Press, 1983.

Daube, David. "The Linguistics of Suicide." *Philosophy and Public Affairs* 1 (1972): 387-437.

Degnan, Daniel A. "Two Models of Positive Law in Aquinas: A Study of the Relationship of Positive Law and Natural Law." *Thomist* 46 (1982): 1-32.

D'Entrèves, A. P. *Natural Law: An Historical Survey.* New York: Harper & Row, 1965.

Denyer, Nicholas. "Is Anything Absolutely Wrong?" In *Human Lives: Critical Essays on Consequentialist Bioethics*, edited by David S. Oderberg and Jacqueline A. Laing, 39-57. New York: St. Martin's Press, 1997.

Desmond, Charles S. "Natural Law and the American Constitution." *Fordham Law Review* 22 (1953): 235-45.

Destro, Robert A. "Quality-of-life Ethics and Constitutional Jurisprudence: The Demise of Natural Rights and Equal Protection for the Disabled and Incompetent." *Journal of Contemporary Health Law and Policy* 2 (1986): 71-130.

Devettere, Raymond J. "Slippery Slopes and Moral Reasoning." *Journal of Clinical Ethics* 3 (1992): 297-301.

Devine, Philip E. *Natural Law Ethics.* Westport, CT: Greenwood Press, 2000.

―――. "The Principle of Double Effect." *American Journal of Jurisprudence* 19 (1974): 44-60.

Diggs, B.J. "The Common Good as Reason for Political Action." *Ethics* 83 (1973): 283-293.

Dolan, John M. "Judging Someone Better Off Dead." *Logos* 2 (1999): 48-67.

Donagan, Alan. "Comment on Wheeler's 'Donagan on *Fiat Justitia Ruat Caelum*'" *Ethics* 96 (1986): 876-77.

―――. *The Theory of Morality.* Chicago, IL: University of Chicago Press, 1977.

————. "The Scholastic Theory of Moral Law in the Modern World." In *Aquinas: A Collection of Critical Essays*, edited by Anthony J. P. Kenny, 325-39. Notre Dame, IN: University of Notre Dame Press, 1976.

Donceel, Joseph. "A Survey of Some Neo-Scholastic Theories." *New Scholasticism* 39 (1965): 295-315.

Donovan, G. Kevin. "Decisions at the End of Life." *Christian Bioethics* 3 (1997): 188-203.

Donne, John. *Biathanatos*, edited by Michael Rudick and Margaret P. Battin. New York: Garland, 1982.

Donner, Wendy. *The Liberal Self.* Ithaca, NY: Cornell University Press, 1991.

Donnelly, John. "Suicide and Rationality." In *Language, Metaphysics, and Death*, edited by John Donnelly, 87-105. New York: Fordham University Press, 1978.

Dougherty, Charles J. "The Common Good, Terminal Illness, and Euthanasia." *Issues in Law and Medicine* 9 (1993): 151-65.

Douglas, R. Bruce, and David Hollenbach, eds. *Catholicism and Liberalism.* Cambridge: Cambridge University Press, 1994.

————, Gerald M. Mara, and Henry S. Richardson, eds. *Liberalism and the Good.* New York: Routledge, 1990.

Droge, Arthur J. "*Mori Lucrum*: Paul and Ancient Theories of Suicide." *Novum Testamentum* 30 (1988): 263-86.

————, and James D. Tabor. *A Noble Death: Suicide and Martyrdom Among Christina and Jews in Antiquity.* San Francisco, CA: Harper, 1992.

Dubois, James M. "Physician-Assisted Suicide and Public Virtue: A Reply to the Liberty Thesis of 'The Philosophers' Brief." *Issues in Law and Medicine* 15 (1999): 159-79.

Duff, R. A. "Socratic Suicide." *Proceedings of the Aristotelian Society* 83 (1983): 48-56.

————. "Intentionally Killing the Innocent." *Analysis* 34 (1973): 16-19.

Duncan, Dwight G., and Peter Lubin. "The Use and Abuse of History in Compassion In Dying." *Harvard Journal of Law and Public Policy* 20 (1996): 175-214.

Durkheim, Émile. *Suicide,* translated by J.A. Spaulding and G. Simpson. Glencoe, IL: Free Press, 1951.

Dworkin, Gerald. T*he Theory and Practice of Autonomy.* New York: Cambridge University Press, 1988.

Dworkin, Gerald, ed. *Mill's On Liberty: Critical Essays.* Lanham: Rowman & Littlefield, 1997.

———, R. G. Frey, and Sissela Bok. *Euthanasia and Physician-Assisted-Suicide.* New York: Cambridge University Press, 1998.

Dworkin, Ronald, *et al.* "Assisted Suicide: The Philosophers' Brief." *New York Review of Books* (27 March 1997): 41-7.

———. *Freedom's Law: The Moral Reading of the American Constitution.* Cambridge, MA: Harvard University Press, 1996.

———. *Life's Dominion: An Argument about Abortion and Euthanasia.* London: Harper Collins, 1993.

———. "Autonomy and the Demented Self." *Millbank Quarterly* 64 (1986): 4-15.

———. *Law's Empire.* London: Fontana, 1986.

———. *A Matter of Principle.* Cambridge, MA: Harvard University Press, 1985.

———. T*aking Rights Seriously.* Cambridge, MA: Harvard University Press, 1977.

Dyck, Arthur. "An Alternative to an Ethic of Euthanasia." In *To Live and to Die: When Why and How?,* edited by R. H. Williams. New York: Springer-Verlag, 1973.

Dzur, Albert W. "Function, Convention, and Policy: William Galston and the Redefinition of Liberal Purposes." *Public Affairs Quarterly* 12 (1998): 101-17.

Eippert, Tonya. "A Proposal to Recognize a Legal Obligation on Physicians to Provide Adequate Medication to Alleviate Pain." *Journal of Law and Health* 12 (1998): 381-405.

Elders, Leo J. "Common Good as Goal and Governing Principle of Social Life: Interpretations and Meaning." In *Principles of Catholic Social Teaching*. Milwaukee, WI: Marquette University Press, 1998.

Ely, John Hart. *On Constitutional Ground*. Princeton: Princeton University Press, 1996.

————. *Democracy and Distrust: A Theory of Judicial Review*. Cambridge, MA: Harvard University Press, 1980.

Emanuel, Ezekiel J. "What is the Great Benefit of Legalizing Euthanasia or Physician-Assisted Suicide?" *Ethics* 109 (1999): 629-42.

Engelhardt, H, Tristram. "Privacy and Limited Democracy: The Moral Centrality of Persons." *Social Philosophy and Policy* 17 (2000): 120-40.

————. "The Foundations of Bioethics: Liberty and Life with Moral Diversity." *Reason Papers* 22 (1997): 101-8.

————. *The Foundations of Bioethics*. 2nd ed. New York: Oxford University Press, 1996.

————. "Some Persons are Humans, Some Humans are Persons, and the World is What We Persons Make of It." In *Philosophical Medical Ethics: Its Nature and Significance*, edited by Stuart F. Spicker and H. Tristram Engelhardt. Boston: D. Reidel, 1977.

Faber, M. D. " Shakespeare's Suicides: Some Historic, Dramatic and Psychological Reflections." In *Essays in Self-Destruction*, edited by Edwin S. Shneidman, 30-58. New York: Science House, 1967.

Farberow, Norman L. "Cultural History of Suicide." In *Suicide in Different Cultures*, edited by N. L. Farberow, 1-16. Baltimore and London: University Park Press, 1975.

————, ed. Farberow, Norman L. *Suicide in Different Cultures*. Baltimore and London: University Park Press, 1975.

Fedden, Henry R. *Suicide: A Social & Historical Survey*. London: Peter Davies, 1938.

Feinberg, Joel. *Freedom and Fulfillment: Philosophical Essays*. Princeton, NJ: Princeton University Press, 1992.

————. "Autonomy." In *The Inner Citadel: Essays on Individual Autonomy*, edited by John Christman. New York: Oxford University Press, 1989.

————. *Harm to Self.* New York: Oxford University Press, 1986.

————. "Suicide and the Inalienable Right to Life." In *Suicde: The Philosophical Issues,* edited by Margaret Battin and David Mayo. New York: St. Martin's Press, 1980.

Feldman, Fred. "Some Puzzles about the Evil of Death." *Philosophical Review* C2 (1991): 205-27.

Fenigsen, Richard. "The Report of the Dutch Governmental Committee on Euthanasia," *Issues in Law and Medicine* 7 (1991): 339-44.

Ferngren, Gary B. "The Ethics of Suicide in the Renaissance and Reformation." In *Suicide and Euthanasia: Historical and Contemporary Perspectives,* edited by Baruch A. Brody, 155-81. Dordecht and Boston: Kluwer, 1989.

Findlay, John. *Values and Intentions.* Atlantic Highlands, NJ: Humanities Press, 1978.

Finnis, John M. "Abortion, Natural Law, and Public Reason." In *Natural Law and Public Reason,* edited by Robert P. George and Christopher Wolfe. Washington, DC: Georgetown University Press, 2000.

————. *Aquinas: Moral, Political, and Legal Theory.* Oxford: Oxford University Press, 1998.

————. "On the Practical Meaning of Secularism." *Notre Dame Law Review* 73 (1998): 491-516.

————. "The Fifth Annual Fritz B. Burns Lecture: Euthanasia, Morality, and the Law." Loyola of Los Angeles Law Review 30 (1997): 1473-87.

————. "Unjust Laws in a Democratic Society: Some Philosophical and Theological Reflections." *Notre Dame Law Review* 71 (1996): 595-604.

————. "Misunderstanding the Case Against Euthanasia." In *Euthanasia Examined: Ethical, Clinical and Legal Perspectives*, edited by John Keown. Cambridge: Cambridge University Press, 1995.

————. "Intention in Tort Law." In *Philosophical Foundations of Tort Law*, edited by David G. Owen, 229-46. New York: Clarendon Press, 1995.

————. "Liberalism and Natural Law Theory." *Mercer Law Review* 45 (1994): 687-704.

———. "Law, Morality, and Sexual Orientation." *Notre Dame Law Review* 69 (1994): 1049-76.

———. "The Authority of Law in the Predicament of Contemporary Social Theory." *Notre Dame Journal of Law, Ethics and Public Policy* 1 (1994): 115-37.

———. "The 'Value of Human Life' and 'the Right to Death': Some Reflections on Cruzan and Ronald Dworkin." *Southern Illinois University Law Journal* 17 (1993): 559-71.

———. Bland: Crossing the Rubicon?" *Law Quarterly Review* 109 (1993): 329-37.

———. "Object and Intention in Moral Judgements According to St. Thomas Aquinas." In Finalité intentionnalité: doctrine Thomiste et perspectives modernes, edited by J. Follon and J. McEvoy, 127-48. Paris: Librairie Philosophique J. Vrin/Leuven: Éditions Peeters, 1992.

———. "Intention and Side-Effects." In *Liability and Responsibility: Essays in Law and Morals*, edited by R. G. Frey and Christopher W. Morris, 32-64. Cambridge: Cambridge University Press, 1991.

———. *Moral Absolutes: Tradition, Revision, and Truth.* Washington, DC: Catholic University of America Press, 1991.

———. "Persons and their Associations." *Proceedings of the Aristotelian Society* 63 (1989): 267-74.

———. "The Consistent Ethic: A Philosophical Critique." In *Consistent Ethic of Life*, edited by Thomas G. Fuchtmann, 140-81. Kansas City, MO: Sheed and Ward, 1988.

———. "The Act of the Person." In *Persona Verità, e Morale: Atti del Congresso Internazionale di Teologia Morale*, edited by Aurelio Ansaldo, 159-75. Roma: Citta Nuova Editrice, 1987.

———. "Legal Enforcement of 'Duties to Oneself': Kant v. the Neo-Kantians." *Columbia Law Review* 87 (1987): 433-56.

———. "Natural Inclinations and Natural Rights: Deriving 'Ought' from 'Is' According to Aquinas." In *Lex et Libertas: Freedom and Law According to St. Thomas Aquinas,* edited by Leo J. Elders and K. Hedwig. Vatican City: Liberia Editrice Vaticana, 1987.

————. "Practical Reasoning, Human Goods and the End of Man." *Proceedings of the American Catholic Philosophical Association* 58 (1984): 23-36.

————. *Fundamentals of Ethics*. Washington, DC: Georgetown University Press, 1983.

————. *Natural Law and Natural Rights*. Corr. ed. Oxford: Clarendon Press, 1982.

————. "Natural Law and the "Is –"Ought" Question: An Invitation to Professor Veatch." *Catholic Lawyer* 26 (1981): 266-77.

————. "Scepticism, Self-Refutation, and the Good of Truth." In *Law, Morality, and Society*, edited by Paul Hacker and Joseph Raz, 247-67. Oxford: Clarendon Press, 1977.

————. "The Value of the Human Person." *Twentieth Century (Australia)* 27 (1972): 126-37.

————, Joseph Boyle, and Germain Grisez. *Nuclear, Deterrence, Morality and Realism*. Oxford: Clarendon Press, 1987.

————, and Anthony Fischer, "Theology and the Four Principles." In *Principles of Health Care Ethics*, edited by Raanon Gillon, 31-44. London: John Wiley, 1993.

FitzGibbon, Scott, and Kwan Kew Lai, "The Model Physician-Assisted Suicide Act and the Jurisprudence of Death." *Issues in Law and Medicine* 13 (1997): 173-216.

Fletcher, Joseph. *Morals and Medicine*. Boston: Beacon Press, 1966.

————. *Situation Ethics: The New Morality*. Philadelphia: Westminster Press, 1966.

Foley, David M. "Voluntary Death, Property Rights, and the Gift of Life." *Journal of Religious Ethics* 17 (1989): 103-21.

Foot, Philippa. "Euthanasia." In Phillipa Foot, *Virtues and Vices and Other Essays in Moral Philosophy*, 33-61. Berkley: University of California Press, 1978.

————, ed. *Theories of Ethics*. Oxford: Oxford University Press, 1967.

Forte, David F., ed. *Natural Law and Contemporary Public Policy*. Washington, DC: Georgetown University Press, 1998.

Frankena, W. K. *Ethics*. 2nd ed. Englewood Cliffs: Prentice-Hall, 1973.

Frey, R. G. "Hume on Suicide." *Journal of Medicine and Philosophy* 24 (1999): 336-51.

————. "Did Socrates Commit Suicide." *Philosophy* 53 (1978): 106-8.

————. "Some Aspects of the Doctrine of Double Effect." *Canadian Journal of Philosophy* 5 (1975): 259-83.

————, and Christopher W. Morris. *Liability and Responsibility: Essays in Law and Morals*. Cambridge: Cambridge University Press, 1992.

Fried, Charles. *Right and Wrong*. Cambridge, MA: Harvard Press, 1978.

Fuechtmann, Thomas G., ed. *Consistent Ethic of Life*. Kansas City, MO: Sheed and Ward, 1988.

Furness, S. H. "Medical Ethics, Kant and Mortality." In *Principles of Health Care Ethics*, edited by Raanon Gillon, 763-74. London: John Wiley, 1993.

Furrow, Barry R., *et al.* Health Law. 3rd ed. St. Paul, MN: Westlaw, 1997.

Gallagher, D. "Aquinas on Moral Action: Interior and Exterior Acts." *Proceedings of the American Catholic Philosophical Association* 64 (1990): 118-29.

Galston, Miriam. "Rawlsian Dualism and the Autonomy of Political Thought." *Columbia Law Review* 94 (1994): 1842-59.

Galston, William A. "Two Concepts of Liberalism." *Ethics* 105 (1995): 516-34.

————. *Liberal Purposes: Goods, Virtues, and Diversity in the Liberal State*. New York: Cambridge University Press, 1992.

————. "Pluralism and Social Unity." *Ethics* 99 (1989): 711-26.

————. "On the Alleged Right to do Wrong." *Ethics* 93 (1983): 320-24.

Gangi, William. *Saving the Constitution from the Courts*. Norman, OK: University of Oklahoma Press, 1995.

Garcia, J. L. A. "Are Some People Better Off Dead? A Reflection." *Logos* 2 (1999): 68-81.

————. "Double Effect." In *Encyclopedia of Bioethics*, edited by Warren Thomas Reich, 636-41. Rev. ed. New York: Simon & Schuster Macmillan, 1995.

————. "Intentions and Wrongdoings." *American Catholic Philosophical Quarterly* 69 (1995): 605-17.

————. "Better Off Dead?" *APA Newsletter on Philosophy and Medicine* 1 (1993): 85-88.

————. "Intentions in Medical Ethics." In *Human Lives: Critical Essays on Consequentialist Bioethics,* edited by David S. Oderberg and Jacqueline A. Laing, 161-81. New York: St. Martin's Press,1997.

Garland, R. "Death Without Dishonor. Suicide in the Ancient World." *History Today* 33 (Jan. 1983): 33-37.

Gaut, Berys. "The Structure of Practical Reason." In *Ethics and Practical Reason*, edited by Garrett Cullity and Berys Gaunt, 161-88. Oxford: Clarendon Press, 1997.

Geach, Peter T. "Good and Evil." *Analysis* 17 (1956): 33-42.

Gennaro, Rocco J. "The Relevance of Intentions in Morality and Euthanasia." *International Philosophical Quarterly* 36 (1996): 217-27.

George, Robert P. *In Defence of Natural Law*. Oxford: Clarendon Press, 1999.

————. "Public Reason and Political Conflict: Abortion and Homosexuality." *Yale Law Journal* 106 (1997): 2475-95.

————. *Making Men Moral.* New York: Clarendon Press, 1993.

————. "Liberty Under the Moral Law." *Heythrop Journal* 34 (1993): 175-82.

————. "Natural Law and Civil Rights: From Jefferson's 'Letter to Henry Lee' to Martin Luther King's 'Letter from Birmingham Jail'." *Catholic University Law Review* 43 (1993): 143-57.

————. "A Problem for Natural Law Theory: Does the Incommensurability Thesis Imperil Common Sense Moral Judgments?" *American Journal of Jurisprudence* 37 (1992): 345-89.

————. "Natural Law and Human Nature." In *Natural Law Theory: Contemporary Essays*, edited by Robert P. George, 31-41. Oxford: Clarendon Press, 1992.

————. "Moralistic Liberalism and Legal Moralism." *Michigan Law Review* 88 (1990): 1415-29.

————. "Individual Rights, Collective Interests, Public Law, and American Politics." *Law and Philosophy* 8 (1989): 245-61.

————. "Recent Criticism of Natural Law Theory." *University of Chicago Law Review* 55 (1988): 1371- 1429.

————, and Gerald Bradley. "Marriage and the Liberal Imagination." *Georgetown Law Journal* 84 (1995): 301-20.

————, ed. *Natural Law and Moral Inquiry*. Washington, DC: Georgetown University Press, 1998.

————, ed. *The Autonomy of Law*. Oxford: Clarendon Press, 1996.

————, ed. *Natural Law, Liberalism and Morality*. Oxford: Clarendon Press, 1996.

————, and Christopher Wolfe, eds. *Natural Law and Public Reason*. Washington, DC: Georgetown University Press, 2000.

Gert, Bernard. "Hobbes's Psychology." In *Cambridge Companion to Hobbes*. In *The Cambridge Companion to Hobbes*, edited by Tom Sorell. Cambridge: Cambridge University Press, 1996.

————, Charles Culver, and K. Danner Clouser, *Bioethics: A Return to Fundamentals*. New York Oxford University Press, 1997.

Gerwith, Alan. *Reason and Morality*. Chicago, IL: Chicago University Press, 1978.

Gilby, Thomas. *Between Community and Society*. New York: Longmans, Green, 1953.

Gillett, Grant R. "Learning to Do No Harm." *Journal of Medicine and Philosophy* 18 (1993) 253-68.

Glover, Jonathan. *Causing Death and Saving Lives*. London: Penguin, 1977.

————. "It Makes no Difference Whether or Not I Do It." *Proceedings of the Aristotelian Society* 49 (1975): 171-90.

Gómez-Lobo, Alfonso. *The Foundations of Socratic Ethics*. Indianapolis, IN: Hackett, 1994.

Gordijn, Bert. "The Troublesome Concept of the Person." *Theoretical Medicine and Bioethics* 20 (1999): 347-59.

Gormally, Luke, ed. *Moral Truth and Moral Tradition: Essays in Peter Geach and Elizabeth Anscombe*. Dublin: Four Courts, 1994.

———— ed. *Euthanasia, Clinical Practice and the Law*. London: Linacre Centre, 1994.

————. "Definitions of Personhood." *Catholic Medical Quarterly* 44 (1993): 7-12.

————. "Against Voluntary Euthanasia." In *Principles of Health Care Ethics*, edited by Raanan Gillon, 763-74. London: John Wiley, 1993.

————. "Non-Persons, Human Dignity and Justice." In *The Dependent Elderly: Autonomy, Justice, and Quality of Care*, edited by Luke Gormally. New York: Cambridge University Press, 1992.

————. "Euthanasia: Some Points in a Philosophical Polemic." *Linacre Quarterly* 57 (1990): 14-25.

Gourevitch, Danielle. "Suicide Among the Sick in Classical Antiquity." *Bulletin of the History of Medicine* 43 (1969): 501-18.

Grasso, Kenneth L., and Cecilia Rodriguez, eds. *Liberty Under Law*. Lanham, MD: University Press of America, 1997.

————, and Gerald V. Bradley, eds. *Catholicism, Liberalism, and Communitarianism*. Lanham, MD: Rowman & Littlefield, 1995.

Green, Harvey. "Refraining and Responsibility." *Tulane Studies in Philosophy* 28 (1979): 103-13.

Green, Paul D. "Suicide, Martyrdom and Thomas More." *Studies in the Renaissance* 19 (1972): 135-55.

Greenawalt, Kent. "On Public Reason." *Chicago-Kent Law Review* 69 (1994): 669-89.

Griffin, Miriam. "Roman Suicide." In *Medicine and Moral Reasoning*, edited by K. W. M. Fulford, Grant R. Gillett, and Janet Martin Soskice, 106-30. Cambridge: Cambridge University Press, 1994.

──── . "Philospohy, Cato, and Roman Suicide." *Greece and Rome* 33 (1986): 64-77.

Grisez, Germain. "The Structures of Practical Reason: Some Comments and Clarifications." *Thomist* 52 (1988): 269-91.

──── . "Natural Law and Natural Inclinations: Some Comments and Clarifications." *New Scholasticism* 61 (1987): 307-20.

──── . "The First Principle of Practical Reason." In *Aquinas: A Collection of Critical Essays*, edited by Anthony J. P. Kenny, 340-82. Notre Dame, IN: University of Notre Dame Press, 1976.

──── . "Towards a Consistent Natural Law Ethics of Killing." *American Journal of Jurisprudence* 15 (1970): 64-97.

──── , Joseph Boyle, and John Finnis, "Practical Principles, Moral Truth, and Ultimate Ends." *American Journal of Jurisprudence* 32 (1987): 99-151.

──── , and Joseph Boyle, *Life and Death with Liberty and Justice: A Contribution to the Euthanasia Debate*. Notre Dame, IN: University of Notre Dame Press, 1979.

──── , and Olaf Tollefsen, *Free Choice: A Self-Referential Argument*. Notre Dame: University of Notre Dame Press, 1976.

Gruman, G. "An Historical Introduction to Ideas About Voluntary Euthanasia." *Omega* 4 (1973): 87-138.

Guernsey, Rocellus S. *Suicide: History of the Penal Laws*. New York: Strouse, 1883. [facsimile reprint]

Guest, Stephen. *Ronald Dworkin*. Stanford, CA: Stanford University Press, 1991.

Gunderson, Martin, and David J. Mayo, "Altruism and Physician Assisted Death." *Journal of Medicine and Philosophy* 18 (1993): 281-95.

Haber, Joram Graf. "Should Physicians Assist the Reaper?" *Cambridge Quarterly of Healthcare Ethics* 5 (1996): 44-50.

Hacker, Paul, and Joseph Raz, eds. *Law, Morality, and Society*. Oxford: Clarendon Press, 1977.

Haksar, Vinit. *Equality, Liberty, and Perfectionism*. New York: Oxford University Press, 1979.

Haldane, John. "Biothics and the Philosophy of the Human Body." In *Issues for a Catholic Bioethic*. London: Linacre Centre, 1999.

―――. "What Future Has Catholic Philosophy?" *American Catholic Philosophical Quarterly* 71 (1997): S79-90.

―――. "The Individual, The State, and the Common Good." *Social Philosophy and Policy* 13 (1996): 59-79.

Hallett, Garth L. *Greater Good: The Case for Proportionalism*. Washington, DC: Georgetown University Press, 1995.

Hancock, Curtis L., and Anthony O. Simon, eds. *Freedom, Virtue, and the Common Good*. Notre Dame, IN: American Maritain Association, 1995.

Hanink, James G. "Some Light on Double Effect." *Analysis* 35 (1975): 147-51.

Hankoff, L. D. "Judaic Origins of the Suicide Prohibition." In *Suicide: Theory and Clinical Aspects,* edited by L. D. Hankoff, 3-20. Littleton, MA: PSG Pub., 1979.

―――, ed. *Suicide: Theory and Clinical Aspects*. Littleton, MA: PSG Pub., 1979.

Hannigan, E.T. "Is It Ever Lawful to Advise the Lesser of Two Evils?" *Gregorianum* 30 (1949): 104-29.

Hardie, W. F. R. *Aristotle's Ethical Theory*. 2nd ed. Oxford: Clarendon Press, 1980.

Hare, R. M. *Moral Thinking: Its Levels, Method and Point*. Oxford: Clarendon Press, 1981.

Harris, Errol. "Natural Law and Naturalism." *International Philosophical Quarterly* 23 (1983): 115-24.

Harris, John. "Euthanasia and the Value of Life." In *Euthanasia Examined: Ethical, Clinical and Legal Perspectives,* edited by John Keown. New York: Cambridge University Press, 1995.

————. *Value of Life*. London: Routledge & Kegan Paul, 1985.

Harris, J.W. *Legal Philosophies*. 2nd ed. London: Butterworths, 1997.

Harrison, Jonathan. *Hume's Moral Epistemology*. New York: Oxford University Press, 1976.

Harrison, Ross. *Bentham*. London: Routledge, 1983.

Hart, H.L.A. *The Concept of Law*. 2nd ed. New York: Oxford, 1994.

Hartmann, Klaus. "The Foundations of Bioethics." *Journal of the British Society for Phenomenology* 20 (1989): 166-69.

Häyry, Heta. "Legal Paternalism and Legal Moralism." *Ratio Juris* 4 (1991): 202-18.

Helm, Paul. *Divine Commands and Morality*. Oxford: Oxford University Press, 1981.

Hendin, Herbert. *Seduced By Death: Doctors Patient, and the Dutch Cure*. New York: W.W. Norton & Co., 1997.

————. "The Slippery Slope: The Dutch Example." *Duquesne Law Review* 35 (1996): 427-42.

————. "Seduced by Death: Doctors, Patients, and the Dutch Cure." *Issues in Law and Medicine* 10 (1994): 123-68.

————, and G. Klerman, "Physician-Assisted Suicide: The Dangers of Legalization." *American Journal of Psychiatry* 150 (1993): 143-45.

Hendle, Robert J. "St. Thomas Aquinas and American Law." In *Thomistic Papers II*, edited by Leonard A. Kennedy and Jack C. Marler, 59-84. Houston: University of St. Thomas, 1986.

Herbert, Gary B. "Fear of Death and the Foundations of Natural Right in the Philosophy of Thomas Hobbes." *Hobbes Studies* 7 (1994): 56-68.

Herman, Barbara. "On the Value of Acting from the Motive of Duty." *Philosophical Review* 90 (1981): 358-82.

Hickey, Michael B. "Reading the Mystery Passage Narrowly: A Legal, Ethical and Practical Argument against Physician Assisted Suicide." *Notre Dame Journal of Law, Ethics and Public Policy* 12 (1998): 567-603.

Higgins, Thomas J. *Man As Man: The Science and Art of Ethics*. Milwaukee, WI: Marquette University Press, 1958.

Hill, Thomas E. *Autonomy and Self-Respect*. Cambridge: Cambridge University Press, 1991.

Hittinger, Russell. "Private Uses of Lethal Force: The Case of Assisted Suicide," *Loyola Law Review* 43 (1997): 151-78.

———. "John Rawls, 'Political Liberalism'." *Review of Metaphysics* 3 (1994): 585-602.

———. "Natural Law in the Positive Law: A Legislative or Adjudicative Issue?" *Review of Politics* 55 (1993): 5-34.

———. "Liberalism and the American Natural Law Tradition." *Wake Forest Law Review* 25 (1990): 429-99.

———. *A Critique of the New Natural Law Theory*. Notre Dame, IN: University of Notre Dame Press, 1987.

Hobbes, Thomas. *On the Citizen*, translated by Richard Tuck and Michael Silverthorne. Cambridge: Cambridge University Press, 1998.

———. *Leviathan*. Cambridge: Cambridge University Press, 1996.

———. *A Dialogue Between a Philosopher and a Student of the Common Laws of England*. Chicago, IL: University of Chicago Press, 1971.

Hodgson, D. W. *Consequences of Utilitarianism*. Oxford: Oxford University Press, 1967.

Hodson, John D. *The Ethics of Legal Coercion*. Boston, MA: D. Reidel, 1983.

Hollenbach, David. *Claims in Conflict: Retrieving and Renewing the Catholic Human Rights Tradition*. New York: Paulist Press, 1979.

Holm, Soren. "Secular Morality and its Limits." *Medicine, Healthcare and Philosophy* 1 (1998): 75-77.

———. "The Peaceable Pluralistic Society and the Question of Persons." *Journal of Medicine and Philosophy* 13 (1988): 379-86.

Hostetler, Karl. "Towards a Perfectionist Response to Ethical Conflict." *Studies in Philosophy and Education* 17 (1998): 295-302.

Howsepian, A. A. "Some Reservations about Suicide." *Ethics and Medicine* 12 (1996): 34-40.

Huby, Pamela. "Greek Ethics." In *New Studies in Ethics*, edited by W.D. Hudson, 17-42. New York: St. Martin's Press, 1971.

Hume, David. "Of Suicide." In *Applied Ethics*, edited by Peter Singer, 19-27. Oxford: Oxford University Press, 1986.

————. *A Treatise of Human Nature*, edited by L.A. Selby-Bigge and P.H. Nidditch. Oxford: Clarendon Press, 1978.

Hurd, Heidi M. "The Levitation of Liberalism." *Yale Law Journal* 105 (1995): 795-824.

Immerwahr, John. "God and Morality in Hume's Suppressed Essays." *International Studies in Philosophy* 11 (1979): 91-102.

Irons, Peter H. *Brennan vs. Rehnquist: The Battle for the Constitution.* New York: A. Knopf, 1994.

Irwin, Terence. *Plato's Ethics.* New York: Oxford University Press, 1995.

Jacquette, Dale. "Schopenhauer on the Ethics of Suicide." *Continental Philosophy Review* 33 (2000): 43-58.

Johnston, Curtis. *Aristotle's Theory of the State.* New York: St. Martin's Press, 1990.

Johnstone, Brian. "Sanctity of Life and Quality of Life." *Linacre Quarterly* 52 (1985): 258-70

Jones, Gary E. "Engelhardt on the Abortion and Euthanasia of Defective Infants." *Linacre Quarterly* 50 (1983): 172-81.

Jones, Peter, ed. *The Scottish Enlightenment: Hume, Reid, and Their Contemporaries.* Edinburgh: Edinburgh University Press, 1989.

Kaczor, Christopher. "Faith and Reason and Physician-Assisted Suicide." *Christian Bioethics* 4 (1998): 183-201.

————. "Double-Effect Reasoning from Jean Pierre Gury to Peter Knauer." *Theological Studies* 59 (1998): 297-316.

Kagan, Shelly. *Normative Ethics.* Boulder, CO: Westview, 1998.

Kamisar, Yale. "Against Assisted Suicide—Even in a Very Limited Form." *University of Detroit Mercy Law Review* 72 (1995): 739-45.

————. "Physician-Assisted Suicide: The Last Bridge to Active Voluntary Euthanasia." In *Euthanasia Examined: Ethical, Clinical and Legal Perspectives*, edited by John Keown, 225-60. Cambridge: Cambridge University Press, 1995.

Kamm, F. M. *Morality, Mortality: Death and Whom to Save form It*. Oxford: Oxford University Press, 1993.

————. Why is Death Bad and Worse than Pre-natal Non-existence?" *Pacific Philosophical Quarterly* 69 (1988): 161-64

Kant, Immanuel. *Groundwork of the Metaphysic of Morals*, translated by H. J. Paton. New York: Harper & Row, 1964.

————. "On a Supposed Right to Lie from Altruistic Motives." In *Critique of Practical Reason,* edited by Lewis White Beck. Chicago, IL: University of Chicago Press, 1949.

Kappelhoff, Mark John. "Bowers v. Hardwick: Is There a Right to Privacy." *American University Law Review* 37 (1988): 487-511.

Kass, Leon. "Is There a Right to Die?" *Hastings Center Report* 23 (1993): 34-43

Kastenbaum, Robert. "Suicide as the Preferred Way of Death." In *Suicidology: Contemporary Developments*, edited by Edwin S. Shneidman, 425-41. New York: Grune & Stratton, 1976.

Kaveny, M. Cathleen. "Managed Care, Assisted Suicide, and Vulnerable Populations." *Notre Dame Law Review* 73 (1998): 1275-310.

————. "Toward a Thomistic Perspective on Abortion and the Law in Contemporary America." *Thomist* 55 (1991): 343-96.

Kekes, John. *Against Liberalism*. Ithaca, NY: Cornell University Press, 1997.

————. "Moral Intuition." *American Philosophical Quarterly* 23 (1986): 83-93.

Kelly, Matthew J., and George Schedler, "St. Thomas and the Judicial Killing of the Innocent." *Journal of Thought* 14 (1979): 17-22.

Kemp, Kenneth W. "Euthanasia." *American Catholic Philosophical Quarterly* 72 (1998): 315-27.

Kenny, Anthony J. P. "The History of Intention in Ethics." In his *Anatomy of the Soul*. Oxford; Basil Blackwell, 1973.

———. "Intention and Purpose in Law." in *Essays in Legal Philosophy*, ed. R.S. Summers (Berkeley, CA: University of California, 1968), 146-63.

Keown, John, ed. *Euthanasia Examined: Ethical, Clinical and Legal Perspectives*. New York: Cambridge University Press, 1995.

———. "The Law and Practice of Euthanasia in the Netherlands." *The Law Quarterly Review* 108 (1992) 51-78.

Keyserlingk, Edward W. "The Quality of Life and Death." In *Quality of Life, The New Medical Dilemma*, edited by James J. Walter and Thomas A. Shannon, 35-53. New York: Paulist Press, 1990.

Kingston, F. Temple. *French Existentialism: A Christian Critique*. Toronto: University of Toronto Press, 1961.

Kirk, Russell. "Natural Law and the Constitution of the United States." *Notre Dame Law Review* 69 (1994): 1035-47.

Kirwan, Christopher. *Augustine*. New York: Routledge, 1989.

Kluge, E.W. *The Ethics of Deliberate Death*. New York: Kennikat Press, 1981.

Kohl, Marvin. *The Morality of Killing*. New York: Humanities Press, 1974.

Kramer, Matthew H. "How Not to Oppugn Consequentialism." *Philosophical Quarterly* 64 (1996): 213-20.

Kuhse, Helga. "Why Killing Is Not Always Worse—and is Sometimes Better—Than Letting Die." *Cambridge Quarterly of Healthcare Ethics* 7 (1998): 371-74.

———. *The Sanctity-of-Life Doctrine in Medicine: A Critique*. Oxford: Clarendon Press, 1987.

Kultgen, John H. *Autonomy and Intervention: Parentalism in the Caring Life*. New York: Oxford University Press, 1995.

Kupfer, Joseph. "Suicide: Its Nature and Moral Evaluation." *The Journal of Value Inquiry* 24 (1990): 67-81.

Kymlicka, Will. "Liberal Individualism and Liberal Neutrality." In *Communitarianism and Individualism*, edited by Shlomo Avineri and Avner De-Shalit, 165-85. New York: Oxford University Press, 1992.

Lachs, John. "When Abstract Moralising Runs Amok." *Journal of Clinical Ethics* 5 (1994): 10-13.

LaFave, Wayne R., and Austin W. Scott. *Criminal Law*. 2nd ed. St. Paul, MN: West, 1986.

Lake, Peter F. "Liberalism Within the Limits of the Reasonable Alone: Developments of John Rawls' Political Philosophy, its Political Positivism, and the Limits on its Applicability." *Vermont Law Review* 19 (1995):603-42.

Lamb, David. "Down the Slippery Slope." In *Explorations in Medicine*, edited by David Lamb, 199-222. Aldershot: Gower, 1987.

————. *Down the Slippery Slope: Arguing in Applied Ethics*. London: Croom Helm, 1984.

Lanfear, Ray. "Moral Autonomy and Reason." *Journal of Value Inquiry* 20 (1986): 183-93.

Larson, Edward J., and Darrel W. Amundsen. *A Different Death: Euthanasia and Christian Tradition*. Downers Grove, IL: InterVarsity Press, 1998.

Latham, Stephen R. "Aquinas and Morphine: Notes on Double Effect at the End of Life." *DePaul Journal of Health Care Law* 1 (1997): 625-44.

Lee, Patrick. "Human Beings are Animals." In *Natural Law and Moral Inquiry*, edited by Robert P. George, 135-51. Washington, DC: Georgetown University Press, 1998.

————. Is Thomas's Natural Law Theory Naturalist?" *American Catholic Philosophical Quarterly* 71 (1998): 567-87.

————. "Permanence of the Ten Commandments: St. Thomas and His Modern Commentators." *Theological Studies* 42 (1981): 422-43.

Lecky, W. E. H. *A History of European Morals from Augustus to Charlemagne*. London: Longmans, 1869.

Leedes, Gary C. "Rawls's Excessively Secular Political Conception." *University of Richmond Law Review* 27 (1993): 1083-93.

Lewis, C. S. "A Jolly Invention." In *English Literature in the Sixteenth Century Excluding Drama. The Oxford History of English Literature,* vol. III, 167-71. Oxford: Clarendon Press, 1954.

Lichtenberg, Judith. "The Moral Equivalence of Action and Omission." *Canadian Journal of Philosophy* 8 (1982): 19-36.

Liddell, B. E. A. *Kant on the Foundation of Morality.* Bloomington, IN: Indiana University Press, 1970.

Lindley, R. *Autonomy.* Highlands, NJ: Humanities Press, 1986.

Linehan, Elizabeth A. "The Duty Not to Kill Oneself." *Proceedings of the American Catholic Philosophical Association* 58 (1984): 104-11.

Lisska, Anthony J. *Aquinas's Theory of Natural Law.* Oxford: Clarendon Press, 1996.

Locke, John. *Two Treatises of Government*, edited and introduced by Peter Laslett. New York: Mentor, 1963.

———. *Essay Concerning Human Understanding.* London: Dent, 1961.

Long, Steven A. "St. Thomas Aquinas and the Death Penalty." *Thomist* 63 (1999): 511-52.

Lovin, Keith. "The Moral End of Law." *Southwest Philosophical Studies* 5 (1980): 11-17.

Luban, David. "Incommensurable Values, Rational Choice, and Moral Absolutes." *Cleveland State Law Review* 38 (1990): 65-83.

Lund, William R. "Egalitarian Liberalism and Social Pathology: A Defense of Public Neutrality." *Social Theory and Practice* 3 (1997): 449-78

Lyons, David. "Liberty and Harm to Others." In *Mill's On Liberty: Critical Essays,* edited by Gerald Dworkin, 115-36. Lanham: Rowman & Littlefield, 1997.

———. *Ethics and the Rule of Law.* New York: Cambridge University Press, 1984.

———. *Forms and Limits of Utilitarianism.* Oxford: Clarendon Press, 1965.

Mack, Mary P. *Jeremy Bentham.* New York: Columbia University Press, 1963.

Maguire, Daniel C. D*eath by Choice.* New York: Image, 1984.

Mair, A.W. "Suicide (Greek and Roman)." In *Encyclopaedia of Religion and Ethics*, vol. 12, edited by J. Hastings, 26-30. Edinburgh: T & T. Clark, 1992.

Maltz, Earl M. "Brown v. Board of Education." In *Constitutional Stupidities, Constitutional Tragedies*, edited by William N. Eskridge and Sanford Levinson. New York: New York University, 1998.

Mangan, J. T. "An Historical Analysis of the Principle of Double Effect." *Theological Studies* 10 (1949): 41-61.

Mappes, Thomas A., and Jane S. Zembaty. *Biomedical Ethics.* New York: McGraw-Hill, 1981.

Maritain, Jacques. *The Education of Man: The Educational Philosophy of Jacques Maritain*, edited by Donald Gallagher. Garden City, NY: Doubleday, 1962.

————. "Defense of Natural Ethics." *Proceedings of the American Catholic Philosophical Association* 29 (1955): 206-18.

————. *Man and the State.* London: Hollis and Carter, 1954.

————. *The Degrees of Knowledge.* New York: Fordham, 1938

Margolis, James. *Negativities*: *The Limits of Life.* Columbus, OH: Charles Merrill, 1975.

Marneffe, Peter De. "Liberalism, Liberty, and Neutrality." *Philosophy and Public Affairs* 19 (1990): 253-74.

Marquis, Don. "Harming the Dead." *Ethics* 95 (1985): 159-61.

Martin, Robert. "Suicide and Self-Sacrifice." In *Suicide: The Philosophical Issues*, edited by Margaret P. Battin and David J. Mayo, 48-68. New York: St. Martin's Press, 1980.

Martyn, Susan R., and Henry J. Bourguignon. "Physician-Assisted Suicide: The Lethal Flaws of the Ninth and Second Circuit Decisions." *California Law Review* 85 (1997): 371-426.

Marzen, Thomas J., *et al.* "*Suicide: A Constitutional Right?.*" *Duquesne Law Review* 24 (1985): 1-145.

Maurer, Armand. "Descartes and Aquinas on the Unity of a Human Being." *American Catholic Philosophical Quarterly* 67 (1993): 497-511.

Mavrodes, George I. "Innocence and Suicide." *Faith and Philosophy* 16 (1999): 315-35.

May, William E. "What Makes a Human Being to be a Being of Moral Worth?" *Thomist* 40 (1976): 416-43.

McCabe, David. "Private Lives and Public Virtues: The Idea of a Liberal Community." *Canadian Journal of Philosophy* 28 (1998): 557-85.

McCloskey, H. J. "The Concept of a Prima Facie Duty." *Australasian Journal of Philosophy* 41 (1963): 336-45.

McCormick, Donald. *The Unseen Killer: A Study of Suicide.* London: Muller, 1964.

MacDonald, Michael, and Terence R. Murphy, *Sleepless Souls: Suicide in Early Modern England.* Oxford: Clarendon Press, 1990.

McDowell, John. "The Role of Eudaimonia in Aristotle's Ethics." In *Essays on Aristotle's Ethics*, edited by Amélie O. Rorty, 359-76. Berkeley, CA: University of California Press, 1980.

McGowan, Kathleen. "Physician Assisted Suicide: A Constitutional Right?" *Catholic Lawyer* 37 (1997): 245-58.

MacIntyre, Alistair. *After Virtue.* London: Duckworth, 1981.

McInerny, Ralph. *Ethica Thomistica: The Moral Philosophy of Thomas Aquinas.* Rev. ed. Washington, DC: Catholic University of America, 1997.

———. *Aquinas on Human Action.* Washington, DC: Catholic University of America Press, 1992.

Mackie, J. L. *Ethics: Inventing Right and Wrong.* London: Penguin, 1977.

McGray, James W. "Bobby Sands, Suicide, and Self-Sacrifice." *Journal of Value Inquiry* 17 (1983): 65-76.

McKim Robert, and Peter Simpson. "On the Alleged Incoherence of Consequentialism." *New Scholasticism* 62 (1988): 349-52.

Meilaender, Gilbert C. "Terra es animata": On Having a Life." *Hastings Center Report* 23 (1993): 25-32.

Merrill, Kenneth R. "Hume on Suicide." *History of Philosophy Quarterly* 16 (1999): 395-412.

Mikochik, Stephen L. "Assisted Suicide and Disabled People." 46 *DePaul Law Review* 46 (1997): 987-1002.

Mill, John Stuart. *Utilitarianism. On Liberty*, edited by Mary Warnock. London: Fontana, 1962.

Miller, Arthur R. "Acts and Consequences: Squeezing the Accordion." *Metaphilosophy* 18 (1987): 200-7.

Miller, Franklin G., Timothy E. Quill, and Howard Brody. "Regulating Physician Assisted Death." *New England Journal of Medicine* 331 (1994): 119-23.

Miller, Fred D. *Nature, Justice, and Rights in Aristotle's Politics*. Oxford : Clarendon Press, 1995.

Miller, Paul Steven. "The Impact of Assisted Suicide on Persons with Disabilities—Is it a Right Without Freedom?" 9 *Issues in Law & Medicine* 9 (1993): 47-61.

Minogue, B. P., G. Palmer-Fernandez, and J.E. Reagan, eds. *Reading Engelhardt*. Dordrecht: Kluwer, 1997.

Minois, Georges. *History of Suicide: Voluntary Death in Western Culture*. Baltimore: Johns Hopkins, MD: University Press, 1999.

Mirandola, Giovanni Pico della. *Oration on the Dignity of Man*, translated by A. Robert Caponigri. Washington, DC: Regnery/Gateway, 1956.

Mitchell, Basil. *Law, Morality, and Religion in a Secular Society*. New York: Oxford University Press, 1967.

Montaigne, Michel de. *The Essays*, translated by Charles Cotton. Chicago, IL: Britannica, 1952.

Montaldi, Daniel F. "A Defense of St. Thomas and the Principle of Double Effect." *Journal of Religious Ethics* 14 (1986): 296-332.

Moore, G. E. *Principia Ethica*. Cambridge: Cambridge University Press, 1903, repr. 1984.

Moreland, J. P. "Humanness, Personhood, and the Right to Die." *Faith and Philosophy* 12 (1995): 95-112.

Moreno, Jonathan D. *Arguing Euthanasia*. New York: Simon & Schuster, 1995.

Mothersill, Mary. "Death." In *Moral Problems: A Collection of Philosophical Essays*, edited by James Rachels. New York: Harper & Row, 1971.

Mouffe, Chantal. "Political Liberalism, Neutrality and the Political." *Ratio Juris* 7 (1994): 314-24.

Mullady, T. "The Moral Act." *Ethics & Medics* 19 (1994): 1-2.

Müller, Anselm W. "Radical Subjectivity: Morality Versus Utilitarianism." *Ratio* 19 (1977): 115-32.

Murphy, J. C. "Cruel and Unusual Punishments." In *Law, Morality and Rights*, edited by M. A. Stewart, 373-404. Dordrecht and Boston: D. Reidel, 1979.

———. "'Rationality and the Fear of Death." *Monist* 59 (1976): 187-203.

Murphy, Mark C. "Self-Evidence, Human Nature, and Natural Law." *American Catholic Philosophical Quarterly* 69 (1995): 471-84.

Nagel, Thomas. *The View From Nowhere*. Oxford: Oxford University Press, 1986.

———. "Death." In *Applied Ethics*, edited by Peter Singer, 9-18. Oxford: Oxford University Press, 1986.

———. *Moral Questions*. Cambridge: Cambridge University Press, 1979.

Neal, Patrick. "Dworkin on the Foundations of Liberal Equality." *Legal Theory* 2 (1995): 205-26.

———. "Perfectionism with a Liberal Face? Nervous Liberals and Raz's Political Theory." *Social Theory and Practice* 20 (1994): 25-58.

Neeley, Steven G. "The Constitutional Right to Suicide. The Quality of Life and the Slippery Slope: An Explicit Reply to Lingering Concerns." *Akron Law Review* 29 (1994): 53-81.

Nelson, William E. "The Role of History in Interpreting the Fourteenth Amendment." *Loyola of Los Angeles Law Review* 25 (1992): 1177-85.

New York State Task Force. *When Death is Sought: Assisted Suicide and Euthanasia in the Medical Context.* New York: New York State Task Force, 1994.

Nielsen, W. H. "The Slippery Slope Argument Against the Legalization of Voluntary Euthanasia." *Journal of Social Philosophy* 18 (1999): 12-27.

Noon, Georgina. "On Suicide." *Journal of the History of Ideas* 39 (1978): 371-86.

Noonan, John T. *A Private Choice: Abortion in America in the Seventies.* New York: Free Press, 1979.

Norman, Richard. *The Moral Philosophers.* New York: Oxford University, 1998.

————. *Ethics, Killing and War.* Cambridge: Cambridge University Press, 1995.

Norton, David Fate. "Hume, Human Nature, and the Foundations of Morality." In *The Cambridge Companion to Hume.* Cambridge: Cambridge University Press, 1993.

Novak, David. *Suicide and Morality: The Theories of Plato, Aquinas and Kant.* New York: Scholars Press, 1975.

Nowak, John E., and Ronald D. Rotunda. *Constitutional Law.* 5th ed. St. Paul, MN: West, 1995.

Noyes, Russell. "Seneca on Death." *Journal of Religion and Health* 12 (1973): 223-40.

Nozick, Robert. *Anarchy, State and Utopia.* New York: Basic Books, 1974.

O'Connor, D. J. "Aquinas and Natural Law." In *New Studies in Ethics*, edited by W. D. Hudson. New York: St. Martin's Press, 1974.

Oderberg, David S. *Applied Ethics.* Oxford: Blackwells, 2000.

————. *Moral Theory*. Oxford: Blackwells, 2000.

O'Dea, James J. *Suicide: Studies on its Philosophy*. New York: Putnam, 1882. [facsimile reprint]

O'Mathuna, Donal P., and Darrel W. Amundsen. "Historical and Biblical References in Physician-Assisted Suicide Court Opinions." *Notre Dame Journal of Law, Ethics and Public Policy* 12 (1998): 473-96.

Orentlicher, David. "The Supreme Court and Terminal Sedation: Rejecting Assisted Suicide, Embracing Euthanasia." *Hastings Constitutional Law Quarterly* 24 (1997): 947-68.

Otlowski, Margaret. *Voluntary Euthanasia and the Common Law*. New York: Clarendon Press, 1997.

Paden, Roger. "Democracy and Liberal Neutrality." *Contemporary Philosophy* 14 (1992): 17-20.

Pakaluk, Michael. "The Liberalism of John Rawls: A Brief Exposition." In *Liberalism at the Crossroads*, edited by Christopher Wolfe and John Hittinger, 1-18. Landham, MD: Rowman and Littlefield, 1994.

Pannier, Russell. "Finnis and the Commensurability of Goods.*" New Scholasticism* 61 (1987): 427-439.

Partridge, Ernest. "Postumous Interests and Postumous Respect." *Ethics* 91 (1981): 243-64.

Paterson, Craig. "On "Killing" versus "Letting Die" in Clinical Practice: Mere Sophistry with Words?" *Journal of Nursing Law* 6 (2000): 25-44.

————. "Renewing the Moral Life: Some Recent Work in Virtue Theory." *New Blackfriars* 81 (May 2000): 238-44.

Pellegrino, Edmund D. "Decisions to Withdraw Life-Sustaining Treatment: A Moral Algorithm." *Journal of the American Medical Association* 283(8) (Feb. 2000): 1065-67.

————. "The Place of Intention in the Moral Assessment of Assisted suicide and Active Euthanasia." In *Intending Death: The Ethics of Assisted Suicide and Euthanasia*, edited by Tom Beauchamp, 163-83. Upper Saddle River, NJ: Prentice Hall, 1996.

————. "Patient and Physician Autonomy: Conflicting Rights and Obligations in the Physician-Patient Relationship." *Journal of Contemporary Health Law and Policy* 10 (1994): 47-68.

————. "Doctors Must not Kill." *Journal of Clinical Ethics* 3 (1992): 95-102.

Perry, Michael J. *The Constitution in the Courts: Law or Politics?* New York: Oxford University Press, 1994.

————. *Morality, Politics, and Law: A Bicentennial Essay.* New York: Oxford University Press, 1988.

Peterman, John E., and William Paterson, "The Socratic Suicide." In *New Essays on Socrates,* edited by Eugene Kelly, 3-15. Lanham: University Press of America, 1984.

Phillips, Michael. "Are Killing and Letting Die Adequately Specified Moral Categories?" *Philosophical Studies* 47 (1985): 151-58.

Pinckaers, Servais. *Sources of Christian Ethics,* translated by Mary Noble. 3rd ed. Washington, DC: Catholic University of America, 1995.

Pitcher, George. "The Misfortunes of the Dead." *American Philosophical Quarterly* 21 (1984): 183-88.

Plato. *Complete Works: Phaedo,* translated by John M. Cooper. Indianapolis, IN: Hackett, 1997.

————. *The Republic,* translated by G. M. A. Grube. Indianapolis, IN: Hackett, 1992.

————. *The Laws,* translated by G. M. A. Grube. Indianapolis, IN: Hackett, 1984.

Pohier, Jacques, and Dietmar Mieth. *Suicide and the Right to Die.* Edinburgh: T. & T. Clark, 1985.

Porter, Jean. "Basic Goods and the Human Good." *Thomist* 47 (1993): 27-49.

Postema, Gerald J. *Bentham and the Common Law Tradition.* Oxford: Clarendon Press, 1986.

Potter, C. Ann. "Will the "Right To Die" Become a License To Kill? The Growth Of Euthanasia In America." *Journal of Legislation* 19 (1993): 31-62.

Power, David. "The Funeral Rites for a Suicide and Liturgical Developments." In *Suicide and the Right to Die*, edited by Jacques Pohier and Dietmar Mieth, 75-81. Edinburgh: T. & T. Clark, 1985.

Quill, Timothy E. "The Ambiguity of Clinical Intentions." *New England Journal of Medicine* 329:14 (1993): 1039-40.

Quinn, Kevin P. "Assisted Suicide and Equal Protection: In Defense of the Distinction Between Killing and Letting Die." *Issues in Law and Medicine* 13 (1997): 145-67.

———, B. Lo, and D. W. Brock. "Palliative Options of Last Resort: A Comparison of Voluntarily Stopping Eating and Drinking, Terminal Sedation, Physician-Assisted Suicide, and Voluntary Active Euthanasia." *Journal of the American Medical Association* 278:23 (1997): 2099-104.

Rachels, James. *Can Ethics Provide Answers? And Other Essays in Moral Philosophy.* Lanham: Rowman and Littlefield, 1997.

"Euthanasia." In *Matters of Life and Death*, edited by Tom L. Beauchamp and Tom Regan, 30-68. 3rd ed. New York: McGraw-Hill, 1993.

———. *The End of Life: Euthanasia and Morality.* New York: Oxford University Press, 1986.

———. "More Impertinent Distinctions and a Defense of Active Euthanasia." In *Biomedical Ethics*, edited by Thomas A. Mappes and Jane S. Zembaty. New York: McGraw-Hill, 1981.

———. "Active and Passive Euthanasia." *New England Journal of Medicine* 292 (1975): 78-80.

Ramsey, Paul. *The Patient as Person.* New Haven, CT: Yale University Press, 1970.

Raphael, D. D. *Moral Philosophy.* Oxford: Oxford University Press, 1981.

Rasmussen, Douglas B. "The Open Question Argument and the Issue of Conceivability." *Proceedings of the American Catholic Philosophical Association* 56 (1982): 162-72.

Rawls, John. *Political Liberalism.* New York: Columbia University Press, 1996.

———. "The Idea of Overlapping Consensus." *Oxford Journal of Legal Studies* 7 (1987): 232-64.

————. "Justice as Fairness: Political not Metaphysical." *Philosophy and Public Affairs* 14 (1985): 223-51.

————. *Theory of Justice*. Cambridge, MA: Harvard University Press, 1971.

Raz, Joseph. *Ethics in the Public Domain: Essays in the Morality of Law and Politics*. New York: Clarendon Press, 1994.

————. "Facing Diversity: The Case of Epistemic Abstinence." *Philosophy and Public Affairs* 3 (1990): 3-46.

————. "Liberalism, Skepticism and Democracy." *Iowa Law Review* 74 (1989): 761-86.

————. *The Morality of Freedom*. Oxford: Clarendon Press, 1986.

————. "Liberalism, Autonomy, and the Politics of Neutral Concern." *Midwest Studies in Philosophy* 7 (1982): 89-120.

Reck, A. J. "Natural Law and the Constitution." *Review of Metaphysics* 42 (1989): 483-511.

Reeve, Andrew F. "Incommensurability and Basic Values." *Journal of Value Inquiry* 31 (1997): 545-52.

Regan, Augustine. "Moral Argument on Self-Killing." *Studia Moralia* 18 (1980): 299-332.

————. "The Human Body in Moral Theology: Some Basic Orientations." *Studia Moralia* 17 (1979): 151-88

————. "The Accidental Effect in Moral Discourse." *Studia Moralia* 16 (1978): 99-127.

————. "The Worth of Human Life." *Studia Moralia* 6 (1968): 207-77.

Rhonheimer, Martin. *Natural Law and Practical Reason: A Thomistic View of Moral Autonomy*. New York: Fordham University Press, 2000.

Rice, Charles E. "Some Reasons for a Restoration of Natural Law Jurisprudence." *Wake Forest Law Review* 24 (1989): 539-71.

————. "The Problem of Unjust Laws." *Catholic Lawyer* 26 (1981): 278-85.

Richards, David A. J. "Moral Rationality." *Synthese* 72 (1987): 91-101.

———. "Kantian Ethics and the Harm Principle." *Columbia Law Review* 87 (1987): 457-71.

———. *Toleration and the Constitution.* New York: Oxford University Press, 1986.

———. *Sex Drugs, Death and the Law.* New Jersey: Rowman & Littlefield, 1982.

———. "Autonomy and Rights." *Ethics* 92 (1981): 3-20.

———. *The Moral Criticism of Law.* Encino, CA: California Dickenson, 1977.

Riley, Jonathan. *Mill on Liberty.* London: Routledge, 1998.

Rist, James. *Stoic Philospohy.* Cambridge: Cambridge University Press, 1969.

Rooney, Paul. *Divine Command Morality.* Aldershot, Eng.: Avebury, 1996.

Rommen, Heinrich. *The Natural Law.* St. Louis, MO: Herder, 1947.

Rosen, George. "History." In *A Handbook for the Study of Suicide*, edited by Seymour Perlin, 2-29. New York: Oxford University Press, 1975.

———. "History in the Study of Suicide." *Psychological Medicine* 1 (1971): 267-85.

Rosenn, Jonathan R. "The Constitutionality of Statutes Prohibiting and Permitting Physician-Assisted Suicide." *University of Miami Law Review* 51 (1997); 875-904.

Ross, W. D. *Foundations of Ethics.* Oxford: Oxford University Press, 1939

Rousseau, Mary. "Elements of a Thomistic Philosophy of Death." *The Thomist* 43 (1979): 582-601.

Rowe, Christopher. *Greek Ethics.* London: Hutchison, 1976.

Sacharoff, Mark. "Suicide and Brutus." *Journal of the History of Ideas* 33 (1972): 115-22.

Sachs, Greg A., *et al.* "Good Care of Dying Patients: The Alternative to Physician-Assisted Suicide and Euthanasia." *Journal of the American Geriatrics Society* 43 (1995): 553-62.

Sandbach, F. H. *The Stoics*. 2nd ed. Indianapolis, IN: Hackett, 1989.

Sandel, Michael J. *Democracy's Discontent: America in Search of a Public Philosophy*. Cambridge, MA: Harvard University Press, 1996.

————. "Political Liberalism." *Harvard Law Review* 107 (1994), 1765-94.

Sandoe, Peter. "Quality of Life." *Ethical Theory and Moral Practice* 2 (1999): 11-23.

Saugstad, Jens. "Abortion: The Relevance of Personhood: A Critique of Dworkin." *Zeitschrift fur philosophische Forschung* 49 (1995): 571-83.

Scalia, Antonin. *A Matter of Interpretation: Federal Courts and the Law*. Princeton, NJ: Princeton University Press, 1997.

————. "Originalism: The Lesser Evil." *University of Cincinnati Law Review* 57 (1989): 849-65.

Scarlett, Brian. "The Moral Uniqueness of the Human Animal." In *Human Lives: Critical Essays on Consequentialist Bioethics,* edited by David S. Oderberg and Jacqueline A. Laing, 78-95. New York: St. Martin's Press,1997.

Scarre, Geoffrey. *Utilitarianism*. London: Routledge, 1993.

Schall, James V. *Maritain: Philosopher in Society*. Landham, MD: Rowman and Littlefield, 1998.

Schauer, Frederick. "Slippery Slopes." *Harvard Law Review* 99 (1985): 361-83.

Scherer, Jennifer M., and Rita J. Simon. *Euthanasia and the Right to Die: A Comparative View*. Lanham, MD: Rowman & Littlefield, 1999.

Scheffler, Samuel. *The Rejection of Consequentialism*. Oxford: Clarendon Press, 1982.

Schneewind, J. B. "Autonomy, Obligation, and Virtue: An Overview of Kant's Moral Philosophy." In *The Cambridge Companion to Kant*, edited by Paul Guyer. Cambridge: Cambridge University Press, 1992.

Secker, Barbara. "The Appearance of Kant's Deontology in Contemporary Kantianism: Concepts of Patient Autonomy in Bioethics." *Journal of Medicine and Philosophy* 24 (1999): 43-66.

Seidler, Michael J. "Kant and the Stoics on Suicide." *Journal of the History of Ideas* 44 (1983): 429-53.

Sher, George. *Beyond Neutrality: Perfectionism and Politics*. New York: Cambridge University Press, 1997.

Sherlock, Richard. *Preserving Life: Public Policy and the Life Not Worth Living* (Chicago, IL: Loyola University Press, 1987.

Shneidman, Edwin S., ed. *Essays in Self-Destruction*. New York: Science House, 1967.

Showalter, J. Stuart. *The Law of Hospital and Health Care Administration: Cases and Materials*. Ann Arbor, MI: Health Administration Press, 1993.

Sidgwick, Henry. *Methods of Ethics*. Chicago, IL: University of Chicago Press, 1962.

Silverstein, Harry. "The Evil of Death." *Journal of Philosophy* 77 (1980): 401-24.

Silving, Helen. "Suicide and Law." In *Clues to Suicide*, edited by Edwin Schneidman and Norman L. Farberow, 79-95. New York: McGraw-Hill, 1957.

Simmons, A. John. "Inalienable Rights and Locke's Treatises." *Philosophy and Public Affairs* 12 (1983): 175-204.

Simmons, Lance. "On Not Destroying the Health of One's Patients." In *Human Lives: Critical Essays on Consequentialist Bioethics,* edited by David S. Oderberg and Jacqueline A. Laing, 144-60. New York: St. Martin's Press,1997.

Singer, Peter. "Is the Sanctity of Life Ethic Terminally Ill?" *Bioethics* 9 (1995): 327-42.

———. *Practical Ethics*. 2nd ed. New York: Cambridge University Press, 1993.

———. "Life's Uncertain Voyage." In *Metaphysics and Morality: Essays in Honour of J.J.C. Smart,* edited by P. Pettit, R. Sylvan and J. Norman, 154-72. Oxford: Blackwells, 1987.

———, and Helga Kuhse, "More on Euthanasia." *The Monist* 76 (1993): 158-74.

Slote, Michael. *From Morality to Virtue.* Oxford: Oxford University Press, 1992.

Smart, J. J. C. "Extreme and Restricted Utilitarianism." In *Theories of Ethics,* edited by Philippa Foot, 171-83. Oxford: Oxford University Press, 1967.

————, and Bernard Williams, *Utilitarianism: For and Against.* Cambridge: Cambridge University Press, 1973.

Smith, Janet E. "The Pre-eminence of Autonomy in Bioethics." In *Human Lives: Critical Essays on Consequentialist Bioethics,* edited by David S. Oderberg and Jacqueline A. Laing, 182-95. New York: St. Martin's Press, 1997.

————. *Humanae Vitae: A Generation Later.* Washington, DC: Catholic University of America Press, 1991.

Smith, Michael. "Did Socrates Kill Himself." *Philospohy* 55 (1980): 253-4.

Smith, Michael A. "Common Advantage and Common Good." *Laval Theologique et Philosophique* 51 (1995): 111-25.

Smith, Wesley J. "Our Discardable People." *Human Life Review* 24 (1998): 78-87.

Sobel, David. "Full Information Accounts of Human Well-Being." *Ethics* 104 (1994): 784-810.

Sobel, J. H. "Rule-Utilitarianism." *Australasian Journal of Philosophy* 48 (1968): 33-39.

Sprott, Samuel E. *The English Debate on Suicide from Donne to Hume.* La Salle, IL: Open Court, 1961.

St. John-Stevas, Norman. *Life, Death and the Law: Law and Christian Morals in England and the United States.* New York: Meridian, 1964.

Steinbock, Bonnie, and Alastair Norcross. *Killing and Letting Die.* 2nd ed. New York: Fordham University Press, 1994.

Stempsey, William E. "Laying Down One's Life For Oneself." *Christian Bioethics* 4 (1998): 202-24.

Stern-Gillet, Suzanne, "The Rhetoric of Suicide." *Philosophy and Rhetoric* 20 (1987): 160-70.

Stewart, M. A., ed. *Law, Morality and Rights.* Dordrecht and Boston: Reidel, 1979.

Stone, Isidor F. *The Trial of Socrates.* Boston: Little, Brown & Co., 1988.

Sullivan, William M. *Reconstructing Public Philosophy.* Berkeley, CA: University of California Press, 1982.

Sulmasy, Daniel P. "Killing and Allowing to Die: Another Look." *Journal of Law, Medicine and Ethics* 26 (1998): 55-63.

―――. "Managed Care and Managed Death." *Archives of Internal Medicine* 155 (1995): 133-36.

―――. "Death and Human Dignity." *Linacre Quarterly* 61 (1994): 27-36.

Sundstrom, Per. "Peter Singer and Lives Not Worth Living." *Journal of Medical Ethics* 21 (1995): 35-38.

Sunstein, Cass R. *One Case at a Time: Judicial Minimalism on the Supreme Court.* Cambridge, MA: Harvard University Press, 1999.

―――. *Legal Reasoning and Political Conflict.* New York: Oxford University Press, 1996.

Szasz, Thomas. *Fatal Freedom: The Ethics and Politics of Suicide.* Westport, CT: Praeger, 1999.

Tak, Peter J.P. *Euthanasia in the Netherlands.* Leipzig: Leipziger, 1997.

Tarlton, Charles D. "To Avoid the Present Stroke of Death: Despotical Dominion, Force, and Legitimacy in Hobbes's "Leviathan"." *Philosophy* 74 (1999): 221-45.

Tassi, Aldo. "Anarchism, Autonomy, and the Common Good." *International Philosophical Quarterly* 17 (1977): 273-83.

Teichman, Jenny. *Social Ethics.* Oxford: Blackwells, 1996.

―――. "The Definition of Person." *Philosophy* 60 (1985): 175-85.

Ten, C.L. "Mill on Self-Regarding Actions." *Philosophy* 43 (1968): 29-37.

Tooley, Michael. "An Irrelevant Consideration: Killing Versus Letting Die." In *Killing and Letting Die,* edited by Bonnie Steinbock and Alastair Norcross, 103-11. 2nd ed. New York: Fordham University Press, 1994.

Tribe, Laurence H., and Michael C. Dorf, *On Reading the Constitution.* Cambridge, MA: Harvard University Press, 1991.

Trotter, Griffin. "Assisted Suicide and the Duty to Die." *Journal of Clinical Ethics* 11 (2000): 260-71.

Tuck, Richard. "Hobbes's Moral Philosophy." In *The Cambridge Companion to Hobbes*, edited by Tom Sorell, 184-93. Cambridge: Cambridge University Press, 1996.

Udoidem, Iniobong. *Authority and the Common Good in Social and Political Philosophy*. Lanham,MD: University Press of America, 1988.

Uhlmann, Michael M. "Western Thought on Suicide: From Plato to Kant." In *Last Rights? Assisted Suicide and Euthanasia Debated*, edited by Michael M. Uhlmann, 11-44. Grand Rapids,MI: Eerdmans, 1998.

———, ed. *Last Rights? Assisted Suicide and Euthanasia Debated.* Grand Rapids: Eerdmans, 1998.

Uniacke, Suzanne M. "The Doctrine of Double Effect." *Thomist* 48 (1984): 188-218.

Urofsky, Melvin I. "Justifying Assisted Suicide: Comments on the Ongoing Debate." *Notre Dame Journal of Law, Ethics & Public Policy* 14 (2000): 893-906.

Van Hooff, Anton J. L. From Autothanasia to Suicide: Self-Killing in Classical Antiquity. New York: Routledge, 1990.

Vaux, Kenneth L. *Death Ethics: Religious and Cultural Values in Prolonging and Ending Life*. Philadelphia, PA: Trinity Press International, 1992.

Veatch, Henry B. *Swimming Against the Current in Contemporary Philosophy.* Washington, DC: Catholic University of America Press, 1990.

———. *Human Rights: Fact or Fancy?*. Baton Rouge, LA: LSU Press, 1985.

———. "Review of 'Natural Law and Natural Rights'." *American Journal of Jurisprudence* 26 (1981): 247-59.

———. *For and Ontology of Morals*. Ivanston, IL: Northwestern University Press, 1971.

———. *Rational Man: A Modern Interpretation of Aristotelian Ethics*. Bloomington, IN: Indiana University Press, 1962.

Velasquez, Manuel G. "Defining Suicide." *Issues in Law & Medicine* 3 (1987): 37-51.

Vitoria, Francisco de. *Reflection on Homicide & Commentary on Summa Theologiae II-II Q. 64*, translated with introduction by John P. Doyle. Milwaukee, WI: Marquette University Press, 1997.

Waldron, Jeremy. "Autonomy and Perfectionism in Raz's Morality of Freedom." *Southern California Law Review* 62 (1989): 1127-38.

Wall, Steven. *Liberalism, Perfectionism, and Restraint*. New York: Cambridge University Press, 1998.

Walton, Richard E. "Socrates' Alleged Suicide." *Journal of Value Inquiry* 14 (1980): 287-99.

Warnock, Mary. "Introduction" in *Utilitarianism*, edited by Mary Warnock. London: Fontana, 1962.

Wasserman, David. "Justifying Self-Defense." *Philosophy and Public Affairs* 16 (1987): 356-78.

Watt, Jeffrey R. "Calvin on Suicide." *Church History* 66 (1997): 463-76.

Weinreb, Lloyd L. *Natural Law and Justice*. Cambridge, MA: Harvard University Press, 1987.

Weir Robert F., ed. *Physician-Assisted Suicide*. Bloomington: Indiana University Press, 1997.

Werth, James L., ed. *Contemporary Perspectives on Rational Suicide*. Philadelphia: Brunner/Mazel, 1999.

Westley, Richard. *When It's Right to Die*. Mystic, CT: Twenty Third Publications, 1995.

———. *The Right to Die*. Chicago, IL: St. Thomas More Press, 1980.

Whelan, C. M. "The Higher Law Doctrine in Bracton and St. Thomas." *Catholic Lawyer* 8 (1962): 218-32.

————. *Partisan or Neutral? The Futility of Public Political Theory.* Lanham, MD: Rowman and Littlefield, 1997.

Whitman, Jeffrey P. "The Many Guises of the Slippery Slope Argument." *Social Theory and Practice* 20 (1994): 85-97.

Wilder, Alfred. "The Meaning and Place of the Principle of Double Effect in St. Thomas Aquinas." In *Sanctus Thomas De Aquino Doctor Hodiernae Humanitatis,* edited by Leo Elders, 571-80. Rome: Pontificia Accademia di S. Thommaso, 1995.

Wildes, Kevin Wm., and Alan C. Mitchell, eds. *Choosing Life: A Dialogue on Evangelium Vitae.* Washington, DC: Gergetown University Press, 1997.

Williams, Bernard. *Ethics and the Limits of Philosophy.* London: Fontana, 1985.

Williams, Glanville. *The Sanctity of Life and the Criminal Law.* New York: Alfred Knopf, 1968.

Williams, T.C. *The Concept of the Categorical Imperative: A Study of the Place of the Categorical Imperative in Kant's Ethical Theory.* Oxford: Clarendon Press, 1968.

Williamson, Brett J. "The Constitutional Privacy Doctrine After Bowers v. Hardwick." *Southern California Law Review* 62 (1989): 1927-1929.

Willke, Jack C. *Assisted Suicide and Euthanasia: Past and Present.* Cincinnati, OH: Hayes Pub., 1998.

Windstrup, G. "Locke on Suicide." *Political Theory* 8 (1980): 169-82.

Wolf, Susan M. "Physician-Assisted Suicide in the Context of Managed Care." *Duquesne Law Review* 35 (1996): 455-79.

Wolfe, Christopher. *Judicial Activism: Bulwark of Freedom or Precarious Security?* Rev. ed. Lanham, MD: Rowman and Littlefield, 1997.

————. *How to Read the Constitution: Originalism, Constitutional Interpretation, and Judicial Power.* Lanham, MD: Rowman and Littlefield, 1996.

Woods, John. "Slippery Slopes and Collapsing Taboos." *Argumentation* 14 (2000), 107-34.

Wreen, Michael. "Nihilism, Relativism, and Engelhardt." *Theoretical Medicine and Bioethics* 19 (1998): 73-88.

———. "Importune Death a While." *Public Affairs Quarterly* 17 (1996): 153-62.

———. "The Definition of Euthanasia." *Philosophy and Phenomenological Research* 48 (1988): 637-53.

———. "Defining Death." *Public Affairs Quarterly* 8 (1987): 87-99.

———. "The Logical Opaqueness of Death." *Bioethics* 1 (1987): 366-71.

———. "Passing the Bottle." *Philosophia* 16 (1986): 427-44.

———. "My Kind of Person." *Between the Species* 2 (1986): 23-8.

———. "In Defense of Speciesism." *Ethics and Animals* 5 (1984): 47-60

Wright, R. George. "Does Free Speech Jurisprudence Rest on a Mistake? Implications of the Commensurability Debate." *Loyola of Los Angeles Law Review* 23 (1990): 763-90.

www.ingramcontent.com/pod-product-compliance
Lightning Source LLC
Chambersburg PA
CBHW062121280526
45788CB00001B/14